WITTGENSTEIN
and the Turning-Point
in the Philosophy
of Mathematics

S.G. SHANKER

State University of New York Press

First published in U.S.A. by
State University of New York Press, Albany

For information, address State University of New York Press,
State University Plaza, Albany, N.Y. 12246

Printed in Great Britain

Library of Congress Cataloging-in-Publication Data

Shanker, Stuart.
    Wittgenstein and the turning point in the philosophy
of mathematics.

    Bibliography: p.
    Includes index.
    1. Mathematics — Philosophy. 2. Wittgenstein,
Ludwig, 1889-1951. I. Title.
    QA8.4.S53   1987   510'.1   86-23053
    ISBN 0-88706-482-5
    ISBN 0-88706-483-3 (pbk.)

To My Parents

CONTENTS

(trans.), amended 2nd edn (Oxford, Basil Blackwell, 1980)

RPP   *Remarks on the Philosophy of Psychology/Bemerkungen über die Philosophie der Psychologie*, vol. I, G.E.M. Anscombe and G.H. von Wright (eds), G.E.M. Anscombe (trans.) (Oxford, Basil Blackwell, 1980)
Remarks on the Philosophy of Psychology/Bemerkungen über die Philosophie der Psychologie, vol. II, G.H. von Wright, G.H. and H. Nyman (eds), C.G. Luckhardt and M.A.E. Aue (trans.) (Oxford, Basil Blackwell, 1980)

Lectures and Conversation Notes

LWL   *Wittgenstein's Lectures, Cambridge 1930–1932*, D. Lee (ed.) (Oxford, Basil Blackwell, 1980)

AWL   *Wittgenstein's Lectures, Cambridge 1932–1935*, A. Ambrose (ed.) (Oxford, Basil Blackwell, 1979)

LA   *Lectures and Conversations on Aesthetics, Psychology and Religious Belief*, C. Barrett (ed.) (Oxford, Basil Blackwell, 1966)

LFM   *Wittgenstein's Lectures on the Foundations of Mathematics, 1939*, C. Diamond (ed.) (Hassocks, Sussex, The Harvester Press, 1976)

Derivative Primary Sources

IMT   Friedrich Waismann, *Introduction to Mathematical Thinking: The Formation of Concepts in Modern Mathematics*, T.J. Benac (trans.) (London, Hafner, 1951)

PLP   Friedrich Waismann, *The Principles of Linguistic Philosophy*, R. Harré (trans.) (London, Macmillan, 1965)

PREFACE

On the first page of *Culture and Value* we read: 'There is no religious denomination in which the misuse of metaphysical expressions has been responsible for so much sin as it has in mathematics.' Here is a charge that must either be exploded or primed; on no account can it be ignored, whatever one's attitude towards Wittgenstein's conception of philosophy. Unfortunately, the widespread obloquy that Wittgenstein's work in the philosophy of mathematics has provoked tends to dampen enthusiasm for such an initiative. Even sympathetic admirers are cowed into submission by such disparaging assessments as Dummett's reproach that 'Many of the thoughts [in *Remarks on the Foundations of Mathematics*] are expressed in a manner which the author recognised as inaccurate or obscure; some passages contradict others; some are quite inconclusive; some raise objections to ideas which Wittgenstein held or had held which are not themselves stated clearly in the volume; other passages again, particularly those on consistency and on Gödel's theorem, are of poor quality or contain definite errors.'[1] It is the spectre of technical mistakes which must be particularly haunting for the aspiring Wittgensteinian; but this issue must be squarely confronted, if only to certify whether or not *Remarks on the Foundations of Mathematics* is an area which would best be left undisturbed by the prudent Wittgensteinian.

The origin of this work was a commission to undertake the first step of this unenviable task by identifying the specific mistakes that critics were alluding to in their passing asides on Wittgenstein's failure to grasp the mechanics of Gödel's second incompleteness theorem. It quickly became manifest, however, that far more was involved here than was immediately apparent. It was obvious that Wittgenstein's remarks on Gödel's theorem could not be grasped without a prior understanding of his attack on meta-mathematics and Hilbert's Programme, yet these latter issues could not be broached before Wittgenstein's discussions of the nature of mathematical propositions and proof had been addressed. But how could the latter topics be understood without placing them in the context of Wittgenstein's attack on the use of 'prose' in the interpretation of mathematics, his many examples of the philosophical confusions that had resulted from the indiscretions of prose, and most importantly of all, his striking new approach to the character of mathematical necessity and the propriety of scepticism in the philosophy of mathematics?

Running through all this was a growing awareness that Wittgenstein's attack on Gödel's interpretation of his second incompleteness theorem could not be dissociated from his proposed resolution/dissolution of the 'foundations crisis'. If anything, the critique of Gödel's theorem was merely a by-product of the much larger investigation into what Wittgenstein regarded as the conceptual confusions inspiring the foundations dispute. Thus, what began as a short paper on Wittgenstein's attitude to Gödel's theorem had soon blossomed into a full-scale monograph on Wittgenstein's extensive involvement in the philosophy of mathematics. For one thing had become all too apparent: Wittgenstein was assailed by the early reviewers of *Remarks on the Foundations of Mathematics* for the mistakes which purportedly riddle the book, yet invariably these 'errors' were only listed, never actually substantiated as such. Obviously the great appeal of such a polemic is that it is much easier to dismiss an argument on technical grounds than to refute it philosophically. But what were presented as *corrections* were, in fact, covert *philosophical objections* which, because of the prior assumption, were developed without any effort to clarify, let alone challenge, the philosophical background on which Wittgenstein had based his approach to the foundations dispute. Whether or not Wittgenstein's criticisms hit their mark is obviously an issue which we cannot hope to consider until we have first established the grounds for the points which he raised; and whether these grounds are warranted will depend on whether or not Wittgenstein's criticisms hit their mark. It was all too clear that any satisfactory treatment of Wittgenstein's writings in the philosophy of mathematics would have to satisfy both of these demands.

Ironically, there is no discussion of Gödel's theorem in what follows; that remains to be pursued in a subsequent work which will be devoted solely to the clarification of Wittgenstein's attack on the standard — meta-mathematical — conception of Gödel's second theorem in light of his philosophical scrutiny of the framework which underpins Gödel's interpretation of his proof. The present book might be seen as a prolegomenon to this subsequent exercise; its primary goal is to establish the outlines for a fresh approach to Wittgenstein's remarks on the philosophy of mathematics by concentrating on the material of the early 1930s. For unless we carefully retrace the steps which Wittgenstein took from his return to Cambridge and philosophy in 1929 (the time at which the above quotation from *Culture and Value* was written) the obstacles to understanding his mature writings on philosophy — particularly in the philosophy of mathematics — are formidable, if not insuperable. The great importance of *Philosophical Remarks* and *Philosophical Grammar* for our understanding of Wittgenstein's later investigations in the philosophy of mathematics is that Wittgenstein discussed here in considerable detail the various technical themes in higher mathematics that are generally only alluded to in *Remarks on the Foundations of Mathematics*. It is thus by focusing on these works that we can best expose the fallacies underlying the currently prevailing interpretations that Wittgenstein was intent on some form of 'Anti-realist' attack on the foundations of mathematics, or that he was interested in a species of 'full-blooded conventionalist' or 'radical constructivist' critique. Freed from these critical incubuses, we shall then be in a position to grasp the full implications of Wittgenstein's anti-metaphysical exertions in the philosophy of mathematics.

It gives me great pleasure to thank Gordon Baker and Peter Hacker here for their unstinting help and encouragement. I am especially grateful to Peter Hacker for his showing me the details of an immense landscape which I could not possibly have known my way around. I would also like to thank Brian McGuinness and Bede Rundle for their valuable comments. I am deeply indebted to the generous funding which I have received from the Canada Council, first as a Doctoral and then as a Postdoctoral Fellow. Finally, I would like to thank Richard Stoneman and Mark Barragry for services rendered far above and beyond the call of duty. To my wife ...

S.G.S.
Christ Church, Oxford

Note

1. Michael Dummett, 'Wittgenstein's Philosophy of Mathematics', in S.G. Shanker (ed.), *Ludwig Wittgenstein: Critical Assessments*, vol. III (London, Croom Helm, 1986), p. 121.

ABBREVIATIONS

Works by Wittgenstein

NB   *Notebooks 1914–1916*, G.E.M. Anscombe and G.H. von Wright (eds), G.E.M. Anscombe (trans.) (Oxford, Basil Blackwell, 1961)

TLP   *Tractatus Logico-Philosophicus*, D.F. Pears and B.F. McGuinness, (trans.) (London, Routledge & Kegan Paul, 1961)

RLF   'Some Remarks on Logical Form', *Proceedings of the Aristotelian Society Supplement*, vol. 9 (1929), 162-71

WWK   *Ludwig Wittgenstein and the Vienna Circle: Conversations recorded by Friedrich Waismann*, B.F. McGuinness (ed.), J. Schulte and B.F. McGuinness (trans.) (Oxford, Basil Blackwell, 1979)

PR   *Philosophical Remarks*, R. Rhees (ed.), 2nd edn, R. Hargreaves and R. White (trans.) (Oxford, Basil Blackwell, 1975)

PG   *Philosophical Grammar*, R. Rhees (ed.), A.J.P. Kenny (trans.) (Oxford, Basil Blackwell, 1974)

BB   *The Blue and Brown Books: Preliminary Studies for the 'Philosophical Investigations'*, 2nd edn (Oxford, Basil Blackwell, 1969)

RFM   *Remarks on the Foundations of Mathematics*, G.H. von Wright, R. Rhees and G.E.M. Anscombe (eds), G.E.M. Anscombe (trans.) 3rd edn (Oxford, Basil Blackwell, 1978)

PI   *Philosophical Investigations*, G.E.M. Anscombe and R. Rhees (eds), G.E.M. Anscombe (trans.), 2nd edn (Oxford, Basil Blackwell, 1958)

Z   *Zettl*, G.E.M. Anscombe and G.H. von Wright (eds), G.E.M. Anscombe (trans.), 2nd edn (Oxford, Basil Blackwell, 1981)

OC   *On Certainty*, G.E.M. Anscombe and G.H. von Wright (eds), D. Paul and G.E.M. Anscombe (trans.) (Oxford, Basil Blackwell, 1977)

CV   *Culture and Value*, G.H. von Wright (ed.), P. Winch

WITTGENSTEIN'S TURNING-POINT

I am persuaded that we are at present in the midst of an alto-gether final change in philosophy, and are justly entitled to consider the fruitless conflict of systems at an end. The present age, I maintain, is already in possession of the means to make all such conflict essentially unnecessary; it is only a matter of reso-lutely using them. ... The methods proceed from *logic*. Their beginnings were obscurely perceived by Leibniz; in recent decades important stretches have been opened up by Gottlob Frege and Bertrand Russell; but the decisive turning-point was first reached by Ludwig Wittgenstein.

Moritz Schlick, 'The Turning-Point in Philosophy'

Philosophy's Debt to Schlick

For all the accolades, Schlick has received rather uncharitable press in the memoirs of his colleagues from the Vienna Circle, largely because of the sentiments which are expressed in the above quo-tation. Herbert Feigl seems to have been particularly disturbed by 'the enormous effect of Wittgenstein, which set a quite new stamp on Schlick's thinking during the last ten years of his life'.[1] In 'No Pot of Message' he recalled: 'To my chagrin Schlick ascribed to Wittgenstein philosophical ideas that he (Schlick) had already expounded much more lucidly in his 1918 book on epistemology. I was also disappointed with Schlick's compromise with positivism (phenomenalistic version) — and the abandonment of his critical realism as "metaphysically suspect".'[2] Whether or not this censure is regarded as unjust will depend, of course, on one's attitude towards Wittgenstein's later philosophy. What would be unpardonable, how-ever, would be to sympathise with Schlick's appraisal and yet do nothing to defend his reputation. For the fact of the matter is that Wittgenstein studies owe a tremendous debt to Schlick.

We shall never know just how much Schlick contributed to Wittgenstein's decision to return to philosophy, nor how much the rapid evolution of Wittgenstein's thought during what Alice Ambrose has so aptly described as the 'Olympian years' of 1932–5 owes to Schlick's success in persuading Wittgenstein to undertake the joint project with Waismann of writing *Logik, Sprache, Philo-*

sophie.[3] Finally, there is the question of how much Schlick was able
to influence Wittgenstein's thought during the conversations on
philosophy which took place from 1929–32. That Wittgenstein had
an enormous impact on Schlick's thought — and through Schlick, on
such younger members of the Circle as Waismann and Juhos — has
been amply recorded by various members of the Vienna Circle. But
there is some evidence to suggest that, if only by the nature of the
questions and objections which he persistently expressed — which,
not surprisingly, all demonstrate his pre-established 'logical
empiricist' bias — Schlick forced Wittgenstein to clarify themes that
were to become central to his development during the 1930s.

This is an issue of more than passing relevance to our interpretation of Wittgenstein's writings on the philosophy of
mathematics. There is a widespread feeling today that Wittgenstein
was engaged in a sceptical assault on the foundations of mathematics; a subject that had already been rocked by serious
epistemological doubts. Yet this is the very opposite of
Wittgenstein's basic objectives in the philosophy of mathematics.
Rather, Wittgenstein was intent on demonstrating that, like all
philosophical sceptical issues, the principal problems in the foundations dispute stem from conceptual confusion, and thus call for
logical clarification as opposed to epistemological refutation. This is
obviously a crucial — indeed, perhaps the single most important —
issue in the interpretation of Wittgenstein's remarks on the philosophy of mathematics. If we start — as some influential
commentators have recently suggested — with the premise that
Wittgenstein was engaged in a species of 'rule-following scepticism',
we shall inevitably be led to view Wittgenstein's arguments as
intended to take us ever further down a sceptical path whose purpose was to dislodge us from the prevailing truth-conditional
conception of semantics. If, on the other hand, we accept that
Wittgenstein never wavered from his fundamental belief that
'Scepticism is *not* irrefutable, but *obviously nonsensical,* when it tries
to raise doubts where no questions can be asked' (TLP 6.51; NB
44), then we shall see these arguments as *attacks,* each of which was
intended to *dissolve* some philosophical problem in the foundations
of mathematics.

Fortunately, we have the precedent of the discussions which
resulted from Schlick's own confusion on this score, as recorded in
Wittgenstein and the Vienna Circle, to corroborate the latter interpretation. For, as we shall see, Schlick posed very much the same

sort of questions as those which have come to the fore in the 'sceptical' interpretation, and Wittgenstein's answers provide a perspicuous indication of the anti-sceptical direction in which his thought was moving. Schlick repeatedly responded to the innovations which Wittgenstein was proposing to introduce into the fabric of the *Tractatus* with the anxiety that Wittgenstein had failed to clarify the epistemological orientation of his new argument, thereby threatening to undermine the great service which the *Tractatus* had performed for philosophy by providing an 'insight into the nature of the logical itself'.[4] Just as persistently, however, Wittgenstein responded that epistemology had nothing whatsoever to do with the current issue: that he was solely concerned with clarifying what at the time he described as the *logical syntax* of those expressions which had resulted in philosophical problems. Indeed, it will be argued that, in a fundamental sense, Wittgenstein perceived his essential task in the philosophy of mathematics as that of removing the epistemological framework from the foundations dispute altogether, without which the 'foundations crisis' would simply collapse. Before commencing these investigations, however, some explanation is perhaps called for to account for why this theme should have been so largely misunderstood or unappreciated.

In large part these misconceptions would seem to be due to the manner in which Wittgenstein's *Nachlass* has been published, together with the philiosophical trends that have been dominant at the time of their appearance. Confronted with *Remarks on the Foundations of Mathematics* — a work which by any standards must be judged unusually opaque — philosophers not unnaturally attempted to penetrate Wittgenstein's highly enigmatic remarks in terms of the problems and approaches that currently preoccupied them. In particular, recent analytic philosophy had become increasingly interested in the so-called 'sceptical' consequences which could be drawn from the paradoxes in set theory and natural language. Since Wittgenstein was demonstrably interested in developing paradoxes of his own, it seemed conceivable that his writings could be cited as an important authority — if not the source — of the various sceptical dilemmas that had captured the imagination of philosophers of mathematics and language. That Wittgenstein was primarily interested in constructing paradoxes as a method of *deflating* metaphysics could not even be considered; for a *reductio ad absurdum* that was intended to undermine philosophical scepticism could certainly have no place in a sceptical

Weltanschauung. The very question from whence this 'sceptical' interpretation springs could not allow for this possibility; for if we begin with the premise that every philosophy must fall into either the category of 'Realism' or 'Anti-realism' in Dummett's sense (cf. Chapter 2), we soon find ourselves grappling with the thorny question of which camp can rightly claim Wittgenstein as an adherent. But if the premise is wrong — if Wittgenstein belongs to neither school of thought, for the very reason that he had embarked on a course which would undermine the very foundation of the Realist/Anti-realist distinction — the 'sceptical' interpretation of *Remarks on the Foundations of Mathematics* is itself undermined at a stroke. Thus, the first task of this book will be to establish that Wittgenstein's arguments are in a crucial sense fundamentally opposed to the basic premise underlying this approach: a fact which accounts for much of the strain in recent exegesis.

To make matters worse, for stylistic reasons — not to mention the method whereby Wittgenstein compiled his manuscripts from his notebooks — these themes can be exceptionally difficult to comprehend solely on the basis of reading *Remarks on the Foundations of Mathematics.* In his 1931 paper 'The Future of Philosophy' Schlick compared Wittgenstein to Socrates on the grounds that we can discern an important parallel between their similar approaches to the solution of philosophical problems.[5] Wittgenstein must have been fully aware of this comparison, and perhaps even sanctioned such an allusion (if only by his silence); certainly the style of his arguments became increasingly Socratic over the next two decades. In this vein, one of the most notable themes, frequently repeated in the manuscripts and the lectures, is Wittgenstein's insistence that he would refrain from the dogmatic assertion of any opinion or thesis; his route would be one which proceeded to philosophical clarification via completely banal assertions. And yet this is hardly what happened: at least in the realm of the philosophy of mathematics. For here Wittgenstein's comments often seem anything but uncontroversial, and some of his more notorious remarks — such as those on consistency — have struck his critics as positively bizarre, if not proof of his technical incompetence in the field. Furthermore, by the end of the 1930s, Wittgenstein had purged his style of almost any remaining elements of a direct approach. (In Book III §6 of *Remarks on the Foundations of Mathematics* he insisted that 'In philosophy it is always good to put a *question* instead of an answer to a question. For an answer to the philosophical question may easily be unfair; disposing of it by means of another question is not.') We are thus left with a series of questions, metaphors and analogies which, although they can be strikingly evocative, often seem to fail to advance matters significantly, or even to clarify what constitutes the central point at issue. Indeed, the effect achieved is often the reverse from that which Wittgenstein intended, only serving to confuse or even undermine the invariably logical point of clarification that he was striving to establish.

Unlike the obscure discussions presented in *Lectures on the Foundations of Mathematics* and *Remarks on the Foundations of Mathematics*, however, the arguments developed in *Philosophical Remarks* and *Philosophical Grammar* are noticeably detailed and explicit, and thus provide an invaluable introduction to the later work. They also furnish the much-needed explanation for why Wittgenstein should have concentrated to such an inordinate extent on problems drawn from elementary arithmetic in *Remarks on the Foundations of Mathematics.* This feature of Wittgenstein's approach was quickly seized on by his critics as proof of his technical limitations in the philosophy of mathematics. But no such accusation can be levelled against *Philosophical Remarks* and *Philosophical Grammar.* It is only when we read through these early works that we can begin to understand the important stylistic and thematic development which Wittgenstein experienced during the 1930s. The more he addressed the fundamental confusions underlying the 'foundations crisis' the more strongly he began to feel that the philosophical problems which surface in the various realms of higher mathematics are merely more complex versions of the same issues which arise in elementary arithmetic. For example, the type of problems that emerged with the construction of the Transfinite Cardinals are essentially the same as those that characterise the construction of any new number system. Hence, Wittgenstein sought to gain in perspicuity what he lost in detailed application by presenting his criticisms of the questions which prefigure in higher mathematics in the context of the problems which occur in elementary arithmetic.

The benefits of adopting a critical approach which takes *Philosophical Remarks* and *Philosophical Grammar* as its starting-point are principally twofold, therefore: the first is simply that the task of clarifying exactly what themes Wittgenstein was objecting to in the philosophy of mathematics and what position he was arguing for becomes far more straightforward. But there is a further reason why it is essential to study this material if we are to appreciate fully the arguments of the later work. Wittgenstein's development as a mature philosopher was in many ways remarkably self-contained. Thus, the arguments which evolved over the next decade were based as much on criticisms of his own earlier views as on those of other philosophers. For exegetical purposes the significance of this fact is that we must try to enter into the concrete details of Wittgenstein's development as he himself perceived them. In other words, we must try to follow as closely as possible the actual steps which Wittgenstein took following his return to active philosophy in 1929. Otherwise, the result is likely to be, as Wittgenstein so rightly feared, that his arguments would be largely misunderstood.

The origin of Wittgenstein's approach to the foundations of mathematics lies in the rapid development of his thought following his return to Cambridge and philosophy in 1929. Wittgenstein's immediate problem was to remedy the glaring error in the *Tractatus* account of logical necessity (which Ramsey in particular was pressing home). In his curt remarks on the colour-exclusion problem at 6.375-6.3751 Wittgenstein had argued that: (i) it is 'logically impossible' for two colours to be in the same place at the same time, and that 'the statement that a point in the visual field has two different colours at the same time is a contradiction'; (ii) that this exemplifies the fundamental principle that 'the only necessity that exists is logical necessity'; and (iii) that it follows from this that 'red' cannot be the name of a simple, and thus that 'A is red' is not fully analysed. But, as Ramsey objected in his review of the *Tractatus*, this argument only serves to push the problem back to a deeper level: 'even supposing that the physicist [can provide] an analysis of what we mean by "red", Mr. Wittgenstein is only reducing the difficulty to that of the *necessary* properties of space, time, and matter or the ether.'[6] Ramsey would undoubtedly have pressed home this point when Wittgenstein returned to Cambridge, and it thus seems likely that 'Some Remarks on Logical Form' reflects Ramsey's success in persuading Wittgenstein that the argument at 6.375-6.3751 needed emendation.[7]

In order to correct this defect, Wittgenstein introduced two major innovations which he believed would enable him to resolve the colour-exclusion problem in such a way as to preserve the *Tractatus*'s rigid demarcation between logical and empirical truth. His first step was to abandon the *Tractatus*'s sweeping model of a single amorphous calculus underlying natural language, and to shift to what he described as a '*Satzsysteme*' conception, in which language was seen as comprising a complex network of interlocking calculi: auto-nomous 'propositional systems' each of which constitutes a distinct 'logical space'. This would enable Wittgenstein to reconcile the principle that colour-statements 'exclude' one another with the *Tractatus'* insistence that 'all necessity is logical necessity'. Such a change necessitated, however, a radical shift from the *Tractatus* conception of inference. Thus, as Wittgenstein explained to Waismann and Schlick: '[When I wrote the *Tractatus*] I believed that elementary propositions must be independent of one another, that you could not infer the non-existence of one state of affairs from the existence of another. But if my present conception of a system of propositions is correct, it will actually be the rule that from the existence of one state of affairs the non-existence of all the other states of affairs described by this system of propositions can be inferred.' (WWK 64) That is, 'A is red' does indeed entail that 'A is not blue, green, yellow ...'. But Wittgenstein now accepted that 'A is red' is an atomic proposition; i.e. not all entailments are to be accounted for by inner propositional complexity. Hence the truth-tabular definition of the logical connectives is demonstrably inadequate as a means of determining all the forms of inference that are permissible in a language. For, in the case of a determinate exclusion, we can only be said to have grasped the meaning of the determinate if we have grasped the entire *Satzsystem*; i.e. to grasp the meaning of a determinate is to grasp how it *logically excludes* the possibility of the combination of the other determinates in that system. As we shall see, this notion of *logical exclusion* came to play an ever more prominent role in Wittgenstein's approach to the 'foundations crisis'.

The price which Wittgenstein was forced to pay for this proposed resolution of the colour-exclusion problem, therefore, was to abandon the hallmark of the 'absolute' logical atomism which characterises the *Tractatus*: the premise that elementary propositions are logically independent. But how was Wittgenstein going to reconcile the introduction of *Satzsysteme* with another of the *Tractatus*'s major themes: the argument that, *contra* Frege, names have meaning (*Bedeutung*) but not sense (*Sinn*)? The answer here was to abandon the referential conception of meaning: the *Tractatus* argument that the meaning of a name is the object which it denotes. In place of this Wittgenstein now argued that a word only has meaning in the context of its propositional system, and that the meaning of a word is the totality of rules governing its use in that system. When a word is used outside the context of its legitimate system it becomes a 'wheel turning idly'. Generally we can simply ignore the obvious *Satz-systeme* confusions which proliferate in language (in as much as these belong to the province of the grammarian), but occasionally *Satzsysteme* confusions arise which from the grammarian's point of view are perfectly well-constructed, but which none the less seem to generate a profound 'ontological' or 'epistemological' perplexity. Such, Wittgenstein now wanted to argue, are the unique source of philosophical problems: they result from the transgression of the rules, not of ordinary grammar, but rather, of *logical syntax*. In order to understand the confusion underlying this type of 'idly turning wheel', we must clarify the logico-syntactical system in which the word properly belongs, a task which can often be extremely taxing, and which we accomplish by considering the use of the term in question. This theme led Wittgenstein to articulate the principle that 'the sense of a proposition is the method of its verification' (WWK 66). The method of verification manifests to which *Satzsystem* a proposition belongs, and hence reveals when words which belong to multiple or different systems are being used meaningfully or illicitly (cf. Chapter 2).

On the basis of these developments in his conception of language Wittgenstein set about the task of salvaging what remained of the *Tractatus*'s grand design. When he first introduced *Satzsysteme* in 1929 it was not with the intention of repudiating the *Tractatus*'s calculus theory of meaning *per se*; rather Wittgenstein was arguing that the *Tractatus* conception of a global calculus underlying natural language failed to account for the complex 'multiplicity' of logical syntax, and what was needed was a 'network' conception of over-lapping 'logical spaces'. The price that Wittgenstein was thus prepared to pay in 1929 in order to shore up the crumbling foundations of the *Tractatus* edifice was to abandon the pristine simplicity of the structure which he had earlier envisaged. Thus he repudiated the Frege–Russell notations in *Philosophical Remarks* as far too oversimplified to serve as concept-scripts for natural languages. He may have still been committed to the universal calculus model at this time, but it was with the important proviso that this turns out to be enormously more complicated than he had anticipated when writing the *Tractatus*. It is hardly surprising, therefore, that Russell should have been so alarmed by the direction that Wittgenstein's thought was taking in 1930. In his report on Wittgenstein's most recent work to Trinity College (made on behalf of Wittgenstein's application for a research grant) Russell concluded his brief summary of Wittgenstein's new *Satzsysteme* conception of language on a note of personal dismay: 'The Theories contained in this new work of Wittgenstein's [*Philosophical Remarks*] are novel, very original, and indubitably important. Whether they are true, I do not know. As a logician who likes simplicity, I should wish to think that they are not.'[8]

There thus arose from the ashes of the colour-exclusion problem a bold new argument which more than anything else heralded the turning-point in Wittgenstein's approach to the philosophy of language, and thence, the philosophy of mathematics. It was this picture of language as compartmentalised into distinct, autonomous systems, each of which operates on its own specific internal rules, which was to lead him ever further from the *Tractatus*'s conception of the formal isomorphism between language and reality. In a short time the last vestiges of the calculus model would also disappear, and from these *Satzsysteme* would evolve 'language games': artificial microcosms of language whose sole purpose was to clarify various aspects of actual linguistic practice. Perhaps the most important point to come to terms with here, however, is the fact that this thesis was intended solely as a matter of clarifying *logical syntax*, which as such was devoid of any epistemological overtones. This is brought out particularly forcefully in Wittgenstein's exchanges with Schlick on the question of whether there is 'nothing that can be said in reply to the question, "How can I know that one syntax is right while another is not. ... In what relation does empirical knowledge stand to syntax?"' (WWK 65).

The argument which developed between the two on this point is somewhat curious, in so far as each seems to have been intent on a different issue. Schlick's main concern was to ensure that Wittgenstein did not allow the dreaded ' synthetic *a priori* truth' to slip back into philosophy, this time under the auspices of the 'logical exclusions' which characterise *Satzsysteme* inference. Thus he asked Wittgenstein, 'What answer can one give to a philosopher who believes that the statements of phenomenology are synthetic *a priori* judgements?' To which Wittgenstein responded: 'Let us take the statement, "An object is not red and green at the same time." Is all I want to say by this that I have not yet seen such an object? Obviously not. What I mean is, "I *cannot* see such an object," "Red and green *cannot* be in the same place." Here I would ask, What does the word "*can*" mean here? The word "can" is obviously a grammatical (logical) concept, not a material one' (WWK 67). But this did nothing to soothe Schlick's qualms. He appreciated that Wittgenstein was urging that we treat the colour-exclusion statement as a necessary proposition, but that in itself was really the cause of his apprehension.

What principally disturbed Schlick was the worry that, if we treat the colour-exclusion proposition as a 'rule of logical syntax', we have then to identify the source of the necessity which governs the 'rules of colour grammar'. For it was hard to see how Wittgenstein's reading could treat the colour-exclusion proposition as 'analytic *a priori*' given that it seems *prima facie* to be synthetic, and on Schlick's rigid approach to the problem of necessity there was only room for a strict demarcation between analytic *a priori* and synthetic *a posteriori* truths. Would it not be safer to pursue an explanation of the colour-exclusion statement in terms of the synthetic *a posteriori*? Thus he asked Wittgenstein: 'How do I know that such-and-such rules of syntax are valid? How do I know that red and blue cannot be in one place simultaneously? Have we not in this case a kind of empirical knowledge?' (WWK 76,7). Wittgenstein answered vaguely: 'Yes and no. It depends on what you mean by empirical. If what you mean by empirical knowledge is not such that it can be expressed by means of a proposition, then this is not empirical knowledge. If it is something different you mean by empirical thinking, then syntax too is empirical' (WWK 77). Not surprisingly, Schlick was far from satisfied with this response, and he returned to exactly the same point: 'But how do I know that precisely these rules [of logical syntax] are valid and not others? Can I not be wrong?' (WWK 77). Once again, however, Wittgenstein avoided Schlick's objection. This was indeed a problem to which Wittgenstein was to devote considerable attention; the direct answer to Schlick's dilemma can be found in the conventionalist argument presented at §§4 ff. in *Philosophical Remarks* which, as we shall see in Chapters 7 and 8, came to form the backbone of Wittgenstein's remarks on the necessity of mathematical propositions and the autonomy of mathematical systems. But this was the not the problem which Wittgenstein chose to take up in his answer to Schlick. Rather, Wittgenstein replied:

> In grammar you cannot discover anything. There are no surprises. When formulating a rule we always have the feeling: That is something you have known all along. We can do only one thing — clearly articulate the rule we have been applying unawares. If,

then, I understand what the specification of a length means, I also know that, if a man is 1.6 m tall, he is not 2 m tall. I know that a measurement determines only *one* value on a scale and not several values. If you ask me, How do I know that? I shall simply answer, Because I understand the sense of the statement. (WWK 77,8)

One can sympathise with the frustration Schlick must have felt, yet if the argument proceeded in a different direction from that which he had intended it was ultimately his own fault. For, despite his awareness and emphasis on the role of logic in the turning-point wrought by Wittgenstein's work, Schlick remained committed to the very epistemological framework which Wittgenstein was struggling to remove. It was this premise which led Schlick to introduce in their first exchange on this issue the theme which clearly captured Wittgenstein's imagination. Schlick had asked Wittgenstein: 'You say that colours form a system. Does that mean something logical or something empirical? How would it be, for example, if a person was locked in a red room for his whole life and could not see any colour but red? Or if a person's entire visual field contained only a uniform red? Could he then say to himself, "I see only red; but there must also be other colours?"' (WWK 65-6). The latter part of this question introduces a new element into the discussion, however, and it is this which Wittgenstein seized on, rather than the former point about the source of the necessity which distinguishes the rules of logical syntax. Thus Wittgenstein responded:

Does it ... make sense to ask, How many colours must a person have experienced, in order to come to know the system of colours? NO. Here there are two possibilities:

a) Either his syntax is the same as ours: red, redder, bright red, yellowish red, etc. In this case he has our complete system of colours.

b) Or his syntax is not the same. In that case he does not know a colour in our sense at all. For if a sign has the same meaning, it must also have the same syntax. (WWK 66)

Wittgenstein then closed the discussion on a brusque note: 'The crucial point is not how many colours one has seen, but the syntax' (WWK 67). In other words, from a philosophical point of view it is not at all clear, nor is it necessary for us to speculate, how the man in the red room might have acquired his understanding of the meaning of 'red'. If there is a genuine issue here it would be one for the psychologist to investigate, but not the philosopher! The sole point that concerns the latter is that by the term 'red' either his syntax includes 'redder', 'bright red', etc., or else he quite simply does not mean red.

In *Philosophical Remarks* this argument was pared down to read: 'The possibility of explaining these things always depends on someone else using language in the same way as I do. If he states that a certain string of words makes sense to him, and it makes none to me, I can only suppose that in this context he is using words with a different meaning from the one I give them, or else is speaking without thinking' (§7). But how can we be certain that someone else's syntax is the same as ours when we cannot be sure what he will say on future — novel — occasions? Herein lie the distinct outlines of the problem which has become all too familiar in recent critical debates on Wittgenstein's intentions. It is clearly imperative, therefore, that we digest the full implications of the position which Wittgenstein adopted in the early 1930s before we approach the discussions on rule-following presented in *Philosophical Investigations* and *Remarks on the Foundations of Mathematics*. For already in these early works we can discern the substance of his later argument: we can no more be certain about the future of the syntax that x will employ than we can be about our own future linguistic behaviour. But that has no bearing on the philosophical issue of whether what x means is 'red'. For the question of whether his syntax is the same as ours — and whether we can be certain that it is — is conceptually distinct from the question of whether it will remain the same as ours in the future. The former is a *logical*, the latter an *empirical* matter. But the brunt of this argument has been passed over by philosophers who, obsessed by the sceptical worries which Wittgenstein subsequently tried to demonstrate were absurd, ultimately identified Wittgenstein as the proponent of the very themes which he had sought to exclude from philosophy. It is clear, therefore, that before we can proceed to examine Wittgenstein's remarks on the foundations of mathematics, we must exorcise this 'sceptical' demon from the interpretation of Wittgenstein's later remarks on rule-following.

2. Sceptical Confusions about Rule-following

The 'sceptical' interpretation of Wittgenstein's remarks on rule-following is not a recent development. Certainly, it has found its most authoritative expression in Saul Kripke's *Wittgenstein: on Rules and Private Language*, but as Kripke himself pointed out, the origins of this book date back to lectures that he delivered and which were widely circulated in the 1960s. Still earlier, we can find the seeds for the interpretation in Dummett's 1958 article, 'Wittgenstein's Philosophy of Mathematics', and even before that, there are traces of the interpretation in Waismann's *Lectures on the Philosophy of Mathematics*, which were delivered in Oxford in the 1950s.[9] For our purposes, however, Kripke's book provides, not just a definitive exposition of the central themes underlying the 'sceptical' interpretation, but also, a damning illustration of the distortions which result from the uncompromising attempt to reconcile a sceptical reading of the remarks on rule-following with the bulk of Wittgenstein's harsh remarks on the incoherence of philosophical scepticism.

Wittgenstein: on Rules and Private Language belongs to that genre of commentary that wavers precipitously between grudging respect and open hostility. Unfortunately, the latter wins out irrevocably over the former. It is thus with a profound sense of uneasiness that we encounter Kripke's claim that 'Wittgenstein's professed inability to write a work with conventionally organized arguments and conclusions stems at least in part, not from personal and stylistic proclivities, but from the nature of his work.' For, in order to prepare the ground for his interpretation, Kripke must convince us that 'Wittgenstein, perhaps cagily, might well disapprove of the straightforward formulation' of the 'sceptical thesis' that is presented in *Wittgenstein: on Rules and Private Language.* The emphasis here is on 'cagily'; Kripke has no choice but to find Wittgenstein guilty of an ingenuousness bordering on duplicity. On Kripke's reading, Wittgenstein had seen the force of the point that if 'we do not state our conclusions in the form of broad philosophical theses, it is easier to avoid the danger of a denial of any ordinary belief'.[10] Kripke's interpretation is thus presented as a revelation of Wittgenstein's *real* motives; and it is merely a symptom of Wittgenstein's extraordinary guile that these should be so diametrically opposed to Wittgenstein's expressed intentions.

Kripke is quite right to be wary of Wittgenstein's exceptionally condensed and often opaque discussion of rule-following. But it is useful to bear in mind Schlick's warning of the distinctively Socratic character of his approach to philosophy before convicting Wittgenstein of any such premeditated subterfuge. Wittgenstein relentlessly pursued questions that were meant to clarify rather than undermine our understanding of fundamental concepts, thereby exposing the primary sources of confusion that have bedevilled philosophy. Far from operating as a sceptic, one of Wittgenstein's earliest and most enduring objectives was, as we saw above, to undermine the sceptic's position by demonstrating its unintelligibility. 'For doubt can exist only where a question exists, a question only where an answer exists, and an answer only where something *can be said.*' (TLP 6.51; cf. NB 44). And yet we find Kripke insisting that, even though 'Wittgenstein never avows, and almost surely would not avow, the label "sceptic"', still 'Wittgenstein has invented a new form of scepticism': it is 'the most radical and original sceptical problem that philosophy has seen to date'.[11] But how could any philosopher, let alone one of Wittgenstein's genius, be mistaken on so fundamental a point as the relationship of his argument to scepticism? This is surely a question which must give us pause before we fling ourselves headlong into the arms of the 'sceptical' interpretation.

As Kripke emphasises, the discussion of rule-following plays one of the central roles in Wittgenstein's inquiry into the nature of meaning and understanding in *Philosophical Investigations.* Thus, it is clearly crucial that we grasp the strategy behind the conclusion which Wittgenstein drew in the famous dilemma stated at §201: 'This was our paradox: no course of action could be determined by a rule, because every course of action can be made out to accord with the rule. The answer was: if everything can be made out to accord with the rule, then it can also be made out to conflict with it. And so there would be neither accord nor conflict here.' Kripke bases his interpretation on the assumption that we are here meant to confront the gravity of the 'sceptic's attack'. Interestingly, Kripke never considers — if only to dismiss — the possibility that this passage is the culmination of a sustained *reductio ad absurdum.* On the contrary, his whole reading proceeds from the conviction that Wittgenstein has ruthlessly mounted a sceptical campaign in order to expose us to the extraordinary possibilty that, as Kripke describes it: 'There can be no such thing as meaning anything by any word. Each new application we make is a leap in the dark; any present intention could be interpreted so as to accord with anything we may choose to do. So there can be neither accord, nor conflict. This is what Wittgenstein said in

§202' [sic].[12] It is precisely this assumption which then forces Kripke to conclude that Wittgenstein was either unaware of or else concealing the fact that he was presenting the most radical sceptical problem in the history of philosophy. Neither alternative is terribly plausible.

At the very least one would have expected such a dramatic charge to have been supported with a careful argument seeking to rule out the possibility that §201 was intended to state the conclusion of a powerful *reductio*. But on Kripke's reading we immediately find ourselves thrust into the desperate attempt to escape from the 'sceptic's' formidable 'dilemma'. Before we abandon all hope that language is conceptually possible, however, the worry must surely arrest us that the problem is spurious precisely because Kripke has ignored the intention of the argument, interpreting as proven the very premise that we are intended to reject. Indeed, not only does the 'sceptical dilemma' disappear when we read §201 as the final proof of the *reductio*, but equally welcome is the fact that we can then incorporate into a unified reading all of the various points that Wittgenstein made about rule-following *vis-à-vis* the explanation of meaning which perforce go unexplained in the 'sceptical' interpretation.[13]

Wittgenstein began the discussion of rule-following at §143, where he introduced the example of instructing a pupil to continue the series '0,1,2,3,4,5, ...'. It may seem straightforward to argue that in order to expand the series correctly the pupil must first grasp the rule of the series, but at §185 Wittgenstein introduced the complication that preoccupies Kripke. We instruct the pupil to 'continue the series "add 1" up to 1000', which he does correctly, but when we tell him to 'continue from that point with the series "add 2"' he responds, '1004, 1008, 1012 ...'. Obviously he has not done what we wanted: has not followed the rule 'add 2'. But if that is possible how can we ever be certain that a pupil has grasped a rule when the finite series of his answers can fit an indefinite number of different functions? Since the pupil's answers are compatible with myriad possible rules, how can we ever be certain that a pupil has grasped the rule we meant? But in what exactly did my 'meaning' him to continue the series with '1002, 1004, 1006 ...' consist? Obviously I intended him to continue, '1002, 1004, 1006 ...', but had I 'meant' him to write '13680, 13682 ...'? How does my *meaning* traverse the infinite expansion of the series? This question forces us to consider in what *grasping* a rule — applying it in the same way — consists. At

§147 Wittgenstein generalised this problem so that it applies no less forcefully to the case of first-person use: what does my knowledge consist in when I grasp how to apply this rule? Does the rule *guide* me, so that in some way the expansion of the series *follows* from the rule? Despite the arithmetical nature of the example, Wittgenstein clearly intended us to see the problem here as applying to any rule: to using the words 'red' and 'green' for example, or even to such basic examples as continuing the pattern '-..-..-..' (cf. RFM, VI §17, BLB 141-3). And what if the pupil had insisted that he did continue to do the same thing after '1000' as before? Here the question is not quite so clear-cut as might at first appear, as Wittgenstein brought out with the example of asking the pupil to continue the series '2,2,2,2, ...' and he responds '3,3,3,3,4,4,4,4, ...'. Does this mean that the problem really lies with an indeterminacy inherent in the word 'same'? Must — and indeed, can — what I mean by 'same' be rendered absolutely unambiguous?

The reason why Wittgenstein dwelt to such an extent on arithmetical examples in his argument was simply because they exemplify the conception of rule-following that Wittgenstein believed lies at the heart of our confusion. They provided him with an ideal opportunity to attack what he described as the *Bedeutungskörper* conception of meaning: the idea that there are 'meaning bodies' underlying and determining the use and extensions of a word. We shall return to this theme in Chapters 7 and 8 when we come to address the issue of Wittgenstein's conception of mathematical necessity. For the moment, however, it is important to see that the arithmetical examples were intended to provide a perspicuous illustration of what we mean by 'being guided by a rule': of how the applications follow, or are derived from a rule. The picture which Wittgenstein was attacking is that which thinks of rules as determining their applications: the rule 'add 2' must somehow ensure that '1002' follows '1000', and hence, the rule 'add 2' must mysteriously reach across the infinite table of values which the function maps onto arguments even before anyone actually begins to calculate it. Wittgenstein saw the fallacy of thinking of a rule as determining the indefinite totality of its applications as a consequence of the misguided attempt to treat rules as akin to mathematical functions in order to treat the calculation of functions as a paradigm for rule-following behaviour. Calculation by algorithm is set up as the ideal standard of rule-following because it seems immune from error. Mathematical functions are thus seen as determining values for any of the indefinite number of arguments which they take, and likewise, rules are seen as determining the indefinite totality of their applications. Both conceptions commit the same fallacy, however: neither rules nor functions can — on their own, as it were — determine their instantiations. Rather, *we* fix what constitutes following a rule and calculating a function.

Wittgenstein set out, therefore, to overthrow the quasi-causal picture that we have of rule-following. There is a feeling that a rule *compels* us to apply it in such and such a way, that we are able to apply a rule because we are *guided* by it (as if rule were an abstract object which engages with a mental mechanism). Our conception of rule-following rests on a principle of necessity: if you *grasp* a rule, then you *must* apply it in such and such a way:

> 'I have a particular concept of the rule. If in this sense one follows it, then from that number one can only arrive at this one.' That is a spontaneous decision.
>
> But why do I say 'I *must*', if it is my decision? Well, may it not be that I must decide?
>
> Doesn't its being a spontaneous decision merely mean: that's how I act; ask for no reason!
>
> You say you must; but cannot say what compels you (RFM VI §24)

We must perceive the causal picture which grips us here in order to liberate ourselves from it. It is not the rule which compels me, but rather, I who compel myself to use the rule in a certain way: 'Why do I always speak of being compelled by a rule; why not of the fact that I can *choose* to follow it? But I don't want to say, either, that the rule compels me to act like this; but that it makes it possible for me to hold by it and let it compel me' (RFM VII §66; cf. VII §27). We are logically compelled to continue the series '1002, 1004, 1006 ...' because this itself is a criterion for grasping 'add 2': to understand the rule is to grasp the fact that the relation between the rule and its application is *internal*. To say, therefore, that grasping a rule compels one to apply it in such and such a way is merely to express our inexorability in deciding what constitutes the correct calculation of the function '+2': 'For the word "must" surely expresses our inability to depart from *this* concept. (Or ought I to say "refusal"?)' (RFM IV §30). It is not that the rule mechanically determines its applications, therefore, but rather that we determine in our practice of using the rule as a paradigm, what is to count as complying with the rule. Rules guide our behaviour because we guide our actions by reference to rules. The impression of necessity is illusory; the apparent inexorability of a rule reflects our *inexorability in applying it.*

The discussion of rule-following in *Philosophical Investigations* was thus intended to undermine the picture of *guidance* which grips our thought. We implicity treat the indefinite application of a rule like infinitely long rails which compel us to move in a certain way, thinking of rules as somehow containing and determining in advance the totality of their applications. By meticulously following through the slippery slope on which this conception of rule-following places us, Wittgenstein finally arrived at the point at §201 where we are forced to accept that either we abandon this picture, or else conclude that language itself must prove to be impossible. The inescapable consequence of the interlocutor's line of attack, Wittgenstein here emphasised, is that we cannot even understand what he is saying. But that is plainly absurd, and it thus emerges that the purpose of the *reductio* is to demonstrate that the interlocutor's argument is ultimately self-defeating precisely because it is nonsensical.

How exactly could we treat the argument leading up to §201 as stating a genuine paradox? Is it not extremely confusing even to label this as a species of 'scepticism'? Far from constituting the 'most radical' pyrrhonism that philosophy has ever seen, this argument does not even manage to state a coherent sceptical objection. At the very least a sceptical argument — as we commonly understand the term — must proceed on the basis of some piece of shared knowledge to which both parties will agree; only on the basis of this agreement is the sceptic able to generate an argument that is intended to undermine some further conviction held by his opponent. But what Kripke describes as 'scepticism' denies even the absolute minimum of shared knowledge: the possibility that we can understand one another. The conclusion which Wittgenstein drew at §201, however, is that the interlocutor's proposed attack *must* be unintelligible; otherwise language itself would be ruled impossible. Faced with someone who wanted to treat this as a genuine argument we could only conclude that here indeed is a 'hitherto unknown type of madness', which simply collapses into incoherence. This is not at all the conclusion which Kripke draws, however; according to Kripke, 'Ridiculous and fantastic though it is, the sceptic's hypothesis is not logically impossible.'[14] But this is the very opposite to the conclusion that §201 forces us to draw: viz. that the interlocutor's hypothesis just is logically impossible.

It is imperative that we do not misconstrue the attack on the guidance-picture as an attack on the concepts of *rules* and *rule-following*. But this is the very step which Kripke takes, leading him to suggest repeatedly that Wittgenstein's 'sceptical' argument forces us to accept that we apply rules 'blindly'.[15] Kripke cites Wittgenstein's argument at §198 as proof of this, in so far as Wittgenstein there concluded that we cannot justify our application of a rule by appealing to an interpretation. Wittgenstein argued that 'any interpretation still hangs in the air along with what it interprets, and cannot give it any support. Interpretations by themselves do not determine meaning.' Kripke concludes from this precisely the opposite of what Wittgenstein intended: 'How can I justify my present application of such a rule,' he asks 'when a sceptic could easily interpret it so as to yield any of an indefinite number of other results? It seems that my application of it is an unjustified stab in the dark. I apply the rule *blindly*.'[16] But the fact that there is an indefinite number of possible interpretations of following a given rule does not entail that anything could constitute following that rule. Far from demonstrating the uncertainty of rule-following, the multiplicity of possible interpretations brings us face to face with the *reductio* that Wittgenstein was pursuing: 'It can be seen that there is a misunderstanding here from the mere fact that in the course of our argument we give one interpretation after another; as if each one contented us at least for a moment, until we thought of yet another standing behind it. What this shews is that there is a way of grasping a rule which is *not* an *interpretation*, but which is exhibited in what we call "Obeying the rule" and "going against it" in actual cases' (PI §201). Perhaps the most striking feature of the 'sceptical' interpretation is the complete absence of any reference to this passage, which obviously provides the focus of the 'dilemma' presented in the first half of §201.

The purpose of the *reductio* at §201, therefore, far from seeking to undermine our concept of rule-following, is to coax us away from a false conception in order to prepare us to see rule-following correctly. For Wittgenstein's aim was to clarify the grammar of rules in the context of the larger discussion of the nature of meaning which begins at §138. Wittgenstein first established that 'meanings' are neither abstract entities nor objects in the (mental or physical) world. But in what, Wittgenstein asked, does the understanding of a word consist? Is it that one *grasps* the rules for applying that word? Consequently, Wittgenstein had to address the problem of what the understanding of a rule consists in when someone grasps how to apply it. The initial discussion of rule-following which begins at §143 was thus placed within the context of a general inquiry into the nature of concept-acquisition, and the examination of rules must be seen against the background of the attempt to establish that it only makes sense to speak of *meaning* or *rules* when we are able to speak of *practices.*

The existence of rules, Wittgenstein emphasised, is a practice. The criteria for the existence of a rule lie in the public manifestation of normative behaviour. Hence there is a strong case to be made that the existence of rules is language-dependent. But why is that, and does it mean that e.g. animals, if they lack a language, cannot follow rules? The question is an important one, for it lies at the very heart of understanding the essentially normative character of rule-following. Clearly the concept of rules is internally related to regularity, but following rules is not mere regularity. In order to constitute rule-following, the regularity must be deemed *normative*:

> If one of a pair of chimpanzees once scratched the figure | — | in the earth and thereupon the other the series | — || — | etc., the first would not have given a rule nor would the other be following it, whatever else went on at the same time in the mind of the two of them.
>
> If however there were observed, e.g., the phenomenon of a kind of instruction, of shewing how and of imitation, of lucky and misfiring attempts, of reward and punishment and the like; if at length the one who had been so trained put figures which he had never seen before one after another in sequence as in the first example, then we should probably say that the one chimpanzee was writing rules down, and the other was following them. (RFM VI §42)

In other words, in order to *ascribe* normative behaviour there must be both regularity and a considerable degree of complexity. Indeed, it would seem to be the case that any behaviour complex enough to indicate rule-following would *ipso facto* signify that the actors were speaking a language. There is no more reason to deny *a priori* the possibility of animals following rules than to deny it of someone communicating by means of semaphore. The point is that rule-following is language-dependent and thus, that it only exists in the context of instructing, explaining, correcting, justifying or referring (etc.) to a rule. In the absence of language a creature cannot display the degree of complexity which is necessary in order to render 'regular' behaviour rule-following behaviour.

The question which this raises, however, is whether, if Wittgenstein was right and we cannot make sense of the notion of a 'private language', and if rule-following is language-dependent, then is Kripke not at least right in his claim that rule-following is 'community-dependent'? The problem with this latter argument is that, on Kripke's reading, it entails a denial that an individual can follow a rule in isolation: 'if one person is considered in isolation, the notion of a rule as guiding the person who adopts it can have *no* substantive content.'[17] Kripke cannot accept this:

> Does this mean that Robinson Crusoe, isolated on an island, cannot be said to follow any rules, no matter what he does? I do not see that this follows. What does follow is that *if* we think of Crusoe as following rules, we are taking him into our community and applying our criteria for rule following to him. The falsity of the private model need not mean that a *physically isolated* individual cannot be said to follow rules; rather that an individual, *considered in isolation* (whether or not he is physically isolated), cannot be said to do so.[18]

But Wittgenstein stated in one of the unpublished manuscripts that Robinson Crusoe, considered in isolation, obviously is capable of following rules: 'He would have to play language-games with himself — and that he can do *for sure*: think of a Robinson Crusoe, who employs a language for his own private use; imagine that you watched him do it' (Man. 116).

According to Kripke, however, what Wittgenstein really wanted to say is that we can ascribe rule-following to the physically isolated, but not to the socially isolated individual. But what exactly does it mean to say that 'we take Robinson Crusoe into our communtiy'? Kripke has simply confused the criteria of the regularity and complexity of behaviour with conformity to our social conventions. To say of a creature that he/it is following a rule is not to co-opt him/it into our linguistic community (i.e. interpret his behaviour by reference to our own social conventions). Rather, it is to make a judgement based on the regularity and the complexity of the creature's behaviour. Such a judgement will certainly be facilitated if we can understand the purpose of this behaviour, but even here Wittgenstein seems to have been prepared to overlook this as a necessary condition (cf. RFM VI §45). The crucial point is that, to say that Robinson Crusoe is following rules does not entail that he is following *our* rules; it is rather to judge that, based on the behaviour which he manifests, his activity is normative.

Kripke is only led into his 'community' view because without it rules threaten to slip away from him altogether. But far from being a mere expediency, the 'community view' supplies Kripke with the *raison d'être* for the 'sceptical' interpretation. Thus Kripke insists that Wittgenstein 'accepts his own sceptical argument and offers a "sceptical solution" to overcome the appearance of paradox'.[19] A 'sceptical solution of a sceptical philosophy problem', he explains, 'begins by ... conceding that the sceptic's negative assertions are unanswerable. Nevertheless our ordinary practice or belief is justified because — contrary appearances notwithstanding — it need not require the justification the sceptic has shown to be untenable.' On Kripke's reading, Wittgenstein adopts a devious approach to his objective in order to disguise the fact that he is introducing a new conception and justification of an ordinary practice. In order to accomplish this, Wittgenstein's first move was to ensnare us in his startling 'sceptical paradox' so that he could then extricate us from this 'dilemma' by revealing that rule-following does not require the type of justification which would lead the 'sceptic' to conclude that language is conceptually impossible. The 'sceptical paradox' states that 'There can be no fact as to what I mean by "plus", or any other word at any time.'[20] Therefore, Wittgenstein is supposed to have concluded, meaning must not be determined by facts. That is, in order to escape from the 'sceptic's dilemma', we are forced to conclude that meaning is not given by facts-in-the-world. The only viable option left open for us is to define meaning in terms of 'assertion-conditions'. Hence, the 'sceptical dilemma' was simply part of Wittgenstein's covert strategy to shift us away from a truth-conditional account of meaning to an explanation of meaning in terms of assertion-conditions.

The obstacles introduced by this argument, however, are insurmountable. There can be no doubt that the purpose of §201 was to undermine what Wittgenstein saw as the twin misconceptions of meaning and understanding which interpret the former as determined by rules and the latter as grasping those rules. But Wittgenstein did not simply equate meaning with 'use'; he also correlated meaning with what is explained by an explanation of meaning. Nor did he want to deny that we can understand the meaning of an expression 'in a flash'; rather, he tried to reconcile such a phenomenon with this conception of meaning by treating understanding as akin to an ability: the mastery of the technique of using an expression according to the rules laid down for its use. But this hardly amounts to a theory of meaning in terms of assertion-conditions, and as Kripke himself is aware, Wittgenstein went out of his way to stress the multiplicity of expressions whose meaning cannot be explained in terms of assertion-conditions. Moreover, it is difficult to see how this move is supposed to resolve Kripke's 'sceptical dilemma'.

Kripke undertakes to explain how the 'community view' provides us with 'rough assertability conditions for such a sentence as "Jones means addition by 'plus'".' That is, '*Jones* is entitled, subject to correction by others, provisionally to say, "I mean addition by 'plus'", whenever he has the feeling of confidence — "now I can go on!" — that he can give "correct" responses in new cases; and *he* is entitled, again provisionally and subject to correction by others, to judge a new response to be "correct" simply because it is the response he is inclined to give.'[21] The most remarkable feature of this argument, however, is that — as the inverted commas inadvertently reveal — Kripke has recognised and accepted that the concept of 'correct' has been rendered entirely dubious. For the problem is, of course, that my 'inclinations' have nothing whatsoever to do with what justifies my judgement that I know what an expression means. Kripke undertakes to penetrate the veil that enshrouds the criterion of 'correctness', only to discover that it rests on nothing more than 'agreement of inclinations'. But, although the fact that we follow rules at all is contingent, what we *call* rule-following is not. It is not at all clear how Kripke hoped to salvage from these 'shared inclinations' the normativity of rule-following, and thus, the certainty of knowing that someone has mastered a concept.

In a significant aside at the conclusion of 'The Wittgensteinian Paradox', Kripke suggests: 'For Wittgenstein, Platonism is largely an unhelpful evasion of the problem of how our finite minds can give rules that are supposed to apply to an infinity of cases.'[22] We shall deal with this theme in much greater depth when we examine Wittgenstein's attack on mathematical platonism in Chapter 8; suffice it here to remark that, far from suggesting that platonism in general is an 'unhelpful evasion', Wittgenstein felt that it is a confused muddle because it succumbs to the spell which the shadows of grammar cast on the philosophical intellect, leading us to mistake the conventions that we have laid down for deep metaphysical truths. What should principally concern us in this passage is Kripke's subsequent claim that Wittgenstein was determined to explain 'how our finite minds can give rules that are supposed to apply to an infinity of cases'. This returns us to the 'man in a red room' argument which we considered at the close of the preceding section. Kripke's problem here is one of explaining how our 'finite minds' can correctly follow rules in an indefinite number of novel applications. But in what sense is this a *philosophical* question? The problem as so stated apparently stems from the worry that, unless we are able to describe the fact whereby a subject masters a rule, we will lack the criterion for establishing when a rule has been correctly applied. This difficulty leads Kripke himself to propound what sounds very much like a Platonist conception of rule-following: rules exist, together with the 'infinite totality' of their applications, and our minds somehow grasp these mysterious abstract entities (even though we cannot explain the mechanics of this process).

Clearly the question of the 'mastery of a concept' is topic-relative; the criteria we adopt are determined by the framework of the particular concept we are discussing. Suppose, then, that we are considering Kripke's example of addition for the positive integers, and we are asked to explain when and how we are certain that a pupil has mastered the concept. In order to satisfy the conditions for our saying that he has mastered the rule the pupil must be able to apply the rule correctly, to answer questions about the application of the rule, to give certain types of explanation for the answers he has supplied, etc. I can be as certain that the pupil has mastered the rule as that I have done so; which is to say, according to the criteria that we lay down to satisfy the concept *mastery of a rule*, he/I have mastered it. This does not entail, however, that such a judgement must be indefeasible; it can always emerge subsequently that one of us had not mastered the rule. So let us suppose that after 57 the pupil does give the wrong answer consistently (i.e. there is a pattern to his wrong answers): does this mean that he had never mastered the rule? The story as it stands is obviously incomplete, for how we should answer will depend on the more precise details that we create. We might say 'he never understood how to add' (e.g. we might say this of a monkey trained to 'calculate' with ten pebbles, who could only give us the 'right' answer if blue pebbles were used, or if pebbles but not marbles were used, etc.); we might say, 'he no longer knows how to add'; or we might simply conclude, 'he only knows how to add up to 57'. What matters here is *what we would be entitled to say*: not whether we can discover some 'fact in the world' to determine whether or not the subject has mastered the concept.[23]

This issue provides us with an excellent illustration of Wittgenstein's insistence that the source of a philosophical problem lies in the form of the questions that are asked, and that the route to enlightenment lies in the reorientation of our point of view. The attempt to explain in what the 'mastery' or 'grasp' of a concept consists can only be resolved when it is interpreted as asking the genuine question, 'what characterises understanding?', where this is seen, not in quasi-psychological terms, but rather as searching for a clarification of what we mean by 'understanding'. It is because he approaches the question of 'clarifying in what the "mastery" of a concept consists' in terms of discovering the 'fact' that would license such a judgement that Kripke finds himself desperately trying to escape from the 'sceptical dilemma' he has constructed for himself. The purpose of the *reductio* is certainly not to question the intelligibility or certainty of the practice of rule-following. The problem is that, as Kripke's quandary demonstrates, we cannot hope to clarify the grammar of rules and rule-following by probing ever deeper into what we believe must be the 'mechanics' of rule-following. Rather the road to a solution lies in the point which Wittgenstein first emphasised in his arguments with Schlick: 'In this matter it is always as follows. Everything we do consists in trying to find the liberating word' (WWK 77). And Wittgenstein clearly felt that, in general terms, that word was 'grammar', not 'epistemology'. Our task now must be to uncover the grounds and the consequences of this thought, for it introduces a theme which became increasingly important in Wittgenstein's attempts to eliminate the sources of epistemology — and *a fortiori*, epistemological scepticism — from the philosophy of mathematics.

Dispersing the Clouds of Epistemological Confusion

Philosophers of mathematics who unwittingly continue to search for the distinction (or identity, as the case may be) between mathematics and science by comparing the epistemological frameworks involved in each have clearly failed to grasp the fundamental principle of Wittgenstein's remarks on the foundations of mathematics. But the temptation to approach the issue in this manner is, so to speak, built into the system. For the classical account of the nature of mathematical propositions is that they are known *a priori*, and as Philip Kitcher explains in *The Nature of Mathematical Knowledge*: 'when philosophers allege that truths of logic and mathematics are *a priori* ... [t]heir aim is to advance a thesis about the epistemological status of logic and mathematics.'[24] To be sure, a considerable amount of effort has been spent on trying to establish that they can, in fact, be known *a posteriori*; but that is still to argue within the parameters of this epistemological framework (cf. Chapter 4). The basic thrust of Wittgenstein's remarks on the foundations of mathematics in the early 1930s, as opposed to this, was to force us to abandon this established approach and restrict our attention instead to questions of logical syntax.

There must be no confusion, however, about the extent of this critique. Wittgenstein remained vitally concerned with the question of the nature of mathematical and scientific truth, and the relation which the propositions of each bear to one another. It was not this issue which Wittgenstein was attacking, but solely the Cartesian tradition of trying to resolve these questions epistemologically. Thus, the background to Wittgenstein's remarks on the foundations of mathematics lies in his approach to epistemology in general. For the question of 'How we know that a mathematical proposition is true?' was, as Kitcher has pointed out, traditionally regarded as providing the key to resolving the 'mathematics versus science' controversy. Wittgenstein's response was that, in the context of mathematics, such a question is extremely misleading, if not ultimately unintelligible (cf. Chapter 7). All that matters, as far as the philosophical comparison of mathematical versus scientific propositions is concerned, is the manner in which we use each, and thence, how such use underpins our concept of the logical demarcation between the two disciplines. Epistemology sets us off on entirely the wrong track, however, leading us more often than not straight into the arms of Platonist metaphysics — where meaningless pictures are called upon to do the work of philosophical clarification — or else into the realm of pseudo-scientific jargon where the logico-grammatical barriers separating mathematics from science are consistently transgressed.

Indeed, perhaps the most important theme in Wittgenstein's work in the philosophy of mathematics is his claim that the nature of the demarcation between science and mathematics is obscured by the very epistemological premises underlying the foundations dispute, and that without these epistemological confusions the 'foundations crisis simply vanishes'. As Max Black so rightly pointed out, Wittgenstein 'was attempting something very different from "tentatively offering" another set of "foundations". A critic of the game is not another player.'[25] It is quite clear that this sentiment captures the spirit of how Wittgenstein viewed his work in the philosophy of mathematics. The only problem with it is: what exactly does it mean? Black may regrettably have ignored this crucial question but we cannot; for it is all too easy for the advocates of the 'sceptical' interpretation to cite this very theme in their own defence: viz. that to be a critic of the game is to show that the notion of mathematical certainty is without justification. But this would be to confuse a 'critic of the game' with a 'fanatic' who was intent on preventing anyone else from playing. Far from trying to establish that the nature of our epistemological framework forbids us from ever attaining the apodeictic knowledge which we assumed was the hallmark of mathematics, Wittgenstein's whole argument was designed to push us towards recognising that the very nature of mathematical truth is such that it forces us to divorce any such epistemological considerations from the philosophy of mathematics.

How is it that this strategy has for so long now been overlooked? We have already touched on the primary factors in the first section, but clearly there must be something further operating here as well: the grip of the framework must be such that the suggestion that the premise itself is spurious — that what we are really concerned with are logical, not epistemological problems — is far too great a heresy to contemplate; many philosophers would appear to be much more comfortable with the supposition that mathematics is irretrievably unjustifiable (an obviously exaggerated form of scepticism which can be safely disregarded). The great innovation introduced by Crispin Wright and Kripke's work on the 'sceptical' interpretation did not so much concern the outline of this standard interpretation as insist that the 'problems' raised by Wittgenstein pose an important 'sceptical dilemma'. It is a curious position to attribute to the philosopher who was also demanding: 'Why should a certain configuration of signs not be allowed to arise? Why this dread? Why the tabu?' (WWK 119). Clearly the prelude to perceiving the importance of Wittgenstein's remarks on the foundations of mathematics, therefore, is to locate and remove the source of this *punctum caecum*.

The first step towards this goal is to consider the spirit in which Wittgenstein turned to the philosophy of mathematics in 1929–30.

Armed with the weapon of his new *Satzsysteme* conception of language Wittgenstein set out to do battle with the philosophical issue that was the current centre of attention: the 'foundations crisis'. Wittgenstein believed, as he told Russell, Waismann and Schlick, that he would be able to resolve the foundations dispute by *dissolving* it with the same techniques that he was introducing into the philosophy of language. Wittgenstein had now begun to argue that philosophical problems are entirely due to *Satzsysteme* confusions: the failure to demarcate between different propositional systems, and thus to perceive when concepts are being applied illicitly in 'foreign' systems. The solution to such characteristically 'philosophical' problems lies, not in discovering an *answer*, but rather, in ridding ourselves of the question itself by clarifying the logical syntax of the various systems involved which have generated our confusion. Thus he told his students in 1930: 'What we are in fact doing is to tidy up our notions, to make clear what *can* be said about the world. We are in a muddle about what can be said, and are trying to clear up that muddle. This activity of clearing up is philosophy' (LWL 21-2).

Notice that the emphasis here is on philosophy *simpliciter*, and not on any specific branch of the subject. This implies that, not only one and the same method, but even one and the same themes will surface in the various disparate domains of philosophical investigation. It is the recurrence of just such a leitmotif which led to the critical position examined above that the so-called 'sceptical' remarks on rule-following were originally developed in the philosophy of language and then subsequently found their way into the philosophy of mathematics. On this reading *Remarks on the Foundations of Mathematics* was intended as a corollary to the sceptical inquiry that had been initiated in *Philosophical Investigations*. But then, that would mean that it was not a *method* to which Wittgenstein had remained constant but rather, a *philosophical thesis*. And both aspects of such a claim war with Wittgenstein's own oft-repeated explanation of the nature of his approach. Admittedly, the author may be a notoriously poor guide to the significance of his own work; but, as we have just seen, before Wittgenstein's *obiter dicta* are ruled out of court, it is wise to approach his remarks on rule-following with the emphasis on the continuity of his *method* restored. The same is no less true for Wittgenstein's approach to the 'foundations crisis'.

It is notoriously difficult, however, to understand the protestations of someone who insists that his arguments fall outside the traditional parameters of a debate. Even more difficult to comprehend is the nonconformist who insists that it is the framework itself which he is attacking, and not one of the primary positions established within that system. Our reaction is generally one of either confusion or disbelief. With a sense of perplexity or annoyance (heightened if the figure in question possessed what Kreisel describes as a 'sparkling intellect') we set about to expose either his failure to grasp the complex issues involved, or else the 'real' motives underlying his puzzling attack. And such has clearly been the fate of Wittgenstein's remarks on the foundations of mathematics. From the earliest allusion to his new ideas on the subject that we have — the tantalising reference to Wittgenstein's evolving ideas in the 'Vienna Circle Manifesto' (*infra*) — it is clear that Wittgenstein believed that the solution to the foundations problem lay in its dissolution. Rather than seeking to defend any particular position within the traditional framework, Wittgenstein would demonstrate that it was a confusion contained in that framework itself which had led philosophers on the vain quest for an impossible solution to an unintelligible 'question'. It is thus crucial that we recognise at the outset just how misleading was the Logical Positivists' view of the *nature* of Wittgenstein's approach to the 'foundations crisis'.

On the logical positivist reading, there were three serious contenders in the race for a solution to the 'foundations crisis': logicism, formalism and intuitionism. But since each particular theory expressed some unique insight, it seemed most likely that 'the essential features of all three will come closer in the course of future development'.[26] However, Wittgenstein's vaunted ambition to resolve the issue was not, as was assumed by the signatories of the 'Vienna Circle Manifesto', 'to unite the various schools in an ultimate solution';[27] it was to demonstrate that a 'solution' to the problem does not exist because the 'questions' leading up to the 'crisis' are themselves unintelligible. In other words, Wittgenstein did not approach the foundations dispute on an equal footing with the other schools; the target of his remarks was the framework itself which had inspired the dispute. Hence, his intention was not to develop yet another (e.g. 'conventionalist') *theory* in the foundations dispute, but rather, to illustrate a new *method* which would dissolve the 'foundations crisis'. Yet, as we shall see throughout this book, the cornerstone of Wittgenstein's remarks on the philosophy of mathematics was his emphasis on the *normativity* of mathematical constructions. Mathematical propositions, he argued in *Philosophical Remarks*, are 'rules of logical syntax'; mathematical proofs 'convince us' to accept 'grammatical propositions'. In *Remarks on the Foundations of Mathematics* he bluntly stated: 'What I am saying comes to this, that mathematics is *normative*'. But then, how are we to avoid the charge that this itself is a *philosophical thesis*?

Certainly that was the manner in which Wittgenstein's new ideas were received by the Logical Positivists: an understandable reaction to Waismann's initial summary of Wittgenstein's latest ideas which, significantly, was entitled 'Theses'. It is imperative, therefore, that we consider the tone of Wittgenstein's reaction to these notes. Wittgenstein warned Waismann:

> As regards your *Theses*, I once wrote, If there were theses in philosophy, they would have to be put in such a way that every-one would say, Oh yes, that is of course obvious. As long as there is a possibility of having different opinions and disputing about a question, this indicates that things have not yet been expressed clearly enough. Once a perfectly clear formulation — ultimate clarity — has been reached, there can be no second thoughts or reluctance any more, for these always arise from the feeling that something has now been asserted, and I do not know whether I should admit it or not. If, however, you make the grammar clear to yourself, if you proceed by very short steps in such a way that every single step becomes perfectly obvious and natural, no dis-pute whatsoever can arise. (WWK 183; cf. PR §2; AWL 93; LFM 103)

But how can this — obviously crucial — guideline be reconciled with the radical claim that mathematical propositions are 'rules of logical syntax'? Surely no one could regard this striking innovation as a per-fectly obvious assertion: one which would excite 'no dispute whatsoever'?

The answer to this *argumentum ad hominem* can be found in the paper which Waismann was deputised to read at the 1930 Königsberg conference, 'The Nature of Mathematics: Wittgenstein's Standpoint'. The reception of this paper must have been bitterly dis-appointing for Wittgenstein, for in the discussion which followed, Hans Hahn curtly dismissed Waismann's argument as an unwarranted attack on Russell's logicism, rendered all the more puzzling by the fact that it shared the same basic logicist framework.[28] But the assembled members of the Circle had totally failed to recognise just how novel and important were the brief remarks which Waismann had presented at the beginning of his 'sketch'. 'The goal of [Wittgenstein's] efforts', Waismann explained at the outset, 'is quite generally a clarification of our understanding of mathematics.'[29] The 'fundamental idea' of Wittgenstein's new approach was that 'only facts can be described, and they can be described distinctly. If one tries to describe something other than facts then one misuses the symbolism; that is to say, one offends against the deep internal rules of syntax which lie in the essence of our methods of communication.'[30] And 'these thoughts', Waismann concluded, 'lead to a definite starting-point with respect to mathematics; or to put this more precisely: they lead to a method — a manner of thinking — with which to look at related questions in the foundations of mathematics.' He then emphasised that 'This method — which should always be obeyed in investigations of this kind — consists of two elements. The first is: in order to ascertain the meaning of a mathematical concept, one must pay attention to the *use* that is made of it; that is to say, one must pay attention to what the mathematician really does in his work. The second is: in order to visualise the significance of a mathematical proposition one must make clear how it is *verified.*'[31] The idea that problems in the philosophy of mathematics can only be resolved by clarifying the rules of logical syntax governing the use of mathematical concepts marked a major departure in the foundations dispute: one that would lead Wittgenstein to demonstrate the confusions which result by treating mathematical propositions as a species of descriptive (empirical) proposition. In order to bring out the — quintessentially *normative* — character of their use, Wittgenstein naturally compared mathematical propositions to a unique species of rules, which he dubbed 'rules of logical syntax'. What they have in common with rules is that they do not say what is the case, but rather, *stipulate* what must be the case; that is, they fix the use of concepts.

To a considerable extent, the appearance that a philosophical thesis has been postulated here is due to the exegetical strategy that has been adopted, rather than to any shortcomings on Wittgenstein's part. For the centrepiece of this interpretation is that any approach to Wittgenstein's remarks on the philosophy of mathematics must proceed from his claim that mathematical propositions fix the use and transformation of mathematical concepts. It is the desire to indicate the starting-point for the following interpretation in clear and forthright terms which is responsible for this somewhat dogmatic presentation. But the putative normativity of mathematics is something which can only be truly borne out in our actual examinations of specific mathematical theories and the philosophical issues which they have engendered. And yet, without some idea of what we are searching for, these discussions are apt to become directionless and inconclusive. The only excuse for this lapse from Wittgenstein's stringent demands, therefore, is that the very complexity of the subject makes it necessary for us to find our bearings before we set out on the task. What is presented in this opening chapter is thus only the outline for much that is to follow, and it is hoped, be substantiated: both in terms of the interpretation, and the significance of the argument which is thereby developed. Indeed, it is a crucial element of this interpretation that these two aspects cannot be separated: the aim here is not just to explain the nature of Wittgenstein's attack on the 'foundations crisis', but in so doing, to show why his argument is anything but the idle 'lexicographical' pastime which some have supposed.

What we need to consider in this opening chapter, however, is not the details of this argument, but solely its orientation. In their exchanges on the nature of *Satzsysteme*, Schlick continually pressed Wittgenstein to declare himself on the issue of the epistemological status of necessary truths: are they *a priori* or *a posteriori*? As we shall see in Chapter 7, Wittgenstein was tempted to say in *Philosophical Remarks* that, if anything, mathematical propositions could best be compared to 'synthetic *a priori*' propositions: a possibility which, had he communicated it to Schlick, might have had a devastating effect on their relationship. But the question itself is awry: you might compare mathematical propositions to what had traditionally been classified as 'synthetic *a priori* truths' in so far as the latter come closest amongst the traditional epistemological categories to accounting for the uses of mathematical propositions, but there is simply no need for us to become embroiled in these venerable quarrels. Wittgenstein's emphasis on examining the use which is made of mathematical concepts does not — *contra* Schlick — constitute a covert approach to epistemological riddles, but rather, a deliberate method for avoiding them altogether.

Thus, by concentrating on the logical syntax of mathematical propositions, Wittgenstein hoped to bypass completely the traditional 'epistemological' and 'ontological' problems which have afflicted — if not sustained — the foundations dispute. We grasp what renders a mathematical proposition 'unshakably certain' by clarifying the nature of its use as a 'rule of logical syntax'. The reason why such an apparently straightforward task can prove so difficult is simply because one and the same expression can operate in different *Satzsysteme*, while the meaning of a proposition is strictly determined by the rules governing its use in a specific *Satzsystem*. There is no such thing as a *formal* criterion for propositional status, for how a sentence is used determines whether it is a 'rule of logical syntax' or an empirical proposition: one and the same expression can be used to stipulate a rule in one *Satzsystem* and yet describe a fact in another — completely autonomous — *Satzsystem*. 'Expressions which look like *a priori* propositions must be clarified. Just as the same expression can be a proposition or an hypothesis, so the same expression can be an equation or an hypothesis. Unless we distinguish confusions occur' (LWL 76). The route to resolving these matters lies in shunning traditional epistemology entirely, therefore, and concentrating instead on the philosophically prior issue of clarifying the logical syntax of the expression.

Unfortunately, the perceptions and preconceptions of the Vienna Circle have persisted, and with them, the misinterpretation of Wittgenstein's argument. For example, in *Mathematical Knowledge* Mark Steiner describes at some length 'Wittgenstein's epistemological attack upon logicism, a discussion aimed at proving that it is not possible to come to know mathematical truths through the medium of logic, because we cannot come to know enough logic'.[32] According to Steiner, Wittgenstein shared with Poincaré 'the conviction that the reduction of mathematics to logic does not offer an explanation of mathematical knowledge which can withstand philosophical scrutiny'.[33] Thus, regardless of Wittgenstein's protestations or declared intentions, the rationale for such an interpretation is simply: how else could Wittgenstein be attacking the reductionist programme, except by trying to establish the epistemological flaws in the logicist account of mathematical knowledge? The key to answering this question must be to clarify Wittgenstein's conception of the nature of epistemological problems and their philosophical resolution.

Whereas traditional epistemology maintains that the source of our beliefs must be identified or their grounds be justified in order to *eliminate* sceptical doubts, Wittgenstein insisted in *Philosophical Remarks* that the proper concern of epistemology is to remove the logical confusions that are exemplified by the entertainment of sceptical theses in situations where doubt is *logically excluded.* Such an argument does not entail, however, that Wittgenstein was repudiating epistemology *per se.* In *Groundless Belief,* Michael Williams explains how 'unless the foundational view' (that 'our justification for holding beliefs of a certain kind must be traceable, ultimately, to a body of knowledge "epistemologically prior" to such beliefs') is assumed, 'there would be no call for epistemological theories as we know them'.[34] In essence this is precisely what Wittgenstein was arguing. But this theme certainly did not commit Wittgenstein to a species of 'anti-epistemology'. From the important premise that Wittgenstein wanted to undermine the foundationalist programme, Richard Rorty draws the much stronger conclusion that Wittgenstein intended to 'set aside epistemology as a possible discipline'.[35] But this is not at all the position that Wittgenstein wanted to adopt. Rather, Wittgenstein sought to demonstrate the unintelligibility of foundationalism and in the process to elucidate the proper nature of epistemology. Whether this would undermine much of the distinctive character of epistemology as it has hitherto been conceived is, of course, another matter. But the same is no less true for the philosophy of mathematics; and no one has yet suggested that, because he was intent on dissolving the 'foundations crisis', Wittgenstein had 'set aside the philosophy of mathematics as a possible discipline'.

The distinctive character of epistemology, Wittgenstein argued in *Philosophical Remarks,* lies in the clarification of the logical syntax of epistemic concepts. Thus, we are not engaged in the construction of a theory of 'epistemologically prior knowledge', but rather, in the clarification of those propositions which we treat as epistemologically basic. Such propositions are grammatically 'basic', but not foundational in the reductivist sense. For it is not that the truth of such propositions is 'self-evident' or 'evident to the senses', but simply, that it makes no sense to speak of evidence in connection with these truths. If pressed to identify the source of our knowledge or to justify the basis for our conviction that such propositions are true, we can ultimately only respond by explaining the rules governing the use of the epistemic operator in question: 'How do I know that the colour of this paper, which I call "white", is the same as the one I saw here yesterday? By recognising it again; and recognising it again is my only source of knowledge here. In that case, "That it is the same" *means* that I recognise it again. Then of course you also can't ask whether it really is the same and whether I might not perhaps be mistaken; (whether it *is* the same and doesn't just *seem* to be)' (PR §16). By concentrating on the logical syntax of such propositions, the task of clarifying the nature of belief, knowledge and justification becomes one of *excluding* rather than *refuting* doubt. For '"I cannot tell whether ..." only makes sense if I *can* know, not when it's inconceivable' (PR §69). Philosophical problems, whether in epistemology proper or the foundations of mathematics, will often rest on the need to clarify the grammar of what constitute our foundational beliefs, but this enterprise must in no way be confused with the misguided search for foundations in order to secure our beliefs against sceptical attacks.

> Philosophy solves, or rather gets rid of, only philosophical problems; it does not set our thinking on a more solid basis. What I am attacking is above all the idea that the question 'what is knowledge — e.g. — is a crucial one. That is what it seems to be: it seems as if we didn't yet know anything at all until we can answer *that* question. In our philosophical investigations it is as if we were in a terrible hurry to complete a backlog of unfinished business which has to be finished or else everything else seems to hang in the air. (MS 219, 10)

Wittgenstein's attitude to epistemological scepticism in *Philosophical Remarks* remained fundamentally committed, therefore, to the early themes formulated in the *Notebooks* and the *Tractatus*. Indeed, in what appears to be a direct reference to the argument enunciated at 6.5, Wittgenstein emphasised this point: 'I said: Where you can't look for an answer, you can't ask either, and that means: Where there's no logical method for finding a solution, the question doesn't make sense either' (PR §149). Only this time he added what, for our purposes, is the crucial rider that 'What "mathematical questions" share with genuine questions is simply that they can be answered' (PR §151; cf. AWL 199 ff.). We shall examine in some detail in Chapter 3 the significance which Wittgenstein drew from this thought for his proposed resolution of the 'Decision Problem'. For the moment, it is important to see in which direction this pointed Wittgenstein's remarks on the foundations of mathematics: the question of justifying the truth of mathematical propositions is seriously misconstrued, not because mathematics is 'immune from doubt', but because *it makes no sense* to speak of 'epistemological doubt' in the context of mathematical propositions. Not surprisingly, the route to this point proceeds via the new picture of language. By locating the source of sceptical issues in *Satzsysteme* confusions, Wittgenstein sought to demonstrate that the problem in question 'simply vanishes' once we have grasped the appropriate uses of the expressions. For, as Wittgenstein told Waismann and Schlick: 'The only thing we can do is *to tabulate rules.* If by questioning I have found out concerning a word that the other person at one time recognises these rules, and at another time, those rules, I will tell him, In that case you will have to distinguish exactly *how* you use it; *and there is nothing else I wanted to say*' (WWK 184). Thus, in much of what follows in this book, our basic problem will be to shift our point of view from traditional epistemological or ontological perspectives to Wittgenstein's emphasis on the rules of logical syntax.

This theme is partially illustrated by the question which Wittgenstein believed would suffice to expose the confusion underlying intuitionism: 'When the intuitionists speak of the "basic intuition" — is this a psychological process? If so, how does it come into mathematics?' (PG 322). The crux of Wittgenstein's attack on intuitionism was that it allows spurious 'epistemological' considerations — which manifest themselves in psychologistic confusions — to interfere with its examination of the logical grammar of mathematical propositions. The popular idea that the 1928 Brouwer Lecture might have been the catalyst for a radical conversion from *Tractatus* Realism to intuitionistically-inspired Anti-realism is a fallacy inspired by the epistemological framework which Wittgenstein was struggling to escape. What did interest Wittgenstein in intuitionism was the new light that had been shed on the grammar of mathematical propositions. We cannot hope to understand the full significance of his remarks on this subject, however, until we have placed them in their proper — non-epistemological (and *a fortiori* anti-sceptical) — context. Only thus will we be able to come to terms with Wittgenstein's notorious attacks on such issues as the 'consistency problem' or the 'foundations crisis'. For the mainstay of all of these issues — even if it is seldom recognised as such — is that what we are concerned with are *au fond* classical epistemological problems; and in each case it is this premise itself that Wittgenstein was striving to illuminate and subvert. But since so much hangs on this point for the interpretation of Wittgenstein's remarks on the foundations of mathematics, we must consider these issues in far greater depth before we can proceed to the concrete details of Wittgenstein's investigations.

Notes

1. Herbert Feigl, 'Moritz Schlick, A Memoir', in Moritz Schlick, *Philosophical Papers*, Vol. I, Mulder, H.L. and van de Velde-Schlick, Barbara F.B. (eds) (Dordrecht, D. Reidel Publishing Company, 1979), p. xx.
2. Herbert Feigl, 'No Pot of Message', in *Inquiries and Provocations: Selected Writings, 1929-1974*, Cohen, R.S. (ed.) (Dordrecht, D. Reidel Publishing Company, 1981), p. 8.
3. Cf. G.P. Baker, 'Verehrung und Verkehrung: Waismann and Wittgenstein', in *Wittgenstein: Sources and Perspectives*, Luckhardt, C.G. (ed.) (New York, Cornell University Press, 1979).
4. Moritz Schlick, 'The Turning-Point in Philosophy', in *Philosophical Papers*, Vol. II, p. 156; cf. S.G. Shanker, 'The Significance of the *Tractatus*', in S.G. Shanker (ed.), *Ludwig Wittgenstein: Critical Assessments*, vol. I (London, Croom Helm, 1986).
5. Cf. M. Schlick, 'The Future of Philosophy', in *Philosophical Papers*, Mulder, H. and van de Velde-Schlick, Barbara F.B. (eds) (Dordrecht, D. Reidel Publishing Company, 1979), pp. 213-17.
6. F.P. Ramsey, 'Critical Notice of the *Tractatus*', in *Ludwig Wittgenstein: Critical Assessments*, vol. I, Shanker, S.G. (ed.) (London, Croom Helm, 1986), pp. 41-2.
7. In the Preface to *Philosophical Investigations*, Wittgenstein recorded the important role which Ramsey had played in forcing him to 'recognise the grave mistakes' contained in the *Tractatus* (PI p.viii).
8. B. Russell, *The Autobiography of Bertrand Russell* (London, Unwin Books, 1975), pp. 439-40.
9. E.g., cf. 'Discovering, Creating, Inventing', in *Lectures on the Philosophy of Mathematics*, Grassl, W. (ed.) (Amsterdam, Rodopi, 1982)
10. Saul A. Kripke, *Wittgenstein: On Rules and Private Language* (Oxford, Basil Blackwell, 1982), pp. 69-70.
11. Ibid., pp. 63, 61.
12. Ibid., p. 55.
13. Cf. G.P. Baker and P.M.S. Hacker, *Wittgenstein: Rules, Grammar and Necessity. Volume 2 of an Analytical Commentary on the Philosophical Investigations* (Oxford, Basil Blackwell, 1985).
14. Ibid., p. 9.
15. Cf. ibid., p.87.
16. Ibid., p. 17.
17. Ibid., p. 89.
18. Ibid., p. 110.
19. Ibid., p. 68; cf. Robert Fogelin, 'Wittgenstein and Intuitionism', in *Ludwig Wittgenstein: Critical Assessments*, vol. III.
20. Ibid., p. 21.
21. Ibid., pp. 90-2.
22. Ibid., p.54.
23. Fortunately, the etymology of 'calculate' does not enter into this issue!
24. Philip Kitcher, *The Nature of Mathematical Knowledge* (Oxford, Oxford

University Press, 1983), p. 21.

25. Max Black, 'Verificationism and Wittgenstein's Reflections on Mathematics', in *Ludwig Wittgenstein: Critical Assessments*, vol. III, p. 69.

26. 'Wissenschaftliche Weltauffassung: Der Wiener Kreis', in Otto Neurath's *Empiricism and Sociology*, Neurath, M. and Cohen, R.S. (eds) (Dordrecht, D. Reidel Publishing Company, 1973) p. 311.

27. Ibid.

28. Cf. Hans Hahn, 'Discussion about the Foundations of Mathematics', in *Empiricism, Logic and Mathematics* (Dordrecht, D. Reidel Publishing Company, 1980), p. 37.

29. Friedrich Waismann, 'The Nature of Mathematics: Wittgenstein's Standpoint', in *Ludwig Wittgenstein: Critical Assessments*, vol. III, p. 60.

30. Ibid., pp. 60-1.

31. Ibid., p. 61.

32. Mark Steiner, *Mathematical Knowledge* (New York, Cornell University Press, 1975), p. 15.

33. Ibid., p. 23.

34. Michael Williams, *Groundless Belief* (Oxford, Basil Blackwell, 1977), pp. 13,20.

35. Richard Rorty, *Philosophy and the Mirror of Nature* (Oxford, Basil Blackwell, 1980), p. 6.

2 THE STRAINS IN THE REALIST/ANTI-REALIST FRAMEWORK

> Some people have turned [my] suggestion about asking for the verification into a dogma — as if I'd been advancing a *theory* about meaning.
>
> Gasking and Jackson, 'Wittgenstein as a Teacher'

Wittgenstein's Verificationism

There is a serious danger inherent in the practice of reinterpreting a work in the context of an explanatory framework which is wholly extraneous to the 'horizons' of meaning — as the hermeneuticians would say — of the original book. For the framework itself soon begins to take over, introducing themes and obstacles which distort what the author himself believed he was engaged in or had accomplished, and which initiate heated controversies that are unrelated to the central concerns of his work. Subtle shifts in emphasis and perception are thus produced which lead one into over-hasty generalisations, and perhaps into misinterpretation. It may be true that alternative critical frameworks can open up an entirely new and profound dimension to a text, but the allure of such potential insights must not blind us to the ever-present need for meticulous study of the new terms which we seek to impose on the author and their relevance to his thought.

To a remarkable extent recent criticism of Wittgenstein's later philosophy has been overtaken by just such a critical model: the distinction between 'Realism' and 'Anti-realism' propounded by Michael Dummett. Dummett presented this as an all-embracing framework, and that is precisely the manner in which it has been received. Thus, in his introduction to Waismann's *Lectures on the Philosophy of Mathematics*, Wolfgang Grassl declares that 'There are essentially two rival accounts, realist and antirealist, of the sense of mathematical propositions.'[1] This is not the place to examine in any detail the various philosophical problems that have been raised by Dummett's distinction — problems in conception as much as detail; but we must scrutinise carefully the application of Dummett's framework to Wittgenstein's approach to the philosophy of mathematics. For despite Grassl's confidence, it is extremely difficult to place Wittgenstein's remarks on the nature of mathematical propositions in either school. And that in itself deals a serious blow to the Realist/Anti-realist distinction, not simply because of its global pretensions, but even more significantly, because Wittgenstein's so-called 'conversion' occupies a very special place in the Realist/Anti-realist cosmology.

One frequently encounters the theme that the transition from the *Tractatus* to the post-1929 writings *exemplifies* the shift from 'Realism' to 'Anti-realism. There is even a subtle undercurrent in Anti-realist writings that it was Wittgenstein's 'conversion' which inspired the first accounts of the 'Realist/Anti-realist' distinction (a point which is subtly reinforced by referring to the development of Wittgenstein's thought as a 'conversion'). Certainly some parallels can be found to support such an interpretation, but in large part this is due to the fact that the terms 'Realism' and 'Anti-realism' incorporate a number of distinct theses, some of which touch on parts of Wittgenstein's work while major areas are left where the framework breaks down, thereby undermining any of the critical insights that might otherwise have been afforded. For in many crucial respects the classification becomes intolerably strained, and worse, sets us off in directions which virtually oppose the very arguments that Wittgenstein was trying to present. Before we can address this issue, however, we must consider the Logical Positivists' claim that, whatever his attitude to verificationism in the *Tractatus*, Wittgenstein had become an enthusiastic convert to the logical empiricist cause in the early 1930s. For in many ways the Anti-realist interpretation has merely carried over — and thus suffers from — the same confusions that were present in the verificationist interpretation of the *Tractatus*.

Much of the *Tractatus* was devoted to the clarification of the 'general form of the proposition'.[2] But with the introduction of the *Satzsysteme* conception of language Wittgenstein immediately began to emphasise the breakdown of the *Merkmale* model of 'proposition', and hence to stress the multiplicity of propositional forms. 'The word "proposition"', he now insisted, 'does not signify a sharply bounded concept' (PG 113). The rules for what constitutes a meaningful expression are *Satzsystem*-defined, and *Satzsysteme* are autonomous grammatical constructions, each of which defines its own rules of logical syntax. Hence 'propositional form' is *Satzsysteme*-variable. Nevertheless, Wittgenstein did not abandon his antagonism — which underlies the *Tractatus*'s search for general propositional form — to Russell's abortive account of 'logical experience'.[3] Wittgenstein never wavered in his opposition to Russell's idea that we need a specifically *logical experience* in order to recognise that an expression has sense. He insisted in the *Tractatus* that it is quite simply unintelligible to suppose that we might not have foreseen that an expression constitutes a proposition (TLP 4.5). For to accept Russell's proposed idea would be to suppose that there is an intermediate quasi-epistemological act involved in our 'recognition' of a string of symbols as meaningful.

Wittgenstein remained equally adamant in the early 1930s that this way of stating the matter is completely misguided: the question is not, 'How do we recognise that an expression is meaningful?'; rather, the proper question must be along the lines, 'What renders an expression meaningful?' For the latter is entirely a matter of logical syntax, not a pseudo-epistemological affair. Wittgenstein may have abandoned the quest for 'general propositional form' in *Philosophical Remarks*, therefore, yet it was without relinquishing the emphasis that whether an expression is a proposition is determined by the rules of logical syntax (now Satzsystem-defined). But what if an expression does not belong to a *Satzsystem*; what means would we have of ascertaining whether or not it is a significant proposition? To put this another way, does it make sense to speak of a *Satzsystemlos proposition*? This is one of the immediate problems which Wittgenstein was struggling to resolve in his discussion of the nature of mathematical propositions and proof. For, given the parallels which Wittgenstein was to draw between *Satzsysteme* and *Beweissysteme*, a '*Satzsystemlos* proposition' in mathematics would amount to an 'unproved proposition'. On this issue hangs, therefore, the whole question of whether the 'Decision Problem' can be resolved.

The key to Wittgenstein's answer lies in the unique role which the verification principle was called upon to play (in *Philosophical Remarks* in particular, and less pronouncedly, in *Philosophical Grammar*). Wittgenstein argued that the meaning of a sentence is given by its method of verification in so far as the method of verification manifests to which *Satzsystem* a proposition belongs. But Wittgenstein was not interested in verificationism as a means of limiting knowledge to the bounds of — or defining 'meaning' in terms of — perceptual experience. Admittedly, there is some evidence to suggest that Wittgenstein passed through a 'positivist interlude' shortly after he returned to active work in philosophy in the late 1920s;[4] but it must have been an extremely short-lived phase, for already in *Philosophical Remarks* we can see Wittgenstein carefully distancing himself from this earlier position (cf. PR §§1, 53; WWK 45). Yet he continued to emphasise the importance of his own version of the verification principle in the early 1930s, for he saw verificationism primarily as a method of clarifying the meaning of a proposition by revealing how it relates to the other propositions in a *Satzsystem*. Thus, even if the origins of Wittgenstein's use of the verification principle do trace back to his 'positivist interlude', his continued use of the principle was solely to highlight the techniques involved in clarifying the logical syntax of a proposition. In this latter sense, verificationist sentiments continue to suffuse his mature writings, but it is a verificationism shorn of any interest in epistemological considerations (PI §353). The distinction between Wittgenstein's version of the verification principle and that propounded by the Logical Positivists is thus subtle but extremely important.

There are those, however, who insist that Wittgenstein was never interested in verificationism;[5] while others see Wittgenstein's adoption of verificationism as proof of his conversion from 'Realist' to 'Anti-realist' semantics.[6] Both claims are misguided. Wittgenstein's obvious interest in verificationism in *Philosophical Remarks* and in the discussions recorded in *Wittgenstein and the Vienna Circle* is beyond dispute. Indeed, there are even sufficient grounds to suggest that although the empiricist orientation of the Logical Positivists' verificationism can be traced back to the influence of Russell, Boltzmann, Mach, and perhaps above all else, to Schlick's *Allgemeine Erkenntnislehre*, nevertheless it was Wittgenstein who formulated the verificationist guideline which was promptly communicated to the Circle by Waismann and Schlick, where it was immediately elevated into the 'verification principle'.[7] But then, how are we to account for Wittgenstein's own disclaimer of the slogan, as reported by Gasking and Jackson (*supra*)? The answer to this clearly lies in the remarks which immediately preceded the recantation — if such it was — recorded at the outset of this chapter. Gasking and Jackson recall how, 'At a time when the "Verification Principle" was fashionable in many quarters, Wittgenstein remarked at the Moral Sciences Club: "I

used at one time to say that, in order to get clear how a certain
sentence is used, it was a good idea to ask oneself the question:
'How would one try to verify such an assertion?' But that's just one
way among others of getting clear about the use of a word or
sentence. For example, another question which it is often very useful to ask oneself is: 'How is this word learned?' 'How would one
set about teaching a child to use this word'"?[8] As he makes clear
here, Wittgenstein saw verificationism as part of the general
method for resolving philosophical problems which Waismann had
emphasised at the beginning of 'The Nature of Mathematics:
Wittgenstein's Stand-point' (cf. Chapter 1). But there is a deeper
reason involved, a theme which we can see Wittgenstein continually returning to in his discussions of verificationism in the context of mathematics.

In the hands of the Logical Positivists/Empiricists the verification principle was — not surprisingly — based on epistemological
considerations. If the meaning of a proposition consists in our
method of verifying it, then it only stands to reason that a
meaningful expression cannot (by definition) transcend our veri-
ficational abilities. The bounds of sense are thus firmly tied to what
we are capable of grasping: to our 'recognitional capacities'. In one
sense the former part of this last proposition struck Wittgenstein as
entirely correct; but where it breaks down is in the qualifying
clause, 'recognitional capacities'. Given the fundamentally
epistemological basis of this concept, we suddenly find ourselves
exposed to all sorts of sceptical problems. But such problems are
absurd, Wittgenstein argued, for the very reason that this epistemological premise is spurious. The sense in which a sentence can
only be significant if it is 'graspable' is not concerned with quasi-
epistemological considerations. Rather, this too is solely a matter
of the logical grammar of expressions: the *Satzsystem-consistency*
of expressions. An expression is meaningful when it adheres to the
logical syntax of a *Satzsystem*, and conversely, meaningless if there
are no such *Satzsystem*-rules to determine its use. Both points are
entirely concerned with grammatical intelligibility and not perceptual capabilities. They amount to the claim that, strictly
speaking, '*Satzsystemlos* proposition' is a contradiction in terms.
As we shall see throughout this work, this two-sided argument was
constantly called upon to resolve such problems in the philosophy
of mathematics as the 'decision problem' or the nature of infinity,
and ultimately, to resolve by dissolving the 'foundations crisis'.

It is clear that early on in the 1930s this became the fundamental purpose that Wittgenstein had in mind for the version of
the verification principle that he was interested in: a point which
we can see Wittgenstein labouring to develop in the Ambrose
Lectures when he told his students that 'If you want to know the
meaning of a sentence, ask for its verification. I stress the point
that the meaning of a symbol is its place in the calculus, the way it
is used. ... Attending to the way the meaning of a sentence is
explained makes clear the connection between meaning and verification (AWL 28-9; AWL 61). In *Philosophical Remarks*,
Wittgenstein sought to apply this argument as rigorously as
possible to the philosophy of mathematics: mathematics consists of
a network of calculi, and the meaning of any particular mathematical proposition is *Satzsystem*-specific, and thus must also be
given by its method of verification, which in the case of mathematics is given by its *method of proof.*[9] The emphasis on verification is thus meant to establish the *Satzsysteme*-complexity of the
subject-matter under study, and hence the confusions that have
resulted from an oversimplified framework, or from ignoring the
manner in which mathematical expressions are actually used.

Wittgenstein clearly felt that he had discerned an important
parallel between this verificationist account of mathematics and
constructivism. Thus, for example, he told Waismann and Schlick
that 'what is wrong with the Frege–Russell definition of number is
that it does not specify a method of verification. ... The definition
of a concept points the way to a *verification*, the definition of a
number word (a form) points the way to a *construction*' (WWK
226). This argument was meant to accord with the principle constructivist theme that in order to establish that a mathematical
object exists we must specify a procedure to posit that object. But
for Wittgenstein, to construct a 'mathematical object' was simply
to create a system of rules governing the use of a mathematical
concept within a calculus. Wittgenstein was quite anxious, therefore, that his argument should not be confused with the intuitionists' psychologistic version of constructivism, and when he
discussed the latter he was careful to stress that what he was thinking of was the rule-governed application of a concept: '"The
highest point of a curve" doesn't mean "the highest point among
all the points of the curve" — after all, we don't see these — it is a
specific point yielded by the curve. ... The curve exists, independently of its individual points. This also finds expression in the

fact that I construct its highest point: that is, derive it from a law and not by examining individual points' (PR §172). The wording of such a passage must not mislead one, however, into believing that Wittgenstein was secretly harbouring platonist convictions.[10] Quite the contrary, his point was that the curve just is the law giving its formulation, as opposed to the — platonist — extensional confusion which supposes that this amounts to saying that the curve exists in the sense of its being the totality of its points. Wittgenstein was not suggesting that the curve can be described in terms of, or is separate from, the rule governing its development; rather, the curve simply is the rule.

The objection to intuitionist versions of constructive existence proofs that particularly concerned Wittgenstein was not the issue of 'strict' versus 'moderate' finitism. (E.g. whether it is enough to specify a procedure by which an object could, at least in principle, be constructed.) What especially disturbed Wittgenstein was the suggestion that there is a general form of constructive existence proof. The burden of his argument was to establish that corresponding to the different kinds of mathematical calculi are different kinds of mathematical propositions (and hence, different kinds of *proof*). 'One could say "proof" has as many different meanings as there are proofs. All the proofs form a family, and the word "proof" does not refer to any one characteristic of those processes called proofs' (AWL 116; cf. AWL 117, PG 374). It is this idea which led Wittgenstein to insist that 'each new proof in mathematics widens the meaning of "proof"' (AWL 10). We employ different techniques or forms of argument to put a mathematical expression 'in the archives', and there is no predeterminate set of (syntactic or semantic) conditions which an argument must satisfy in order to qualify as a proof (PG 374). Certainly epistemological considerations have no bearing on what we are permitted to count as a proof (*infra*).

It is quite commonly argued now, however, that Wittgenstein's interest in constructivism and verificationism are proof of his conversion to 'Anti-realism'. Indeed, the school of criticism which Michael Dummett inaugurated with his work on Anti-realism exploited Wittgenstein's obvious interest in constructivism from 1929 onwards as proof of his whole-hearted conversion from 'Realist' to 'Anti-realist' semantics. It was this fundamental philosophical shift which supposedly led Wittgenstein to attempt to employ this new conceptual model in a wide-ranging sceptical attack on the classical problems in the foundations of mathematics. The rationale for this interpretation is quite straightforward: platonism and constructivism are identified as sub-species of a sweeping distinction between Realism and Anti-realism which encompasses virtually every area of philosophical inquiry. According to Dummett:

> What distinguishes platonists from constructivists is that, for the latter, an explanation of the meaning of a mathematical statement essentially involves reference to, and in fact consists in, a stipulation of what is to count as a proof of it; understanding a statement amounts to being able to recognise, for any mathematical construction, whether or not it is a proof of it. For the platonist, on the other hand, the meaning of a mathematical statement is given ... by a determination of its truth-conditions, thought of as determined independently of whether we can recognise the truth-value of the statement or not.[11]

Hence, since Wittgenstein converted from a platonist — or at least. bearing in mind the obscurity of the *Tractatus* remarks on mathematics, from Platonism *simpliciter* — to a constructivist philosophy of mathematics, it follows that in general terms, Wittgenstein converted from a Realist to an Anti-realist conception of 'meaning' in the philosophy of mathematics as well as in the philosophy of language.

This is a difficult argument to come to terms with, not simply in trying to identify who these 'platonists' and 'constructivists' that Dummett alludes to are, but more importantly, to grasp what it means to describe the meaning of a mathematical statement as given by a determination of its truth-conditions. For surely the essence of a mathematical proposition — at least as far as platonists are concerned — is that it is true under all conditions? Dummett's framework attempts to substitute a precise description for what is, after all, merely a picture. But the danger with his proffered explanation is ultimately that a new, 'meta-linguistic' set of pictures is substituted for the old classical version. The principal theme in the classical platonist/constructivist dispute revolved upon the question of whether the mathematician *discovers* or *creates* mathematical truths. It is, of course, precisely this aspect which Dummett hopes to capture with his explanations of the different conceptions of *meaning* which are involved in these pictures. But there is also a much more technical side to the platonist/constructivist dispute which goes largely ignored (or distorted) in Dummett's version, and it is precisely this aspect which most concerned the original protagonists.

In particular, Kronecker's influence on the development of constructivism — which was obviously paramount — fades into the background. Kronecker had insisted that in order to prove that a mathematical object exists it is necessary to show how that object can be constructed. It is an admittedly obscure idea, made even more opaque by the stipulation that the objects we are concerned with are mental entities. But what this really amounted to was an attack on the mathematical use of indirect proofs. Arguing by *reductio* may be a clever debating technique, but it is entirely inadequate for mathematical purposes, where what we need above all else is a precise procedure for constructing the various entities we have posited. We quickly lose sight of this crucial point on the Realist/Anti-realist account, however, as we engage in internal wrangles about the relative merits of rival 'theories of meaning'. For example, Dummett argues in 'Realism' that 'Since in mathematics there is neither a reductive class nor any conclusive indirect evidence, no sense can attach, for a constructivist, to the notion of a statement's being true if this is to mean any less than that we are actually in possession of a proof of it.'[12] This theme of 'the possession of a proof' is a leitmotif running throughout Anti-realist writings on constructivism. Perhaps there is a sense in which this applies to the constructivist prohibition of proof by *reductio ad absurdum*, but then, the focus of emphasis has shifted imperceptibly from a controversy over the *nature* of proof to one over the *possession* of proof, where the latter seems to be based on epistemological as opposed to logical considerations (*infra*). Thus, whereas the former is a controversy over the logical status of a mathematical proof, the latter carries with it a disturbing hint of sceptical overtones (viz. how can we be certain that someone is in possession of a proof, or indeed, that a proof *really is* a proof!).

Admittedly Dummett wants to encourage the shift from talking about the nature to the possession of proof in order to remove the original dispute to an entirely different conceptual plane, where what is at issue is 'a dispute concerning the kind of *meaning* which [the statements of the disputed] class have'.[13] It is a novel suggestion that has proved extremely powerful in the existing climate of meta-linguistic analysis. The basic problem with it as far as Wittgenstein's writings on the philosophy of mathematics are concerned, however, is that Wittgenstein was clearly concerned with the classical framework, and what is more, trying to resolve the problems at issue by showing how their very genesis was due to the assumptions buried in that framework. And as was emphasised in the first chapter, it was not as a participant, but rather, as a critic of the very structure of that game that Wittgenstein was trying to operate. But the Anti-realist would have us accept that it was that very stance — from an entirely new point outside the established approaches to the foundations dispute — which, unbeknownst to Wittgenstein himself, constituted the first tentative formulation of what we now identify as an Anti-realist semantics. Let us see, then, how well the Realist/Anti-realist framework accords with both the spirit and the content of Wittgenstein's pre- and post-*Tractatus* thought.

Wittgenstein's 'Conversion'

We can quickly dispense with the suggestion that the *Tractatus* account of mathematics was platonist in the Realist terms that Dummett lays down.[14] In response to such an assumption we need only recall how Wittgenstein insisted point-blank at 6.2-6.21 that 'The propositions of mathematics are equations, and therefore pseudo-propositions. A proposition of mathematics does not express a thought.' In which case it is obviously impossible to apply Dummett's scheme that 'For the platonist, the meaning of a mathematical statement is to be explained in terms of its truth-conditions.'[15] If this is what mathematical platonism in the Realist sense means, then quite simply the *Tractatus* account of mathematics lies completely outside of its ken. It might be thought, however, that even though the *Tractatus* cannot be thus described as 'platonist', nevertheless it could at any rate still be described as Realist in the larger sense, on the grounds that since Dummett's definition of Realism — the meaning of a statement is to be explained in terms of its truth-conditions — only applies to meaningful statements, then the *Tractatus* account of equations leaves this theme intact, on the grounds that mathematical propositions are removed by fiat from what Dummett calls the 'disputed class'. Such a reading might be awkward in so far as it would mean classifying Wittgenstein as a Realist in one area and at least a potential Anti-realist in another, but perhaps that is the necessary price for preserving the 'conversion' picture? There are further serious obstacles, however, to this Realist interpretation of the *Tractatus*.

For one thing, Wittgenstein never openly suggested that we can understand propositions which 'transcend our recognitional capacities'; notoriously, the Vienna Circle interpreted Wittgenstein's stress on the principle of bivalency as committing him to the exact opposite — verificationist — position. Admittedly, agnosticism does not amount to repudiation, but there are deeper problems in store for the Realist interpretation of the *Tractatus*. For what Wittgenstein argued is that the meaning of *molecular propositions* is to be explained in terms of their truth-conditions; but that immediately rules out *elementary* propositions. For the term *truth-conditions* is specifically applied only to the meaning of molecular propositions which are constructed out of truth-functional operators (those whose meaning can be exhibited by truth-tables). They thus presuppose significant elementary propositions: logically simple propositions whose meaning is given by the objects which they denote, and thus which cannot themselves be explained by truth-conditions. Hence, far from licensing us to apply the truth-conditional account of meaning to every proposition of natural language and mathematics, the *Tractatus* explicitly limited the application of the concept to the circumscribed class of molecular propositions.[16]

What we have, then, is a situation where the Realist model touches the *Tractatus* at the point of the explanation of the meaning of molecular propositions in which a logical constant occurs — which is hardly surprising, seeing that the *Tractatus* account of the meaning of molecular propositions serves as one of the paradigms for the definition of Realism — and yet where large areas of the 'disputed class' fall outside of the framework. The danger is thus that an over-hasty attempt to classify the *Tractatus* as Realist will lead us to misconstrue what Wittgenstein was actually saying about the meaning of elementary or mathematical propositions. Furthermore, the framework itself can become the source of unnecessary confusion, for there are distinctly constructivist elements in the brief remarks on mathematics in the *Tractatus*, but these can no more be fitted into the Anti-realist model of constructivism than into the Realist model of platonism.

The basic stumbling-block to this move remains in the fact that Wittgenstein classified equations as meaningless 'pseudo-propositions' (6.2). With all of the mounting difficulties confronting us, it is difficult to see what benefit the model can serve as an exegetical device with which to approach the *Tractatus*; particularly as far as the *Tractatus* account of mathematics is concerned. Of course, it would greatly facilitate the Anti-realist reading of *Philosophical Investigations* and *Remarks on the Foundations of Mathematics* if Wittgenstein's repudiation of the *Tractatus* could be seen as a repudiation of Realism; but then, the needs of the framework must not be allowed to function as their own justification.

The situation is even more complicated when we turn to *Philosophical Remarks*. Part of the appeal of Dummett's Anti-realist version of constructivism is that it seems to open up a method of interpreting the later Wittgenstein as a constructivist of sorts even though he was so intent on destroying the constructivists' picture of mathematical objects as mental entities. But although Dummett's version allows us to classify Wittgenstein as a constructivist while escaping the psychologism of the classical versions, it opens up an entirely different problem. The apparent strength of Dummett's account is that it draws a parallel between the constructivist notion of an *effective procedure* for constructing a mathematical object and the Anti-realist notion of explaining the meaning of a proposition in terms of the assertion-conditions which justify its use. But the problem with Dummett's move from constructivism to Anti-realism is that he is imposing a model specifically based on empirical propositions onto mathematical propositions. As we shall see in Chapter 3, Dummett wants to argue that Wittgenstein was extremely interested in an empiricist philosophy of mathematics: an idea which would no doubt help to smooth the way towards his Anti-realist/constructivist interpretation of *Remarks on the Foundations of Mathematics*. But the fundamental purpose of Wittgenstein's remarks on the nature of mathematical propositions was to stress the logical demarcation between mathematical and empirical propositions in order to highlight the manner in which mathematical propositions are rules of logical syntax whereas empirical propositions are (contingently true or false) descriptions of the world. But the picture is far more complicated in *Philosophical Remarks*, and it is here where the proponents of the Anti-realist/constructivist thesis can have most hope of finding a foothold for their theory.

On the one hand, Wittgenstein stressed in *Philosophical Remarks* that mathematical propositions are rules of logical syntax, i.e. grammatical constructions, which are *ipso facto* conceptually different from empirical propositions. In which case, the Anti-realist thesis bogs down before it can even get started, for if a mathematical proposition is a species of rule or convention, then the idea of 'what we count as evidence for its truth' can have no bearing. To be a rule just is to be placed outside of this evidential framework; nothing counts as evidence of either its truth or falsity *because* we have elected to treat it as a rule. This is precisely the point that Wittgenstein wanted to make clear in *Remarks On the Foundations of Mathematics* when he asked: '*What* is unshakeably certain about what is proved? To accept a proposition as unshakeably certain — I want to say — means to use it as a grammatical rule: this removes uncertainty from it' (III §39). Having said that, it is also true that Wittgenstein was preoccupied in *Philosophical Remarks* with discerning the similarities between mathematics and natural language, and as part of his general inquiry into what licenses us in even talking of mathematical theorems and equations as 'propositions' he compared the meaning of a mathematical proposition and its method of proof to the meaning of an empirical proposition and its method of verification.

Wittgenstein might thus seem to have been articulating a parallel very much along the lines that Dummett is seeking at §148 of *Philosophical Remarks*, where he argued that 'in a very important sense, every significant proposition must teach us through its sense how we are to convince ourselves whether it is true or false. "Every proposition says what is the case if it is true." And with a mathematical proposition this "what is the case" must refer to the way in which it is to be proved.' But we must not allow the verificationist overtones which predominate in *Philosophical Remarks* to undermine the fundamental point about the *contrast* between the two types of expression which Wittgenstein was ultimately illustrating, and the point that it makes sense to speak of a mathematical proposition as (normatively) certain precisely because it makes no sense to speak of the *evidence* for the truth of that proposition. For Wittgenstein's overall concern was to elucidate the nature of the logical demarcation between empirical and mathematical propositions while at the same time describing the nature of the parallels which account for our placing them both within the larger 'family' relationship of being *propositions*. That is, the dual problem confronting us here is: Why do we refer to mathematical propositions as 'propositions', and how do they differ from empirical propositions?

The answer to both these questions lies in the fact that we use one and the same method — the verification principle — in order to clarify the logical difference between the two species of proposition. 'If you want to know what a proposition means, you can always ask "How do I know that?" Do I know that there are 6 permutations of 3 elements in the same way in which I know there are 6 people in this room? No. There the first proposition is of a different *kind* from the second' (PR §114). In one sense we can speak of the construction of a proof as similar to the process of verifying an empirical proposition, therefore, but the very term 'constructing a proof' highlights the difference: that in the one case we are concerned with grammatical stipulation versus empirical verification or falsification in the other. This is the very point which Wittgenstein soon came to emphasise so strongly. We must not allow the subtle parallels, therefore, to blind us to the fact that mathematical propositions are divorced from the evidential framework as it is empirically understood. But the Anti-realist picture is *intrinsically* based on the logical nature of empirical propositions as opposed to grammatical conventions. Hence, when we try to treat Wittgenstein's constructivism as merely a mathematical application of Anti-realist sentiments, the interpretation becomes intolerably strained precisely because we are now violating the distinction between rule and empirical proposition: we are seeking to impose a model which by its very nature is ill-equipped to deal with this categorially distinct species of expression.

It is thus entirely misleading to classify the two grammatically disparate types of expression involved here under the same category. That is not to sanction the 'Anti-realist' model for empirical propositions, however; only to clarify the unintelligibility of the framework as far as mathematical propositions are concerned. (The problems involved in the former issue are of an entirely different character.) What exactly does it mean when Dummett says that 'the meaning of mathematical statements are tied directly to what we count as evidence for them', albeit not in the same way as occurs for empirical propositions? The essence of Wittgenstein's account is that the meaning of a mathematical proposition is characterised by the fact that it is *not* tied directly to the production of evidence in the way that is true of empirical propositions; that it makes no sense to speak of evidence in the context of mathematical propositions. Thus, it is not that we are dealing with a different 'species of evidence', but rather, that the concept of evidence is *logically excluded* from this domain. If what we are interested in is why we refer to equations as 'propositions', or why we treat them as necessary truths, then we must seek for enlightenment in some other aspect of their use.

Of course, Dummett seeks to fill out his Anti-realist picture by treating the proof of a mathematical proposition as a mathematical *analogue* for tying the meaning of a proposition to what counts as evidence for it. Hence he argues that 'Wittgenstein adopts a version ... of constructivism; for him it is of the essence of a mathematical statement that it is asserted as the conclusion of a *proof.*'[17] That is, this identifies Wittgenstein as a constructivist in Dummett's Anti-realist sense because 'in mathematics an anti-realist (i.e. a constructivist) position involves holding that a mathematical statement can be true only in virtue of *actual* evidence, that is, our actually possessing a proof.'[18] Disregarding the appeal to evidence here — the problem of what exactly it means to describe a proof as an 'analogue of a method of verification' — this interpretation fits in with some of the arguments presented in *Philosophical Remarks*. But this becomes the very picture that Wittgenstein wanted to overthrow. A mathematical proposition is not in some sense a free-floating expression, standing in need of a proof; rather, a mathematical proposition is *internally* tied to its proof: we cannot even speak of the existence of a mathematical proposition in the absence of a proof (cf. Chapter 3). It is not that we can only be certain that a mathematical proposition is true if we possess a proof; it is that the two concepts — proposition and proof — are *inextricably* bound together. The purpose of this argument is quite simply to bring out the point that a mathematical proof is a *grammatical construction*, and thus a mathematical proposition is a *grammatical convention*, whose role is carved out by the internal relations established in the proof. It makes no sense to speak of producing a proof as evidence of the truth of a mathematical proposition, therefore, for the proof determines the essence of the mathematical proposition, and it is as unintelligible to suggest that the proof provides the evidence for itself as it is to assert that rules stand in need of evidence.

Thus, although Wittgenstein drew a parallel between mathematical and empirical propositions — between methods of proof and methods of verification — in order to clarify why both are described as 'propositions', his ultimate aim was to highlight their difference: viz. that the one is concerned with the construction of rules of logical syntax whereas the other is concerned with the description of reality. That is not to deny that Wittgenstein succumbed to some extent at the time of writing *Philosophical Remarks* to the fascination of developing a so-called 'verificationist' account of mathematics. A classic illustration of this influence can be found in Waismann's insistence in 'The Nature of Mathematics: Wittgenstein's Standpoint' that 'the meaning of a mathematical concept is the manner of its use, and the significance of a mathematical proposition is the method of its verification.'[19] Without the background to this somewhat curious remark — such as is provided in *Philosophical Remarks* — it can be difficult indeed to distinguish the anti-epistemological intention of Wittgenstein's approach. As we shall see in Chapter 7, Wittgenstein turned to this format largely because he was so intent on undermining the argument that mathematical propositions are tautologies. Yet all the while Wittgenstein was exploring parallels, not identities, between mathematical and empirical propositions in order to bring this out. Which leads us to what is perhaps the most important danger in trying to place Wittgenstein's remarks on the philosophy of mathematics within an Anti-realist framework.

We have so far been exploring the problems involved in reading Wittgenstein's arguments in the light of Dummett's conception that 'For the constructivist, the general form of an explanation of meaning must be in terms of the conditions under which we regard ourselves as justified in asserting a statement, that is, the circumstances in which we are in possession of a proof.'[20] The problems we have hitherto been concerned with all arise from trying to apply a conception which is specifically based on the nature of empirical propositions to Wittgenstein's remarks on the normative status of mathematical propositions. The very use of the central theme, 'the justification of the assertion of a statement', is proof enough of this. But we must also confront a related problem which results from the temptation to tie this notion of 'regarding ourselves as justified in asserting a statement' to the important gloss on the blatantly vague concept of 'possession of a proof'. In 'The Reality of the Past', Dummett argues that 'For the contructivist ... there is nothing for the truth of a mathematical statement to consist in save our possession of a proof of it: our understanding of a mathe-matical statement does not reside in our grasp of what it is for the statement to be true, independently of any proof of it, but rather in our capacity to recognise a proof or a disproof of the statement when we see one.'[21] It is not surprising, given the veiled verifi-cationist origins of the framework, that 'possession of a proof' should have been interpreted by Dummett and those who have followed him as 'the capacity to recognise a proof'. It is this notion of 'recognitional capacities' which has increasingly come to dominate the Anti-realist interpretation of Wittgenstein's interest in constructivism. But it introduces a theme — indeed, very much the same sort of theme that Russell introduced into his account of logical analysis — which undermines much of what Wittgenstein intended.

The closest that Wittgenstein came to suggesting that our under-standing of a mathematical proposition resides in our capacity to recognise a proof of it is at §121 in *Philosophical Remarks*: 'An equation is a rule of syntax. Doesn't that explain why we cannot have questions in mathematics that are in principle unanswerable? For if the rules of syntax cannot be grasped, they're of no use at all. And equally, it explains why an infinity that transcends our powers of comprehension cannot enter into these rules.' But before we hasten to embrace the Anti-realist thesis on the basis of this passage (and the similar thoughts which suffuse the later works) we must be careful that we have interpreted the argument accurately in terms of the context in which it was developed. For what has struck many as proof of Wittgenstein's Anti-realist proclivities was actually presented as a gloss on what the intuition-ists meant by speaking of the infinite as 'transcending our powers of comprehension' in the strictly grammatical terms of logical syntax: not in the quasi-epistemological terms of a 'recognitional ability'. Clearly the moral being drawn in the above passage was that the explanation for why such 'questions' are unanswerable lies firmly in the realm of logical syntax: in the theme that mathe-matical propositions *qua* rules of syntax *must* (by definition) be *grammatically* — as opposed to *epistemologically* — intelligible.

The notion of a 'recognitional ability' is obscure. If what is meant is simply that understanding is akin to an ability — to use a proposition correctly — then the motto reads as a trivial reformu-lation of Wittgenstein's later explanation of understanding. Cer-tainly one of the points that Wittgenstein was making in §16 of

Philosophical Remarks (*supra*) was that to say that I understand what 'white' means entails that I am able to recognise white things. But it is quite clear that the emphasis placed on 'recognitional abilities' is intended to capture the essence of the dispute over the application of the law of excluded middle in such recondite areas as 'questions involving infinite extensions'. In this respect Goldbach's Conjecture is said to 'transcend our recognitional capacities' because our powers of comprehension are 'finitely bound'. But such a way of describing the problem is illicit: a result of the confusion of *possibility* with *totality* (cf. Chapter 5). Moreover, there is more than a distinct hint here that, as far as the philosophy of mathematics is concerned, this is the direct result of spurious epistemological considerations creeping forward once again. After all, if the understanding of a mathematical proposition resided in a recognitional capacity, this would have the disastrous result that whether an expression was meaningful would be a question that could only be answered relative to some particular individual at a specific moment. For recognitional capacities might vary from subject to subject, and over time. Certainly this theme would open the door to all sorts of bizarre sceptical worries; and indeed, has done so.

We can see Wittgenstein moving forcefully in *Philosophical Remarks* towards the goal of demonstrating the absurdity of this reading by hinting at the unintelligibility of such consequences. Far from entertaining any such 'quasi-epistemological' thesis, Wittgenstein took the verificationist principle — in the form commonly expressed by e.g. Schlick — and purged it of any spurious epistemological overtones. Or rather, he demonstrated that the only issue we are genuinely involved with here is a logical issue, and our task is thus to translate the misguided epistemological version into the legitimate logical problem with which we should be concerned. In other words, we must demonstrate how the thesis that 'we cannot understand a proposition which transcends our recognitional capcities' is a muddled version of a logical principle which as such is completely unconnected with any 'medical limitations'. And in essence, the key to the argument is that, far from resting on any sceptical considerations, the reason why we cannot understand a 'statement that transcends our recognitional capacities' is that the very notion is itself nonsensical. This argument turns completely on the rules of intelligibility as laid down by *Satzsysteme*. A 'question' such as 'Are there four 7s in the expansion of π?' — where the expansion is treated as a predeterminate totality — is unintelligible in much the same way as a 'question' such as 'Is the chair despondent?'. In the latter case we have a clear-cut example of grammatical confusion created by *Satzsysteme* transgression: it is logically absurd to suggest that some other being with a more refined perceptual or empathetic faculty might be able to tell us whether the chair was feeling depressed. And the same considerations are operating in the question of the number of 7s that occur in the predeterminate expansion of π. It is not recognitional limitations which render the latter unanswerable; it is logical grammar which renders it unintelligible. Hence it is absurd in the same sense to suppose that a being with an 'infinite intellect' would be able to answer such a 'question', since he would be able to survey this infinite expansion (cf. Chapter 3).

At the beginning of *Frege's Conception of Numbers as Objects*, Crispin Wright asks, is it not 'natural to say that Goldbach's Conjecture must be determinately either true or false?'[22] It has certainly become the norm to approach the issue in this manner; so much so that we are likely to overlook the fact that the problem thus phrased cannot encompass what Wittgenstein actually said. For Wittgenstein's argument was that the conjecture is *meaningless*, whereas only a proposition is logically part — by definition — of the true/false game. Wittgenstein was not denying, as the Anti-realist interpretation would have it, that there is not some 'fact in the world' which determines whether the conjecture is true or false; rather, Wittgenstein was insisting that the very manner in which this problem has been framed is the source of our difficulties. If it makes no sense to treat a mathematical conjecture as a meaningful proposition, then the very question whether such a conjecture is determinately true or false is expunged: and with it, the entire Realist/Anti-realist dispute which hinges on the answer to this question. The fact that we cannot in principle determine whether a sentence is true or false — that we cannot apply the law of excluded middle — is a *criterion* (*contra* the Anti-realist thesis) for our saying that the expression is meaningless. *Not* that the thought expressed by the sentence 'transcends our recognitional capacities', but rather, that no thought has been expressed! But as part of his anti-revisionist policy, Wittgenstein conceived of his philosophical responsibility here as that of explaining what the verificationists and intuitionists really meant when they employed this notion of *transcends*. Thus, the Anti-realist interpretation confuses

Wittgenstein's position for the very conception that he had set out to rectify.

The problem here is not to obliterate the distinction between mathematical propositions and conjectures by treating the latter as a 'shadow' (i.e. meaningful) proposition on the grounds that the rules for its use already — tacitly — exist, and our job is merely to disclose those rules. Rather, our task here is to liberate ourselves from the platonist confusions which underlie this argument and clarify precisely what logical-syntactical role an expression plays when there are no rules as yet for its use. That is, we must clarify that strictly speaking a mathematical conjecture is only an heuristic device, while the proposition created by the construction of a proof is inseparable from the proof itself, and is thus not the conjecture in a different garb. Hence we must not confuse or conflate the two notions that we are dealing with and suppose that Wittgenstein was arguing that mathematical conjectures cannot be determinately true or false until a proof has been constructed. Mathematical conjectures will *never* be true or false; to be a mathematical conjecture is *ipso facto* to be divorced from the concepts of *meaning* and *truth*. Whereas the *proposition* that the conjecture may guide us to construct is by definition (i.e. *internally*) related to the concepts of *meaning* and — in the peculiarly normative sense — *mathematical truth* (cf. Chapter 3).

The argument turns, therefore, on the logical syntax of the notions of *mathematical conjecture* and *proposition*, and is thus completely divorced from any epistemological considerations about our powers of recognition. The problem is not that we cannot be certain whether a mathematical conjecture is true or false; rather, it is that it makes no sense to apply the concept of certainty to a mathematical conjecture. The reason for this is epistemological only in the purely negative sense that by clarifying the grammar of the concept *mathematical conjecture* we recognise that it is logically absurd to speak of 'truth' or 'certainty' at all as far as these expressions are concerned. The problem, therefore, is quite simply one of clarifying the nature of nonsense, which by its very nature excludes sceptical considerations. Wittgenstein was not suggesting, as the Anti-realist interpretation contends, that we cannot understand *statements* that transcend our recognitional capacities: the very notion is unintelligible. What he was saying is that we cannot understand expressions that transgress logical barriers. That such expressions are unintelligible is solely a matter for logical syntax to decide, and it is for this reason that Wittgenstein continued to insist that what he was doing in no way related to raising matters of *doubt*. Our task is not to eliminate the possibility of doubt so as to achieve epistemological certainty: it is to exclude the very possibility of expressing doubt by recognising that what we are concerned with are purely questions of logical syntax. In the ensuing chapters we must try to fill out some of the details of this admittedly highly schematic outline of Wittgenstein's argument, as well as consider how strongly it bears on the resolution of some of the more intransigent issues in the philosophy of mathematics; but first it will be helpful if we conclude the present chapter by looking at a theme which is fast becoming a critical orthodoxy among Anti-realists.

The Objectivity of Mathematical Knowledge

It happens not infrequently in the violent arena of critical trends that what was originally intended as a passing aside suddenly becomes the rallying-cry for a militant new school of criticism. If not for Dummett's acute powers of perception, Kreisel's brief comment on the objectivity of mathematics would no doubt have suffered the fate of countless other forgotten footnotes (whether to Plato or otherwise). As it is, the so-called 'Kreisel dictum' — that the essential issue between platonists and constructivists has more to do with the objectivity of mathematical truths than with the existence of mathematical objects — has become the slogan for Anti-realist writings on the philosophy of mathematics. It is not at all clear, however, that either of these alternatives adequately characterises the key element of the conflict between the two schools; yet, as further evidence of the Anti-realists' general disregard for the attitudes or conceptions of the original protagonists, it little matters that the classical platonists and constructivists might have thought that they were disputing the nature of mathematical reality or the criteria for satisfactory existence proofs. For what these early antagonists were really manifesting, as far as the Anti-realist interpretation is concerned, was their instinctive philosophical attitude to the notion of a 'verification transcendent' species of mathematical proposition.

Thus, according to Dummett, the 'real disagreement' between platonists and intuitionists 'relates to the kind of meaning we succeed in conferring upon mathematical statements'.[23] It is not the ontological issue about mathematical reality which provides the grounds for the dispute about the nature of the 'meanings' of mathematical statements, therefore, but the reverse: 'It is more tempting to suppose that there is a dependence in the opposite direction. If one believes, with the platonists, that we have conferred on our mathematical statements meanings such as to render them all determinately either true or false independently of our knowledge, then one will find it natural to adopt the picture of a mathematical reality existing, fully determinate, independently of us.'[24] The notion of a transfinite cardinal number as subsisting in an external mathematical reality may be a totally opaque picture, but this counter-explanation of the central thesis underlying platonism — and the 'Objectivist/Anti-objectivist' distinction which has sprung from it — is no more perspicuous.

It is one thing to suggest that classical Platonists and intuitionists might be unhappy with this formulation of their dispute over the question of whether we discover or invent mathematical truths, but it is not at all clear that the budding Anti-realist will himself be fully comfortable with this transformation. He too will want to clarify whether the essential issue between platonists and constructivists concerns the argument that 'mathematical reality lies outside us [and] our function is to discover or *observe* it';[25] or is rather whether there is a distinction between a mathematical proposition's being true and being judged to be true. Yet if it is the latter, then one would naturally have supposed that the antithesis to the 'Objectivity' thesis would be *subjectivity*, in which case one suspects that quite a few Anti-realists would promptly disown the argument. After all, the Anti-realist principle that meaning cannot be secured by any 'facts-in-the-world' is hardly intended to result in the claim that there is no such thing as objective meaning. Indeed, the whole purpose of the community view just is to render rule-following a perfectly objective phenomenon.

That matters are not quite so straightforward on the Realist/ Anti-realist framework is merely an indication that the 'Objectivist/Anti-objectivist' distinction is not quite what one would expect. The antithesis to the 'Objectivity' thesis, Crispin Wright tells us, is the 'Anti-objectivity' thesis that the truth-value of a statement cannot be determinate irrespective of whether we can recognise the fact as holding.[26] But the danger in this line of thought (as Wright himself appreciates[27]) is that the 'Objectivity/

Anti-objectivity' thesis will not so much mirror as simply recapitulate under a different name the basic Realist/Anti-realist distinction. It certainly begins to look as though the 'Anti-objectivity' principle that 'there are no transcendent mathematical facts' means nothing more than that the meaning of a mathematical proposition is not secured by 'facts-in-the-world'. But, of course, the two are very different propositions indeed, as becomes particularly clear when we consider the application of the thesis to Wittgenstein's approach to the foundations dispute. For whatever the hidden subtlety involved in this issue might be, it soon emerges that the 'Objectivity/Anti-objectivity' distinction must also break down irretrievably as far as Wittgenstein's arguments are concerned.

In 'Rule-Following, Objectivity and the Theory of Meaning', Wright maintains that 'the Wittgenstein of the *Investigations* and *Remarks on the Foundations of Mathematics* is, rightly or wrongly, sceptical about investigation-independence, and ... the grounds for that scepticism are embedded in his discussion of rule-following.'[28] 'Investigation-independence' is one of those quasi-technical terms that seem to proliferate in Anti-realist writings, which purport to be solely concerned with logical questions, but which harbour the very assumptions that Wittgenstein regarded as 'epistemological' confusions. In *Wittgenstein on the Foundations of Mathematics*, Wright explains that 'it is a presupposition of the intelligibility of the realist's attitude to "$(x)FX$" that sense can be made of the idea that each "Fa" has an investigation-independent, determinate truth-value — is true, or false, independently of our investigation. ... It is the conception of objectivity thus outlined which the Wittgensteinian is opposing: the idea of the investigation-independent determinacy in truth-value of decidable statements — henceforward, for short, *investigation independence*.'[29] But no one apart from an idealist would seriously wish to dispute this notion of truth as far as ordinary empirical propositions are concerned. Given that 'My desk is in my study' is a 'decidable statement', then Realist and Anti-realist alike would surely agree that the truth-value of this assertion is 'investigation-independent'. Of course, the idea underlying this argument is that it must in principle be possible to investigate whether the facts are as so stated, but if that is all that is meant, why bother to dignify the verification principle with nothing more than a misleading new title? For this revised version of the dogma creates a false impression, suggesting Berkleian as opposed to positivist intentions.

Clearly we are meant to be concerned here, however, with a rather more subtle type of problem than that which is offered by ordinary empirical propositions. Or, for that matter, by ordinary mathematical propositions; for, as we shall see below, the truth of '2 + 2 = 4' also seems to be 'investigation-independent', albeit not quite in the manner envisaged by the 'Anti-objectivist' thesis. But the obvious intention of this argument is conveyed by the select example which is chosen in Wright's exposition: quantification over 'infinite totalities'. Thus we return once again to the question of the status of 'verification-transcendent propositions'; only now an entirely new suggestion has been infiltrated into the discussion, for we find the rejection of the notion of a predeterminate truth-value for questions involving quantification over 'infinite extensions' reinterpreted as evidence of a basic hostility to the 'investigation-independence' of true propositions *tout court.* Certainly there is no indication in the passage from 'Rule-following, Objectivity and the Theory of Meaning' quoted above that we are dealing with a highly specialised type of expression. Consequently, an argument that was intended to be a demonstration of the confusions resulting from the unintelligible concepts *infinite extension* and *universal quantification* (cf. Chapter 5) has been seized upon as proof of Wittgenstein's disguised incursion against the Objectivity of mathematical knowledge *per se.*

The very suggestion that Wittgenstein was engaged in an 'Anti-objectivist' critque is redolent of the spurious epistemic overtones that we have been struggling to expose in this and the preceding chapter. That this is the very sort of conception which he wanted to undermine is certainly reinforced by such passages as that in *Philosophical Investigations* in which Wittgenstein argued that 'what a mathematician is inclined to say about the objectivity and reality of mathematical facts, is not a philosophy of mathematics, but something for philosophical *treatment*' (§254). That is, it is not the reverse or 'Anti-objectivist' position that Wittgenstein argued for; he simply disputed the assumption that it is intelligible to speak *in the normal sense* about the objectivity of 'mathematical facts'. Far from wishing to undermine the objectivity of mathematical knowledge, however, what Wittgenstein was actually trying to do was clarify, in purely logical terms, in what sense mathematical knowledge can be said to be objective. According to

Wittgenstein, this is to be explained in terms of the *form of reality* (viz. the logical syntax of mathematical propositions) rather than in the *description of mathematical objects*, or in some peculiarly mathematical (or logical) 'experience' (PR 113). It was not the objectivity of mathematical propositions *qua* rules of logical syntax that Wittgenstein was attacking: it was the notion that such objectivity is due to the fact that mathematical propositions are descriptive. Once again, therefore, we must be extremely wary of where the Anti-realist framework is leading us.

The whole point of the 'Objectivity/Anti-objectivity' thesis is that it takes us — via the route of Anti-realism — from scepticism about rule-following to scepticism about mathematical knowledge. Moreover, it does so in such a way that we are meant to see these two species of scepticism as inextricably tied together: different sides of the same Anti-realist coin. But in order to erect this sceptical bridge the argument is forced to employ the concept of *objectivity* in an equivocal and confusing manner. This becomes particularly manifest when Wright tells us that 'the point of the Positivists' emphasis on verification was, presumably, in the present terms, essentially anti-objective. It was to repudiate any notion of statement-understanding dissociated from experiences which we may have and procedures which we may carry out.'[30] It is symptomatic of the problems involved in this thesis that the one group that made a fetish out of scientific objectivity have now been stigmatised as 'Anti-objectivist'. Certainly the Logical Positivists denied that there is any such thing as a 'verification-transcendent' truth, but that is not at all the same thing as the denial that truth is objective as this is ordinarily understood. Nor indeed, as they themselves understood the matter. In 'Psychological and Physical Concepts' Schlick insisted that 'All experience ... points to the conclusion that only physical concepts fulfill the requirement of objectivity, which is, of course, essential to a language, for without it the language could not serve as a means by which different subjects could arrive at an understanding.'[31] Granted, these are not at all the expressions which concern the Anti-realists, but what this means is simply that the Anti-realists have only introduced a technical term — 'Anti-objectivity' — to describe their conception of 'non-verification-transcendent' proposition: a conception which misleadingly carries with it resonances of subjectivism that are wholly unrelated to the point at issue.

Wright begins his argument with the claim that 'For

Wittgenstein ... it is a dangerous error to think of pure mathematics as descriptive of some objective domain.' This is perfectly true, but then it is important that we consider what sort of work is being performed here by the emphasis placed on 'objective'. The crucial point, as far as Wittgenstein was concerned, is that mathematics does not *describe* any domain, but that hardly entails that mathematical knowledge is not objective. There is a further point involved here, however, which seems to underlie the Anti-realists' assumption that Wittgenstein was committed to 'Anti-objectivism'. According to Dummett, if 'one believes, with the intuitionists, that the content of a mathematical statement resides entirely in our ability to recognise what constitutes a proof of it and what a disproof, so that, when we lack an effective means of arriving at a proof or a disproof, we have no right to declare it either true or false, one will prefer a picture according to which mathematical reality is constructed by us, or, at least, comes into existence only as we become aware of it.'[32] But no such explanation of the constructivist position can serve as an interpretation of Wittgenstein's argument, for Wittgenstein was deliberately seeking to overturn the assumption that we must resolve the problem of when we have acquired the 'right' to assert a mathematical proposition.

His point was not that the use of an unproved proposition is *unjustifiable*; rather, it was that an *unproved expression* has no meaning. It is not that we are unable to assert a proposition until we have constructed a proof for it: it is that we cannot understand a string of symbols until we have constructed rules for their use. To be a well-formed proposition just is to be decidable. Far from constituting — as Dummett suggests in the above passage — a 'picture' of the nature of mathematical reality, the argument was intended solely as one of clarifying the logical syntax of the concept *mathematical proposition* (cf. Chapter 3). Thus, things go wrong right from the start in Wright's exegesis, for he defends the view that Wittgenstein's argument that a mathematical proof is a grammatical construction is an 'alternative picture', the interest of which 'depends at least in large part upon the strength of his reasons for rejecting the platonist picture.'[33] Certainly, Wittgenstein regarded platonism as a picture, but this argument places Wittgenstein's own explanatory efforts in entirely the wrong light, planting the seeds for the subsequent assumption that Wittgenstein attempted to introduce an 'Anti-objectivist picture' of mathematics. What Wittgenstein was really trying to do was supplant a picture with a precise philosophical clarification of mathematical syntax; for in the philosophy of mathematics we are only concerned with the clarification of the logical status of mathematical constructions: it is this which tells us what the mathematician is doing.

Wright's argument is far more complicated, however, than this objection might suggest. He tells us that 'The central question is not so much whether pure mathematics should be viewed as describing an external, changless, abstract reality as whether we ought to admit, at least in principle, a distinction between meeting the most refined cri[t]eria of mathematical acceptability and actually being mathematically true.'[34] This introduces yet another complication into the argument described above. Wright has now moved noticeably away from the important position from whence he started; he began by emphasising how concerned Wittgenstein was to undermine the picture of mathematics as a body of descriptive propositions, but now we are told that this is not at all the 'central question'. The problem which he faces here is essentially that of explaining what it means to say that the platonist is capable of believing that 'we can confer meanings on our statements which render them determinately true or false independently of our knowledge'.[35] This is not a question of probing the platonist's picture of our mental powers, however, but rather, of clarifying how we are to draw the boundary circumscribing the class of 'mathematical statements'. Yet it is not at all the problem which the Anti-objectivist thesis takes up.

Wright attempts to circumvent this problem with his passing reference to 'mathematical acceptability', without making clear exactly what this involves. Is there some unwritten code which determines whether a candidate for mathematical propositional status will be admitted into this august company by the practitioners of the discipline? If, however, what Wright and Dummett are driving at is that according to the platonist a proposition can be well formed yet not decidable, then this is precisely the idea that Wittgenstein hoped to expose as incoherent: to be well formed is by definition to be decidable, and the notion of 'undecidability' is itself meaningless (cf. Chapter 3). Indeed, how could the platonist distinguish between genuine and nonsensical 'mathematical' expressions? The platonist does not want to hold that an *ill-formed* expression is determinately true or false (independently of our knowledge). But his attempt to treat 'undecidable' questions as determinately true or false reveals his dilemma on this point. For example, to say that Fermat's last theorem might be pre-determinately false is quite definitely not, on his conception, to say that it is ill-formed; rather, it is to hold that $(\exists n)\ x^n + y^n \neq z^n$. But how can he ascertain that this expression is *false*, as opposed to *unintelligible*? This reading merely *presupposes* the central point at issue: viz. that it is intelligible to quantify over infinite series.

The Objectivity thesis cannot provide any further justification for this premise — nor was it designed to do so — for it ultimately comes down, Wright tells us, to the principle that a 'statement may be determinate in truth-value irrespective of whether we can recognise what its truth-value is'.[36] But, as the wording of this sentence demonstrates, the question of how 'we can confer meanings on verification-transcendent statements' is not at all the point that the Anti-realist/Objectivist critique pursues; as far as the latter is concerned, there is no question as to whether the expression constitutes a genuine proposition, but only whether the thought expressed by this 'proposition' transcends our 'recognitional capacities'. And that is precisely the reason why we cannot apply this framework to Wittgenstein's approach. Wittgenstein was not denying that a 'verification-transcendent statement' might be determinately or 'objectively' true; rather, he was insisting that a *nonsensical expression* cannot be true: that the very notion of a 'verification-transcendent statement' is unintelligible. It is this logical fallacy underlying the platonist argument, and not any pseudo-epistemological considerations about 'recognitional capacities', which he attacked. And that certainly does not amount to a denial of the objectivity of mathematical knowledge.

There is, however, a still deeper problem lurking in Wright's argument. We must be careful how we employ the concept 'truth' when we speak of rules as opposed to empirical propositions. The latter are certainly not true 'because of us': they are true or false according to how things are in the world. But the situation is considerably different when we look at rules. Are we to say that, because we construct mathematical propositions, their truth is somehow 'dependent on us'? Ignoring the prior question of what it means to describe rules as 'true' in the first place (cf. Chapter 7), we can see that Wright has confused legislation with anarchy in his 'Anti-objectivist' reading. There are two separate themes involved in the question of whether a rule is binding, but this distinction is obliterated on the 'sceptical' interpretation. Wittgenstein argued that no rule is binding in the sense that we must adopt that rule; there is no sort of logical coercion compelling us to construct certain rules, or preventing us from replacing them with new rules. In other words, there is nothing forcing us to play some particular language-game, nor to continue playing some game once it has been constructed. (Pragmatic considerations are another matter; cf. Chapter 8.) But if we do change the rules of a language-game then we change the game itself. It is in the latter sense, therefore, that rules *are* binding: in order to play *this* game, we must follow *these* rules.

We are not bound to follow any particular rule, but neither are we at liberty to say that anything constitutes following an established rule. Once the rules of a *Satzsystem* have been constructed the meanings of the expressions governed by that *Satzsystem* are objectively fixed; it is typically a completely determinate matter whether or not someone's use of an expression accords with the rules laid down in a *Satzsystem*. A large part of the Anti-realist confusion in this area derives from the manner in which they feel that we can 'modify' the rules of a *Satzsystem* without changing the system; e.g. by adding to the rules, such as in the case of extending the application of the concept 'number'. But Wittgenstein's point was that there can be no such 'modification' — there are no 'gaps' in a system or concept; rather, we have constructed a new *Satzsystem*, which bears a strong 'family resemblance' to the pre-existing system (cf. Chapter 8). Thus we must be careful not to confuse the construction of a rule with the 'objective meaning' of a rule. Although the actual existence of a rule may, so to speak, be dependent on us, the 'truth' of the rule is dependent on the rule itself. Assuming that it is not too confusing to speak of 'dependency' at all here, this leaves the far more important confusion of speaking of the truth of rules in the same way that we speak of the truth of empirical propositions, where the concept of objectivity finds its proper bearings. Once again, we encounter the problem of sorting through the confusions created by applying a concept to mathematical propositions that is fundamentally connected to the logical category of empirical statements.

Wright explains that if we 'believe in the objectivity of mathematics', then 'we commit ourselves to regarding truth for these statements as not simply a matter of our — human — judgement; to supposing that for such statements it is not human judgment which *constitutes* truth, but something else; precisely, "objective reality".[37] It is, of course, absurd to suppose that only a platonist can believe in the objectivity of mathematics. And, as we shall see in Chapter 8, it is not any sort of 'external reality', however this is defined, that makes a mathematical proposition true. Furthermore, this passage places the argument in the very philosophical framework that Wittgenstein was trying to overthrow in the *Tractatus*. Interestingly, it is a framework which is far more reminiscent of nineteenth-century conceptions of logic than of the emphasis on sentential logic that Wittgenstein introduced in the *Tractatus*. Wright insists that 'the central intuitive idea of objectivity [is that] being true is not the same thing as being judged to be true by human beings, even when their judgement is at its most sophisticated. ... The root idea of objectivity is that truth is not constituted by but is somehow independent of human judgement.'[38] Close as this may sound, it is not quite the same thing as the crucial point of Wittgenstein's argument, which is that 'human judgement' has nothing whatsoever to do with what constitutes the truth or falsity of mathematical propositions. This is entirely a question of the syntax of mathematical propositions: of their use as grammatical conventions.

The problem with this argument, however, is that *prima facie* it seems difficult to reconcile Wittgenstein's claim that he was not involved in any form of mathematical revisionism with the principal theme that we can best elucidate the logical grammar of mathematical propositions by comparing them to rules. After all, rules do not, strictly speaking, belong to the true/false language-game, whereas mathematical propositions have traditionally been taken to exemplify a paradigm of true propositions. Opponents and adherents alike of the thesis that mathematics and science exhibit different *types* of true proposition have all agreed on the premise that they both do yield true propositions. To be sure, the formalists rejected this premise, but then Wittgenstein went out of his way to stress his disapproval of the formalists' attempt to treat mathematical propositions as strings of meaningless marks. But such an argument did not commit Wittgenstein to the further rejection of the formalist thesis that the concept of truth does not apply to mathematical propositions, and in his discussion of the Hilbert/Frege controversy it often seems that the compromise that Wittgenstein sketched out took from Frege the idea that mathematical propositions are meaningful while from Hilbert the idea that they are not true in the empirical sense of 'true'.

Still, it is noteworthy that Wittgenstein avoided any outright endorsement of this position, and tended to move away from its revisionary implications by the end of the 1930s. Indeed, he conspicuously avoided discussing the very question of the truth of mathematical propositions. This may largely be due to his desire to undermine the picture that mathematical propositions are descriptive; for to discuss their uniquely normative 'truth' may cloud this enterprise. And yet it is clear that if he was to remain faithful to his non-revisionist principles he certainly must confront the issue. The schematic outline of a redundancy theory of truth at Appendix I §6 of *Remarks on the Foundations of Mathematics* has struck some as proof of Wittgenstein's unwillingness to discuss this issue, and his equivocal attitude to the principles of non-revisionism. But the real source of our problem here is that Wittgenstein's attitude to conventions fell outside of the traditional parameters in the foundations debate, and to argue that he was a 'conventionalist' in any of the received senses of the term is as confusing as to insist that he was not a conventionalist in any sense whatsoever. The solution which we shall pursue in Chapter 7 will be to ignore the established attitudes and approach Wittgenstein's argument afresh. For our immediate purposes, it bears remarking that Wittgenstein may, justifiably, have felt that the topic was adequately covered; certainly all of the materials for his solution were present. The point revolves upon the idea that 'truth' and 'proposition' are family resemblance concepts which are internally related to one another (cf. PI §§136, 225). From this it follows that different logical species of significant expression will yield different kinds of truth or certainty, as the case may be. What matters here is not whether it is 'legitimate' to describe mathematical propositions *qua* rules of logical syntax as 'true', but rather, in what sense this 'truth' should be understood; i.e. how this differs from empirical contexts.

This points still further to the difficulties involved in applying a concept specifically based on the nature of empirical propositions to rules or conventions. There may seem to be some rationale for saying that mathematical propositions are not 'objectively true' in the same manner as empirical, but this in no way casts any doubt on the *objectivity* of mathematical knowledge: it merely underscores the logical demarcation between empirical and mathematical propositions. For that matter, the logico-grammatical difference between empirical propositions and rules is such that it suggests the very opposite of the 'Objectivity' thesis as it is defined in terms of 'investigation-independence'. One might even argue that it is rules — which qualify if indeed anything does as truths which are known *a priori* — that are certain independent of our investigation. But, apart from the noted problem of describing rules as true or false, even this way of stating things distorts the issue; for the real point is that the concept of *investigation* as it applies to empirical propositions is completely inapplicable to the case of rules. It is not so much that rules are 'true' *independently* of investigation as that the empirical concept of *investigation*, like *evidence*, is logically divorced from the concept of a rule. Indeed, this virtually amounts to a defining characteristic of rules. (Even in the case of empirical propositions the thesis is misleading, for it tends to obliterate the distinction between what makes a proposition true and how we know that it is so.)

None of this has any bearing, however, on the question of the objectivity as ordinarily understood of rules and empirical propositions; and it is precisely this ordinary meaning that is used to generate the 'sceptical' thesis. For Wright's 'sceptical/Anti-objectivist' interpretation proceeds from the same premise that we examined in the first chapter that Wittgenstein 'seems to want to disallow that it is ever pre-determinate what counts as "doing the same thing again" or "applying the rule in the same way".'[39] But this, as we have already seen, is the very picture that Wittgenstein was trying to undermine. His point was that it is not the rule itself which somehow mysteriously determines the full range of its applications, but how we use the rule which establishes what counts as applying it in the same way. To be sure, Wittgenstein was saying that the certainty of rules cannot be justified, but that is not because they are *unjustifiable*; rather, it is because the concept of 'justification' has no relevance or application for rules of logical syntax. The two are grammatically prohibited from operating together: 'I do not call a rule of representation a convention if it can be justified in propositions: propositions describing what is represented and showing that the representation is adequate. Grammatical conventions cannot be justified by describing what is represented. Any such description already presupposed the grammatical rules. That is to say, if anything is to count as nonsense in the grammar which is to be justified, then it cannot at the same time pass for sense in the grammar of the propositions that justify it' (PR §7).

Ultimately, therefore, we must recognise that the whole issue of the objectivity of mathematical truth is a matter of logical syntax: a consequence of the fact that 'The mathematical proposition has, as it were, officially been given the stamp of incontestability' (OC §655). The point of the 'Anti-objectivity' thesis, however, just is to introduce the possibility of doubt into the question of objectivity, with the result that we are exposed to the so-called 'sceptical dilemma' presented at §201 in *Philosophical Investigations* that there is no such thing as objective meaning and language proves to be impossible. Once we recognise that the objectivity of mathematical truth consists in the very fact that doubt is logically excluded from its domain, we shall likewise see that the denial of mathematical objectivity does not result in an 'alternative picture' of the meaning of mathematical statements, but rather, in unintelligibility: in the chaos that results when we do not grasp that an expression functions as a rule of grammar. Our confusions in this area largely derive, therefore, from the fact that there are different meanings of 'truth' and 'certainty': a point which Wittgenstein dwelt on extensively in *On Certainty*. Indeed, one might almost say that one of the principal goals of *On Certainty* was to undermine the very grounds which were subsequently to give rise to the 'Objectivist/Anti-objectivist' thesis.

Wittgenstein explained: '"I have compelling grounds for my certitude." These grounds make the certitude objective. What is a telling ground for something is not anything I decide' (OC §§270-1). The fatal flaw in the 'Objectivity/Anti-objectivity' thesis is that, in order to introduce the possibility of doubt into the question of mathematical objectivity, it is forced to trangress the *Satzsysteme* barriers separating rules from empirical propositions. The propositions of mathematics are *objectively* certain — unassailable by doubt — because, as was emphasised in the preceding chapter, the very notion of epistemological doubt has been *logically excluded* from the normative province of mathematics: 'With the word "certain" we express complete conviction, the total absence of doubt, and thereby we seek to convince other people. That is *subjective* certainty. But when is something objectively certain? When a mistake is not possible. But what kind of possibility is that. Mustn't mistake be *logically* excluded?' (OC §194). It is this grammatical feature of the use of conventions — i.e. the fact that the logical syntax of mathematical propositions is such that the possibility of doubt or justification cannot intelligibly arise — which renders mathematical knowledge objectively certain.

The only question that we can intelligibly ask in this context is: What are the grammatical features which render mathematical knowledge objectively certain? Thus Wittgenstein remarked: 'Knowledge in mathematics: Here one has to keep on reminding oneself of the unimportance of the "inner process" or "state" and ask "Why should it be important? What does it matter to me?" What is interesting is how we *use* mathematical propositions. *This* is how calculation is done, in such circumstances a calculation is *treated* as absolutely reliable, as certainly correct' (OS §§38-9). Hence, when Wright asks, 'What exactly is it to believe in the objectivity of mathematics',[40] he commits himself to the very sort of question that undermines the logical basis of the objectivity of mathematical knowledge.

We shall return to this theme in Chapters 7 and 8 when we examine in much greater detail how Wittgenstein's proposed resolution of the 'foundations crisis' turned on the point that the certainty of mathematics rests, not in the *refutation* of doubt, but rather, in the logical *exclusion* of doubt. That is, not in the refutation of the sceptical problems that had been raised, but rather, in the demonstration that such problems are logically unintelligible. This, as we shall see, is why Wittgenstein's proposed solution of the 'foundations crisis' can best be described as a *dissolution* of the problem. For 'Where you can't look for an answer, you can't ask either, and that means: Where there's no logical method for finding a solution, the question doesn't make sense either' (PR §149).

Notes

1. F. Waismann, *Lectures on the Philosophy of Mathematics*, Wolfgang Grassl (ed.) (Amsterdam, Rodopi, 1982), p. 11.

2. Cf. TLP 5.47 ff.; PI §134; A.N. Prior, *Objects of Thought*, Geach, P.T. and Kenny, A.J.P. (eds) (Oxford, The Clarendon Press, 1971), pp. 38 f.; G.P. Baker and P.M.S. Hacker, *Wittgenstein: Understanding and Meaning* (Oxford, Basil Blackwell, 1980), pp. 565 ff.

3. Cf. Bertrand Russell, *Theory of Knowledge: The 1913 Manuscript*, Eames, E.R. (ed.) (London, George Allen & Unwin, 1984); and D.F. Pears, 'The Relation between Wittgenstein's Picture Theory and Russell's Theories of Judgement', in S.G. Shanker (ed.) *Ludwig Wittgenstein: Critical Assessments*, vol. I (London, Croom Helm, 1986).

4. Cf. P.M.S. Hacker, *Insight and Illusion* (Oxford, Oxford University Press, 1972), chapter 4 §4.

5. Cf. Bernard Harrison, *An Introduction to the Philosophy of Language* (London, The Macmillan Press, 1979), p. 208.

6. Cf. Crispin Wright, *Wittgenstein on the Foundations of Mathematics* (London, Duckworth, 1980), Chapters X–XII.

7. Cf. Hacker, *Insight and Illusion*, pp. 105 ff.; Béla Juhos, 'The Methodological Symmetry of Verification and Falsification', in *Selected Papers on Epistemology and Physics*, Frey, G. (ed.) (Dordrecht, D. Reidel Publishing Company, 1976), pp. 137 ff.; Oswald Hanfling, *Logical Positivism* (Oxford, Basil Blackwell, 1981), pp. 24 ff., 115ff.; Dahms, Hans-Joachim, 'Verifikationismus und Mathematik bei Wittgenstein', in *Ethik: Grundlagen, Probleme und Anwendungen*, Morscher, E. und Stranzinger, R. (Hrsg.) (Vienna, Hölder–Pichler–Tempsky, 1981).

8. Cf. D.A.T. Gasking and A.C. Jackson, 'Wittgenstein as a Teacher', in *Ludwig Wittgenstein: The Man and his Philosophy*, Fann, K.T. (ed.) (Sussex, Harvester Press, 1967), p.54.

9. Cf. F. Waismann, 'The Nature of Mathematics: Wittgenstein's Standpoint', S.G. Shanker (trans.) in Shanker (ed.), *Ludwig Wittgenstein: Critical Assessments*, vol. III.

10. E.g. David Schwayder describes Wittgenstein as a 'trans-Platonistic conceptualist' in 'Wittgenstein on Mathematics', in *Studies in the Philosophy of Wittgenstein*, Winch, P. (ed.) (London, Routledge & Kegan Paul, 1969).

11. Michael Dummett, 'Realism', in *Truth and Other Enigmas* (London, Duckworth, 1978), p. 153.

12. Ibid., p. 164.

13. Ibid., p. 146.

14. Such a claim would seem to be accepted without reservation by Crispin Wright, in *Wittgenstein on the Foundations of Mathematics* (London, Duckworth, 1980), p. 9.

15. M. Dummett, 'Wittgenstein's Philosophy of Mathematics', in *Truth and Other Enigmas* (London, Duckworth, 1978), p. 121.

16. Cf. G.P. Baker and P.M.S. Hacker, *Language, Sense & Nonsense* (Oxford, Basil Blackwell, 1984), Chapter 4.

17. Dummett, 'Wittgenstein's Philosopy of Mathematics', op.cit., p. 123.

18. Dummett, 'Realism', op.cit., p. 163.

19. Waismann, 'The Nature of Mathematics: Wittgenstein's Standpoint', op.cit., p. 61.

20. Dummett, 'Wittgenstein's Philosophy of Mathematics', op.cit., p. 122.

21. Michael Dummett, 'The Reality of the Past', in *Truth and Other Enigmas*, p. 361.

22. Crispin Wright, *Frege's Conception of Numbers as Objects* (Aberdeen, Aberdeen University Press, 1983). p. xv.

23. Dummett, *Truth and Other Enigmas*, op.cit., p. xxviii.

24. Ibid.

25. G.H. Hardy, *A Mathematician's Apology* (Cambridge, Cambridge University Press, 1969), pp. 123-4.

26. Wright, *Wittgenstein on the Foundations of Mathematics*, op.cit., p. 9.

27. Cf. ibid., p. 198.

28. Crispin Wright, 'Rule-following, Objectivity, and the Theory of Meaning', in *Wittgenstein: To Follow a Rule*, Holtzmann, S. and Leich, C. (eds) (London, Routledge & Kegan Paul, 1981), p. 206.

29. Wright, *Wittgenstein on the Foundations of Mathematics*, op.cit., p. 206.

30. Ibid., p. 9.

31. Moritz Schlick, 'Psychological and Physical Concepts', in *Philosophical Papers*, vol. II, op. cit., p. 426.

32. Dummett, *Truth and Other Enigmas*, op. cit., pp. xxviii-xxix.

33. Wright, *Wittgenstein on the Foundations of Mathematics*, op.cit., p. 5.

34. Ibid., p.7.

35. Cf. the passage quoted from Dummett's introduction to *Truth and Other Enigmas*, quoted at the beginning of this section, pp. 59-60.

36. Wright, *Wittgenstein on the Foundations of Mathematics*, op.cit., p. 7.

37. Ibid., p. 197.

38. Ibid., pp. 197, 199.

39. Ibid., p. 20.

40. Ibid., p. 197.

3 THE NATURE OF PROOF

We hear within us the perpetual call: There is the problem. Seek its solution. You can find it by pure reason, for in mathematics there is no *ignorabimus.*

David Hilbert, 'Mathematical Problems'

Only where there's a method of solution is there a problem.

(PR §149)

The Burden of Proof

Wittgenstein had an extraordinary gift, not simply for looking at stale problems from some entirely fresh perspective, but perhaps even more significant, for recognising problems where none was suspected. For example, philosophers of mathematics continue to debate the implications of Gödel's second incompleteness theorem for the 'foundations crisis' without ever having considered the soundness of the 'meta-mathematical' framework on which Gödel's proof rests. Only Wittgenstein sought to clarify the significance of the latter by scrutinising the *cogency* of the former. So too, Wittgenstein warned that before we struggle with the Decision Problem — the question whether it is possible to construct an algorithm which will enable one to arrive in a finite number of steps at an answer to any question belonging to a given mathematical system — we must consider that most basic of all problems in the philosophy of mathematics: the nature of mathematical proof.

It might seem something of an exaggeration to suggest that Wittgenstein was the first to propose an intensive philosophical investigation of the concept of 'proof'. After all, was this not the crux of the foundations dispute, and had not Kronecker, Frege, Russell, Hilbert and Brouwer all stimulated considerable interest in this very issue? The distinction operating here turns, however, on what we understand by a 'philosophical' investigation. For there is a crucial difference between the various foundations approaches to the question of what *should* or *should not* be admitted as a legitimate proof, and Wittgenstein's focus on what *does* qualify as a legitimate proof. Wittgenstein was not interested in participating in the debate on what sorts of technique and methodology should be permitted in the ongoing search for ever greater rigour in the pursuit of mathematics. Rather, his intention was to clarify the features of those constructions which mathematicians *do* present and accept as proofs. Wittgenstein's concern was by no means taxonomic, however; his goal was not to identify the various types of proof (e.g. mathematical induction, transfinite induction, *reductio ad absurdum*, constructive proof, etc.) that mathematicians employ, and leave the matter at that. For it was not the mores of mathematics that Wittgenstein undertook to disclose, but rather, the logical syntactical features of mathematical constructions that he sought to clarify. His interest was not in whether any particular proof or species of proof should be admitted as a *bona fide* method of reasoning, therefore, but simply, what *we mean* when we say that *this figure* is a proof of *this proposition* (LFM 36).

Still, even this approach is not unique, nor is it immune from similar dangers to those which ensnared the adversaries in the foundations dispute. In one of the rare papers devoted solely to this problem, Raymond Wilder announced at the outset of 'The Nature of Mathematical Proof' that 'it is chiefly the following aspects of mathematics that I should like to discuss: (1) The nature of this process or procedure that we call "proof," and (2) the relation of the end result of the process to "truth". Specifically, what position does proof occupy in mathematics, and how does it influence the so-called truth or certainty of our results?'[1] What Wilder was really hoping to find was the 'essence' which all of the various types of proof share. This, as we saw in the preceding chapter, was an objective which Wittgenstein carefully rejected (cf. AWL 116 quoted on p. 45 above). The great problem with this approach is that what serves as a proof can be a highly variable affair, depending not only on the demands of the particular system, but also on each reader's own level of mathematical sophistication. (Notoriously, some of the 'proofs' offered by the great mathematicians are little more than skeletal clues to the convoluted pattern of their thought.) Since he could find no *formal* criterion — without seeing his argument collapse into one of the foundations positions — Wilder was led to conclude that the common feature he was searching for must lie in the 'role of proof'. This, he insisted, is nothing more than '*a testing process that we apply to the suggestions of our intuition*'.[2] But such an argument gets us nowhere, for the fatal problem with 'tests', as far as mathematics is concerned, is that no matter how stringent we might make them they remain ineluctably falsifiable. And 'Nothing is more fatal to philosophical understanding than the notion of proof and experience as two different but comparable methods of verification' (PG 361).

To be sure, some have willingly accepted this result and endeavoured to make a virtue out of necessity by embracing the more orthodox scientific status which this seems to bestow upon mathematics. But even those who, like Wilder, may have begun with the intention of identifying the basis for our conviction that 'the results of mathematics are certain and absolutely true',[3] have found themselves forced to concede at the end of their arguments that, as Wilder himself accepted: 'Obviously we don't possess, and probably will never possess, any standard of proof that is independent of time, the thing to be proved, or the person or school of thought using it. And under these conditions, the sensible thing to do seems to be to admit that there is no such thing, generally, as absolute truth in mathematics, whatever the public may think.'[4] Vainly struggling to dissociate himself at this point from the charge that this compromise exposes him as little more than a closet intuitionist, Wilder pleaded that: 'Our intuition suggests certain results, and they seem mathematically desirable — and moreover, prove to be generally liked by the mathematical public. We test them by what we call a proof. ... Naturally, we cannot assume a dogmatic attitude about them ... but we can rely, I think, upon the combined evidence of our intuition and the test which we call "proof", even though the latter may be rejected by some of our colleagues who have somehow attained, possibly from psychic sources, a preferred position among the gods that they think rule over the mathematical universe.'[5] Not even cynicism can disguise the fact, however, that on Wilder's approach, the absolute truth of mathematics has been abandoned, and proof has been relegated to the sad fate of inverted commas.

What is most striking about Wilder's paper is not the relatively commonplace solution which he adopted, but the mere fact that, at such a late date in the evolution of mathematics, it should still be necessary to address such an issue. After all, one of the questions which has most vexed historians of mathematics is whether the Babylonians and Egyptians possessed the concept of proof. It has traditionally been argued that the concept of proof was first introduced by Thales, and from there it has remained essentially unchanged, albeit it has gradually become more formalised over the ages. It is curious, however, that despite the heated debates which this issue has aroused amongst historians of mathematics, the prior question of what they understand by the term 'proof' has gone virtually untouched. Or indeed, the basic question of what it means to speak of Egyptian *mathematics* in the absence of proof? In one sense this may simply be due to the fact that our major source of Egyptian mathematics — the Rhind papyrus — consists solely of 85 arithmetical problems and their solutions, presented much more in the manner of a recipe book than as a mathematics treatise. It is conceivable that the problems were presented in this manner in order to stimulate the reader to discover the proofs for himself; the danger here, of course, is that we are merely reading our own expectations into the text. Whatever Ahmes' intentions, his solutions have largely been denied the status of proofs on the grounds that, as Jourdain complained in *The Nature of Mathematics*, 'there are no theorems properly so-called [in the Rhind papyrus]; everything is stated in the form of problems, not in general terms, but in distinct numbers'.[6] But then, Jourdain does not explain the basis for 'The generally accepted account of the origin and early development of geometry' — to which he himself subscribed — 'that the ancient Egyptians were obliged to invent it in order to restore the landmarks which had been destroyed by the periodical inundations of the Nile'.[7]

Jourdain implicitly lent his imprimatur to this usage with his argument that we distinguish between two senses of the term 'mathematics': 'the methods used to discover certain truths', and 'the truths discovered'. But can these two elements be divorced in this strict manner: if indeed there really are two separate elements here? After all, we do not confuse cartography with geometry, or accounting with arithmetic. And in which of these senses would we attribute primitive mathematical concepts to the Egyptians? Jourdain hinted that it is in the latter sense that the Egyptians could be said to have been engaged in mathematics; but it is not at all clear what it means to credit the Egyptians with the discovery of mathematical truths whilst using non-mathematical methods. For example, using the method of *regula falsi* (i.e. assuming a preliminary solution and then correcting it) Ahmes set out to calculate the volume of various geometrical figures. According to both James R. Newman and Peter Beckmann, Ahmes would base his solutions of problems involving the volume of cylindrical containers on the assumption that $\pi = 3.16$. In Beckmann's words: 'Ahmes assumes that the area of a circular field with a diameter of 9 units is the same as the area of a square with a side of 8 units. Using the formula for the area of a circle $A = \pi r$ this yields $\pi(9/2)^2 = 8^2$, and hence the Egyptian value of π was $\pi = 4 \times (8/9)^2 = 3.16049$.'[8] As Newman describes it, 'In solving this problem a rule is used for determining the area of a circle which comes to area $= (8/9d)^2$, where d denotes the diameter. Matching this against the modern formula, area $= \pi r^2$, gives a value for π of 3.16 — a very close approximation to the correct value.'[9] Both arguments are extremely confusing. A student who was set the task of calculating the volume of a cylinder with a diameter of 9 units would not be credited with the mastery of a mathematical concept — let alone the discovery of the value of π — if he ascertained by trial and error that the contents of the cylinder almost matched those of a square container with a side of 8 units. What matters here, however, is not the question of whether Ahmes should be credited with a 'primitive' concept of π — whatever that might actually mean — but rather, the framework in which Beckmann and Newman must present such a thesis. For the former describes Ahmes as in possession of *the formula for the area of a circle*, and the latter refers to the *rule for determining the area of a circle*.

To see the premises underlying their interpretation, we need only consider the precise terms in which this debate has proceeded. No less an authority than Neugebauer also claimed that 'special rules are followed which are explicitly summarised in one of our main sources, the mathematical Papyrus Rhind.'[10] Indeed, he too explained how, 'for the [area of a] circle a rule is used which we can transcribe as $A = (8/9d)^2$ if d denotes the diameter'.[11] Most important of all, perhaps, is the argument which Richard J. Gillings offers in his attempt to exonerate the Egyptians from the charge that they lacked the concept of proof. In a section which is suitably entitled 'The Nature of Proof' he maintains: 'It is true that the Egyptians did not show exactly how they established their rules or formulas, nor how they arrived at their methods of dealing with specific values of the variable. But they nearly always proved that the numerical solution to the problem at hand was indeed correct for the particular value or values they had chosen. For them, this constituted both method and proof, so that many of their solutions concluded with sentences like the following: The producing of the same.'[12] As Gillings rightly indicates, unsatisfying as it might be, neither of the first two lacunae seriously affects the status of Ahmes' solutions *qua* proofs. Indeed, the same could be said for many of the abstract proofs in higher mathematics. Rather more worrying, however, is the conclusion which Gillings draws in the latter part of this passage: for what is to prevent the same theme from applying to mere empirical regularity? Notoriously, the fact that you will nearly always end up with twelve pebbles when you add piles of five and seven together does not in itself constitute a mathematical proof. Thus, Gillings does not help matters when he concludes his defence on the note that 'What they did was to explain and define in an ordered sequence the steps necessary in the proper procedure, and at the conclusion they added a verification or proof that the steps outlined did indeed lead to a correct solution of the problem.'[13] For what we want to know precisely is the *difference* between these two 'tests': that is, not just why 'the steps outlined did indeed lead to a correct solution of the problem', but why *they must do so*!

Wittgenstein supplied what you might call the philosophical clarification for the critical theme which is implicit in all of these accounts. On Wittgenstein's approach we begin to see why it is that the concept of mathematics is inextricably (i.e. *internally*) tied to the notion of proof. Wittgenstein did not supply us, however, with the means to decide whether or not the Egyptians possessed the concept of proof; that is an issue which, conceivably, will only be decided by future archaeologists and historians of mathematics. What Wittgenstein did clarify is simply what it means to say that the Egyptians were engaged in an activity that can be described as *mathematics*, as opposed to a primitive science. If there is sufficient evidence to suggest that the Egyptians followed the rule outlined above for calculating the area of a circle — that is, if they really did employ this proposition *as a rule* — then this would indeed constitute genuine grounds for crediting them with the possession of mathematical propositions and proofs: not because this enabled them to achieve 'a very close approximation to the correct value of π', nor even that they employed this as a standard for what must be counted as the ratio of the length of the circumference of a circle to the length of its diameter — terms which merely serve to reintroduce the concept of π under another guise — but simply because they used some such rule as that described above as their *paradigm* for how to measure the area of a circle.

Hence, we would need some evidence to suggest that e.g. they would have regarded it, not as false, but as *unintelligible* if someone were to suggest that the area of a circular field with a diameter of 9 units might be the same as the area of a square with a side of 8 units on some occasions and a square with a side of 10 units on others, depending (say) on the kind of material which was being stored. Admittedly, such information may never be forthcoming, but what matters here — from our philosophical point of view — is not so much whether the issue can be decided on the basis of the evidence which is already contained in the existing mathematical papyri as the type of conditions which are entailed by the various attempts to attribute the possession of *mathematical* — as opposed to primitive *scientific* — concepts to the Egyptians.

The subtle links between mathematics and science are the source of both the glory of mathematics in western culture and the misery which the philosophy of mathematics has suffered over the past century, and continues to endure despite the constantly growing influence and success which mathematics enjoys. If the difference between the two types of activity lies in the nature of their truth, then it is only at this fundamental level that the issue will be settled: in the nature of the 'tests' which the two types of activity employ. Perhaps the most influential mathematician in this area has been Morris Kline. As we shall see in the penultimate chapter of this book, Kline has meticulously charted the course of what he describes as 'The Loss of Mathematical Certainty': a calamity which he has tried, unsuccessfully, to reconcile with the great utility of mathematics. Wittgenstein's approach can be described as the exact antithesis to Kline's: where Kline struggles to identify the key 'débâcles' resulting in the 'withering of mathematical truth', Wittgenstein set out to clarify the unintelligibility of the picture which has led to such an interpretation of the development of non-Euclidean geometries and abstract algebras. Both begin, however, from the same starting-point: the significance of proof to the evolution of mathematics.

It is clear that, to Kline, 'proof' means axiomatisation. The problem with attributing the concept of proof to the Egyptians, he explains, is that 'No one believes that the Egyptians had a deductive structure based on sound axioms that established the correctness of their rules.'[14] Not surprisingly, therefore, Kline sees the 'most vital contribution of the Greeks to mathematics' as lying in 'the insistence that all mathematical results be established deductively on the basis of explicit axioms'.[15] This renders proof, not just coextensive, but synonymous with 'axiomatisation'. To be sure, this picture suggests that the distinction we are searching for between mathematical and scientific 'tests' lies in the logical demarcation between deductive and inductive inference; but it none the less raises serious questions in its wake. The first is simply: is it warranted? Or to put this another way: *why* must every proof be part of a deductive system? There might well be strong reasons for such a condition: the question is whether this is a theme which can merely be assumed? Forgoing until Chapter 8 any discussion of the hazards involved in what would amount to the 'postulational method' if we were to abandon this important premise, the objection which surfaces here is that such an argument does little to clarify the logical character of proof: the question of how deductive inference renders mathematical truth 'absolutely certain', and in what the distinguishing feature of a successful proof consists. It may seem tempting to dismiss this as a self-evident matter, but it is important to bear in mind that many philosophers who share Kline's explanation — and indeed Kline himself — see no conflict between this premise and the conclusion that 'proof is subject to a constant process of criticism and revalidation. Errors, ambiguities, and misunderstandings are cleared up by constant exposure. Proof is respectability. Proof is the seal of authority.'[16] But how there can be any room for doubt as far as the status of a proof is concerned? Is this simply a case of human fallibility, and if so, how can we ever be absolutely certain that a proof can be accepted as such? A 'seal of authority' which can always be over-ruled is at best a token device, forever waiting to be discarded. Thus Wittgenstein stressed that perhaps our main objective here is to clarify why it is that 'to say, e.g.: we must be able to be certain, it must hold as certain for us, that we have not overlooked a sign in the course of the proof. That no demon can have deceived us by making a sign disappear without our noticing, or by adding one, etc. One might say: When it can be said: "Even if a demon had deceived us, still everything would be all right," then the prank he wanted to play on us has simply failed of its purpose' (RFM III §21).

No less insidious, however, is the question of in what sense every proof could be part of a pre-existing deductive system. The main objection to logicism, first raised by Poincaré at the beginning of the century, was that it fails to explain how mathematics grows:

how we can *prove* something that lies outside the domains of an axiomatic system, and if we cannot, how we are to escape the conclusion that mathematics reduces to an 'immense tautology'? It was precisely this latter problem which Wittgenstein took up. There is a subtle trap waiting here, however, for as was already stressed, Wittgenstein saw his task as that of clarifying — not of legislating on — the nature of proof. Hence, if the Greeks succeeded in convincing mathematicians that the paradigm of proof should be confined to deductive inference from explicit axioms, it was not for Wittgenstein to challenge this practice. Yet this is very much the manner in which Wittgenstein's remarks on the foundations of mathematics have been interpreted. The 'anarchy' which Wittgenstein has been found guilty of wishing to excite is precisely one of abandoning the logical constraints established by deductive systems (cf. Chapter 8). But it was not axiomatisation *per se* which Wittgenstein attacked, but rather, a fallacy to which the standard picture of axiomatisation exposes us.

It may seem paradoxical, but the difficult part of Wittgenstein's argument is not that he disputed, but rather that he confronted the obvious. As we saw above, Wittgenstein's concern was not so much to emphasise that different forms of argument can serve as legitimate proofs as it was to clarify the logico-syntactical nature of proof *per se*. The starting-point for this investigation was the plain fact that, bearing in mind the myriad *Beweissysteme* which proliferate in mathematics — and hence the 'MOTLEY of techniques of proof' (RFM III §46) — there is none the less a crucial distinction to be drawn between two basic *kinds* of proof: those which operate within an *existing* axiomatic system, and those which serve to establish a *new* axiomatic system. For example, there is a categorial difference between e.g. an elementary proof in Euclidean geometry that if the right-angled triangle *abc* with sides of length *a* and *b* and hypotenuse of length *c* has an area of $z^2/4$ then the triangle *abc* is isosceles, and Gauss's proof that the abandonment of Euclid's parallel postulate did not result in an inconsistent geometrical system, even though many of its geometrical concepts would be markedly different from the Euclidean. Whatever specific method the pupil adopts will hinge on his mastery of basic concepts in Euclidean geometry: e.g. of the Pythagorean theorem and the definition of an 'isosceles triangle'. But there were no such constraints operating in Gauss's proof; and indeed, the essence of Gauss's great discovery, after trying to resolve the problem of the status of Postulate 5 by showing that the abandonment of Euclid's parallel postulate would result in a contradiction, just was to grasp that, as Gauss wrote to Bessell, Euclidean geometry could no longer claim to be the sole candidate for geometrical truth.[17]

It was with this fundamental distinction in mind that Wittgenstein differentiated between merely doing a 'piece of homework', and creating a new — autonomous — system (PR §158). The Euclidean example is an obvious instance of the former: the pupil's problem does not allow him to take any liberties with Euclid's axioms; rather, he must apply the existing rules of the system in order to arrive at the proof. It is curious that Wittgenstein should have been charged with the premeditated intention of undermining deductivism even though he asked: 'What is in common between the purpose of a Euclidean construction, say the bisection of a line, and the purpose of deriving a rule from rules by means of logical inferences? The common thing', he answered, 'seems to be that by the construction of a sign I compel the acceptance of a sign' (RFM III §29). Where this theme tends to be overshadowed is in such comments as that 'What *proves* is not that this correlation leads to this result — but that we are persuaded to take these appearances (pictures) as models for what it is like if ...' (RFM III §39). Such a thought recalls one of the central points which we saw in the discussion of rule-following in Chapter 1. Wittgenstein's noticeable reticence in the first of these two quotations is a reminder of the warning that we should avoid stating that rules *force* us to apply them in such and such a way; so too, we should be wary of the picture that the rules of Euclidean geometry force the pupil to construct such and such a proof. To revert to this formulation is to fall victim to the causal confusions about rule-following which we examined in Chapter 1: it is not the rules of Euclidean geometry which force the pupil to construct a given proof if he grasps them, but rather, we who instruct the pupil to use those rules in this way. That is, to say that grasping the rules of Euclidean geometry compels the pupil to show that e.g. $(a^2 + b^2) = c^2$ in order to establish that a = b is merely to express our inexorability in deciding what constitutes a correct proof of the problem.

There is a rather more significant reason, however, why Wittgenstein's remarks on the nature of proof have been misconstrued. As we shall see in the following sections, Wittgenstein laid great emphasis on the point that the rules of an existing deductive system cannot in any sense *compel* us to construct certain rules in a novel axiomatic system; such an assumption leads directly into the unintelligibility of a platonist conception of mathematical truth. The great danger here for the interpretation of Wittgenstein's argument is that his critique of platonism might be mistaken for an attack on deductivism *per se*. It is a problem which is heightened by the fact that the greater part of Wittgenstein's argument was concerned with the construction of new axiomatic systems. It is not surprising that much of Wittgenstein's remarks on the nature of proof should have been concerned with the latter, and not the former type of proof. After all, these are not simply the more interesting, but for the philosophy of mathematics they are vastly more important, given the role which some of them have played in the genesis of the 'foundations crisis'. 'The difficult mathematical problems', Wittgenstein argued, 'are those for whose solution we don't yet possess a *written* system. The mathematician who is looking for a solution then has a system in some sort of psychic symbolism, in images, "in his head", and endeavours to get it down on paper. Once that's done, the rest is easy' (PR §151). The difficult task which remains for the philosophy of mathematics, however, is to clarify the logico-syntactical status of the problem which sets the mathematician off on this exercise and the bearing which the successful proof has on the original conjecture. Before we can approach this issue, however, it is imperative that we grasp the nature and the independence of Wittgenstein's remarks on the grammatical nature of the two kinds of proof, so that we do not confuse his discussion of mathematical invention for an attack on axiomatisation.

This is precisely the fallacy which most frequently occurs, however, in the hostile reactions to Wittgenstein's discussion of proof which have proliferated. For example, critics immediately complained that according to Wittgenstein, a proposition can only have one proof; yet, as is clear in the above example, it seems that there are multiple proofs for the proposition in question. The pupil could equally well begin his proof by establishing — again using the Pythagorean theorem — that $(x - y)^2 = (x^2 - 2xy + y^2) = 0$. This criticism only arises, however, from the failure to distinguish between Wittgenstein's remarks on two kinds of proof. For Wittgenstein did not dispute the possibility of a single proposition having what are ordinarily described as 'multiple proofs' *within* an axiomatic system. What he did insist, however, was that 'Proofs proving the same thing may be translated into one another, and to that extent are the same proof' (PR §153). That is, in terms of the above problem, the two proofs are the same in the sense that, whether we adopt a forward or a backward approach, we shall still be applying the same rules (for the application of the Pythagorean theorem and the definition of an isosceles triangle) in the solution. But, as Wittgenstein continued: 'The only proofs for which this doesn't hold are like: "From two things, I infer that he's at home: first his jacket's in the hall, and also I can hear him whistling". Here we have two independent ways of knowing' (PR §153). The example is rather weak, perhaps, but the point that Wittgenstein was driving at is clear: what matters here is that, in so far as the internal relations laid down between concepts constitutes the essence of a mathematical proof, then you cannot have two different methods or 'ways of knowing' (i.e. drawn from autonomous *Beweissysteme*) for constructing the same proposition. A better example of Wittgenstein's point might thus be that the proof in Euclidean geometry that you can bisect a line using ruler and compasses cannot be interchanged with the proof of — what before Wittgenstein would have been regarded as the 'same' — proposition in modern algebra. The upshot of Wittgenstein's argument, however, is that the two propositions cannot be treated as synonymous, and thus the warning which Wittgenstein issued in *Remarks on the Foundations of Mathematics* that we must 'remember that it is not enough that two proofs meet in the same propositional sign. For how do we know that this sign says the same thing both times? *That* must proceed from other connexions' (RFM III §62). But notice that, even here, Wittgenstein was careful not to rule out the possibility of meeting such a condition within an existing *Beweissystem* (*infra*).

The key to all this is to grasp the normative character of a mathematical proof: 'A proof', Wittgenstein repeatedly emphasised, 'leads me to say: this *must* be like this' (RFM III §30). The essence of a mathematical proof, Wittgenstein explained, is that it carves out a rule of grammar: 'Let us remember that in mathematics we are convinced of *grammatical* propositions; so the expression, the result, of our being convinced is that we *accept a rule*' (RFM III §27). That is, the proof establishes the grammatical conventions which constitute the proposition's role as a *rule of grammar*: 'For the proof is part of the grammar of the proposition!' (PG 370). What matters here, therefore, are the internal relations that are forged between the various concepts which underpin the proposition: 'the proof changes the grammar of our language, changes our concepts. It makes new connexions, and it creates the concept of these connexions' (RFM III §31). Admittedly, such an argument departs in the above respect from the orthodox conception of proof: on the standard approach a proof is simply any series of inferences which leads up to the theorem. But what matters on Wittgenstein's account are not the particular steps which are taken, but rather, the connections which are created. Hence, we do not distinguish between proofs according to the specific steps which are presented, but rather, according to whether or not they construct the same rule: '"Two proofs prove the same when what they convince me of is the same." — And when is what they convince me of the same? — How do I know that what they convince me of is the same? Not of course by introspection. I can be brought to accept this rule by a variety of paths' (RFM III §58). Thus, pupils are taught how to construct proofs in Euclidean geometry using various complementary proof techniques; but whereas on the ordinary conception we would distinguish as separate two proofs of the same proposition using these different techniques, on Wittgenstein's conception we have, strictly speaking, the *same* proof here, albeit under different guises. For what matters is the *grammar* of the proof, and not its style.

Assuming for the moment that this argument answers at least some of the queries that have been posed about the question whether, according to Wittgenstein, a proposition can have but one proof, we have still not clarified precisely in what relation a mathematical proposition stands to its proof, and thus the significance of Wittgenstein's puzzling suggestion that the sense of a mathematical conjecture is changed by a proof. For if the latter is the case it is no longer clear how we can ever succeed in proving the conjecture with which we started out. Indeed, some have gone further than this and credited Wittgenstein with the claim that we can never prove the proposition which we intended. Clearly, then, we have not by any means settled the highly contentious matters that have been raised by Wittgenstein's discussion of proof with these preliminary remarks; nor have we digested the full implications of his intentions. All that we have accomplished is to bring us to the point where we can address his proposed resolution of the Decision Problem, and thence his comments on the heuristic role of mathematical conjectures. But these latter themes are themselves integral aspects of his argument, and thus we shall not be finished with Wittgenstein's discussion of the nature of proof until we have properly dealt with these issues, and still further, the complications which they in turn present.

Observing the Law of Excluded Middle

In the foregoing chapters we have seen that in the early 1930s Wittgenstein drew a strong parallel between his *Satzsysteme* conception of natural language and a *Beweissysteme* conception of mathematics, with a corresponding parallel drawn between *methods of verification* and *methods of proof.* And furthermore, that he saw in constructivism, interpreted as the rule-governed application of concepts, the means for establishing this affinity. The conceptual similarities thus understood between mathematics and natural language enabled Wittgenstein to incorporate the philosophy of mathematics within the broad parameters of his approach to philosophy *simpliciter,* and thus to concentrate on the *use* of mathematical concepts as a method for resolving our problems in the philosophy of mathematics. But the analogy between mathematical and empirical propositions can only go so far if the type of confusions which Mill suffered in the philosophy of mathematics are to be avoided. For, short of embracing an ultra-empiricist account of mathematical propositions, Wittgenstein's attempt to establish the broad similarity between natural language and mathematics must soon come up against the necessity of mathematical propositions; and Wittgenstein's first priority was to clarify — not undermine — the hallmark of mathematical truth (cf. Chapter 7).

What is most noticeable about Wittgenstein's argument in *Philosophical Remarks* and *Philosophical Grammar,* however, is that not only did he refrain from saying that mathematical and empirical propositions are *toto caelo* different, but if anything, he appears to have been trying to minimise their disparity (PR §120). Dummett goes so far as to suggest that Wittgenstein was 'obsessed with an empiricist philosophy of mathematics'.[18] That Wittgenstein was not interested in the theory that mathematical propositions express 'high-level empirical generalisations' is made abundantly clear; throughout his writings and lectures in the early 1930s, Wittgenstein constantly stressed that whatever account we give of the logical character of mathematical propositions, it must be one which remains fully committed to the overriding need to preserve the basic distinction between the two species of propositions (AWL 197). But certainly, he was obsessed with the question of the nature of the distinction between mathematical and empirical propositions, and in many respects the argument presented in *Philosophical Remarks* does indeed seem more interested in the similarities than the differences.

For that very reason, the empiricist interpretation of Wittgenstein's remarks is not without some plausibility. It is intriguing that in 'The Nature of Mathematics: Wittgenstein's Standpoint' Waismann described how

> For Mill the propositions and concepts were empirical. For Russell the propositions of mathematics are, to be sure, *a priori* — they are tautologies — but the concepts are empirical. [Millian empiricism thus continues in part in Russell.] This is a half-way measure, an impossible construction in itself. If one pursues this line, one ends up with Wittgenstein. It is a straight path which leads from Mill via Russell to Wittgenstein. Wittgenstein's point of view is the consequence of thinking through the Russellian interpretation to the end, where it has been purified of the remains of a false empiricism.[19]

One wonders how Wittgenstein must have responded to this passage. Certainly this is, at least in part, how the Vienna Circle saw the matter, but did Wittgenstein himself actually sanction — and perhaps even encourage — this impression? Such a possibility is not as startling as may at first appear; for there are two crucial themes present in Waismann's account here, which are deceptively easy to overlook in the haste to assimilate this 'empiricist' gloss on Wittgenstein's intentions. Wittgenstein's point of view was intended to 'purify the remains of a false empiricism': his account differs, Waismann emphasised, from *both* Mill's and Russell's versions. That is, mathematical propositions, on Wittgenstein's approach, can *neither* be reduced to empirical propositions *nor* to tautologies. But the force of the latter point was lost on the Logical Positivists (cf. Chapter 7), and the former is, so it would appear, lost on Dummett.

Wittgenstein's argument is rendered even more complicated by the fact that, in addition to exploring the similarities between mathematical and empirical propositions, he wanted at the same time to clarify the essential logico-syntactical demarcation between 'decidable' and 'undecidable' mathematical problems. His reason for conflating these two issues was the belief that efforts to answer the former question had been frustrated precisely because the latter had been misunderstood. The key to both these distinctions lies in the fact that 'A proof is a proof of a particular proposition if it goes by a rule correlating the proposition to the proof. That is, the proposition must belong to a system of propositions, and the proof to a system of proofs' (PG 376). Thus, one and the same picture — the conception of mathematics and language as composed of networks of calculi — was employed to explain both the basis for the parallel which exists between mathematical and empirical propositions (i.e. the underlying pattern in their use which accounts for our common application of the term 'proposition' for expressions of both sorts), and the nature of the logical difference between 'decidable' and 'undecidable' mathematical expressions. The correspondence lies in the 'system' which links *Satzsysteme* to *Beweissysteme*: 'For example, the proposition $26 \times 13 = 419$ is essentially one of a system of propositions (the system given in the formula $a \times b = c$), and the corresponding question one of a system of questions. The question whether 26×13 equals 419 is bound up with one particular *general method* by means of which it is answered' (AWL 197).

Thus, just as to understand the meaning of an empirical proposition presupposes that we are familiar with the method of verification for all the propositions that belong to a given *Satzsystem*, so to understand the meaning of a mathematical proposition presupposes that we are familiar with the method of proof for the family of propositions that are members of a given *Beweissystem*, and it is for this reason that 'What "mathematical questions" share with genuine questions is simply that they can be answered' (PR §151). This similarity had hitherto been obscured, Wittgenstein maintained, by philosophers' preoccupation with the 'prose' of mathematics: the verbal expressions in which the results of a proof are inexactly — and often incoherently — presented. 'The main danger' posed by the latter 'is surely that the prose expression of the result of a mathematical operation may give the illusion of a calculus that doesn't exist, by bearing the outward appearance of belonging to a system that isn't there at all' (PG 375). The matter only becomes fully perspicuous when we turn our attention to the proposition in the context of its *Beweissytem* (AWL 198,9). All propositions acquire their meaning from their method of verification in the sense that we know how to use them, how to set about verifying (in mathematics, proving) them; in the case of familiar mathematical propositions, we can understand their meaning before their specific proof in the sense that we have already developed a general method of verification (constructed a *Beweissystem*), and thus possess an effective means for proving the proposition: 'The cases in which a mathematical question is similar to an ordinary one are those in which we have a general method for answering it. For example, since we have a general way of deciding whether $m \times n = r$, the question whether $26 \times 13 = 1560$ resembles an ordinary question, although it does differ from an ordinary question since we cannot imagine what it would be like for the answer to be true if it were false, or false if it were true' (AWL 199-200).

Given this interdependence — or rather, inseparability — between a mathematical proposition and its proof, it obviously emerges that we must carefully reconsider what we understand by a *mathematical problem*. The difficulty is that the 'verbal expressions' of mathematics which often go by the name of 'mathematical proposition' can be highly misleading, and thus our first task is to investigate in what sense 'undecidable questions' either constitute or else relate to genuine mathematical problems. To accomplish this, we must clarify what is meant by the term 'mathematical proposition', and see how this excludes the 'verbal expressions' which Wittgenstein pejoratively identified as 'prose'. When Wittgenstein concluded that 'a mathematical proposition is the last link in a chain of proof' (PR §162) he was neither suggesting that the final theorem of the proof can be divorced from the body of proof, nor that the final line of the proof expresses a proposition which is distinct from 'the proposition stated in the first line of the proof'. At one point in *Philosophical Remarks* he proposed that 'We could say: a mathematical proposition is an allusion to a proof' (PR §122); elsewhere, that 'a mathematical proposition is only the immediately visible surface of a whole body of proof and this surface is the boundary facing us' (PR §162). Perhaps the most important comment is that 'the completely analysed mathematical proposition is its own proof' (PR §162).

The foundation for this last thought goes back to the *Tractatus* account of the significance of truth-tables in logical analysis (TLP

5.1 ff.). Truth-tables do not analyse a proposition in the sense that they describe the meaning of that proposition; rather, truth-tables are simply a more explicit formulation — a 'translation' —of that proposition (AWL 135-6). In much the same way, 'A mathematical proof is an analysis of the mathematical proposition' (PR §153). It articulates the network of internal relations which underpin the role of the mathematical proposition *qua* 'rule of syntax'. We cannot treat any expression as a mathematical proposition unless it belongs to a proof-system, therefore, for 'What we call a proposition is not one thing, aloof and isolated. When people ask whether the question, "Are there three 7's in π?" is sense or nonsense, they are up against the difficulty of saying under what conditions we would call "There are three 7's" a proposition' (AWL 199). Thus, until an expression has been located within the specific confines of the grammatical structure that is laid out in a proof, we have no grounds for describing it as a *mathematical proposition*, since we possess no rules for its use within a calculus. To understand an expression as a mathematical proposition just is to grasp the body of internal relations governing its use.

There might well seem to be a distinctly finitistic overtone to Wittgenstein's attack on 'undecidable questions', and indeed to the extent that Wittgenstein denied the intelligibility of the notion of 'a proof carried out in an infinite number of steps', this is certainly the case. But it would be misleading to describe his argument in orthodox finitistic terms — i.e. as pertaining to the 'limits of human understanding' — for the very reason that Wittgenstein once again based his argument on the *Beweissysteme* conception of mathematics. Just as we can distinguish two basic kinds of mathematical proof among the 'motley of proof techniques', so it follows that among the myriad expressions which are loosely grouped together under the rubric 'mathematical proposition' we can distinguish two basic kinds, which Wittgenstein described as those that 'belong to a system of propositions' and those that are 'aloof and isolated': in other words, those for which we possess an effective decision procedure (which characterises the *Beweissystem* to which they belong), and those which remain problematic because they resist all attempts to, as it were, 'systematise' them. The question of 'undecidability' turns on our understanding of the latter phenomenon, and the resolution of the Decision Problem which Wittgenstein pursued, far from having anything to do with quasi-epistemological considerations involving 'recognitional capacities', turns on the logico-syntactical question of whether it is intelligible to speak of a '*Beweissystemlos proposition*'.

In the *Tractatus* Wittgenstein had characterised entailment and logical truth in terms of, what for an omnipotent deity would amount to, a universal decision procedure (6.1251, 6.1262). He modified this approach in *Philosophical Remarks* with the obvious intention of reconciling the *Tractatus* account with the *Beweissystem* conception of inference. Thus, he amended his *Tractatus* position in the light of his network model, conceding that there is no such thing as a *universal* decision procedure, but holding fast to the principle that it is unintelligible to speak of 'undecidable propositions'. The key to his argument lies in the shift to the principle that decision procedures must be *Beweissystem*-specific. With this new approach he undertook to refute the intuitionists' claim that the philosophy of mathematics cannot hope to eliminate 'undecidable propositions' — those for which the law of excluded middle does not hold — from mathematics entirely, while at the same time avoiding the finitistic leanings of which he has frequently been accused. But his argument has little to do with the powers of intuition versus the limits of reason (or formal systems!); rather, it is solely a consequence of clarifying the logical grammar of mathematical *vis-à-vis* 'undecidable' propositions.

Following in Brouwer's footsteps, Weyl had insisted that the latter can only be grasped by some form of intuition. Thus he warned in *Philosophy of Mathematics and Natural Science* that the completeness of an axiomatic system

> would only be ensured by the establishment of such procedural rules of proof as would lead demonstrably to a solution for every pertinent problem. Mathematics would thereby be trivialised. But such a philosopher's stone has not been discovered and never will be discovered. Mathematics does not consist in developing the logical consequences of given assumptions omnilaterally, but intuition and the life of the scientific mind pose the problems, and these cannot be solved by mechanical rules like computing exercises. The deductive procedure that may lead to their solution is not predesigned but has to be discovered in each case. Analogy, experience, and an intuition capable of integrating multifarious connections are our principal resources in this task.[20]

Wittgenstein seized on what he regarded as the key phrase underlying this argument: the question whether the law of excluded middle applies to *every pertinent proposition*. Everything turns here on what we understand by 'pertinent': 'Weyl puts the problem of decidability in the following way. Can every *relevant* question be decided by means of logical inference? The problem must not be put in this way. Everything depends on the word "relevant." For Weyl, a statement is relevant when it is constructed from basic formulae with the help of seven principles of combination (among which are "all" and "there is"). This is where the mistake lies. A statement is relevant if it belongs to a *certain system*. It is in this sense that it has been maintained that every relevant question is decidable. What is not visibly relevant, is not relevant at all' (WWK 37). It is because he failed to take the *Beweissysteme* character of mathematics into consideration that Weyl was led to assume — and hope! — that the Decision Problem was destined to remain unsolvable. But 'where there's no logical method for finding a solution, the question doesn't make sense either' (PR §149). The resolution of the Decision Problem must therefore lie in the realm of philosophy as opposed to mathematical logic: what is called for is clarification of the question itself, rather than completeness proofs.

Wittgenstein thus set out to show that it is the very manner in which the Decision Problem has been approached that has been the source of our difficulties: 'Does the question of relevance make sense? If it does, it must always be possible to say whether the axioms are relevant to this proposition or not, and in that case this question must always be decidable, and so a question of the *first* type has already been decided. And if it can't be decided, it's completely senseless' (PR §149). Wittgenstein saw this issue as compelling grounds, therefore, to scrutinise the intuitionists' interpretation of these expressions as 'undecidable propositions'. This was precisely the point which Wittgenstein broached when he told his students that 'The reason I have brought up this comparison [with $a \times b = c$] is to see what sort of proposition "There are three 7's in π" is' (AWL 198). That is, he was trying to bring them to see that 'There are three 7's in π' is not a *mathematical proposition*:[21] to understand why, if this is an intelligible proposition, it cannot be one that belongs to the province of mathematics.

Far from attacking the law of excluded middle (i.e. the classical interpretation of disjunction), therefore, Wittgenstein saw the latter as the essential key to resolving the Decision Problem by revealing the unintelligibility of speaking of an undecidable *proposition*: 'I need hardly say that where the law of the excluded middle doesn't apply, no other law of logic applies either, because in that case we aren't dealing with propositions of mathematics. (Against Weyl and Brouwer)' (PR §151). Once this point has been grasped there will no longer be any temptation to question the validity of the law of excluded middle for all significant propositions. Or rather, one might equally — if not more accurately — say: once the significance of the law of excluded middle has been grasped (viz. its role as the fundamental criterion whereby propositional status, in whatever context, is determined) the Decision Problem collapses of its own accord. For 'Every proposition in mathematics must belong to a calculus of mathematics. (It cannot sit in solitary glory and refuse to mix with other propositions)' (PG 376). Every (meaningful) proposition — whether mathematical or empirical — is 'decidable' just because it is a *proposition*: because it is a member of a *System* for which there exists a general method of verification.[22] Even to ask if a proposition is 'decidable' is thus in a crucial sense otiose: to grasp the meaning of an expression (i.e. to grasp that it is a proposition!) just is for it to be decidable. 'A proposition construed in such a way that it can be uncheckably true or false if completely detached from reality and no longer functions as a proposition' (PR §225). For if to know the meaning of a mathematical proposition is to know the method of its solution, then how could we understand any proposition for which there exist no such rules of comprehension?

The emphasis on the 'method of solution' which characterises a 'system of proofs' is a recurrent theme throughout Wittgenstein's writings and lectures on the philosophy of mathematics during this period. Wittgenstein thought of this argument in terms of a point which he drew attention to in the *Tractatus* as his *Grundsatz*: 'Our fundamental principle is that whenever a question can be decided by logic at all it must be possible to decide it without more ado' (5.551). In *Philosophical Remarks* and *Philosophical Grammar* he interpreted this as a consequence of the fact that we cannot understand an expression unless it belongs to a *Satzsystem*, simply because without the rules constituted by a *Satzsystem* we have no method for knowing how to verify an expression. As we can see from the above, the argument was then carried over — with the requisite changes demanded by the fundamental shift from verification to proof — into the context of mathematics. Yet the latter brings with it a special — and obviously crucial — problem: how are we to characterise those mathematical expressions which are *Beweissystemlos*: the 'undecided' problems 'to which the mathematician tries to find an answer which are stated without a method of solution' (AWL 185). If the only significant questions are, by definition, those which we already know how to answer, then how did mathematics ever manage to progress beyond its elementary stages? Wittgenstein rather brusquely insisted that 'Where we can only expect the solution from some sort of revelation, there isn't even a problem. A revelation doesn't correspond to any question' (PR §149). Here, Wittgenstein concluded, the mathematician must 'Do something which I shall be inclined to accept as a solution, though I do not know now what it will be like' (AWL 186). Is this a foretaste of the anarchy which so many commentators have warned was to follow?

Postponing until the following section any consideration of the significance which this argument has for our understanding of mathematical conjectures, the   immediate problem which this approach to mathematical problems raises is whether it does not simply gloss over what — on his own terms — constituted a fatal omission in Wittgenstein's account: viz. those questions which occur within an existing mathematical system, but for which no 'general method of solution' exists? If, on Wittgenstein's interpretation of mathematical significance, there are only two species of mathematical problems — those which occur within an existing proof-schema and those which can only be resolved by constructing a new system — then this would surely play havoc with Wittgenstein's subsequent efforts to clarify the nature of mathematical invention. For it would entail that we could never prove *new* propositions within an existing system, in which case it is difficult to see how e.g. Euclidean geometry could have grown so prodigiously over the ages. But Wittgenstein himself was mindful of the dangers that loomed here. Thus he cautioned: 'My explanation mustn't wipe out the existence of mathematical problems. That is to say, it isn't as if it were only certain that a mathematical proposition made sense when it (or its opposite) had been proved. (This would mean that its opposite would never have a sense (Weyl).) On the other hand, it could be that certain apparent problems lose their character as problems — the questions as to Yes or No' (PR §148). It is this last, highly subtle point which Wittgenstein was struggling to clarify in his discussion of the significance of the law of excluded middle.

The problem which Wittgenstein was principally concerned with was to show that the common characterisation of all mathematical problems as 'mathematical conjectures' is unworkable, and indeed the source of considerable confusion in the philosophy of mathematics. For it conflates — and thus confuses — three separate species of mathematical problem: (i) straightforward mathematical questions, which are similar to empirical in the sense that a general method of proof already exists for their solution; (ii) mathematical conjectures, whose solution can either be realised within an existing system (but which none the less demand the construction of a new rule within that system), or which can only be settled by constructing an entirely new system;[23] and (iii) 'undecidable questions'. The first two categories are those which can, in principle, be proved: whether within an existing system or by the construction of a new system. The latter problems are those which are barred — for reasons which have wholly to do with logical grammar — from being incorporated into a *Beweissystem*. It is with this last issue that the remainder of the present section will be concerned.

It was chiefly for reasons of perspicuity that Wittgenstein focused on the notorious question, 'Are there four 7's in the expansion of π?' Unfortunately, the very intransigence of the epistemological framework in which this problem is entrenched makes it difficult to recognise the manner in which Wittgenstein was trying to shift our outlook. The key point is to grasp the full import of the law of excluded middle: the fact that in no sense could a *picture* be said to violate the law of excluded middle. For only propositions are governed by this fundamental logical principle. The conclusion that Wittgenstein drew from Brouwer's attack on platonist violations of the law of excluded middle lay precisely in the theme that, as we saw above, the law serves as our fundamental *criterion* for what constitutes a mathematical proposition: 'The word "proposition", if it is to have any meaning at all here, is equivalent to a calculus: to a calculus in which $p \vee \neg p$ is a tautology (in which the "law of the excluded middle" holds). When it is supposed not to hold, we have altered the concept of proposition. But that does not mean we have made a discovery (found something that is a proposition and yet doesn't obey such and such a law); it means we have made a new stipulation, or set up a new game' (PG 368). That is, the law of excluded middle is given by the rule that '"p v ¬p" is a tautology': 'p v ¬p and ¬ (p. ¬p) are rules, rules which tell us what a proposition is. If a logic is made up in which the law of excluded middle does not hold, there is no reason for calling the substituted expressions propositions' (AWL 140). Hence, 'Brouwer has actually discovered something which it is misleading to call a proposition. He has not discovered a proposition, but something having the appearance of a proposition' (AWL 140).

Given the Brouwerian influence, it is not surprising that Wittgenstein's arguments often seem to proceed from a concern with the limitations on understanding imposed by 'recognitional capacities'. For example, he told Waismann and Schlick:

> $\pi = 3.14159625 \ldots$
> The extension of such a number can only be an induction. There can be no such question as, do the figures 0, 1, 2, ... 9 occur in π? I can only ask if they occur at one particular point, or if they occur among the first 10,000 figures. No expansion, however far it may go, can refute the statement 'They do occur' — therefore this statement cannot be verified either. What is verified is an entirely different assertion, namely that this sequence occurs at this or that point. Hence you cannot affirm or deny such a statement, and therefore you cannot apply the law of the excluded middle to it. (WWK 71)

Admittedly, this sounds like the standard constructivist attack on non-finitary procedures, and when joined to the rigid emphasis on verificationism it is no wonder that Wittgenstein has been regarded as a strict finitist. But it would be a serious mistake to conclude from this overlap that Wittgenstein was forced into any form of finitism. The verificationist sentiments that Wittgenstein expressed in *Philosophical Remarks* led him to reformulate his account of logical syntax in a manner designed to clarify, rather than impugn the meaning of infinitary statements (PR §121).

The crucial point in Wittgenstein's argument is that he went on to rebuke Brouwer: Brouwer had reached the right conclusion, but for the wrong reasons, for he had failed to understand the basis and hence the implications of his own discovery: 'Brouwer is right when he says that the properties of his pendulum number are incompatible with the law of the excluded middle. But, saying this doesn't reveal a peculiarity of propositions about infinite aggregates. Rather, it is based on the fact that logic presupposes that it cannot be *a priori* — logically — impossible to tell whether a proposition is true or false. For, if the question of the truth or falsity of a proposition is *a priori* undecidable, the consequence is that the proposition loses its sense and the consequence of this is precisely that the propositions of logic lose their validity for it' (PR §173). That is, Brouwer's '*a priori* undecidable' expression rests on an infinitary statement that has been unintelligibly formulated in an extensional *Beweissystem*, which as such permits no coherent translation into a properly intensional mode (AWL 196). It treats an infinite series as a totality, and any 'question' that rests on this type of confusion could never be answered, for we cannot construct any rules for the use of an expression which regards infinity as a quantity. The point that Wittgenstein was making about the unintelligibility of 'Do four 7's occur in the expansion of π?' thus had nothing to do with any Anti-realist considerations about 'psychological limitations'.[24] The problem with such an interpretation is that it confuses our inexorability in deciding what is to count as the correct expansion of π (application of the law) with a 'predetermined expansion'. Wittgenstein's objection to the latter was that it rests on a straightforward *Beweissysteme* confusion: '"Can God know all the places of the expansion of π?" would have been a good question for the schoolmen to ask. In all such cases the answer runs, "The question is senseless"' (PR §128). Thus he concluded that 'Here again it is grammar which, as always in the sphere of the infinite, is playing tricks on us' (PR §172).[25]

The crux of Wittgenstein's argument thus proceeds from the familiar objection that, since no matter how far you have developed the expansion of π you could never be satisified whether you had proved or disproved that 'There are four 7's in the expansion of π' if such a sequence had not yet appeared, then this proposition must — *qua* mathematical proposition — be meaningless. But for Wittgenstein this constituted irrefutable evidence of the confusion which results when intensional contexts are irrevocably confused with an extensional *Beweissystem*. This does not entail that we can only understand finitistic statements, or that we cannot speak intelligibly about infinite sequences; rather, it portends simply that questions about infinity cannot be confused with finitary *Beweissysteme*. The fact that this confusion arises is proof of the puzzles which result when we try to treat propositions about infinity in the same manner as propositions about finite totalities. To be sure, the intuitionists had themselves insisted that we must distinguish between infinite processes and finite totalities, yet they had, Wittgenstein believed, unwittingly continued to be ensnared by the same confusion. Wittgenstein thus seized on the intuitionists' terminology as the key to grasping the nature of infinity, a problem which hinges on the stringent *Beweissystem* demarcation between *infinite processes* and *finite totalities*[26] (cf. Chapter 5).

The bridge separating the infinite conjunction of finite statements about the expansion of π ('"550" occurs in the first n places of π') and a statement about the infinite expansion of π is entirely conceptual: '[I] find it intelligible that one can give an infinite rule by means of which you may form infinitely many finite propositions. But what does an endless proposition mean?' (PR §127; cf. AWL 189-90). Hence the barrier preventing us from extending our reading of the quantifiers ranging over finite to 'infinite totalities' is a consequence of the *Beweissysteme* conditions for the use for these different kinds of propositions. It is quite true that no 'explicit rejection' of the law of excluded middle is to be found in Wittgenstein's discussion,[27] but this is for the simple reason that Wittgenstein explicitly emphasised its validity for propositions of both finite and infinite *Beweissysteme*. But the reason for this is hardly because Wittgenstein agreed that the significance of the principle for 'statements involving quantification over infinite totalities' cannot be interpreted extensionally. On the contrary, it is because the validity of the principle entails that we cannot make sense of the notion of 'quantification over an infinite totality': 'If someone says (as Brouwer does) that for $(x).f_1x = f_2x$, there is, as well as yes and no, also the case of undecidability, this implies that "$(x) \ldots$" is meant extensionally and we may talk of the case in which all x happen to have a property. In truth, however, it's impossible to talk of such a case at all and the "$(x) \ldots$" in arithmetic cannot be taken extensionally (PR §174; cf. PR §173).

The seeds of Wittgenstein's critique of the *Tractatus* account of quantification can be found early on in *Wittgenstein and the Vienna Circle*. The *Tractatus* account of *determinacy of sense* (cf. 2.021, 3.23, 4.26) hinges on our being able to decide, for any object in the denumerable infinity which forms the substance of the world (cf. 4.221) whether or not it is 'ø'. So the *Tractatus* semantics, which assumes the coherence of the claim that 'we can describe the world completely by means of fully generalised propositions' (5.526) rests on the unrestricted application of the law of excluded middle, whatever the domain of the quantifiers. With the pronounced objections to the notion of the 'actual infinite' which are so predominant in *Philosophical Remarks* it is no wonder that Wittgenstein should have questioned the *Tractatus* explanation of the quantifiers. Significantly, however, Wittgenstein's initial objections were concerned with a failure in what he described as the 'logical multiplicity' of the Russellian notation (which he had adopted), which is independent of the worries of 'quantifying over infinite totalities'. Thus, it might well have been the contact with Brouwer's ideas that stimulated Wittgenstein to reconsider the application of the law of excluded middle to quantified expressions ranging over infinite totalities, but Wittgenstein was quickly led to formulate a basic objection to the interpretation of the existential quantifier that obtains independently of his attack on the 'actual infinite'. Wittgenstein explained to Waismann and Schlick that the Russellian notation for the quantifier breaks down when its inner scope is negated (WWK 40). What this amounts to is the denial of the intelligibility of the law of excluded middle when the inner scope of existential generalisation is negated. But, far from establishing the failure of the principle, this constitutes irrefutable evidence of the failure of the Russellian notation to conform with the 'logical multiplicity' of what it is trying to represent (WWK 39). The important point that Wittgenstein expressed in his discussions with Waismann and Schlick is that the objection does not simply apply to quantification over infinite totalities; what he showed is just how widespread the occasions are when the existential quantifier is not understood in terms of an enumeration (a complexity brought out by Wittgenstein's special use of the verification principle).

This in turn leads us to see one reason why Wittgenstein insisted that a 'piece of prose' — such as 'Do four 7's occur in the expansion of π?' — may lead us to something entirely different after we have completed its proof from what we had initially contemplated. The point is that, encouraged by the extensional picture, we have a hazy impression of what the verbal expression means, but once we have carried out a proof (i.e. which either adheres rigidly to or else constructs the rules of a *Beweissystem*) we shall be led to discover/invent a *meaning* which is logically different from the picture 'conjured up by a particular image — as it were, of something lost in infinity' (AWL 196; PR §130). This itself is not 'revisionary' mathematics based on Anti-realist considerations, but rather, a philosophical method based on *Satzsysteme* clarification. Wittgenstein was certainly not suggesting that we cannot prove a question about e.g. infinite periodicity; rather, it is that it must be proved by a completely different method than that which is used to prove finite (extensional) mathematical questions (e.g. 'Do three 7's occur in the first *n* places of π') (PR §123, AWL 200; cf. Chapter 4). To see the force of this objection, we need only consider the nature of e.g. the Shanks and Wrench method for computing the value of 'π'.

Many have argued that the intuitionist-inspired objections to 'Do four 7's occur in the expansion of π?' have been left stranded by such recent high-powered calculations as that performed by Shanks and Wrench. Using the Störmer formula

$$\pi = 24 \arctan (1/8) + \arctan (1/57) + 4 \arctan (1/239)$$

they programmed a computer to calculate the value of 'π' to 100,265 places. As far as one can tell from looking at their results — which itself is a highly significant remark! — there are four consecutive 7's beginning at the 1589th place.[28] How could anyone still deny, in the face of this evidence, that the answer was predeterminedly true, and *a fortiori*, that the original question was intelligible? The immediate answer to this objection, however, is that it shifts implicitly — and illicitly — from the question 'Do four 7's occur in the first 100,265 digits of π?', to 'Do four 7's occur in the expansion of π?' The essence of Wittgenstein's argument is that, even if it were true, the premise that Shanks and Wrench proved the former would not entail that they had demonstrated the intelligibility of the latter. As it happens, however, the initial premise itself is far from trouble-free, for it raises problems of a different order, which centre on the question of the surveyability of proof.

There was never any obstacle to treating 'Do four 7's occur in the expansion of π?' as a legitmate (i.e. meaningful) *hypothesis*: and indeed, this is much the way in which the Shanks–Wrench solution was achieved. In this context, we perform an experiment: viz. we ascertain whether, if we perform such and such an operation (e.g. program a computer to perform some reiterated symbol-manipulation) to see whether a string of four 7's will appear. What we cannot conclude from such a successful experiment, however, is that the four 7's *must* have appeared: that we have *proved* that there are four 7's in the expansion of π. If it really is a hypothesis, then our result is condemned to remain inductive, no matter how high the probability; for how can we be *absolutely certain* that, e.g. the program contained no bugs? (cf. Chapter 4). If what we want to say, however, is that it was the rule for the expansion of π that *determined* that there must be four 7's in the expansion, then we are no longer using the expression as an hypothesis. For now we have shifted back to a mathematical context, and the objection to this latter usage is that it is based on a *Beweissysteme* confusion: it does not make sense to ask any sort of question about an infinite series as if it were an 'infinite extension'.[29]

The upshot of Wittgenstein's argument, therefore, is that we must clarify the nature of the context in order to distinguish between empiricial and mathematical questions. Wittgenstein's intention was not that we must rid mathematics of a sizeable proportion of those problems which have stimulated the most interest, but rather, that we must free ourselves from the lingering fallacy that epistemology plays a role in the classificaton of mathematical problems. For the battle that Wittgenstein was fighting here was not with the adherents of classical mathematics, but rather, with the defenders of the thesis that we can understand yet be unable to prove *propositions* which transcend our 'recognitional capacities'. Perhaps the most difficult aspect of this argument to come to terms with is that, despite the licence which this seems to provide for adjudicating between *legitimate* mathematical problems, no such philosophical authority has been sanctioned. We must be careful, therefore, not to overstate the case (as, perhaps, even Wittgenstein himself was occasionally prone to do): all that has been removed is a philosophical confusion, the seeds of which have inspired various epistemological theories, and thence mathematical revisionism. A highly relevant illustration of the subtleties involved here can be found in the section on the Appel–Haken solution of the four-colour problem (cf. Chapter 4). Philosophy's involvement in this issue is confined to clarifying the status of the Appel–Haken solution. If the result of this investigation is that the Appel–Haken solution must be denied the status of a *proof*, this in no way entails that their solution is flawed, nor that there *never* could be a four-colour theorem: only that their solution does not yield a four-colour *theorem*, and that we must be careful not to describe the four-colour problem which they addressed as a *mathematical* conjecture. But before we can approach this issue, we must next clarify the logical syntax of 'mathematical conjectures' *per se*.

Mathematical 'Stimuli'

The success of the foregoing resolution of the Decision Problem is contingent upon the elimination of 'undecidable propositions' in such a way that the 'trivialisation' of mathematics which Weyl warned against — or worse — is not incurred. Wittgenstein may have been perfectly well aware of the dangers that lurked here, but it has seemed to many that the price of his forcible removal of the former confusion is that his approach breaks down at this second obstacle. For, as we saw in the preceding section, Wittgenstein's argument turns on the principle that, in mathematics no less than in natural language, the concept of a *question* presupposes the existence of an established method for answering it: 'A question makes sense only in a calculus which gives us a method for its solution' (PG 387). The method is established by the logical syntax of the *Beweissystem* to which it belongs. A proof 'determines the meaning of a question' in the sense that it establishes the method of deciding that question: 'the proof belongs to the *sense* of the proved proposition, i.e. determines that sense' (PG 375). Thus, when Wittgenstein argued that we cannot understand 'undecided questions' in mathematics until a proof has been constructed for their use, it was on the firm understanding that we are not using the word 'question' in the same sense as when we speak of answering ordinary questions (AWL 200). For if a 'question' belongs to no *Satzsystem*, then it fails by definition to be meaningful in the sense in which this normally applies to questions. Spurious 'questions' such as 'Do green ideas sleep furiously?' are unintelligible, therefore, precisely because we have not yet established any rules for the manner in which these words have been used. And the same considerations apply *pari passu* to such meaningless 'questions' as 'Does $26 \times 13 =$ sine a?' (AWL 200; PR §151). But then, as Wittgenstein himself warned, 'Wouldn't all this lead to the paradox that there are no difficult problems in mathematics, since if anything is difficult it isn't a problem?' (PG 380). For all that we appear to be left with are instantiations of problems for which we already possess the general method of solution!

The answer to this dilemma, Wittgenstein explained, lies in the very theme that '"the difficult mathematical problems", i.e. the problems for mathematical research, aren't in the same relationship to the problem "25 × 25 = ?" as a feat of acrobatics is to a simple somersault. They aren't related, that is, just as very easy to very difficult; they are "problems" in different meanings of the word' (PG 380). Wittgenstein's next challenge was thus to elucidate in exactly what sense these 'undecided questions' — the mathematical conjectures on which the progress of mathematics revolves — are *mathematical questions*: '"You say 'where there is a question, there is also a way to answer it', but in mathematics there are questions that we do not see any way to answer." Quite right, and all that follows from that is that in this case we are not using the word "question" in the same sense as above' (PG 380). Saying this is clearly not enough, however; we need to know in what way these 'questions' do constitute genuine mathematical problems. And, it goes without saying, the clarification of this latter issue — the solution to the problem of 'How can there be conjectures in mathematics? Or better, what sort of thing looks like a conjecture in mathematics?' (PG 359) — must proceed without inadvertently permitting the return of the spurious notion of 'undecidable propositions' (PG 377).

Wittgenstein's argument must also satisfy those who are disturbed by the *prima facie* paradoxicality of suggesting that 'a proof alters the grammar of a proposition' (PG 367). For, among other things, Wittgenstein's conception of proof would seem to force us to conclude that, in so far as the last line of a proof must mean something different from the first line, it would be impossible to prove the proposition we intended. This objection results, however — like so much of the criticism that has been raised against Wittgenstein's remarks on the nature of proof — from the failure to recognise the significance of the distinction which he drew between *mathematical questions* and *mathematical conjectures*. As far as the former are concerned, the proof does *not* alter the meaning of the mathematical proposition; on the contrary, the essence of a mathematical question (i.e. a problem for which we already possess a general method of solution) is that the rules of the *Beweissystem* 'give the question sense' (AWL 196). When we turn to mathematical conjectures, however — where Wittgenstein's comments on the grammatical alterations wrought by proof were intended — the objection collapses as a result of the logical syntax of 'mathematical conjecture'. For the latter are —

again, by definition — *Beweissystemlos,* and 'Where there is no method of looking for an answer, there the question too cannot have any sense' (PG 377). Hence, the distinction urged here — between the sense of the first and last propositions of a proof — does not arise. The real distinction is to be drawn between the 'verbal expression' expressed in the first line and the mathematical proposition at the end of the proof. 'You might say that an hypothesis in mathematics has the value that it trains your thoughts on a particular object' (PG 359), but whatever the heuristic function which it exercises (*infra*), the sense of the *Beweissystemlos* verbal expression does not *change* after a proof has been constructed: rather, it *emerges.*

This grammatical transformation can occur in either of the two ways discussed in the preceding sections, and it was for this reason that we distinguished between two species of mathematical conjecture: those whose solution can be realised within an existing system but which none the less demand the construction of a new rule within that system, and those which can only be settled by constructing an entirely new system. It would obviously be absurd to suggest that e.g. Euclid's proof in Proposition 34 of the *Elements* — that the opposite sides and angles in a parallelogram are equal to one another — is categorially indistinguishable from Lobatchevsky's proof that the sum of the angles of a triangle — which is always less than π — decreases as the area of the triangle increases, and converges on π as the area approaches zero. Whereas the former proceeds from Postulate 5 and the definitions of straight line, angle, and the proof in Proposition 33 that straight lines joining equal and parallel straight lines are themselves equal and parallel, the latter is a direct consequence of the displacement of Postulate 5 with the alternative assumption that, given a line AB and a point C, all lines through C fall into two classes with respect to AB: viz. those which meet AB and those which do not. Among the latter are the two boundary lines, p and q, henceforward defined as parallel lines. Thus, whereas Euclid's proof can be seen to extend his system by developing new concepts which are complementary to the primitive definitions, Lobatchevsky's abandonment of the Parallel Postulate obviously served to produce an alternative geometrical system: one in which, where the definition of parallels is concerned, leads to concepts that, as the above proof demonstrates, are radically divorced from their Euclidean counterparts.

On a simpler level, we might try to elucidate this distinction by considering the options open to a municipal council who are deciding how to expand their city's transport system. They might simply choose to build a new road linking two previously unconnected points, or they might lay down a tram line where hitherto there had only been roads, developing their transportation facilities in an entirely new direction. In either case, the crucial point to bear in mind would be that we may have an inchoate picture of what sort of sense we think the *Beweissystemlos* verbal expression possesses (and it is this feature which accounts for the regulative function which such expressions can serve). But such associations must not be confused with meaning. Meaning in mathematical systems is only given by a proof outlining the rules which govern the use of expressions. By constructing a proof which is 'guided' by such pictures, therefore, we are not *clarifying* the *meaning* of the picture, but rather, constructing the rules which create a meaningful mathematical proposition. The natural objection to this argument, however, is whether there is not still a third species of proof — or perhaps, an alternative interpretation of the first kind of mathematical conjecture: the case in which the council discovers that there was, in fact, no need no expand the transportation system in the first place, for it transpires that it was already possible to get from point A to B via the existing road network, and all that was needed were some new road signs to advertise this route. Indeed, most would argue that this is by far the most characteristic form of mathematical proof, and the model rather than the exception for what we regard as a successful proof.

There are profound conceptual subtleties buried in this topic, both for our understanding of the nature of mathematical proofs and the possibility of error in the construction of proof, which we shall pursue further in Chapters 4 and 8. For the moment, however, it is important to see that, on Wittgenstein's approach, we are still engaged in even the most elementary of mathematical conjectures in the construction of a new rule: namely, the theorem proved within the framework of a pre-existing network of rules, which functions as a new rule in the system precisely because the old rules have been rearranged to accommodate this new format, thereby extending the internal relations between the basic concepts in the system. On Wittgenstein's account the municipal metaphor is misleading, therefore, precisely because grammatical constructions are unlike empirical discoveries in this crucial respect:

'The edifice of rules must be *complete*, if we are to work with a concept at all — *we cannot make any discoveries in syntax*. For, only the group of rules *defines* the sense of our signs, and any alteration (e.g. supplementation) of the rules means an alteration of the sense' (PR §154). Hence, the relation of a mathematical conjecture to a proof — of an heuristic expression to a grammatical construction — is invariant, no matter what type of proof may be involved, and it is for this reason that 'It is impossible to make discoveries of novel rules holding of a form already familiar to us (say the sine of an angle). If they are new rules, then it is not the old form' (PG 378).

This last line contains what might properly be identified as the crux of the issue. To be sure, there are many cases where we do not construct a new rule when solving a mathematical problem; but those are simply the cases where we are 'doing our homework'. That is, in these problems we are not dealing with mathematical conjectures, but rather, with mathematical questions. For if the rules of the system already provide the means for deriving an answer — as on the standard picture of axiomatics — then the question itself was just that: a *mathematical question*, whose sense as such was determined by the rules of the *Beweissystem*. The natural objection to this argument is, of course, that the whole point of studying e.g. the *Elements* is that the pupil learns as he goes along that various theorems can be derived from the axioms, so these 'questions' must really be conjectures *for him*. But this argument merely reverts to a subtle variation of the rule-following confusions examined in Chapter 2, which swiftly leads us back into the very epistemological muddles that we are struggling to overcome. The question here is not whether the pupil knows the general procedure whereby the problem is solved; it is whether the *calculus* caters for the question. What we are concerned with is entirely a matter of the logical syntax of the system, not the individual's mastery of mathematical concepts: 'We call it a problem, when we are asked "how many are 25×16", but also when we are asked: what is $\int \sin^2 \times dx$. We regard the first as much easier than the second, but we don't see that they are "problems" in different senses. *Of course*, the distinction is not a psychological one; it isn't a question of whether the pupil can solve the problem, but whether the calculus can solve it, or which calculus can solve' (PG 379). Hence, there is simply no room here for 'rule-following scepticism' to enter; for 'Whether a pupil *knows a rule* for ensuring a solution to ∫ sin ² × dx is of no interest; what does interest us is whether the *calculus* we have before us (and that he happens to be using) contains such a rule. What interests us is not whether the pupil can do it, but whether the calculus can do it, and *how* it does it' (PG 379).

What this objection does draw attention to, however, is the tension which is present in the claim that we can distinguish on Wittgenstein's account between the two different kinds of mathematical conjecture outlined above. The nature of the distinction operating here depends ultimately on what we understand by a *Beweissystem*. If we define a system strictly in terms of its axioms (or axioms and postulates), then it is manifestly necessary to distinguish between mathematical conjectures which can be proved within an existing system and those which can only be settled by constructing an entirely new system. But Wittgenstein repeatedly insisted that to construct a new rule is *ipso facto* to construct a new system: 'The system of rules determining a calculus thereby determines the "meaning" of its signs too. Put more strictly: The form and the rules of syntax are equivalent. So if I change the rules — seemingly supplement them, say — then I change the form, the meaning' (PR §152). In which case, 'Euclid doesn't show us how to look for the solutions to his problems; he gives them to us and then proves that they are solutions. And this isn't a psychological or pedagogical matter, but a mathematical one. That is, the *calculus* (the one he gives us) doesn't enable us to look for the construction. A calculus which does enable us to do that is a *different* one' (PG 387). That is, the relationship between the axioms and propositions of a system is reciprocal, not one-sided: the meanings of the concepts which are implicitly defined by the axioms are altered by each new rule extending their use. It is the totality of rules governing their use in a system — and not just the axioms — which constitutes the meaning of the primitive concepts. Likewise, if the identity of a system is determined by the sum total of its rules, then to construct a new concept on the basis of the primitive definitions of the system is *ipso facto* to construct a new system.

In either case, the distinction between these two species of mathematical conjecture is less pronounced than was indicated above, and what we must differentiate between is constructing a new calculus in the evolution of a family-resemblance system and constructing an entirely new system. In other words, we would distinguish between e.g. the evolution of the family of Euclidean geomotries that were developed over the ages — or indeed, the family of Euclidean geometries which are developed in the *Elements* itself, as each successive book introduces a new set of primitive definitions — and the introduction of an entirely new type of — non-Euclidean — geometry. The axioms of a system do not implicitly *contain* or *predetermine* which rules can be constructed: whether this be rules for the use of new concepts, or rules for the modification of a primitive concept (cf. Chapter 8). The only constraint operating here is that which we impose on the issue of what counts as developing the family system (e.g. we treat the proof of Proposition 29 by 'Playfair's axiom' rather than the Parallel axiom as a staunch Euclidean proof) as opposed to what constitutes passing outside the boundaries of the family system (as in the construction of Bolyai–Lobatchevskian geometry). The key point is that 'the verbal expressions in mathematics which we use to describe the results of proofs are used highly metaphorically. They only get their strict sense from a method, and when the method has been evolved, then questions in that system become very like ordinary empirical questions' (AWL 198-9).

The source of our confusion in this issue is the premise that a mathematical conjecture has a meaning prior to the proof: that a proof merely clarifies or confirms the truth of a conjecture. The solution Wittgenstein pursued is to show us that the meaning of the mathematical proposition constructed by the proof is not equivalent to the sense of the mathematical conjecture; for the proof lays down new rules of use. Indeed, since the conjecture has by its very nature no underlying proof it has no sense in the manner in which it is presently being employed. The fact that the expression is being used in a *Beweissystemlos* context is precisely what establishes its existence as a mathematical conjecture! Thus, as was touched on in Chapter 2, the construction of a proof does not mark the *consolidation*, but rather, the *construction* of a 'logical space' in which the conjecture can begin to operate. The essence of this conception of mathematical conjectures can thus be appreciated by considering just what sort of proof could establish whether e.g. 'green ideas sleep furiously'. No amount of psychological or chromatic research will settle this issue. But neither will a careful examination of the logical implications of each of the constituent concepts as combined in this expression. Hence, any successful solution of this 'question' would not be one which had rigorously deduced its proof from the established rules which constitute the meanings of these concepts. Rather, a proof would be such in virtue of its having *created* a meaning for this combination. And this will be accomplished, not by a deductive process, but rather by the creation of new rules. Why we should agree to this grammatical innovation may be a psychological, practical, or aesthetic matter, but it is not a logical issue; it is not because the previous meanings of these concepts *compel* us to accept this new grammatical structure, but because the proof *persuades* us to enact this piece of linguistic legislation (usually because of the images commonly associated with the concepts in question) (cf. Chapter 8). In any event, the question as to why we accept an argument as a proof is empirical; the primary philosophical issue involved here is to clarify the logical status of a grammatical construction that we *call* a mathematical conjecture.

The heart of Wittgenstein's argument thus lies in the attempt to reorient the point of view from which we explain the logical status of a mathematical conjecture. Wittgenstein's argument was concerned neither with the epistemological status of a mathematical conjecture nor with the psychological explanation of mathematical discovery. Rather, the focus of his investigation was the assumption that a mathematical conjecture is identical to the mathematical proposition subsequently proved, and that the proof merely licenses us to apply the conjecture in the manner which we had originally envisaged. That is, that a proof does not in any way change the meaning of the original conjecture: we supposed that such and such would be the case and the proof merely confirms the validity of this intuition. But a subtle grammatical equivocation occurs in this argument. For what it really states is that, with a mathematical conjecture, we have the basic mathematical proposition shorn of the various internal relations which the proof subsequently establishes. That is, we know that the conjecture is connected with a host of other mathematical concepts, but we do not yet quite know how. But these relations are not accidental or external: they are what *constitutes* an expression as a mathematical proposition. The problem here is simply that a mathematical proposition cannot be divorced from the internal relations which a proof constructs for its use. Thus, in the absence of these rules, it simply makes no sense to describe a mathematical expression as a species of 'meaningful proposition', and *a fortiori*, one which can be either true or false. Which is precisely why we distinguish between mathematical conjectures and mathematical questions in the first place.

Despite the radical consequences which this argument has for our understanding of the Decision Problem the conception of mathematical conjectures from whence it proceeds is by no means unorthodox. Indeed, one frequently encounters this very picture of the heuristic function performed by mathematical conjectures in writings by mathematicians interested in the process of mathematical discovery. Throughout *The Act of Creation* Koestler gathered a number of illustrations of this theme. A notable example is the passage which he quoted from Jacques Hadamard's *The Psychology of Invention in the Mathematical Field*: 'I distinctly belong to the auditory type; and precisely on that account my mental pictures are exclusively visual. The reason for that is quite clear to me: such visual pictures are more naturally vague, as we have seen it to be necessary in order to lead me without misleading me. ... The mental pictures ... are most frequently visual, but they may also be of another kind, for instance, kinetic. There can also be auditive ones, but even these ... quite generally keep their vague character.'[30] Wittgenstein's involvement with this issue is fundamentally different, however, from this concern with the mechanics of mathematical discovery. Whereas the mathematicians who have written on this subject are (understandably) interested in the psychology of discovery (e.g. whether, as Hadamard considers, sitting, walking, or taking two baths may best contribute to mathematical discovery[31]), Wittgenstein was unique in working through the philosophical implications of this conception of mathematical conjectures.

His problem here was to explain the manner in which *Beweissystemlos* expressions can be said to *guide* us in the construction of a proof even though lacking sense, and in what relation they stand to the newly-constructed proof (PR §151). What Wittgenstein had to avoid, however, was the suggestion that the process of mathematical discovery is blind, or that mathematical progress is essentially fortuitous. And yet this is just the sort of impression conveyed by such passages as when Wittgenstein — responding to an image first introduced into the context of mathematical discovery by Zermelo — remarked:

The comparison between a mathematical expedition and a polar expedition. There is a point in drawing this comparison and it is a very useful one.

How strange it would be if a geographical expedition were uncertain whether it had a goal, and so whether it had any route whatsoever. We can't imagine such a thing, it's nonsense. But this is precisely what it is like in a mathematical expedition. And so perhaps it is a good idea to drop the comparison altogether.

It would be an expedition, which was uncertain of *the space* it was in! (PR §161; cf. PG 365, PLP 398)[32]

Read as a statement about the phenomenology of mathematical discovery this sounds remarkably thin. But that is only because this was not at all what Wittgenstein intended; rather, he was trying to clarify the logical syntax of mathematical conjectures and their subsequent proofs. Thus he hastened to explain: 'Fermat's proposition makes no *sense* until I can *search* for a solution to the equation in cardinal numbers. And "search" must always mean: search systematically. Meandering about in infinite space on the look-out for a gold ring is no kind of search. You can only *search* within a system: And so there is necessarily something you *can't* search for' (PR §150; cf. PR §152). This certainly intimates that Wittgenstein's interpretation of mathematical 'conjectures' was similar to Kant's description of 'heuristic' principles; i.e. that they exercise a 'regulative' influence on our imagination, setting us off on the search for proofs. 'A mathematician is of course guided by associations, by certain analogies with the previous system. After all, I do not claim that it is wrong or illegitimate if anyone concerns himself with Fermat's Last Theorem. Not at all! If e.g. I have a method for looking at integers that satisfy the equation $x^2 + y^2 = z^2$, then the formula $x^n + y^n = z^n$ may stimulate me. I may let a formula stimulate me. Thus I shall say, here there is a *stimulus* — but not a *question*. Mathematical problems are always such stimuli' (WWK 144).

All this clearly represents no solution, however, to the problem we are principally concerned with: viz. what is the logical syntactical status of these 'stimuli'? Take the search for a solution to Goldbach's conjecture: 'What is here going [o]n is an unsystematic attempt at constructing a calculus. If the attempt is successful, I shall again have a calculus in front of me, only a different one from the calculus I have been using so far' (WWK 174 f.; cf. PG 381). The problem is thus to clarify what *searching for a solution* means in a mathematical as opposed to an empirical context: 'Suppose someone was investigating even numbers to see if they confirmed Goldbach's conjecture. Suppose he expressed the conjecture — and it can be expressed — that if he continued with this investigation, he would never meet a counter-example as long as he lived. If a proof of the theorem is then discovered, will it also be a proof of the man's conjecture? How is that possible?' (PG 361). In answer to this last question, Wittgenstein immediately went on to emphasise that 'Nothing is more fatal to philosophical understanding than the notion of proof and experience as two different but comparable methods of verification' (PG 362). That is, there is a great temptation to interpret these 'signposts' as quasi-empirical hypotheses, which threatens to confuse proof and experiment: to misinterpret the nature of *search* in mathematical discovery. Moreover, the target for Wittgenstein's argument was not a Popperian theory (such as that which was developed by Imre Lakatos in *Proofs and Refutations*), but rather, the assumption that the relationship between mathematical conjectures and their proofs is — following the paradigm of the *Beweissysteme* instantiations of a proof-schema — *deductive*.

Mathematical conjectures are similar to empirical hypotheses in so far as each plays a heuristic role (which accounts for our use of the term 'conjecture' for these mathematical expressions). But there is a serious danger that this common element might blind us to the considerable grammatical difference between an *empirical* as opposed to a *mathematical* conjecture (PR §162). For the search for the solution to an undecided mathematical 'question' is conceptually completely unlike the search for a solution to a physical hypothesis (PG 370-1). The primary difference between an *experiment* and a *proof* is demonstrated by the difference in the semantic relations that an empirical hypothesis bears to a successful experiment and a mathematical conjecture to a constructed proof. Whatever happens to its probability, the *meaning* of an empirical hypothesis remains unchanged after the completion of an experiment. The same cannot be said for mathematical conjectures, however; yet neither can the opposite. Significantly, Wittgenstein studiously avoided saying that the meaning of the mathematical conjecture changes its sense after the construction of a proof; what he emphasised is that the conjecture '*alters its position in mathematics*'. For the mathematical conjecture simply has no *meaning* that can be changed, and it is for that reason that 'The proposition with its proof doesn't belong to the same category as the proposition without the proof' (PG 371).

It may be tempting to compare Wittgenstein's idea here — bearing in mind the 'obsession' with an empiricist philosophy of mathematics which Dummett describes — to Lakatos's 'heuristic approach to proof-generated concepts'. Admittedly there are passages which bear out such affinities; especially when, as in *Philosophical Grammar,* Wittgenstein curtly declared: 'Unproved mathematical propositions — signposts for mathematical investigation, stimuli to mathematical constructions' (PG 371). It is certainly interesting that Wittgenstein shared with Lakatos the belief that the proofs of mathematical conjectures cannot be accomplished by a mechanical or deductive process.[33] But for Lakatos proof is an explanatory device which renders a mathematical conjecture more convincing, and which, through the process of adducing and responding to counter-examples, produces greater accuracy and plausibility for its conjectures. Despite his opposition to the identification of proof with experiment, Wittgenstein need not have objected completely to the general outlines of Lakatos's picture of mathematical dialogue. Indeed, one might even argue that, far from being hostile to it, Wittgenstein was fundamentally sympathetic to the spirit behind such a model, and that this accounts for the interest in an empiricist philosophy of mathematics that Dummett emphasises. But where Wittgenstein would have fundamentally disagreed with Lakatos is over the latter's interpretation of the logical status of mathematical proofs.

From Wittgenstein's perspective, Lakatos has confused the manner in which we *use* proofs with the actual logical status of a proof. The Wittgensteinian response to Lakatos's picture is that the process of mathematical 'discovery' which Lakatos depicts is not a species of scientific 'discovery', where the criterion of testability constantly goads us on to ever-more sophisticated explanations. Rather, mathematical 'discovery' is a normative activity in which similar pressures to those which motivate the scientist (and the mathematical basis of contemporary physics enhances this affinity) encourage the mathematician to produce increasingly complex normative structures. The logical status of the different types of refutation which Lakatos calls 'local' and 'global' counter-examples (i.e. criticisms of the steps in a proof versus criticisms of the conclusion) remains that of *rules of syntax*: grammatical reformulations which are prompted, perhaps, by the belief that an existing rule does not elucidate some aspect of the mental image

(Lakatos's 'thought-experiment') which is guiding us. Hence, the fundamental objection to Lakatos's account is that it confuses *syntactic* for *explanatory* complexity, and it is this which in turn induced Lakatos to confuse the grammatical nature of proof with the empirical nature of experiment. In describing the phenomenology of mathematical discovery Lakatos was led to overlook the fact that 'discovery' itself is a family-resemblance concept, which entails something radically different in mathematics (viz. the construction of increasingly complex grammatical structures) from what it means in science. (Compare the development of three-dimensional chess: this is not a more accurate account of what chess is 'about', but rather a more complicated game which bears certain resemblances to chess.)

This issue also sheds further light on familiar problems broached in the first two sections. To begin with, given that the meaning of a mathematical proposition is *Beweissystem*-specific, it obviously follows that if such a proposition is used to ask some completely new type of mathematical 'question' — for which there exists no established method of solution — then it is being used as a mathematical conjecture. What we then have to bear in mind is that if we do construct a proof for this novel use, the meaning of the subsequent proposition is not the same as that of the original. In a sense, Wittgenstein was thus describing a variation of the sentence/statement distinction; but whereas the theorist of meaning tends to think of the meaning of a statement as being a function of its *sentential* meaning (the combinatorial rules governing the employment of the sub-sentential expressions) together with contextual factors, Wittgenstein's point was that the same sentence *qua* sign can be used in different *Satzsysteme*, but the statement which it makes in each is solely a matter of the rules governing its use in that particular *Satzsystem* (PG 367). Hence, the immediate significance which this has for the philosophy of mathematics is that (e.g.) ' "this equation has n roots" hasn't *the same* meaning if I've proved it by enumerating the constructed roots as if I've proved it in a different way. If I find a formula for the roots of an equation, I've constructed a new calculus; I haven't filled in a gap in an old one' (PG 373). Thus, when some theorem is given a new (and generally a more comprehensive or abstract) proof, we would say that the proposition does not mean the same for the two different proofs (PG 360, 378). Similarly, one and the same expression (e.g. 'Are there four 7's in the expansion of π?')

can be used in both an empirical and a mathematical context: viz. to formulate either an empirical hypothesis or a mathematical conjecture. And in many cases, the logico-syntactical status of the expression can only be decided by scrutinising the nature of the solution.

This is an extraordinarily powerful conception of mathematical propositions and proofs. If one were to isolate a single theme as the cornerstone of Wittgenstein's approach to the foundations of mathematics, it would be his conception of the normative character of mathematical constructions. For the remainder of this book we shall examine some of the major issues in which Wittgenstein worked through the consequences of this revolutionary insight. But before we consider the implications of this argument, we must first flesh out this schematic outline of the distinction between an experiment and a proof. For as it stands, the argument is unlikely to win many converts among working mathematicians or philosophers of mathematics. We can best assess the force of this insight, therefore, in the light of the controversy that has recently been sparked off by the Appel–Haken solution of the four-colour problem, where it is just this problem which has been raised. Before we can address this issue, however, we must first consider what is, perhaps, the most contentious aspect of Wittgenstein's discussion of proof: the emphasis which he placed on the notion of 'surveyability'. For if there is one theme which militates against the anti-epistemological interpretation which has here been canvassed it is surely this. Our next task is thus to show why the remarks on surveyability were themselves intended to undermine the epistemological approach to the 'foundations crisis', and indeed, how this theme further underscores the logico-syntactical demarcation between experiment and proof.

Notes

1. R.L.Wilder, 'The Nature of Mathematical Proof', *American Mathematical Monthly*, vol. 51 (1944), p. 310.
2. Ibid., p. 318.
3. Ibid., p. 309.
4. Ibid., p. 319.
5. Ibid.
6. Philip Jourdain, *The Nature of Mathematics*, in James R. Newman (ed.), *The World of Mathematics*, vol. 1 (New York, Simon and Schuster, 1956), p. 12.
7. Ibid., p. 10.

8. Petr Beckmann, *A History of* π *(PI)* (New York, St Martin's Press, 1971), p. 24.

9. James R. Newman, 'The Rhind Papyrus', in *The World of Mathematics*, op. cit., p. 175.

10. Otto Neugebauer, 'Egyptian Mathematics and Astronomy', in Douglas M. Campbell and John C. Higgins (eds), *Mathematics: People. Problems. Results*, vol. I (Belmont, California, Wadsworth International, 1984), p. 5.

11. Ibid., p. 7.

12. Richard J. Gillings, 'Mathematics in the Time of the Pharaohs', in *Mathematics: People. Problems. Results*, op.cit., p. 16.

13. Ibid.

14. Morris Kline, *Mathematical Thought from Ancient to Modern Times* (New York, Oxford University Press, 1972), pp. 20-1.

15. Ibid., p. 34.

16. Philip J. Davis and Reuben Hersh, *The Mathematical Experience* (Brighton, Sussex, The Harvester Press, 1981), p. 151.

17. If, indeed, there was such a thing as 'geometrical truth'; cf. his letter to Olbers, quoted in Roberto Torretti's *Philosophy of Geometry from Riemann to Poincaré* (Dordrecht, D. Reidel Publishing Company, 1984), p. 55.

18. M. Dummett, 'Wittgenstein's Philosophy of Mathematics', in S.G. Shanker (ed.), *Ludwig Wittgenstein: Critical Assessments* (London, Croom Helm, 1986), p. 132.

19. Friedrich Waismann, 'The Nature of Mathematics: Wittgenstein's Standpoint', in *Ludwig Wittgenstein: Critical Assessments*, vol. III, p. 86.

20. Hermann Weyl, *Philosophy of Mathematics and Natural Science*, Olaf Helmer (trans.) (Princeton, Princeton University Press, 1949), p. 24.

21. Cf. 'I say that the so-called "Fermat's last Theorem" is no kind of *proposition* (not even in the sense of a proposition of arithmetic)' (PR §189).

22. Despite this emphasis on the meaninglessness of mathematical conjectures *(infra)*, Wittgenstein remained completely opposed to the formalist approach to the Decision Problem. Given Wittgenstein's explanation of meaning, the problem whether some *well-formed formula* is a theorem in a given system is quite simply unintelligible. To recognise an expression as a well-formed formula just is to be able to prove it. To be a well-formed formula is simply to be a mathematical proposition constructed according to the rules governing the use of the constituent expressions. Thus, to recognise that an expression is well formed amounts to the very same thing as to understand its sense *qua* theorem in that system. The formalist conception of the Decision Problem reflects what Wittgenstein believed was the formalists' general attempt to have it both ways in the philosophy of mathematics: they insisted that we are only dealing with meaningless signs, but then immediately reintroduced those concepts which only have significance for *meaningful* propositions. The point here is that such concepts as *decidability* or *entailment* do not have any meaning when applied to *signs*. For example, we can speak of one sign being larger than another, but not of one sign *entailing* another. Thus, this fundamentally formalist version of the Decision Problem mistakenly supposes that it is possible to separate well-formedness from deducibility, when the genuine syntactic question we are concerned with is whether such and such an expression is well formed in a given *Beweissystem*.

23. To be sure, this distinction may in practice be an exceptionally difficult matter to resolve; as was borne out, for example, in the history of the attempts to settle the status of Euclid's parallel postulate. But the philosopher's concern is not how we would differentiate a given problem in practice, but solely to clarify the nature of the categorial distinction between these two species of conjecture.

24. Cf. Crispin Wright, *Wittgenstein on the Foundations of Mathematics*

(London, Duckworth, 1980), p. 144.

25. Cf. Hans Hahn, 'Logic, Mathematics, and Knowledge of Nature', in *Logical Positivism*, A.J. Ayer (ed.) (New York, The Free Press, 1959), p. 159.

26. Interestingly, Russell concluded in his report to Trinity College on Wittgenstein's work that 'what Wittgenstein says about infinity tends ... to have a certain resemblance to what has been said by Brouwer. I think perhaps the resemblance is not so close as it appears at first sight' (*Autobiography*, p. 440).

27. Cf. Wright, *Wittgenstein on the Foundations of Mathematics*, op.cit., pp. 142-3.

28. Cf. J.W. Wrench, Jr, 'The Evolution of Extended Decimal Approximations to π', *The Mathematics Teacher*, vol. 53 (1960), pp. 664-50; and D. Shanks and J.W. Wrench, Jr, 'Calculation of π to 100,000 decimals', *Mathematics of Computation*, vol. 16 (1962), pp. 76-99.

29. Admittedly the argument amounts to a full-scale attack on classical set theory, but this in no way committed Wittgenstein to any sort of finitist dogma.

30. Arthur Koestler, *The Act Of Creation* (London, Picador, 1969), p. 172.

31. Or, as in Poincaré's case, a cup of black coffee drunk just before bedtime; cf. 'Mathematical Creation', in James R. Newman (ed.), *The World of Mathematics*, vol. IV (New York, Simon and Schuster, 1956).

32. But cf. Karl Kraus: 'Science will make one last attempt and send out its arbiters. It is hoped they will establish that there really is a North Pole, because they know it from hearsay, and the Pole will be pleased if it comes out of this affair without a scratch, this self-satisfied spot "from which everywhere is south" and everywhere meanness — a desolate area since it came into contact with things human' ('The Discovery of the North Pole', in *In These Great Times*, Harry Zohn, (ed.), Manchester, Carcanet Press, 1976, p. 55).

33. Cf. Imre Lakatos, *Proofs and Refutations: The Logic of Mathematical Discovery* (Cambridge, Cambridge University Press, 1976). p.4.

4 SURVEYABILITY

If logical inference is to be reliable, it must be possible to survey these objects completely in all their parts, and the fact that they occur, that they differ from one another, and that they follow each other, are concatenated, is immediately given intuitively, together with the objects, as something that can neither be reduced to anything else nor requires reduction.

Hilbert, 'On the Infinite'

Perspicuity is part of proof. If the process by means of which I get a result were not surveyable, I might indeed make a note that this number is what comes out — but what fact is this supposed to confirm for me? I don't know 'what is *supposed* to come out'. (RFM I §154)

The Bounds of Perspicuity

It is noteworthy that Wittgenstein nowhere mentioned the notion of a surveyable proof in *Philosophical Remarks* or *Philosophical Grammar*. To be sure, the grounds for his later discussion are very much in evidence, and it is possible to trace the origins and development of his thought on what emerged as a central element in his treatment of proof in *Remarks on the Foundations of Mathematics* in these early works. But it would seem that the idea that we can clarify what we mean by 'mathematical proof' by recognising that, in order to qualify as such a proof must be surveyable, only occurred to Wittgenstein after he had developed the argument in relation to the grammar of colour-words. This reinforces, perhaps, the widespread impression that the constructivist direction of Wittgenstein's thought in the philosophy of mathematics was heavily influenced by his shift towards verificationism in the philosophy of language, and hence, that it is crucial that we understand the development of the latter if we are to appreciate the subtlety of the former. For if one theme could be said to underpin the epistemological interpretation of Wittgenstein's proposed resolution of the 'foundations crisis', it is the insistence that '"A

120

mathematical proof must be perspicuous." Only a structure whose reproduction is an easy task is called a "proof". It must be possible to decide with certainty whether we really have the same proof twice over, or not' (RFM III §1). Certainly this is a complication which the foregoing interpretation cannot afford to disregard.

As we saw in the preceding chapter, the central idea which Wittgenstein was labouring to develop in *Philosophical Remarks* and *Philosophical Grammar* is that *proof* is a family resemblance concept: that the various constructions which we identify as proofs form a family on the basis of their shared normative function. Proofs produce the mathematical analogue of rules of grammar; thus, 'The point of the remark that arithmetic is a kind of geometry is simply that arithmetical constructions are autonomous like geometrical ones, and hence so to speak themselves guarantee their applicability' (PR §111). Whatever the domain, a proof is very much like the catalogue of rules for a game: it creates the meanings for the pieces which constitute playing that game. One might, of course, object to this that Wittgenstein ignored what should be described as the 'mathematical reality' which accounts for the crucial difference between proofs and the rules of a game: viz. that proofs are not at all arbitrary in the way that applies to games. For the fact is that in constructing a mathematical proof we are primarily constrained by the meanings which govern the use of the concepts we are extending. Wittgenstein's answer to this, as we have just seen, is that the pre-established meaning of concepts can only serve a heuristic role as far as the construction of a new proof is concerned. But certainly, as we shall see in Chapter 8, this in itself militates against the 'arbitrariness' of mathematical constructions. For the moment, however, we must explore the significance of the premise that 'The proof constructs a proposition; but the point is *how* it constructs it' (RFM III §28).

It was natural for Wittgenstein to argue later, in light of the 'conventionalist' account of proof-constructed meaning presented in *Philosophical Remarks*, that a proof *qua* grammatical construction must be what he subsequently described as 'surveyable'. Indeed, he was already beginning to insist in *Philosophical Remarks* that 'If a proposition is to have a definite sense (and it's nonsense otherwise), it must comprehend — survey — its sense completely; a generalisation only makes sense if it (i.e. all values of its variables) is completely determined' (PR §122). It is no easy matter, however, to explain precisely what this means. Even Wittgenstein found it difficult to translate *Übersicht* into English, but it is clear that the fundamental point of an *Übersicht* in philosophical investigations is that it should clarify the logical articulations which are forged by grammatical conventions.[1] The demand that a proof should be surveyable in this sense amounts to the principle that the grammatical conventions that are established by a proof must be perspicuous. The first step is thus to identify proofs as grammatical constructions; a proof in elementary arithmetic, for example, '*defines* "correctly counting together"' (RFM III §24; cf. §§26,28). Which means that proof, *qua* grammatical construction, must be surveyable: 'Proof, one might say, does not merely shew *that* it is like this, but: *how* it is like this. It shows *how* 13 + 14 yield 27. "A proof must be capable of being taken in" means: we must be prepared to use it as our guideline in judging' (RFM III §22). The significance of this step in terms of the shift away from the *Tractatus* conception of logical analysis is clear: there cannot be any hidden (or 'deep') rules governing the use of concepts, and thus grammatical constructions — from whence all conventions spring Athena-like fully-formed — must establish these rules completely and intelligibly. To be a rule of logical syntax is *ipso facto* to be surveyable: 'For if the rules of syntax cannot be grasped, they're of no use at all' (PR §121).

The origin of Wittgenstein's thought on the importance of surveyability for mathematical constructions can thus be found in his discussion of the logical structure of *Satzsysteme* in *Philosophical Remarks*. It would seem, however, that it was not until the late 1930s that Wittgenstein became fully aware of the extent to which his earlier remarks on the surveyability of colour-systems applied no less forcefully to his account of mathematical proof, even though this theme is implicitly developed so extensively in *Philosophical Remarks*. The very fact that a *proof* is interpreted as a species of *Satzsystem* suffices to establish this point. But the initial focus of his thought was the manner in which a colour octahedron might be said to provide us with a concretised model for depicting the grammar of colour-words. The colour octahedron is a 'grammatical representation' of the logical syntax of colour-words which can be 'taken in at a glance'. 'Using the octahedron gives us a surveyable representation of the grammatical rules' (PR §1). The idea underlying his remarks on the logico-syntactical role of the colour octahedron, therefore, was that the grammar of a *Satzsystem* must be fully surveyable, and indeed, perspicuous in the sense that one can literally *see* the logical articulations governing the employment of the rules of the *Satzsystem*. One should be able to tell simply by looking at a proper model of the grammar of colour-words which moves are allowed in this *Satzsystem* (PR §222). For 'The colour octahedron is grammar, since it says that you can speak of a reddish blue, etc.' (PR §39).

When he came to apply this theme to the discussion of mathematical proof in *Remarks on the Foundations of Mathematics* Wittgenstein made no reference to this early suggestion that it is possible to construct a concretised model of the grammar of a *Satzsystem*. Nevertheless, he adhered to the idea that the grammatical conventions constructed by a notation must in some sense be phenomenologically surveyable if they are to be intelligible. The central problem with this argument, however, is that it seems to introduce an epistemological uncertainty which is foreign to the stringently logical point about proof that Wittgenstein was struggling to present, opening up, perhaps, the very sorts of sceptical doubts that, according to Wright, lie at the heart of Wittgenstein's philosophy of mathematics.[2] For example, are we not forced to ask on this picture whether it could be the case that a string of symbols which is unsurveyable today might become a proof in the future if our powers of 'surveyability' should suddenly increase; or that what is currently ensconced as a proof could relinquish that status if our powers should begin to diminish? Moreover, how could I ever be certain that an argument did constitute a proof: that I had genuinely surveyed it, or could trust some eminent authority who claimed to have performed this act?

A brief remark in one of the discussions in *Wittgenstein and the Vienna Circle* indicates, however, the manner in which Wittgenstein intended this emphasis on the surveyability of proofs to conform with his general intention to undercut the possibility of epistemological scepticism: once again, by clarifying the correct logical point of view that is at issue. Significantly, Wittgenstein tied the issue in to Schlick's worry about the ability of a man who had been confined in a red room to understand the colour-spectrum:

It is not possible to say anything, either in the case where a man knows only one red or in the case where he knows several shades of red. I want to give a simple counter-example that is very old. What about the number of strokes that I can *see*? I could also draw the following inference. If I can see 1,2,3,4,5 strokes and seen strokes have the same syntax as counted ones, then I must be able to *see* any number of strokes. This, however, is not the case.

| || ||| |||| |||||

||||||||||||| |||||||||||||||

The crucial point is not how many colours one has seen, but the syntax. (WWK 66-7)

The key to understanding Wittgenstein's point lies in the importance of *Satzsysteme*-clarification in the understanding of logical syntax. Wright obscures this point, however, when he lists the following passage from *Philosophical Grammar* as an example of what he interprets as Wittgenstein's 'surveyability/recognitional' thesis:[3] 'Imagine someone giving us a sum to do in a stroke-notation, say |||||||||| + |||||||||||, and, while we are calculating, amusing himself by removing and adding strokes without our noticing. He would keep on saying: "but the sum isn't right", and we would keep going through it again, fooled every time. — Indeed, strictly speaking, we wouldn't have any concept of a criterion for the correctness of the calculation' (PG 330). Wright believes that Wittgenstein offered this argument as part of a general campaign to introduce pervasive sceptical doubts into our standard conception of the reliability of arithmetical computation. But the pattern which emerges from all such examples is that, whenever Wittgenstein introduced what appears to be a line of sceptical inquiry, it was invariably in order to develop a *reductio ad absurdum* whose purpose was to demonstrate that the manner in which we are looking at the problem is misconceived, and thus to encourage us to reconsider our original questions and premises.

The remainder of the above passage bears out just such an intention:

Here one might raise questions like: is it only *very probable* that $464 + 272 = 736$? And in that case isn't $2 + 3 = 5$ also only very probable? And where is the objective truth which this probability approaches? That is, how do we get a concept of 2 + 3's really *being* a certain number, apart from what it seems to us to be?

For if it were asked: what is the criterion in the stroke-notation for our having the same numeral in front of us twice? — the answer might be: 'if it looks the same both times' or 'if it contains the same number of lines both times'. Or should it be: if a one–one correlation etc. is possible?

How can I know that |||||||||| and |||||||||| are the *same* sign? After all it is not enough that they look *alike*. For having roughly the same gestalt can't be what is to constitute the identity of the signs, but just their being the same in number. (PG 331)

Far from trying to introduce a sceptical doubt based on the unreliability of the Gestalt, therefore, Wittgenstein made it absolutely clear that the premise to be rejected here is that in some way the Gestalt of the stroke-notation could have anything whatsoever to do with the certainty of knowing that $464 + 272 = 736$.

It is clear from the discussion in *Philosophical Remarks* why Wittgenstein felt that it was so important to raise this sceptical absurdity, only to undermine it. For herein lies the fundamental problem with the Fregean explanation of mathematical meaning: Frege's explanation was only an application, not the foundation, of mathematical propositions. The Gestalt of the stroke notation is only mentioned in order to clarify that the reason why '||||| + ||||||| = |||||||||||||' is true is not because we *see* that the right side 'equals' the left side; to try to base the logical status of the equation on the manner in which we apprehend the strokes — on the fact that we see that Frege's knives and forks are 'equinumerous' — just is to open the door to the very sceptical worries that Wright envisages. But far from trying to compose a 'sceptical solution' to overcome these doubts Wittgenstein's point was that the very possibility of such sceptical worries serves as a profound indication that we cannot explain the meaning of arithmetical propositions in this manner (PR §103). That is, the fact that we happen to see some identity between the two sides of the equation in stroke-notation cannot have any bearing on the significance of the equation *qua* mathematical proposition. How an individual sees the strokes may be extremely 'open-textured' (PR §224). But the status of the equation is that of a rule of logical syntax, and this is precisely why ||||| + ||||||| = ||||||||||||| has nothing to do with the Gestalt of the strokes: the reason it is true is because it is an application of the rule '$5 + 7 = 12$' (PR §114).

This disposes, therefore, of Dummett's objection that:

> It is a matter of some difficulty to consider just what our mathe-
> matics would look like if we adopted [Wittgenstein's] 'anthro-
> pologistic' standpoint. Would the Peano axioms survive
> unaltered? 'Every number has a successor' would mean, in this
> mathematics, that if a number is accessible (that is, if we have a
> notation in which it can be surveyably represented) then its
> successor is accessible, and this at first seems reasonable. On the
> other hand, it seems to lead to the conclusion that *every* number
> is accessible, and it is clear that, whatever notation we have,
> there will be numbers for which there will not be a surveyable
> symbol in that notation.[4]

But Wittgenstein intended his argument to be anything but
'anthropologistic'. It is only because he misconstrues the direction
of Wittgenstein's sustained attack on the Frege–Russell attempt to
justify our use of mathematical expressions that Dummett was led
into this conclusion. On the contrary, Wittgenstein's fundamental
concern was to rid us of our misguided preoccupation with the
problem of such 'justification' (for what can we say on this topic,
apart from that my justification for applying a rule in this manner
is that this is the way it is applied), and shift our attention instead
to the much more serious question of clarifying the nature of
mathematical necessity and the logico-syntactical character of
mathematical expressions. As we saw in Chapter 2, the problem
Wittgenstein was concerned with here was not, 'How can I be certain that the pupil knows the rule'; rather, we must circumvent this
bogus sceptical worry and clarify what we mean by 'knowing how
to apply the rule correctly'.

The point which Dummett has confused in this passage is the
distinction which Wittgenstein drew between saying that the series
of numbers must be surveyable and that the law generating the
construction of the series must be surveyable: 'When we teach
someone how to take his first step we thereby enable him to go any
distance' (PR §165). Clearly Dummett's objection is simply a
variation of what Wittgenstein described as the *Beweissysteme*
confusion of infinite processes with finite totalities: i.e. how could
we 'survey' an infinite expansion? (cf. Chapter 5). Moreover, what
does it mean to suggest that our law for constructing e.g. the

infinite series of integers generates numbers that will simply be too long for us to write down in our notation? As if, given that the series runs on to infinity, we must eventually come to a digit with more zeros than any man could physically reproduce. But Wittgenstein dealt with just such a criticism when he argued:

> Our normal mode of expression carries the seeds of confusion right into its foundations, because it uses the word 'series' both in the sense of 'extension', and in the sense of 'law'. The relationship of the two can be illustrated by a machine for making coiled springs, in which a wire is pushed through a *helically* shaped passage to make as many coils as are desired. What is called an infinite helix need not be anything like a finite piece of wire, or something that that approaches the longer it becomes; it is the law of the helix, as it is embodied in the short passage. Hence the expression 'infinite helix' or 'infinite series' is misleading. (PG 430)

Obviously, if it is a point of our actually working with integers that are far too long for us to write out in standard Hindu–Arabic notation we shall need to devise some other form of notation, just as it is easier to work with 10 and 11 than with $||||||||||$ and $|||||||||||$. It is thus instructive to consider some of the confusion which surrounds this issue.

In 'Mathematics and Computer Science: Coping with Finiteness', Donald E. Knuth warns that 'Although we have certainly narrowed the gap between three and infinity, recent results indicate that we will never actually be able to go very far in practice.'[5] To illustrate this thesis, he constructs a new notation to represent enormous — what Knuth calls 'unrealistic' — numbers. For example,

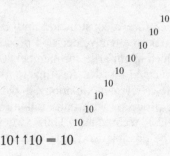

$$10 \uparrow \uparrow 10 = 10$$

The point of this exercise is ultimately to show us that, using this notation, we can see that numbers exist which are simply too long to have ever been written down: 'unsurveyable' in the epistemological sense with which Wittgenstein has been lumbered. For Knuth explains: 'At any rate it seems to me that the magnitude of this number $10\uparrow\uparrow\uparrow\uparrow3$ is so large as to be beyond human comprehension. On the other hand, it is very small as finite numbers go.'[6] It is interesting that Knuth does not notice the paradoxicality of saying that the number he has just presented does not exist. For, of course, the point is that the number is perfectly meaningful, according to the rules which he has laid down for the generation of his series (viz. $x\uparrow\uparrow n = x\uparrow(x\uparrow(\ldots \uparrow x) \ldots))$, where the powers are taken n times). And this rule for the construction of the series is certainly surveyable; hence our ability to understand the number $10\uparrow\uparrow\uparrow\uparrow3$.

The point of Wittgenstein's argument, therefore, as was emphasised above, is not that we can see that $10 + 11 = 21$ whereas we cannot see the same thing in stroke-notation; rather, it is that the truth of the proposition in either notation rests on the rules governing addition. The real question we are concerned with here is not, 'How can I be certain that $10\uparrow\uparrow\uparrow\uparrow3$ is an integer?', but rather, 'What renders such a figure an integer?' But even this way of stating the matter is misleading, for to understand '$10\uparrow\uparrow\uparrow\uparrow3$' just is to grasp its role *qua* 'unrealistic' integer. Once again, we must distance ourselves from the attempts to force Wittgenstein's comments on surveyability into an epistemological and thence a sceptical framework, and recognise instead that what he was concerned with was e.g. the relation of a number to the law which generates the series in which it occurs. It is the law governing the expansion of the series, not the actual expansion of the series, that must be surveyable. The latter interpretation is simply another example of the 'finite totality'/'infinite series' *Beweissysteme* confusion.

In order to constitute a proof, therefore, a construction must be 'surveyable' in the sense that it creates an effective decision procedure for resolving any questions which might arise for members of the *Beweissystem* which it constructs. In order for this to be possible a proof must not contain *Beweissysteme* violations; in particular, it must not confuse infinite processes with finite totalities, or experimental with mathematical techniques. Thus, when Wittgenstein insisted that 'It must be possible to decide with certainty whether we really have the same proof twice over, or not' (RFM III §1) his point, once again, was solely based on the logical syntax of *proof*. The concept of *surveyability* does not introduce, therefore, any spurious worries over 'medical limitations'. Wittgenstein himself may have been partly to blame for this misinterpretation, with his undue emphasis on the need to be able to 'copy a proof'. Nevertheless, this distorts the real significance of his point, which was concerned with the concept of surveyability as resting on *Beweissysteme*-consistency. In part it could be the case that the early interest in the colour octahedron introduced a phenomenological element into Wittgenstein's discussion which threatens to obscure the essentially logical point which he was trying to make, which is simply that *Beweissysteme* erect the bounds of perspicuity no less than of sense.

Over the past decade the significance of this issue has become particularly acute with the proliferation of the so-called 'computer proofs'. Perhaps the best-known example of these is the Appel–Haken solution of the four-colour problem, where the critical 'reducibility lemma' performed by the computer is 'humanly unsurveyable'. Certainly the controversy which has been kindled by Appel and Haken's 'four-colour theorem' (4CT) provides us with an excellent illustration of the very confusions which Wittgenstein was trying to expose. For the question is not whether we could ever be certain that a computer proof of the four-colour problem could be assimilated by the average mathematican, but rather, whether such a proof was surveyable in *Beweissysteme* terms. It is not that a 'proof' of the four-colour problem which provided no law for the generation of 'unavoidable sets of reducible configurations' (*infra*) would be unsurveyable because the calculations involved *transcended* our recognitional capacities (as if such sets were simply too large for us to grasp); it would be unsurveyable precisely because it *would* make sense to speak of our recognitional capacities in relation to such a construction. And yet, this would seem to entail that, *contra* Wittgenstein's pronounced emphasis on the non-revisionist character of his remarks on the philosophy of mathematics, the success of Appel and Haken's solution rests on a philosophical investigation. Before we can judge the outcome of the confrontation between the Appel–Haken proof and Wittgenstein's critique, however, we must first address a proposed 'amendment' to the concept of proof which is rapidly gaining influence.

'Probabilistic Proofs'

The Appel–Haken solution of the four-colour problem — can every (plane or sphere) map be coloured with only four colours in such a way that no two neighbouring regions ever share the same colour — brings into sharp relief the force of the objections which Wittgenstein raised against the confusion of *experiment* with *proof*. The heated debate which Appel and Haken's work has instigated rests on what Thomas Tymoczko somewhat misleadingly describes as 'The new four-colour problem': viz, 'whether the Appel–Haken four-colour theorem really is a theorem'[7] (*infra*). That is, whether the Appel–Haken 'proof' really is a proof, and if so, what consequences this has for Wittgenstein's remarks on the nature of proof and his critique of 'undecidable questions'. Proceeding from the staunchly Wittgensteinian premise that proof must be surveyable, Tymoczko warns that the Appel–Haken 'proof' 'introduces empirical experiments into mathematics. Whether or not we choose to regard the 4CT as proved, we must admit that the current proof is no traditional proof, no *a priori* deduction of a statement from premises.'[8] Yet from this uncompromising position he arrives at the distinctly unWittgensteinian conclusion that 'It is a traditional proof with a lacuna, or gap, which is filled by the results of a well-thought-out experiment. This makes the 4CT the first mathematical proposition to be known *a posteriori* and raises again for philosophy the problem of distinguishing mathematics from the natural sciences.'[9] Whatever the merits of this attempt to turn Wittgenstein's argument on its head, it is highly significant that Tymoczko's paper provoked immediate responses from Paul Teller, Michael Detlefsen and Mark Luker: eloquent testimony to the fact that Tymoczko had touched on a raw nerve.

It is not difficult to see why this issue has attracted such widespread attention lately, far outstripping the bounds of Wittgensteinian scholarship; for herein hangs the fate of our conception of proof, and quite likely as a result, the immediate future of mathematical research. Despite the natural apprehension that the autonomy of mathematics may be threatened by the march of computer mathematics, the general consensus slowly emerging amongst mathematicians — abetted by philosophers who, as always, are eager to assimilate the latest technical advances — is that the development of computer proofs and heuristic programs in pure mathematics is indeed forcing us to reconsider and 'liberalise' our concepts of proof and mathematical discovery. A taste of what is to come was provided by Elsie Cerutti and Philip Davis in their 'pioneering' paper, 'Formac Meets Pappus'. Granted the familiar objections which can be raised against the reliability of computer programs — and programmers — they none the less insist that 'Similar objections ... can be raised with conventional proofs.'[10] *Pari passu*, 'These considerations lead us to a position — which is rarely discussed in works on the philosophy of mathematics and which is very unpopular — that a mathematical proof has much in common with a physical experiment; that its validity is not absolute, but rests on the same foundation of repeated experimentation.'[11]

The problem, as Tymoczko conceives it, is that there clearly seem to be 'medically undecidable' questions (i.e. those whose proofs would be so long that no human, and perhaps no computer as well, could ever write them down); and that these provide us with obvious counter-examples to Wittgenstein's dictates on the 'surveyability' of mathematical proof and the unintelligibility of 'undecidable questions'. Thus, the charge is implicitly pressed that, despite his emphasis that proof is a family-resemblance concept, Wittgenstein remained sadly blind to the possibility of extending the concept in such a way as to allow for the resolution by computer of questions which demand humanly impossible powers. Indeed, the potentially more damaging argument has surfaced that if we allow computer algorithms to enjoy predetermined, low-probability, margins of error, then questions hitherto impossible to answer for computers no less than humans can readily be solved. As, for example, in Michael Rabin's extremely rapid computer program for deciding, for any arbitrarily chosen large number, whether or not it is prime: provided that we allow the program a margin of error of approximately one in a billion. (To be more precise, Rabin's algorithm establishes that the probability of a number's *not* being prime can be virtually insignificant. Thus, in 'Probabilistic Algorithms' Rabin explains: 'The basic idea in both the Solovay–Strassen algorithm and the algorithm presented here, is to find a test for compositeness for which the witnesses, in our terminology, are abundant. If the test fails many times to produce a witness then we are provably confident that the number is prime.'[12]

The conclusion which has been drawn in the light of Rabin's results is that mathematicians must henceforward revise their attitude to what is essentially a matter of little more than the aesthetic appeal of a mathematical proof.[13] In as much as the possibility of human error in proofs has always haunted mathematics, there is a growing number who have followed Cerruti and Davis in the claim that no justifiable reason can be proffered why we should deny the same latitude to computer programs. Thus, as Detlefsen and Luker explain, 'the degree of confidence that one can have in many of the complex and arduous proofs of recent mathematics is limited by the fact that the likelihood of error increases with the complexity of the proof. But even in more traditional mathematics, certitude is limited by the fact of human fallibility, the specter of inconsistent axioms, and the knowledge that mistakes are a commonplace in the history of mathematics.'[14] Given this inescapable — if lamentable — shortcoming, 'the limited but extremely high certitude provided by Rabin's techniques is no reason for not allowing his methods entrance into the methods of mathematical proof.'[15] And once we do permit such minuscule margins of error to computer proofs, questions which for all intents and purposes seemed irrevocably 'undecidable' suddenly become swiftly amenable to computer calculation. Detlefsen and Luker recognise and welcome the fact that 'if they are allowed entrance, the character of mathematical proof will be fundamentally changed, since for the first time in the history of mathematics nondeductive arguments will be allowed to count as proofs.'[16] They are thus prepared to argue that mathematicians must reconsider their widespread 'assumption' that proofs must be *indubitably correct*: that there is any conceptual barrier to marrying the notions of 'probabilistic' and 'proof'.

In a last-ditch attempt to hold off the radical changes which threaten here, Paul Teller objects that the concepts of proof and mathematical discovery have been left unaltered by the development of computer-assisted proofs; only certain *practices* have been affected by their implementation. Contrary to Tymoczko's interpretation of the significance of the Appel–Haken 4CT: 'no new sense or concept of proof has been introduced. We have merely extended our means of checking correctness of proofs in the old sense, and we have anticipated future help from computers in discovering new proofs, again in the old sense, by use of programs embodying methods of proof we use ourselves.'[17] Hence what is needed is, not a repudiation of the notion of surveyability, but rather, a reassessment of its relevance to proof: a recognition of the fact that 'a shift in the means of surveying actually used means only a shift in methods of checking proofs, not a shift in our conception of the things checked.'[18] But, according to Wittgenstein, the 'method of checking' is exactly what determines 'our conception of the things checked'! The question is thus whether this argument — however august its historical antecedents — does not proceed from the same misconception, and thence commit itself *nolens volens* to the same radical shift in our understanding of proof that the foregoing interpretation so boldly embraces.

On either approach the issue has thus, almost imperceptibly, shifted into the 'epistemological' debate on 'mathematical reliability', which has only served to undermine the genuine logical syntactical question with which we should be concerned. Just as in the previous chapter, where the problem was not whether the pupil had mastered the rule but whether the calculus catered for the question, so too the issue here is not whether computer operations can be rendered as trustworthy as human but rather, whether the concept of proof is flexible enough to *incorporate* that of non-deductive arguments. And once again, the problem is complicated by the two conceptually different species of proof that we have been examining. To be sure, once a proof-schema has been constructed it is possible to commit an error in any particular application: especially where the proofs involve the derivation of such large numbers that the possibility of error rises exponentially. If what we are concerned with, therefore, is a case of 'doing our homework', then the question, 'How can we be certain that this is a proof?' really means: 'How can we be certain that we have applied the rules of a proof-schema correctly?' It is principally this issue which arises *à propos* the discussion of 'computer-assisted proofs' (i.e. where the computer performs some intricate calculation, as in the 4CT). If, however, what we are considering is the construction of a new *Beweissystem*, then the concept of error undergoes a radical shift. It is, of course, possible to misuse the basic rules as they have been stipulated at the outset of the proof, but not to misuse the concepts of the new system according to their predetermined meaning in foreign systems. For in this case, we are not bound by any *Bedeutungskörper* in what shall constitute the rules of the new *Beweissystem* (cf. Chapter 8). In which case, the question 'How can we be certain that this is a proof?' is primarily concerned with the evolution of mathematical concepts: e.g. with the utility/significance of the new proof. It is principally this issue which arises *vis-à-vis* the development of heuristic mathematics programs (e.g. Lenat's AM thesis).

In both cases, the screening for errors is a strictly internal mathematical affair. The philosophical question lurking behind each, however, is not how we can be certain whether something is a proof, but rather, what it means to describe it as a proof. Mathematicians have understandably been preoccupied with the former problem, but in their haste to extend the 'checks' deemed suitable for mathematical deployment, they have inadvertently wandered into the latter minefield. Unfortunately, philosophers have followed suit, and the result of their combined efforts is the thesis that Rabin's results demonstrate the legitimacy of 'probabilistic proofs'. To be sure, 'Typical of the reactions of many mathematicians [to Rabin's and similar arguments] is that of one who said he does not accept a probabilistic method of proof because the "glory of mathematics is that existing methods of proof are essentially error-free".'[19] The confusion stems, however, from those who 'report that they have more confidence in results that could be obtained by probabilistic methods such as Rabin's prime test than in many 400-page mathematical proofs'. Thus, Ronald Graham worries that

> long and involved proofs are becoming the norm rather than the exception in mathematics, at least in certain fields such as group theory. He speculates that this situation may arise because there are relatively few interesting statements with short proofs compared to the total number of possible interesting mathematical statements. Fewer and fewer statements with short proofs remain to be worked on. He and Paul Erdös believe that already some of the long proofs being published are at the limit of the amount of information the human mind can handle. Thus Graham and others stress that verification of theorems by computers may necessarily be part of the future of mathematics. And mathematicians may have to revise their notions of what constitutes strong enough evidence to believe a statement is true.[20]

Hence, it is the sheer profusion of modern mathematics/mathematicians which is forcing this 'modification' onto antiquarian practitioners. And quite a shift it is too: for it is difficult to recognise that it is mathematics we are dealing with from the quintessentially empirical terminology of the above passage. Thus, the vanguard have succeeded in transforming the issue into what they regard as a straightforward technical question. The problem is no longer, 'What does people's agreement about accepting a structure as a proof consist in?' (RFM I §153), but rather, 'How do we verify an unsurveyable proof?' Yet this, according to Wittgenstein, is the very question which cannot be asked of a grammatical construction.

If contemporary mathematicians have been reluctant to recognise any deep-rooted conceptual problem lying here, it has not been without important philosophical encouragement. For example, Kripke asks us in *Naming and Necessity* to 'Consider what the traditional characterisations of such terms as "*a priori*" and "*necessary*" are. First the notion of a prioricity is a concept of epistemology. I guess the traditional characterisation from Kant goes something like: *a priori* truths are those which can be known independently of any experience.'[21] Kripke may have little appetite for this picture, but his real quarrel is with those philosophers who 'somehow change the modality in this characterisation from *can* to *must*. They think that if something belongs to the realm of *a priori* knowledge, it couldn't possibly be known empirically. This is just a mistake. Something may belong in the realm of such statements that *can* be known *a priori* but still may be known by particular people on the basis of experience.'[22] But such a contentious issue obviously demands more than a riposte, and to substantiate his claim Kripke offers the — for our purposes highly pertinent — example:

anyone who has worked with a computing machine knows that the computing machine may give an answer to whether such and such a number is prime. No one has calculated or proved that the number is prime: but the machine has given the answer: this number is prime. We, then, if we believe that the number is prime, believe it on the basis of our knowledge of the laws of physics, the construction of the machine, and so on. We therefore do not believe this on the basis of purely *a priori* evidence. We believe it (if anything is *a posteriori* at all) on the basis of *a posteriori* evidence. Nevertheless, maybe this could be known *a priori* by someone who made the requisite calculations. So '*can* be known *a priori*' doesn't mean '*must* be known *a priori*'.[23]

Here, in relatively simple outline, lies the crux of the issue raised by Rabin's 'probabilistic algorithm'. Thus, if this argument were allowed, there would be no obstacle to admitting 'probabilistic proofs' into the mathematical pantheon, and *a fortiori*, no objection to Teller's conclusion 'that the use of a computer in the 4CT is an extension of our means of surveying, not a change in our concept of proof. The relevant lemma is a combinatorial matter, and the computer is used merely to survey the long list of combinations. The novelty is in the means of surveying, not in the means of proof.'[24] But the question which Kripke's argument raises is whether his conclusion does indeed follow from the distinction as he has outlined it, or merely corroborates the confused assumption from which this thesis proceeds.

As we saw in Chapter 2, if anything can be described as 'a truth which is known *a priori*', it is surely a rule of grammar, and hence, a mathematical proposition. We must be careful, however, not to confuse the logical syntactical question — 'What is the grammatical status of this expression?' — with the 'epistemological' question, 'How do we acquire this knowledge?' For the origin of our understanding of both types of proposition may be experiential: I am taught how to apply rules just as I am taught about contingent truths. But even here it is important to see that the latter question need not dogmatically rule out the possibility of innate ideas. From a strictly logical point of view, it simply does not matter where knowledge 'comes from'; all that matters is the logical syntax of the proposition in question, which is determined by the manner in which that proposition is used. Granted that Kripke draws his authority for his use of the expression '*a priori*' from the long tradition of rationalist and empiricist custom, his argument none the less offends against the point that what we are really concerned with here is logical syntax, not whether some proposition can be understood 'independently of experience' (whatever that might actually mean), or on the basis of experience.

Certainly, as we saw in the preceding chapter, one and the same sentence can be used to express either a mathematical conjecture or an empirical hypothesis, depending on the manner in which it is employed. But that does not entail that a mathematical proposition can be known or used empirically. For a rule of syntax cannot somehow shed its normative character and adopt an air of contingency in empirical circumstances. The conceptual gulf which yawns here is that between proof and experiment. Someone who understands the mathematical proposition $a \times b = c$ does so as the result of a proof: i.e. from the rules governing the use of these symbols. But someone who understands that a × b = c on the basis of the LCD readout of his pocket calculator — or rather, for this way of presenting the matter is itself a source of confusion, who understands that pressing 'a', '×', 'b' and '=' caused 'c' to appear — has in effect performed an experiment which, as Kripke quite rightly points out, is based purely on physical evidence. Hence, this will leave him with probabilistic knowledge that the LCD readout he has achieved is empirically — not mathematically — reliable.[25] For the former, a × b *must* equal c; for the latter, it is perfectly *intelligible* to suppose that pressing 'a × b = ' might not result in the symbol 'c'. The barrier between mathematical and empirical propositionhood is thus conceptual, not experiential. The point here is not that what is known *a priori* can also be known experientially, therefore, but rather that the same sentence can be used in either a mathematical or an empirical context, and our interest in this issue lies solely in the area of clarifying the nature of the conditions under which we should register the one or the other: 'I learned empirically that this came out this time, that it usually does come out; but does the proposition of mathematics say that? I learned empirically that this is the road I travelled. But is *that* the mathematical statement — What does it say, though? What relation has it to these empirical propositions? The mathematical proposition has the dignity of a rule' (RFM I §165).

Once again, therefore, the question which concerns us is not the seductive, 'How can I be certain that he is using this sentence as a mathematical proposition?', but rather, 'What does it mean to say that he is using it as a mathematical proposition?' The deeper problem still lying in wait is thus whether the conceptual barricade segregating *proof* and *experiment* no less forcefully inhibits us from trying to shrink the parameters of their distinction so as to allow the postulation of 'probabilistic' and 'computer proofs'. Saaty and Kainen insist in *The Four-Colour Problem* that, 'On a formal level, one may regard all mathematical proofs as thought experiments which contain a nonzero possibility of error. Well-known cases in the literature illustrate how such an error may be missed for years (sometimes because of the small number of times the experiment is repeated). Presumably, some are never found.'[26] But this would mean that the difference between proof and experiment is measured by the *degree* of infallibility which each exhibits; on this reading, the possibility of error is not *excluded* from a particularly lengthy proof, but only minimised. Far from regarding the concept of error as *a priori* precluded from the internal relation between a mathematical proposition and its proof, the problem has now become one of assessing the accuracy of the methods which have been employed for the new species of 'mega' problems which have captured the imagination of a generation of mathematicians who find themselves equipped with CRAYs rather than slide-rules. But the concept of proof is not something which rests on such fluid boundaries that it can incorporate experimental methods — or indeed, accommodate highly probable experiments — as members of the conceptual family. In asking us to allow computers some predetermined margin of error in their proofs the advocates for the case of 'probabilistic proofs' are not importuning us to relax the stringency which we demand from proofs: rather, they would have us completely abandon our concept of proof *qua* grammatical construction.

To suppose that the concept of proof can be 'readjusted' in order to allow for the presence of 'probabilistic proofs' is similar to Quine's suggestion that linguistic conventions can be regarded as high-level empirical generalisations. In each case we are confronted with a conceptual violation masquerading as a technical reformulation. The problem here does not concern the 'epistemological' thesis that we can never be certain — at least for excessively complex problems — that a proof is error-free. If that were the case, we would have to identify proofs relative to the bearer; and there could be few who would be willing to measure their prowess against that of an Erdös. But even this way of stating the matter misrepresents the extent of the damage that would thus be inflicted. It is highly significant that, in order to bolster his probabilistic thesis, Davis argues that: 'the arithmetic of excessively large numbers can be carried out only with diminishing fidelity. As we get away from trivial sums, arithmetic operations are enveloped in a smog of uncertainty.'[27] But why is the arithmetic of smaller numbers any more certain; is it because it is easier to *see* that we have calculated accurately? This is nothing more than a recapitulation of the basic Gestalt argument which we examined in the previous section, and thus subject to the same consequences. For as Wittgenstein pointed out, if we 'raise questions like: is it only *very probable* that $464 + 272 = 736$?', then what is to stop us from wondering whether '$2 + 3 = 5$ [is] also only very probable? And where is the objective truth which this probability approaches?

That is, how do we get a concept of 2 + 3's really *being* a certain number, apart from what it seems to us to be?' (PG 331) This is very much the outcome of the regress to which Cerutti and Davis committed themselves with their initial premise that 'Human processing is subject to such things as fatigue, limited knowledge or memory, and to the psychological desire to force a particular result to "come out".'[28] Which only serves to bring us full circle in the 'sceptical' rule-following argument!

The reason why 66,666 is the sum of 12,345 + 54,321 and not the 'odds-on favourite from a probability distribution of possible answers'[29] is precisely because '12,345 + 54,321 = 66,666' is a rule of arithmetic. The question here is not, 'How can I be certain that I have calculated the sum of this palindrome accurately?', but rather, 'In what does the certainty of this theorem consist?' The very possibility of the sceptical worries that would be opened up by Davis's misguided attempt to interpret this rule of logical syntax as the result of an experiment once again serves as a profound warning that such epistemological considerations have no bearing on the certainty of mathematical truths. For the point here is not, how long can a proof be before the possibility of error can no longer be excluded? Nor the counter-thesis that we should now accept the absurdity of drawing such a limit and hence finally concede the presence of error in the relation between proof and proposition. Both positions proceed from the same confused attempt to conflate the problem of how we can be certain whether a given argument should be admitted into the archives of proof with the logical certainty of the proposition which is established by a proof. That is, the notion of a 'probabilistic proof' shifts from the former, mathematical issue to the latter philosophical confusion that the internal relation between a mathematical proposition and its proof can itself be a matter of probability. Once we describe the relation between argument and proposition as that of proof to mathematical proposition, however, we *exclude* any such possibility for philosophical scepticism to breed. Hence, Wittgenstein's conclusion that if it is intelligible to express such an ineliminable doubt — however remote — this entails, not that the proof is only probable, but rather, *that it is not a proof*!

By all means, we can have probabilistic techniques for arriving at a figure subsequently *proved* to be a prime; such a practice is as old as Archimedes! In *The Method* — the palimpsest which was only discovered in 1906 — Archimedes described the heuristic approach which was the key to his extraordinary fecundity in the calculation of areas and volumes. Archimedes would approach a problem using the methods which he had developed in his mechanics, and then work backwards from the desired result to construct a rigorous proof. 'Archimedes employed his heuristic method, therefore, simply as an investigation preliminary to the rigorous demonstration by the method of exhaustion. It was not a generous gesture that led Archimedes to supplement his "mechanical method" by a proof of the results in the rigorous manner of the method of exhaustion; it was, rather, a mathematical necessity.'[30] A mathematical necessity because, whatever 'non-rigorous' methods Archimedes might have used to discover his preliminary results has absoloutely no bearing on the logical status of the theorems once they has been axiomatically derived: i.e. on the proofs which he would subsequently construct. The question which Rabin's program raises is likewise whether you can have a *probabilistic proof* that x is a prime: whether the proposition 'x is a prime' yielded by logically discrete methods — viz. empirical and mathematical — are *synonymous*.

What complicates this issue is the familiar argument that 'Proofs ⸽utilising computers have been around for quite some time. This is particularly true of the search for Mersenne primes, where the Lucas–Lehmer algorithm has been used in automated tests for Mersenne primes for roughly half a century.'[31] The subtle fallacy contained in this assumption, however, is that, because an algorithm can be suitably encoded for computer manipulation, it makes sense to attribute the calculation of the algorithm to the computer. To be sure, the Lucas–Lehmer algorithm can be used to calculate Mersenne primes; all that the computer performs, however, is the manipulation of bits. The fetters preventing us from moving from the latter electro-mechanical operation to the much stronger conclusion that the computer has calculated the algorithm — has 'followed mechanical rules' — are entirely conceptual: we are prohibited by the logical grammar of normativity, not the 'inflexibility' of computer systems.[32] Hence we really do have two categorially distinct propositions yielded by our calculation of the Lucas–Lehmer algorithm and the results yielded by the 'Lucas–Lehmer program': the one *a priori* and the other *a posteriori.*

The reason why Tymoczko's description of the Appel–Haken 4CT as resulting in a 'new four-colour problem' is misleading, therefore, is precisely because his argument succumbs to the very confusion it was designed to overcome: it misconstrues the nature of the conceptual distinction between proof and experiment, and the nature of the truth yielded by each. It thus transgresses Wittgenstein's fundamental point that 'What is proved by a mathematical proof is set up as an internal relation and withdrawn from doubt' (RFM VII §6). For Tymoczko's conclusion that the Appel–Haken 4CT 'forces us to modify our concept of proof' is based entirely on his premise that 'the 4CT [is] the first mathematical proposition to be known *a posteriori*'.[33] That is, following Kripke, that it provides a clear example of an analytic *a posteriori* truth (although Tymoczko qualifies his support for Kripke's argument by maintaining that the 4CT is an example of an analytic *a posteriori* truth which could not, even in principle, be known *a priori*.[34] Instead of presenting a surveyable proof of the 4CT, the Appel–Haken proof provides us with what Tymoczko accepts as 'mathematically convincing grounds for the 4CT ... where a key lemma is justified by an appeal to certain computer runs ... [which] help establish the 4CT ... on grounds that are in part empirical.'[35] Thus he too concludes that 'The reliability of the 4CT ... is not of the same degree as that guaranteed by traditional proofs, for this reliability rests on the assessment of a complex set of empirical factors. ... The 4CT is a substantial piece of pure mathematics which can be known by mathematicians only *a posteriori*. Our knowledge must be qualified by the uncertainty of our instruments, computer and program.'[36] But in stating this conclusion Tymoczko has clearly already slipped from recognising the problem as conceptual into regarding it as empirical. For the demarcation that is involved here has nothing to do with a matter of *degree*, but has only to do with *kind*: the distinctions between the *a priori* and the *a posteriori*, *convention* and *hypothesis*, *proof* and *experiment*.

For this reason, it is equally misguided to argue that Tymoczko's conclusion is 'unwarranted' because he 'gives us no grounds for thinking that the fallibility of computers and mathematicians are relevantly different'.[37] Teller quite rightly points out that 'the fact that I cannot follow a complex proof produced by a good mathematician does not show that such a mathematician's complex proof is a proof in a different sense of the word from a proof that I can follow.'[38] Were such a disastrous possibility admitted, the bounds of proof would indeed be constantly shifting and the strife of mathematical contention even more pronounced. Yet because he interprets this as an *epistemological* condition,

Teller continues: 'In the same way, the fact that no mathematician may be able to follow a proof produced by a computer does not show that such a computer-produced proof is a proof only in some new sense.'[39] The very assumption that we can meaningfully refer to the latter as a 'proof' only serves to deflect attention from the categorial shift which has thus occurred, and focus it instead on the spurious issue of 'relative fallibility'. To be sure, there is a marked similarity between *my* understanding of the two propositions canvassed above. That is, my knowledge of the former is no less inductive than the latter: in the one case, based on the reliability of the mathematician in question, in the other, on that of the computer system. But this entails, not that both propositions are equally entitled to mathematical status, but rather, that neither can be regarded as a mathematical proposition! This is not at all the distinction which Teller draws, however; for his just is between the mathematical proposition (viz. which only serves as such if the proof *has* been grasped) and the empirical proposition yielded by the computer.

Thus, both sides of this debate are misconstrued, for both proceed from the same misconception of the relevance of surveyability to the nature of proof. Teller maintains that 'Surveyability is needed, not because without it a proof is in any sense not a proof ... but because without surveyability we seem not to be able to verify that a proof is correct. So surveyability is not a part of what it is to be a proof in our accustomed sense.'[40] This is the exact antithesis of the notion of surveyability we have been discussing. The issue we are concerned with here is not the question of *how a proof is checked*, but rather, *how a proposition is used*. To see why this notion of surveyability is more than a relic of 'pre-Turingesque metaphysics', let us now apply it to the test of the Appel–Haken solution of the four-colour problem. Detlefsen and Luker remark that, of the two, Rabin's work probably has 'a much greater potential for altering the fundamental character of mathematical proof than do any of the computer-assisted, deductive proofs — including that of the 4CT.'[41] Yet to some extent, the subtlety of the latter makes it the more insidious. For the start to the slippery slope ending up in the 'alteration' of proof begins with the seemingly innocuous premise that 'proofs involving calculation typically — or at least often — depend upon empirical evidence', in which case 'one may show that much of traditional mathematics — mathematics based upon "surveyable" proof — is empirical in character. And so, it is not "surveyability" which is the crucial factor in determining the empirical character of the proof of the 4CT.'[42] After all, why should Appel and Haken be denied a liberty accorded to Gauss? The ultimate challenge which this last objection raises is whether Wittgenstein's approach can meet this demand without collapsing into revisionism.

The Appel–Haken Solution of the Four-Colour Problem

As we have just seen, the Appel–Haken solution of the four-colour problem presents what has struck some philosophers as a doubly embarrassing result for Wittgenstein's remarks on the nature of proof. For not only do Appel and Haken claim to have proved the four-colour problem using a computer program that relies on a 'humanly unsurveyable' lemma, thereby blurring the sharp demarcation which Wittgenstein drew between proof and experiment; but in so doing, their proof seems to strike a further blow at Wittgenstein's argument that we cannot make sense of the notion of an 'undecidable question'. For the traditional version of the four-colour conjecture (4CC) presents a problem which is *prima facie* similar to such enigmas as Goldbach's conjecture and Fermat's last theorem. The problem asks whether every map can be four-coloured: a question which does not seem all that far removed from asking whether every even number is the sum of two odd primes, or whether for any integer greater than 2, $x^n + y^n = z^n$. But whereas the source of the difficulty with e.g. Goldbach's conjecture lies in the fact that the concept of a prime is defined in terms of multiplication while the problem itself involves addition, the most conspicuous feature of the original 4CC is the extent to which the concept of a 'map' was vaguely defined.

After more than a century of failure mathematicians were beginning to despair of ever disposing of the four-colour problem.[43] To be sure, a limited amount of headway had been made; for example, by the time of Appel and Haken's solution mathematicians had succeeded in raising the 'Birkhoff number' — the number of countries that a five-chromatic map must contain — to 96 (i.e. showing that every map with fewer than 96 countries is four-colourable). But this sort of progress is comparable to Schnirelmann's proof that every positive integer can be represented as the sum of not more than 300,000 primes.[44] Indeed, we might even draw a parallel between the Appel–Haken solution and Vinogradoff's non-constructive proof that every 'sufficiently large' even number can be written in the form 'p + q', where p is prime and q has at most 2 prime factors. (What Vinogradoff actually proved is that the assumption that infinitely many integers cannot be decomposed into at most 4 prime numbers results in a contradiction.[45]) As work on the four-colour problem progressed this century the conviction grew that, if the problem were ever to be solved, it would only be by proving that the concept of a 'minimal five-chromatic map' is impossible. The problem seemed to devolve on the question of whether a fairly large set of 'unavoidable configurations' could be proved to be 'reducible' (*infra*). Hence it seemed that the possibility of solving the four-colour problem rested on the size, if it could be found, of a 'reducible unavoidable set'; had the set which Appel and Haken had to work with been much larger, then the resolution of the problem would for the present have been medically impossible (until such time as e.g. advanced parallel processing systems could be utilised). Thus, although the Appel–Haken solution demonstrated that the original conjecture was only *undecided*, it seemed to indicate — through its very success — the manner in which it could easily have turned out to be *undecidable*.

This latter criticism can be summarily dealt with. The success of the Appel–Haken solution, if such it should prove to be (and bear in mind that this is an issue which does not concern Wittgenstein's argument; what we are investigating here is solely the logico-syntactical status of the Appel–Haken solution), would not force Wittgenstein into the expediency of arguing that if the four-colour problem has indeed been solved, then it must have been the case that the original four-coloured conjecture was merely 'undecided' rather than 'undecidable'. Such a retort would indeed represent all the advantages of theft over honest toil, and we would certainly be entitled to demand an elucidation of where exactly the difference lies. We would quite rightfully feel that, if the 4CC is more similar to (say) Fermat's theorem[46] than it is to Fermat's last theorem, then this is a distinction which we should be able to elicit merely by examining the question itself, rather than having to wait for a successful solution before pronouncing our verdict. But, as we have seen, Wittgenstein would have rejected the very premise that it makes sense to speak of the 4CC as having meaning before it had been located in a *Beweissystem*. Hence the original 4CC was *neither* 'undecided' nor 'undecidable': for in the absence of rules governing its use it was not, strictly speaking, a proposition, and only the latter is subject to the mandate of the law of excluded middle (cf. Chapter 3). What mathematicians were actually working with was a pseudo-proposition which, becaue of the meanings possessed by each of the sub-sentential expressions in their proper *Beweissysteme*, exercised in this novel combination a heuristic influence which encouraged mathematicians to construct a new *Beweissystem* for its use. (This skeleton outline is not intended as a genetic account, but solely as an elucidation of the status of the various expressions and arguments that were developed.) Moreover, as we have already seen, the concept of 'undecidability' applies to those ill-formed 'questions' which are logically incapable of being answered because they rest on irreconcilable *Beweissysteme* conflicts which render them unintelligible. In other words, we cannot make sense of the concept of an 'undecidable 4CC': to be intelligible just is to be decidable, and it is absurd to suppose that a species of 4CC existed which mathematicians could understand but which they were unable to answer because of physical limitations.

Thus, what we might say is that, if it is interpreted as asking a 'question' about the *infinite set* of maps, then the 4CC — like Fermat's last theorem or Goldbach's conjecture — is indeed undecidable: assuming that we take this to mean that it is *a priori* unintelligible. But that does not rule out the possibility of a genuine solution of the 4CC, interpreted in terms of the nature of the rules governing the construction of the (infinite) series of planar maps. Wittgenstein's critique of 'undecidable questions' was directly concerned with the former philosophical confusion — prevalent at the time he was writing — that Fermat's last theorem and Goldbach's conjecture are 'undecidable' because the set of integers is infinite while our powers of comprehension are finitely bound. In order for the 4CC to be 'undecidable' — irrevocably unintelligible — in this sense, it would have to assume that the set of countries contained in a map — and *a fortiori*, the set of unavoidable configurations — is infinite (a confusion which is generally but not invariably avoided; *infra*). Wittgenstein's response to the four-colour problem would surely have been that, provided it is interpreted in the latter sense, there is certainly no *a priori* reason to deny the possibility of discovering a solution for Guthrie's problem (by creating a meaning for his 'question'): but then, neither is there any basis for suggesting that the problem was at any time 'undecidable'. The point is that until such a system has been constructed, it can be profoundly misleading to speak of the 'four-colour problem'.

We must be clear from the start, therefore, precisely where Wittgenstein would have felt committed to respond to the Appel–Haken solution. It is not, according to the arguments that have so far been canvassed, the philosopher's responsibility — nor prerogative — to decide which proofs are mathematically sound; rather, the philosopher's task is, in an issue such as this, to clarify in what a genuine mathematical proof consists. The Appel–Haken solution does, however, raise two separate — although not completely independent — issues which challenge Wittgenstein's strictures. But before we investigate the nature of the Appel–Haken 'reducibility lemma', we should first consider how Wittgenstein might have reacted to the format of the Appel–Haken 'proof'; for the strategy of their argument is classically non-constructive in the sense attacked by the Kroneckerians. The basic premise of the Appel–Haken solution, which they inherited from the original Kempe attempt to prove the 4CC, is that rather than proving directly that *every* map can be four-coloured, we need only show that there is no map which must be drawn with five colours. The Kempe/Appel–Haken 'proof' is thus an orthodox *reductio ad absurdum* which proceeds by assuming that there is at least one map which requires five colours. The burden of their argument is to establish that it is impossible to construct a minimal normal five-chromatic map: to demonstrate that the assertion that 'a minimal normal five-chromatic map exists' leads to a contradiction. From this the conclusion can be drawn that four colours must always be enough to colour a planar map.

Such a method makes no attempt to provide an effective method for actually four-colouring a map. There are no substantial grounds to suggest, however, that Wittgenstein would have been hostile to the basic framework of this approach. On the contrary, Wittgenstein stressed throughout his writings on the philosophy of mathematics that the use of indirect proof is a perfectly respectable mathematical practice; or at least, deemed perfectly respectable by most mathematicians (for this too is a strictly internal mathematical affair).[47] Wittgenstein repeatedly emphasised that his interest in constructivism did not result from any dogmatic foundation (e.g. based in finitism); rather it was a consequence of the account which he pursued of the meaning and understanding of mathematical propositions in terms of the mastery of the rules of a *Beweissystem*. Moreover, as we shall see below, the objections which he would have raised — indeed, which in a prescient way he did raise — against the unsurveyability of such methods as that adopted by the 'reducibility lemma' in the Appel–Haken solution, rest on the conclusions which he drew from his interpretation of the grammatical nature of mathematical propositions and their proofs.

The strategy of the Kempe argument, which Appel and Haken attempt to rescue from Kempe's failed proof for countries with five neighbours, is quite straightforward in outline. We begin by assuming that a 'minimal normal five-chromatic map' exists. A map is said to be 'normal' if no country completely surrounds another; if no more than three countries meet at one point; if no country has zero or one neighbour; and if no country is unconnected. A 'minimal' normal five-chromatic map is the map with the least number of countries requiring more than four colours. The argument already provides us, therefore, with an illustration of the manner in which, as Wittgenstein argued, a proof 'changes' (i.e. creates) the meaning of the expressions stated in a conjecture (in this case, 'country' and 'map'), so that the ultimate meaning of these expressions may not coincide with the sense of the words as they are used in their original *Satz/Beweissysteme*.[48] For example, according to the present definition we would now have to disqualify the map of the United States as a genuine map, if only because Utah, Colorado, Arizona and New Mexico all meet at a single point, and the map of Australia would be excluded since it has no neighbours. And this is even before we consider the changes that were wrought in the concept by Heesch's shift to the triangulation of a map in a planar dual in order to tackle the problem with the techniques developed in graph theory.[49]

Kempe then proved that in every normal map there is at least one country with either two, three, four or five neighbours; i.e. that there is no normal map where every country has six or more neighbours. (De Morgan had earlier proved that it is impossible to construct five mutually adjacent countries.) This is an essential step in the proof: the introduction of the concept of an 'unavoidable set of configurations', such that every normal map contains at least one member of the set. (It might seem from the manner in which this has been expressed that the argument slips dangerously into platonist idiom, but there is, in fact, nothing here to which we need object, provided that we interpret this as stating that the concept of a 'normal map' has been defined in such a way that every normal map is 'unavoidable'. That is, the concept *normal map* is developed in much the same way as (e.g.) *prime number*, and this feature is merely the consequence of the rules governing the construction of the infinite series of normal maps.) The next step in Kempe's argument was to show that, for any normal map M which contains a configuration which is a member of this 'unavoidable set' U, we can derive another map M' which contains fewer countries than M, such that, if M' is four-colourable, then so too is the unavoidable map M. Where such a construction is possible we say that that configuration is reducible. (A 'reducible' configuration is one which cannot be part of a minimal normal five-chromatic map, for if it was there would then be another five-chromatic map with fewer countries. We say that a vertex is reducible if, by removing any vertex of degree k from a graph, the four-colourability of the resulting sub-graph implies the four-colourability of the original graph. A configuration is said to be reducible if the four-colourability of a planar graph containing it is deducible from the four-colourability of the sub-graph which results when that configuration is removed.) That is, we modify any given map in such a way that, from a four-colouring of our reduced map, we can reconstruct a four-colouring of the original map. No matter what the size of our original map, if we keep reducing often enough we shall come to a reduced map with four or fewer countries, from which we can then work backwards to reconstruct the four-colouring of the original map.

It bears reiterating at this point that while the series of normal maps is infinite, a map must itself consist of a finite number of countries/vertices; just as the series of composite numbers is infinite, but each composite number consists of a finite number of factors. To suppose otherwise would defeat at this early stage, if not the proof itself then certainly its interpretation, since the postulation of a 'map with an infinite number of vertices' would rest on an obvious *Beweissysteme* confusion. Interestingly, the significance of this point is not universally recognised. In *The Four Color Problem*, Saaty and Kainen remark: 'A connected graph is one-colorable if and only if it consists of a single vertex. ... The situation for two-colorability is slightly more complicated but still manageable. ... Of course, the infinite checkerboard does not present this problem, but we are interested in maps with a finite number of regions.'[50] But the latter would constitute, not an unmanageable map, but rather, no sort of 'map' whatsoever.

The final stage of the proposed proof is then to show, at each step of the reduction, that we can four-colour the previous map provided that we can four-colour the existing reduced map. This process guarantees that we must eventually come across a map which we are certain can be four-coloured, from whence we can then work backwards to the original map. Whereupon we are forced to conclude that M is four-colourable, contradicting our original assumption. Hence no minimal normal five-chromatic map exists, from which Kempe/Appel–Haken conclude that every normal map is four-colourable. The upshot of the original Kempe programme is thus that it will suffice to prove the 4CC if only we can construct an avoidable set of configurations that is reducible. Kempe's undertaking broke down because he could only prove that four of his five unavoidable vertices were reducible; his attempted proof for countries with five neighbours was soon destroyed by Heawood, who showed that, in general, vertices of degree 5 are not reducible. (There are certain configurations which are exceptions to this rule; e.g. Birkhoff's theorem that a five-degree vertex with three consecutive five-neighbours is reducible.) In order to comply with the inspiration of Kempe's argument, Appel and Haken were forced to alter the nature and size of Kempe's unavoidable set dramatically. Thus they shifted from trying to prove that vertices of degree 5 are reducible to proving that 'configurations' — clusters of vertices — are reducible. Obviously, the problem of finding a set of reducible configurations sufficiently rich that every planar graph contains one member of the set is vastly more complicated than Kempe's original project. The design of Appel and Haken's approach may have remained faithful to Kempe's original strategy in one sense, therefore, in so far as they endeavoured to construct an unavoidable set of configurations that are reducible; but by embarking on a route which must of necessity rely extensively on the use of computers, they completely altered the spirit which had animated Kempe's failed venture.

By their own account, Appel and Haken appear to have developed an extraordinary 'feel' for which set would prove so reducible, but their method remained firmly based on a — from a mathematical point of view — disturbingly random approach: a procedure in which they increasingly followed rather than governed the development of their program. After explaining how in early 1975 they had 'modified the experimental program to yield obstacle-free configurations and forced it to search for arguments that employed configurations of small ring size', Appel and Haken describe how

> At this point the program, which had by now absorbed our ideas and improvements for two years, began to surprise us. At the beginning we would check its arguments by hand so we could always predict the course it would follow in any situation; but now it suddenly started to act like a chess-playing machine. It would work out compound strategies based on all the tricks it had been 'taught' and often the approaches were far more clever than those we would have tried. Thus it began to teach us things about how to proceed that we never expected. In a sense it had surpassed its creators in some aspects of the 'intellectual' as well as the mechanical parts of the task.[51]

Whenever an unavoidable set of configurations could not be proved to be reducible — which is not by any means to be equated with a proof that it was not reducible — they developed a highly effective method of modifying and then testing the new set for reducibility. However, the larger the configuration the more difficult it becomes to prove reducibility. The 'ring size' of a configuration — the number of countries that form a ring around the configuration — provides a direct indication of the complexity involved in proving that the configuration is reducible. Working with formidably large ring sizes, Appel and Haken were not simply forced to rely on a sophisticated system to run through large unavoidable sets of configurations to test for reducibility, but were extremely fortunate that the results from their self-modifying program suggested ways to keep the ring size down to a level where a computer could at least work through the configurations in a reasonable length of time. As it was their ultimate discovery of an unavoidable set of 1500 reducible configurations took approximately 1200 hours of computer time.

The key to this achievement lay in the development of their successful 'discharging algorithm' (basically a rule for redistributing the 'charge' of vertices in a planar triangulation). That is, they devised an effective procedure for constructing a set of so-called 'obstructing configurations' — configurations which 'obstruct' the discharging of positive charges — and since the 'sum charge' of a planar graph is always positive, these 'obstructing' configurations are unavoidable. Hence the discharging algorithm enabled them to enumerate an unavoidable set U, and to revise this set continually by modifying the algorithm. This part of the solution — that every planar graph must contain a configuration which is a member of U — is clearly surveyable. But at the next stage of the argument they were forced to resort to empirical methods to reduce the calculations to manageable proportions. Heesch had described three 'reduction obstacles': embedded configurations which are regularly present in configurations which are irreducible. To establish that none of the 'reduction obstacles' is present in a configuration does not at all serve as a proof that the configuration is reducible, but it does make it highly probable that that will turn out to be the case (in so far as no configuration which contains one of these 'reduction obstacles' has as yet been proved to be reducible). Hence, it provides the mathematician with a fairly — but not necessarily — reliable indication of where such a proof is likely to prove successful. Without this technique the sheer size of the set of configurations that would have had to have been examined would have required an impossible amount of computer time to perform the necessary operations.

Appel and Haken cite this procedure as an example of the manner in which future mathematical investigations will have to rely heavily on computer-assisted routines. But even if, as seems likely, such a prediction should materialise, it will provide no succour for the 'computer/probabilistic proof' thesis. For although this step may have been crucial to the genesis of the Appel–Haken solution, it none the less has no role to play in the actual proof of the four-colour problem. It is part of the general confusion which surrounds this issue that Appel and Haken should have assumed that such an empirical prop could play a role in the rules laid down by a proof. How a mathematician is led to construct a mathematical truth — whether this be by intuition, observation or heuristic programs — may be a vital issue for the psychology of mathematical invention, but it has no bearing on the normative character of that truth. The obvious parallel here is to the relation which Archimedes' 'method' bore to the proofs which he subsequently constructed which, as we saw in the preceding section, was methodological, not logical. As far as the Appel–Haken solution of the four-colour problem is concerned, the point is that how an unavoidable set of reducible configurations might have been discovered does not amount to a proof of the same, platonist confusions notwithstanding.

The experimental use of the computer in the development of the 'reducibility lemma' was thus twofold. First, the computer was used to develop a highly probable approach to determine which configurations might prove to be reducible. The next and final stage of the proof was then to test these likely candidates for reducibility. In essence, the (D-)reducibility program which Appel and Haken employed, tests the configuration to see whether every four-colouring of the ring around that configuration can be extended to a four-colouring of the configuration, and if not, whether it can be modified by one or more interchanges in the 'Kempe chain' of colours (the two-coloured paths leading from one country to another) and then extended, or finally, whether by the identification of distinct vertices it can be extended. Obviously the number of possible four-colourings of a circuit is proportionate to the size of the ring (a circuit with 13 vertices, for example, has 66,430 different four-colourings). And the process of generating these different four-colourings, they argue, is *purely mechanical,* so the problem really comes down to having a powerful enough computer to go through all the permutations in a reasonable length of time. But that is precisely the source of our philosophical problem here: that the process of testing these configurations is 'purely mechanical'. For what we need to know is not *that* there is an unavoidable set of reducible configurations, but *how* to generate it; not a *test,* but rather, a *rule* for their construction.

We must not confuse such a *mechanical operation* with the concepts of recursive proof or calculation (cf. Chapter 5). Wittgenstein was certainly quite prepared to countenance the presence of the latter in the body of a proof, but in doing so he deliberately contrasted recursion with the type of 'arithmetical experiment' that results in the 'reducibility lemma'. In *Philosophical Remarks* he asked: 'Is an arithmetical experiment still possible when a recursive definition has been set up? I believe, obviously not; because via the recursion each stage becomes arithmetically comprehensible' (PR §194). We must consider this last point carefully when assessing the logico-syntactical status of the 'reducibility lemma'. For the problem with the 'reducibility lemma', *qua* grammatical construction, lies precisely in its unsurveyability, which in turn is merely a manifestation of the unintelligibility of describing this part of Appel and Haken's solution as a *lemma* as opposed to an empirical hypothesis. The logical distinction we must clarify here, therefore, is yet again that between experiment and proof: 'In this context we keep coming up against something that could be called an "arithmetical experiment". Admittedly the data determine the result, but I can't see in what way they determine it (cf. e.g. the occurrences of 7 in π). The primes likewise come out from the method for looking for them, as the results of an experiment. To be sure, I can convince myself that 7 is prime, but I can't see the connection between it and the condition it satisfies. — I have only found the number, not generated it' (PR §190). Likewise, the worry here is that the Koch computer program may *convince* us that U is reducible, but we cannot grasp an internal connection between this result and the criteria for reducibility because we cannot *generate* this result as a consequence of applying the rules for reducibility. And this is precisely the source of the logical obstacles to describing the 'reducibility lemma' as a mathematical construction. The critical point is that I cannot understand a mathematical construction as a *lemma* unless I understand the proof underlying it. 'This boils down to saying: If I hear a proposition of, say, number theory, but don't know how to prove it, then I don't understand the proposition either' (PR §155; cf. §§157, 190). Hence the Koch/Appel–Haken program no more provides an answer to Guthrie's conjecture than the Shanks–Wrench program answers the mathematical conjecture 'Do four 7s occur in the expansion of π?'

As we saw above, Wittgenstein argued that the colour octahedron must be surveyable in the sense that the logical articulations forged by the grammatical construction are perspicuous. Likewise, a proof must be surveyable in the sense that we can grasp the 'law' forged by the proof: 'I must be able to write down a part of the series, in such a way that you can *recognise* the law. That is to say, no *description* is to occur in what is written down, everything must be represented' (PR §190). But this is precisely the condition which the Appel–Haken solution fails to meet: what we are given just is a description of U — together with the operations which the computer has performed to test its reducibility — rather than a 'manifestation of the law' for the generation of unavoidable sets of reducible configurations. Hence the 'reducibility lemma' commits the same fallacy which Wittgenstein warned against when he argued that 'A number as the result of an arithmetical experiment, and so the experiment as the *description* of a number, is an absurdity. The experiment would be the description, not the *representation* of a number' (PR §196). Thus the problem here is not at all comparable to the calculation of an 'enormous' number, where the rules of arithmetic are the criteria for what is a correct theorem. In this case the program is not an application, but rather constitutive of what we shall call an 'unavoidable set of reducible configurations'. That is, there are no *rules* for the proposition 'U is an unavoidable set of reducible configurations'; all that we have in the Appel–Haken solution is a *description* of an unavoidable set of reducible configurations and the *test* which led to U. What we need is not — as in the case of the pocket calculator — a causal link, but rather, a *normative* one: not only that U is the result of running the (D-)reducibility program, but that U *must* be an unavoidable set of reducible configurations.

The issue that concerns us here, therefore, is not the *accuracy* of the operations that were performed by the system: it is the lack of an *internal relation* between the notion of an unavoidable set of reducible configurations and the results that were obtained from the (D-)reducibility program. If it were the former, then the way would indeed be open to Detlefsen and Luker's conception of 'the presence of calculation or computation in a proof as injecting an empirical element into that proof'.[52] But what we must distinguish between — if we are not to confuse surveyability with verification — is the execution of a rule versus the construction of a proof. What must be surveyable is the law for the construction of reducible configurations. For this reason it is quite out of place to compare this issue to Gauss's proof that the sum of the first 100 positive integers is 5,050. What must be surveyable in the latter is the rule '101 × 50 = 5050'. The table

1	2	3	4	...	49	50
100	99	98	97	...	52	51

is merely an application of the rules of arithmetic, which can thus be scrutinised for error; and as we shall see in Chapter 6, the grammar of 'scrutinise' rules out the possibility of merely *overlooking* an error. Detlefsen and Luker ask: 'Upon what is our confidence in the results of such a computation based?'[53] The answer to this just is: on the rules of arithmetic. Or rather: the rules of arithmetic render it totally misguided to speak of 'confidence' as far as the certainty of 'the results of such a computation' is concerned. But it is perfectly intelligible to ask: 'Upon what is our confidence in the results of the (D-)reducibility program based?', and therein hangs the crux of this issue. For *shorthand* is not the same thing as *unsurveyability*. In the former the possibility of error can be *excluded*; in the latter it can only be *tested.*

Saaty and Kainen, however, conclude that: 'The crux of the Appel–Haken proof of the four-colour theorem is a subtle and elegant probabilistic argument which establishes an *a priori* certainty that there must exist some discharging procedure producing an unavoidable set all of whose configurations are reducible. That is, they showed that the computer-assisted reducibility proof was overwhelmingly likely to succeed, and they appear to have been right.'[54] It is fascinating to see the ease with which the authors shift back and forth here between the *a priori* and the *a posteriori*. The explanation for this laxity is clear: it is because they regard the *a posteriori* as related to the *a priori* on a scale of relative certainty, with absolute certainty finally reached at the level of the *a priori*, that they slip so effortlessly from the one concept to the other. Thus, they fail to distinguish bewteen the two *kinds* of certainty involved in mathematical as opposed to empirical contexts: viz. normative versus inductive (cf. Chapter 2). The confusion involved in this passage is similar to the misconception which interprets the limit which an infinite series approaches as the actual infinite. As we shall see in the following chapter, just as the focus of Wittgenstein's critique of Cantor's interpretation of the transfinite cardinals lies in Cantor's attempt to elucidate his infinitary constructions in terms of the 'larger than' relation that governs finite totalities, so too the problem with Saaty and Kainen's argument is that they try to describe the relation between probability and certainty in terms of a 'greater than' relation. But mathematical propositions are not *more* certain than empirical: they are certain in a completely different way. For 'I cannot be making a mistake about 12 × 12 being 144. And now one cannot contrast *mathematical* certainty with the relative uncertainty of empirical propositions' (OC §151). The *a priori certain* (i.e. *the logical exclusion of doubt*) is separated from the notion of probability tending towards the limit of (inductive) certainty by the conceptual barrier which sunders *rules of grammar* from *empirical propositions*. Thus, if we tighten up their argument, we see that what Saaty and Kainen really mean is that the Appel–Haken solution established a highly probable *a posteriori* truth because they showed that the (D-) reducibility program is overwhelmingly likely to succeed. (The greater the probability that an arbitrary colouration of a ring is extendable, the greater the probability that the bounded configuration is reducible. When the former reaches a probability $\geq$ .30, the probability of the latter very nearly reaches 1.) And this in itself provides yet a further indication of the reason why Appel and Haken did not succeed in constructing a *proof* for the 4CC.

The fact that this approach forces us to interpret the Appel–Haken solution as what Wittgenstein called an 'arithmetical experiment' does not thereby commit us, however, to the disconcerting corollary that Guthrie's orginial four-colour problem was *ex post facto* an empirical rather than a mathematical conjecture. This is a direct result of the theme that mathematical conjectures cannot be treated as well-formed (i.e. meaningful) mathematical questions prior to the construction of a grammatical structure in which they are rendered decidable. By converse reasoning, the solution which is pursued determines the logico-syntactical fate of its conjecture. Thus, when Waismann remarked that 'Some psychologists believed so firmly that [the logical incompatibility of colours] was a matter of empirical states of affairs that they even performed empirical investigations whether two colours could not be at the same place', Wittgenstein responded: 'That too might be possible — you would have to tell me what methods these psychologists employed, that is, what counted as verification for them. Only then can I say what sense an assumption has. It is thinkable, after all, that such an investigation makes good sense — but it is only the method of answering a question that tells you what the question was really about. Only when I have answered a question can I know what it is aimed at' (WWK 79). Consequently the 4CC, as it is presented at the beginning of the Appel–Haken solution, must be deemed to present an hypothesis, and this is solely because of the empirical nature of their solution: not some hidden aspect of the question which implicitly sets an upper limit on the certainty with which Guthrie's problem can be answered.

It must be stressed that, despite the heavy philosophical presence which intrudes itself, the outcome of this issue ultimately remains a strictly mathematical affair. What concerns us is not the *validity*, but rather, the *significance* of the objections which have been voiced by mathematicians to the Appel–Haken solution. For when mathematicians object to the format of the 'proof' what disturbs them is not so much its length or complexity as what we have described as the 'unsurveyability' of the 'reducibility lemma'. Thus Ian Stewart complains in *Concepts of Modern Mathematics* that the problem with the Appel–Haken solution is that 'it doesn't give a satisfactory explanation *why* the theorem is true. This is partly because the proof is so long that it is hard to grasp (including the computer calculations, impossible!), but mostly because it is so apparently structureless. The answer appears as a kind of monstrous coincidence. Why is there an unavoidable set of reducible configurations? The best answer at the present time is: there just is. The proof: here it is, see for yourself. The mathematician's search for hidden structure, his pattern-binding urge, is frustrated.'[55] In one sense Stewart's objection is too harsh, however, for in an important way we *do* understand why U is reducible. Appel and Haken would undoubtedly — and justifiably — insist that some such account as the above constitutes a perfectly legimate explanation of why there is an unavoidable set of configurations. The epilogue to this discussion, however, is not that Appel and Haken failed to solve the four-colour problem, but that their solution is empirical, not mathematical.

Thus, the above argument in no way seeks to detract from the success of Appel and Haken's accomplishment; its sole ambition is to clarify the logico-syntactical nature of their achievement. And it is at this point that Stewart's criticism finds its mark; for what we are offered is, not a proof for the existence of this unavoidable reducible set of configurations, but rather, a description of the experimental procedure that was used to discover it. It is for this reason that the Appel–Haken solution of the four-colour problem is empirical rather than mathematical, and hence, that it makes no sense to speak of Appel and Haken 'proving' the 'four-colour theorem', let alone of their solution forcing us to modify our understanding of the concepts of proof and theorem. The resistance with which some mathematicians have greeted their results strikes Appel and Haken as evidence of a reactionary attitude fostered by an antediluvian mathematical training.[56] But there is no objection here to the Archimedes-like use of computers as 'tools' which might facilitate the preliminary or extraneous stages of proof-construction. The problem with Appel and Haken's solution is essentially that, as it stands, it is rather like the first half of Archimedes' method: the described result may have been found, but the proof for this proposition has yet to be constructed. There are no grounds to suppose that such a feat is *a priori* precluded, however, any more than that such a 'proof' is tacitly contained in Appel–Haken's solution. The outcome of this critique, therefore, is not a piece of mathematical legislation or revisionism, but simply an example of the impartiality which governs a philosophical investigation.

Notes

1. Cf. G.P. Baker and P.M.S. Hacker, *Wittgenstein: Understanding and Meaning*, Vol. I of *An Analytical Commentary on the Philosophical Investigations* (Oxford, Basil Blackwell, 1980), pp. 531.
2. Cf. Crispin Wright, *Wittgenstein on the Foundations of Mathematics*, Chapter 2, (London, Duckworth, 1980).
3. Cf. ibid., p. 117.
4. M. Dummet, 'Wittgenstein's Philosophy of Mathematics', in S.G. Shanker (ed.), *Ludwig Wittgenstein: Critical Assessments* (London, Croom Helm, 1986), p. 134.
5. Donald E. Knuth, 'Mathematics and Computer Science: Coping with Finiteness', *Science*, vol. 194, no. 4271, p. 1235.
6. Ibid., p. 1236.
7. Thomas Tymoczko, 'The Four-Colour Problem and its Philosophical Significance', *The Journal of Philosophy*, vol. LXXVI, no. 2 (1979), p. 57.
8. Ibid., p. 58.
9. Ibid.
10. Elsie Cerutti and P.J. Davis, 'Formac Meets Pappus', *American Mathematical Monthly*, vol. LXXVI (1969), p. 903.
11. Ibid.
12. Michael O. Rabin, 'Probabilistic Algorithms', in Traub, J.F. (ed.), *Algorithms and Complexity: New Directions and Recent Results* (New York, Academic Press, 1976), p. 37.
13. Cf. G.B. Kolata, 'Mathematical Proofs: The Genesis of Reasonable Doubt', *Science*, vol. 192 (1976), pp. 989-90.
14. Michael Detlefsen and Mark Luker, 'The Four-Color Theorem and Mathematical Proof', *The Journal of Philosophy*, vol. LXXVII (1980), p. 819.
15. Ibid.
16. Ibid.
17. Paul Teller, 'Computer Proof'. *The Journal of Philosophy*, vol. LXXVII (1980), p. 801.
18. Ibid., p. 798.
19. Kolata, 'Mathematical Proofs: The Genesis of Reasonable Doubt', op cit., p. 990.
20. Ibid., p. 990.
21. Saul Kripke, *Naming and Necessity*, (Oxford, Basil Blackwell, 1980), p. 35.
22. Ibid.
23. Ibid.
24. Teller, 'Computer Proof', op.cit., p. 799.
25. It is important to see that the 'pocket calculator' is nothing of the sort: it has not *calculated* anything, and our belief that the readout is 'accurate' relates to

the inductive probability that the device has correlated the symbols which, in a mathematical proof, we would have *derived*. The problem we are faced with here is entirely one of the correct logical description of the mechanical operations of such a device, and how these operations relate to mathematical operations. cf. my 'The Nature of Philosophy', in *Ludwig Wittgenstein: Critical Assessments*, vol. IV.

26. T.L. Saaty and P. Kainen, *The Four-Color Problem: Assaults and Conquest*, (New York, McGraw-Hill, 1977), pp. 97-8.

27. Philip J. Davis, 'Fidelity in Mathematical Discourse: Is One and One Really Two?', *American Mathematical Monthly*, vol. LXXIX (1972), p. 258.

28. Ibid.

29. Ibid.

30. Carl B. Boyer, *The History of the Calculus and its Conceptual Development* (New York, Dover Publications, 1949), p. 51.

31. Detlefsen and Luker, 'The Four-Color Theorem and Mathematical Proof', op. cit., p. 805.

32. The confusions here are extremely subtle, and for that reason, extremely well entrenched. I have looked at this issue in some depth in 'The Nature of Philosophy', op. cit.; and 'The Decline and Fall of the Mechanist Metaphor', in Rainer Born (ed.), *The Case Against AI* (London, Croom Helm, 1986).

33. Tymoczko, 'The Four-Colour Problem and its Philosophical Significance', op. cit., p. 58.

34. Cf. ibid, pp. 62, 63.

35. Ibid.

36. Ibid., pp. 74, 77-8.

37. Teller, 'Computer Proof', op. cit., p. 801.

38. Ibid., p. 800.

39. Ibid.

40. Ibid., p. 798.

41. Detlefsen and Luker, 'The Four-Color Theorem and Mathematical Proof', op. cit., p. 819.

42. Ibid. p. 804.

43. Cf. Kenneth Appel and Wolfgang Haken, 'The Four Color Problem', in L.A. Steen (ed.), *Mathematics Today* (New York, Springer-Verlag, 1978), p. 162.

44. Cf. Ernst Sonheimer and Alan Rogerson, *Numbers and Infinity* (Cambridge, Cambridge University Press, 1981), p.18.

45. Cf. Richard Courant and Herbert Robbins, *What is Mathematics?* (New York, Oxford University Press, 1978), pp. 30 f.

46. That if p is any prime which does not divide the integer a, then $a^{p-1} \equiv 1$ (mod p).

47. Albeit standing in need of philosophical clarification; cf. RFM V §28, and Morris Lazerowitz and Alice Ambrose's 'Assuming the Logically Impossible', in their *Necessity and Language* (London, Croom Helm, 1985), pp. 69-79.

48. In what follows, the words 'map', 'country', 'neighbours', etc. will appear without quotation marks; it should be understood throughout, however, that they are used here in their uniquely mathematical and not an ordinary context.

49. On the latter approach, a 'normal map' is projected into a dual (planar) graph, with each vertex in the graph representing a country, and the straight lines connecting the vertices representing borders, thus dividing the plane into polygonal 'faces'. Heesch established that when the map is normal these faces will all be triangles, in which case the resulting graph is called a 'triangulation of the plane'. We can now describe the number of 'neighbours' which a 'country' has in the planar graph as the 'degree of the vertex': i.e. the number of lines meeting at the vertex, which represents the number of neighbours that the dual country in the original map has. The 'ring size' is defined as the boundary circuit of the

configuration: the path of edges that starts and ends at the same vertex without crossing itself.

50.   Saaty and Kainen, *The Four-Color Problem*, op. cit., p. 23.

51.   Appel and Haken, 'The Four-Color Problem', op. cit., p. 175.

52.   Detlefsen and Luker, 'The Four-Color Theorem and Mathematical Proof', op. cit., p. 809.

53.   Ibid., p. 808.

54.   Saaty and Kainen, *The Four-Color Problem*, op. cit., p. 83.

55.   Ian Stewart, *Concepts of Modern Mathematics* (Harmondsworth, Penguin Books, 1981), p. 304.

56.   Cf. Appel and Haken, 'The Four-Color problem', op.cit., pp. 178-9.

5 THE PERILS OF PROSE

> Good Heavens! For more than forty years I have been speaking prose without knowing it.
>
> Molière, *Le Bourgeois Gentilhomme*

> Our minds are finite, and yet even in these circumstances of finitude we are surrounded by possibilities that are infinite, and the purpose of human life is to grasp as much as we can out of that infinitude.
>
> A.N. Whitehead, *Dialogues*

The Nature of Infinity

Wittgenstein's non-revisionist protestations frequently strain the bounds of credibility, but nowhere more so than in his critique of transfinite number theory. How could he hope to sustain the air of impartiality he so carefully cultivated, and yet ask us to 'Imagine set theory's having been invented by a satirist as a kind of parody on mathematics. — Later a reasonable meaning was seen in it and it was incorporated into mathematics. (For if one person can see it as a paradise of mathematicians, why should not another see it as a joke?)' (RFM V §7) But before we dismiss this as yet another example of Wittgenstein's iconoclastic fervour untempered by technical proficiency, we must clarify exactly what it was that Wittgenstein was attacking. For the problems posed by the mathematical theory of infinity founded by Cantor provide what might best be described as both the testing-ground and the touchstone of Wittgenstein's approach to the philosophy of mathematics. Herein lies the juncture between calculus and prose, and thus, the confrontation between mathematics and philosophy. And yet, according to Wittgenstein, 'It is a strange mistake of some mathematicians to believe that something *inside* mathematics might be dropped because of a critique of the foundations. Some mathematicians have the right instinct: once we have calculated something it cannot drop out and disappear! And in fact, what is caused to disappear by such a critique are names and allusions that occur in the calculus, hence what I wish to call *prose*' (WWK 149). The question is: can this sentiment — however well-intentioned —

be reconciled with the subsequent avowal: 'I would say, "I wouldn't dream of trying to drive anyone out of this paradise." I would try to do something quite different: I would try to show you that it is not a paradise — so that you'll leave of your own accord. I would say, "You're welcome to this; just look about you"' (LFM 103). Is there a genuine distinction here, or was Wittgenstein guilty of sophistry, if not something worse?

The first step to appreciating the significance of Wittgenstein's critique of transfinite number theory is to grasp the evolution of his thought in the early 1930s. It might seem that the accounts of number and infinity in the *Tractatus* and *Philosophical Remarks* could have little in common; after all, the *Tractatus* fragments are exceedingly schematic, while the arguments developed in *Philosophical Remarks* betray a striking Brouwerian influence. Wittgenstein repeatedly referred during this time, however, to the continuity in his thought on this issue. One explanation for this might well be that Wittgenstein was persistently interested in intuitionist-inspired constructivist themes: Poincaréan in the *Tractatus* and Brouwerian in *Philosophical Remarks*. With this in mind, it might be possible to trace the route which led Wittgenstein from the *Tractatus* account of number as the exponent of an operation, through the transitional remarks on arithmetic as the grammar of numerals, to the pronouncedly intuitionistic discussion of the meaning of '$\aleph_0$' in *Lectures on the Foundations of Mathematics* and *Remarks on the Foundations of Mathematics*. Furthermore, we can glean from the remarks on generality and induction in *Philosophical Remarks* an insight into some of the more enigmatic pronouncements in the *Tractatus*, as well as an indication of the route on which Wittgenstein embarked when he returned to Cambridge in 1929.

Wittgenstein claimed in *Philosophical Remarks*: 'I have always said you can't speak of *all* numbers, because there's no such thing as "all numbers"' (PR §129). Perhaps he was alluding to the long argument proscribing the use of 'formal' concepts at 4. 1272. There he insisted that 'It is nonsensical to speak of the *total number of objects*. The same applies to the words "complex," "fact," "function," "number".' We can further reconstruct the development of his thought by considering the following sequence of quotations:

6.03:   The general form of an integer is [0, x, x + 1].
6.031:   The theory of classes is completely superfluous in

mathematics. This is connected with the fact that the generality required in mathematics is not *accidental* generality.

6.1231: The mark of a logical proposition is *not* general validity. To be general means no more than to be accidentally valid for all things.

6.1232: The general validity of logic might be called essential, in contrast with the accidental general validity of such propositions as 'All men are mortal'.

PR §126: It seems to me that we can't use generality — all, etc. — in mathematics at all. There's no such thing as 'all numbers', simply because there are infinitely many. And because it isn't a question here of the amorphous 'all', such as occurs in 'All the apples are ripe', where the set is given by an external description: it's a question of a collection of structures, which must be given precisely as such (cf. PR §107).

PR §142: Generality in mathematics is a direction, an arrow pointing along the series generated by an operation.

PR §142: The infinite number series is itself such a series — as emerges from the single symbol $(1, x, x + 1)$. This symbol is itself an arrow with the first '1' as the tail of the arrow and '$x + 1$' as its tip.

The pattern which emerges from these interlocking quotations reveals a decidedly intuitionistic hostility to set theory running from the *Tractatus* to *Philosophical Remarks*, gathering force in the latter work and subsequently blossoming into a frontal assault on transfinite set theory and the Cantorean notion of the 'actual infinite'. Wittgenstein made two points at 6.031: first, that set theory is 'superfluous'; and second, that this is because the generality required in mathematics *qua* logical method is *essential*. It is a contingent fact that 'all the men in this room are tall', but it is a necessary fact that there are infinitely many natural numbers. Hence the generality required in the latter mathematical context is *internal*: i.e. it is *manifested* by induction. The general form of an integer — which is nothing less than the symbol for the infinite number series — is given by the representation of mathematical induction. Take away the *Tractatus* conception of universal quantification and it 'looks now as if the quantifiers make no sense for numbers. I mean: you can't say "(n).fn", precisely because "all natural numbers" isn't a bounded concept' (PR §126). That is, we are left with the conclusion that we cannot *speak* of generality in mathematics: induction *shows* us what e.g. Russell's use of quantification had tried to *say.*

This provides us with a likely explanation for how the attack on the 'actual infinite' presented in *Philosophical Remarks* grew out of the logico-syntactical considerations that were initiated in the *Tractatus*, which in turn highlights the critical point that Wittgenstein's approach stands in a subtle relation to the 'finitistic' denial of the existence of infinite sets. The finitist insists that the expressions of our mathematical language can only be cashed in terms of transactions that we can — in principle or in practice — carry out, and thus the platonist conception of an infinite totality (viz. as an extensional structure) offends against the laws of empirical possibility, since we could never be capable of executing an infinite number of operations.[1] But, as we saw in Chapter 3, Wittgenstein was intent on clarifying — as opposed to questioning — the significance of the universal validity of the law of excluded middle. The essence of Wittgenstein's argument was thus that the issue does not involve any so-called 'finite limitations' on what we are capable of performing, and the reason why such a conception is absurd is not in the least empirical. For 'The objection that "the finite cannot grasp the infinite" is *really* directed against the idea of a psychological act of grasping or understanding' (RFM V §6). But our concern here is with logical syntax: not pseudo-epistemology. Hence our true task is to clarify the logical grammar of two completely separate concepts: 'the crucial distinction ... between "totality" and "system".'[2] The great problem with transfinite set theory lies in its assumption that 'we can understand the meaning of a class without knowing whether the class is finite or infinite, that that is something we establish only later.' But 'We cannot imagine the same class finite at one time and infinite at another. The truth of the matter is that the word "class" means completely different things in the two cases. It is not one and the same concept at all that is qualified by the addition of "finite" or "infinite".' Such a confusion follows from the creation of 'a symbolism which represents both kinds of classes in exactly the same way'. 'A correct symbolism has to reproduce an infinite class in a completely different way from a finite one. Finiteness and infinity of a class must be obvious from its syntax. In a correct language there must not even be a temptation of raising the question whether a class is finite or infinite.' The crux of this issue, therefore, is that ' "*Infinite*" *is not a quantity*. The word "infinite" has a different syntax from a number word' (WWK 228).

It has seemed to several commentators that it is ultimately a moot issue whether Wittgenstein's argument was intended to develop an alternative to, or simply provide a philosophical rationale for, finitism, in so far as the two routes seem to arrive at very much the same destination. Admittedly, there is an intuitionistic familiarity to Wittgenstein's insistence that 'The infinite number series is only the infinite possibility of finite series of numbers. It is senseless to speak of the *whole* infinite number series, as if it, too, were an extension'[3] (PR §144). But even from this curt remark, subtle nuances of his distinctiveness begin to emerge. For Wittgenstein's argument proceeded from his preoccupation with logical syntax, not epistemology; the emphasis here was on the meaning of 'infinite class', and the categorial difference which this displays from 'finite class'. Thus the intuitionist distinction between finite totality and infinite series was not so much borrowed as *absorbed* into Wittgenstein's new approach. What emerged from the process was the emphasis on the confusion which is bred by the common use of the terms 'class' and 'set' in the two different *Beweissysteme.* The word 'class' means *totality* when it is used in the context of a 'finite' *Beweissystem* (a group of objects all sharing the same property); but in its 'infinite' framework 'class' signifies a rule-governed series (the possibility of constructing a series *ad infinitum* by the reiteration of an operation). This argument — that Cantorean set theory rests on a *Beweissystem* confusion — is perhaps the major theme in Wittgenstein's discussion of infinity, recurring as a leitmotif throughout his examination of number theory *simpliciter.*

The above passage also indicates precisely why it is that we cannot use the notation for generality in mathematics (a point which on Wittgenstein's own authority he had tried to convey in the *Tractatus*). The expression '(n) (n $\in$ N)' only makes sense for a *finite* system: a restriction which cannot be obliterated by stipulating that a class-symbol now stands for an 'infinite class'. Corresponding to the categorial distinction in what the two types of expression convey there must thus be a syntactical distinction in the manner in which this is accomplished. 'A proposition about all propositions, or all functions, is *a priori* an impossibility: what such a proposition is intended to express would have to be shown by an induction' (PR §129). That is, we already employ different notations for these concepts: general and existential quantification for finite classes, and the symbol for mathematical induction for infinite series. On the basis of this logico-syntactical premise the somewhat muted attack on set theory in the *Tractatus* turns into a full-scale denunciation in *Philosophical Remarks*. Mathematics has little to do with set theory: it is as much a mistake to introduce finite sets into the arithmetic of natural numbers as 'infinite sets' for transfinite number theory.[4] The concept of infinity can only be elucidated in terms of the concepts of 'system' and 'operation', and the confusion manifested in theories about 'completed infinities' only enters through the prior confusions instigated by set theory.

If we are to do justice to Wittgenstein's critique of transfinite number theory we must approach it on the firm understanding that Wittgenstein was only interested in what he regarded as the central *philosophical* issues involved. It is clear that the discussion of infinity in *Philosophical Remarks*, which proceeds on the basis of this *Beweissystem*-clarification of the meaning of 'infinite series', was formulated to undermine the postulation of the 'actual infinite', and thus, the Cantorean interpretation of transfinite numbers. But the arguments which Wittgenstein employed are extremely — perhaps excessively — superficial, and his criticisms inevitably suffer from an acute lack of gravitas. His argument has thus been condemned for attacking a somewhat pathetic species of straw man: a crude form of platonism that oversimplifies the complex and powerful theory which Cantor developed.[5] Admittedly, Wittgenstein concentrated on the theme that the notion that transfinite numbers exist because they are attributes of infinite sets is unintelligible, and that this in turn underlies the unintelligibility of the postulation of an 'actual infinite'. Wittgenstein obviously believed that he had perceived deep grammatical confusions undermining the Cantorean interpretation of transfinite number theory, and that this rendered a close examination of Cantor's various proofs unnecessary. Moreover, he was confident enough in his work to show it to Russell in 1930, clearly without any qualms about this lacuna. Nevertheless, we cannot hope to unpack the full significance of his ideas without at least a limited probe of the application of Wittgenstein's thought, rather than a mere description of his intentions.

The key to Wittgenstein's argument lies in his repeated admonition that 'Where the nonsense starts is with our habit of thinking of a large number as closer to infinity than a small one' (PR §138). This theme is undoubtedly intuitionist-inspired, but Wittgenstein developed it in terms of his general *Beweissysteme* conception: there are two distinct kinds of system — the finite and the infinite — and Cantor's initial error was to transgress the boundary between them *in his notation*, thereby leading him to interpret transfinite numbers as concrete proof of the existence of the 'actual infinite' (PR §142). Despite Frege's important criticisms of Cantor's theory (all concerned with the lack of rigour in Cantor's definition of his terms), this fundamental *Beweissysteme* confusion remained embedded in transfinite number theory. Thus, Wittgenstein assumed that by focusing attention on this initial premise, the need to examine the technical apparatus introduced by Cantor and refined by Frege simply does not arise in the context of such a philosophical discussion. This 'mathematical calculus' is fine as it is (or at least, is not the philosopher's concern); it is the conceptual confusion underlying the *interpretation* of the *Beweissystem* that demands our attention. In the present chapter we shall concentrate on the success of Wittgenstein's critique; in the following chapter, on the havoc which this plays for his attempt to maintain an air of philosophical detachment *vis-à-vis* mathematical affairs.

By his own account Cantor crossed the Rubicon of the 'actual infinite' when he came to see the transfinite numbers as 'real' numbers.[6] In the Preface to *Grundlagen* Cantor recalled how 'A couple of years ago I was led to the infinite real whole numbers without having realized that they were concrete numbers of real significance.'[7] But if they were 'real', it must be because they share the same ontological foundation as the finite numbers: viz. they are properties of sets. Thus, to prove that the transfinite numbers are 'real' just was, so it seemed to Cantor, to prove that the 'actual infinite' exists.[8] The *Grundlagen* presented the fruits of his recent 'discovery', offering several independent proofs for the existence of transfinite numbers. The Kroneckerians immediately responded to this epoch-shattering pronouncement with a clamorous attack on the non-constructive methods Cantor had adopted to posit the existence of these 'fictional numbers'. Indeed, Kronecker even tried — with some success — to suppress the publication of Cantor's results. But the same line of criticism was not open to Wittgenstein, assuming that he was to remain faithful to his principle to eschew mathematical revisionism. The only alternative was thus to accept the existence of transfinite numbers, yet divorce this concept from the notion of the 'actual infinite'. The most conspicuous feature of Wittgenstein's account, therefore, is that he never questioned Cantor's claims to have constructed transfinite numbers. On the contrary, his strategy was to demonstrate precisely why and in what way Cantor's claims were justified. He endeavoured to accomplish this on the basis of a grammatical as opposed to a mathematical examination of the concepts of *number, transfinite number,* and the *actual infinite*. The results of this examination would, accordingly, clarify why the existence of Cantor's transfinite numbers and the 'actual infinite' are entirely separate issues.

The source of the confusion which Wittgenstein exposed lies in the initial assumption with which Cantor introduced his theory in *Grundlagen*: the conviction that, as he expressed it in 'Über die vershiedenen Ansichten in Bezug auf die actualunendlichen Zahlen': 'each potential infinite, if it is rigorously applicable mathematically, presupposed an actual infinite'.[9] Much of Wittgenstein's argument was concerned to show that 'potential' does not mean 'incomplete': that 'potential' and 'actual' are not, as it were, complementary aspects of infinity. Part of the problem with the intuitionist conception of infinity is simply that 'The word "possibility" is of course misleading, since someone will say, let what is possible now become actual' (PR §141). And this is very much how Cantor perceived his creation; for, according to Cantor, the transfinite numbers constitute 'an extension of the concept of number.'[10] Significantly, this remark can be interpreted in two widely different ways. Wittgenstein did not dispute the wisdom of this claim, provided that it is intended to suggest that the transfinite numbers represent an extension of the concept of number *simpliciter*, in which case it reveals an intuitive awareness of the family-resemblance character of *number* and the autonomy of individual number-systems.[11] However, should the statement be read as an affirmation of the thesis that the introduction of the transfinite numbers extends the domain of the natural numbers, then it will saddle us with the so-called proof for the existence of the 'actual infinite'. It was Cantor's great accomplishment in *Grundlagen* to recognise the former principle; unfortunately, this insight was immediately undermined by Cantor's further belief in the latter interpretation — the 'prose' of his theory — a confusion which Cantor bequeathed to subsequent transfinite number theory.

Wittgenstein's attack on the 'actual infinite' rests on the principle that this corrective merely subverts the Cantorean *interpretation*, not the *existence* of transfinite numbers; the issue calls for philosophical clarification, not mathematical reconstruction.

Grundlagen marked a crucial stage in Cantor's thought in so far as it explored the consequences of the supposition that transfinite numbers, *qua* numbers, must be 'real' *in exactly the same way* as natural numbers. And on this crucial point Wittgenstein was in complete agreement with Cantor: the philosophical task created by the construction of transfinite numbers consists in the proper elucidation of what their introduction entails. The bone of contention lies in Cantor's interpretation of the nature of this 'reality', and hence, the type of proof which is necessary to establish the manner in which transfinite are no less 'real' than natural numbers. Cantor was increasingly uneasy with the *Grundlagen* demonstration of his thesis, and it was not until the *Beiträge* — where he defined cardinal numbers as 'powers' — that he was finally satisfied with his exposition of the nature of transfinite numbers. But Wittgenstein did not challenge Cantor's decision to supplant the transfinite ordinal with transfinite cardinal numbers; for the introduction of this new species of transfinite number does not resolve the fundamental conceptual predicament afflicting the *Grundlagen*. Indeed, it only serves to obscure still further the source of the trouble, making it that much more difficult to come to terms with the confusion underlying the hypostatisation of the 'actual infinite'. For Cantor was thrust into his dilemma by his interpretation of what it means to say that the transfinite numbers are 'real in exactly the same way as the natural numbers'. The shift from transfinite to cardinal numbers may have provided the crucial step in Cantor's quest to develop a unified account of the finite/infinite number system, but it remains committed to a misconception which prompted the assumption that the construction of the rational numbers are an extension of the whole numbers (cf. Chapter 8). To see why the *Beiträge* strategy failed to resolve the problems raised by the *Grundlagen* — for reasons unrelated to Frege's attack on Cantor's rather obscure accounts of *Mächtigkeit* and the 'principle of abstraction' — therefore, we must consider how Cantor set about to define the transfinite numbers with the aim of achieving 'ontological uniformity' with the natural numbers: viz. by defining them as an extension of the natural numbers.

To a considerable extent this fallacy arose from Cantor's apprehension that transfinite numbers might be dismissed as yet another product of the mathematician's fecund imagination. Cantor's anxiety on this score was understandably exacerbated by Kronecker's response; so much so, that his reaction became increasingly bound up with a religious mania that regarded any suggestion that the transfinite numbers were less 'real' than the natural numbers as blasphemous. In his zeal to leave no stone unturned Cantor offered a battery of arguments in *Grundlagen* to support his thesis, with little regard for mutual compatibility. On the one hand, we are told that 'inner intuition' alone suffices to establish the reality of the transfinite numbers; on the other hand, that their presence is manifested by physical aggregates; they are ideas in the Divine Intellect; and still later, that all that is needed to demonstrate their existence is mathematical consistency. Above all else, however, Cantor believed that in order to show conclusively that the transfinite numbers are as 'real' as the natural numbers, he would have to demonstrate that they are literally an 'extension' of the natural numbers. To accomplish this he believed that it would be necessary to define the transfinite numbers in such a way that the 'larger than' relation would hold both for all transfinite numbers in relation to the natural numbers, and among the transfinite numbers themselves. That is, the finite/infinite number system would be governed and unified under the sway of the same relation: the infinite series of transfinite numbers and the extended system of the finite and infinite number series would be internally ordered by the 'larger than' relation. But Cantor had to accomplish this while at the same time maintaining a type-distinction between the natural and the transfinite numbers; otherwise he would be guilty of the supreme folly of actualising limits within the series of natural numbers. His solution was to distinguish between two different types of numbers — ordinal numbers (*Anzahlen*) and natural numbers (*Zahlen*) — which are none the less governed, both among themselves and in relation to each other, by '$>$'.[12]

In *Grundlagen* Cantor defined a finite natural number as a *unit*, and the infinite natural number series as an unending sequence of successive units. He then explained that even though we cannot speak of the largest element in the set of natural numbers, we can still define ω — the lowest transfinite ordinal number — as the *first* number following the entire sequence of natural numbers (ν). Thus Cantor introduced a striking new twist into the traditional conception of omega as the limit of the natural numbers: omega is the smallest number (*Anzahl*) larger than any integer (*Zahl*). Without treating the concept of limit as actualised *within* the calculus of the natural numbers, Cantor was thus able to distinguish between calling ω the greatest natural number — the traditional interpretation of the actual limit, and a spurious concept which he rightly insisted does not exist — and defining ω as larger than any natural number. For ω is the lowest *ordinal* number: a number expressing the regular order of the entire sequence of natural numbers. The apparent paradox — that ω is not the largest element in ν and yet is the first number following the entire sequence ν — is supposed to disappear when we recognise the categorial distinction we are dealing with. Whatever the merits of his objection to this argument, one can at any rate sympathise with Wittgenstein's feeling that there was a certain amount of 'abracadabra' going on here (PR §144). Indeed, far more than that, for we can already see how the argument represents an illicit attempt to introduce the relationship between ω and ν as one governed by '>' in such a way that ω both is and is not $>$ ν. But if there is a type distinction involved which licenses the assertion that 'ω $>$ ν', then by the same token ω $>$ ν must mean something categorially different than $n + 1 > n$. Somehow this point was lost in the tangled undergrowth of the technical apparatus of the *Grundlagen* argument, and unfortunately, remained buried in the revised *Beiträge* exposition.

Cantor introduced the 'first principle of generation' — the successive addition of units — to define the '>' relation for the infinite natural number series. In order to establish that '>' holds between the transfinite ordinal numbers and the finite natural numbers, Cantor then introduced the 'second principle of generation', which stipulates that for any boundless series (with no largest element) there exists a least (ordinal) number which is larger than any number of this set: 'If any definite succession of defined whole real numbers exists, for which there is no largest, then a new number is created by means of this second principle of generation which is thought of as the *limit* of those numbers, i.e., it is defined as the next number larger than all of them.'[13]

On Wittgenstein's criticism this principle merely stipulates that the relation between ω and the natural numbers is to be characterised by the same symbol — '>' — which we use to describe the relation which governs the rule-ordered generation of the natural numbers; but this arbitrary convention hardly serves to give this new relation the same meaning which '>' signifies among the natural numbers. The meaning of the concept is defined by the totality of rules governing its use within the particular *Beweis-system* in which it occurs. Given the fundamental distinction between natural and 'transfinite' *Beweissysteme*, it is clear that the totality of rules governing the use of such expressions (i.e. the meaning of such expressions) is *ipso facto* different for the two systems.

The second principle of generation was also inadequate for Cantor's purposes, for it only served to establish that ω is '>' ν; it does not entail that '>' holds among the transfinite ordinal numbers. To establish this, Cantor reapplied the first principle of generation to the series which has ω as its first (least) number. Alternate application of the two principles then yields the series:

$$\omega, \omega + 1, \ldots \omega + \nu \ldots$$
$$2\omega, 2\omega + 1, \ldots 2\omega + \nu \ldots$$

.

.

$$\omega^2, \omega^2 + 1, \ldots \omega^2 + \nu \ldots$$

.

.

.

$$\nu_0 \omega^\mu + \nu_1 \omega^{\mu-1} + \ldots + \nu_\mu.$$

In other words, ω is the ordinal number for one progression (e.g. 1,2,3,4,5 ...) while 2ω is the ordinal number for two progressions (e.g. 1,3,5,7 ... $2n + 1$; 2,4,6,8 ... $2n$) and $\omega + 2$ is a 'larger' serial number than $\omega + 1$ (e.g. the series '1,3,5,6,7, ... n ... 2,4,' > '1,3,4,5, ... n ... 2').

The trouble with this account is obviously that $\omega + 2$ is not $>$ $\omega + 1$ in the way that $n + 1$ is $>$ n (i.e. in the sense of possessing greater magnitude). For $\omega + 2$ does not contain more units than $\omega + 1$; $1 + \omega = \omega$, while $\omega + 1 = (\omega + 1)$. It is no coincidence that, when he expounded this argument in *Introduction to Mathematical Philosophy*, Russell explained: 'The serial numbers of these various series are $\omega + 1$, $\omega + 2$, $\omega + 3$, ... 2ω. Each of these numbers is "greater" than any of its predecessors, in the following sense: — One serial number is said to be "greater" than another if any series having the first number contains a part having the second number, but no series having the second number contains a part having the first number.'[14] But inverted commas cannot absolve the strain thus created. The reasoning underlying this ambivalent interpretation of '$>$' is that a progressive expansion of a rule-governed series is somehow *equivalent* to the 'larger than' relation. The problem with this assumption, however, is that while '$>$' is indeed a symbol for such a rule-governed expansion, it specifically deals with the addition of units in order of increasing magnitude. We cannot, therefore, apply '$>$' to just any ascending series; after all, we would hardly wish to describe C# as 'larger than' C$^+$! Nor, for that matter, is $\omega + 2$ '$>$' $\omega + 1$ in the way that ω is supposed to be '$>$' ν. And it is difficult to see any way in which e.g. $\omega^2 + \nu$ is '$>$' $\omega + 1$. Finally, 2ω is not '$>$' ω in the way that ω is 'larger than' ν. For 2ω is formed by the second principle of generation, and therefore by definition has no immediate predecessor. It is difficult, to say the least, to keep track of all the different relations that are operating here, all under the same guise of '$>$'.

In order to realise the idea that the '$>$' relation holds for the transfinite numbers Cantor introduced a third principle, the 'principle of limitation'. This defines a *class* of transfinite ordinals according to the criterion of *power*: all those transfinite ordinals that form a series with the same power belong to the same class (e.g. the first number class is defined by the criterion that they form a denumerably infinite series of transfinite ordinals). However, this explanation in terms of *power* cannot do the work which Cantor demanded of it, since it does not confirm that any transfinite number is larger than another, but rather — because powers have been segregated from the start — it merely serves to establish that different classes of transfinite ordinals possess different powers. There is simply no mechanism to tie this in with the '$>$' relation, or even, at a more profound level, with the concept of magnitude. This difficulty led Cantor in the *Beiträge* to define all cardinal numbers as powers, thus enabling him to explain '$>$' in terms of a single relation that holds internally between the transfinite and the finite cardinal number series. Before examining this argument, however, it is important to note how the original version was led to violate *Beweissysteme* distinctions precisely because it sought to establish the nature of the *extension* provided by the transfinite numbers in terms of the 'larger than' relation holding between the two types of number.

What exactly does it mean to 'add' 1 to ω; how can we add a natural number to an ordinal? Of course, that does not mean that '$\omega + 1, \omega + 2, \ldots \omega + \nu \ldots$' is not a rule-governed series, with the arbitrary symbols $\omega + 1 \ldots$ used to express this series, and thus bearing no relation to the natural numbers. And *qua* series we might perhaps discern a parallel between this rule and the same '$>$'relation that governs the natural numbers. But to be a rule-governed series hardly amounts to being a series governed by the same relation! Moreover, we can no more say that $\omega + 1$ is larger than n than we can say that $+ 7$ is larger than 6. The *Beiträge* shift to defining cardinal numbers as 'powers' appears to overcome this obstacle by stipulating that the finite and transfinite numbers in effect belong to the same 'extended' system. But this artificial manoeuvre is hardly sufficient to remove the *Beweissysteme* confusions which Wittgenstein discerned lying at the heart of transfinite number theory, any more than stipulating that the integers and the whole numbers are all part of the Real numbers would enable us to subtract 6 from $+ 7$ (cf. Chapter 8). Thus, the terms of reference introduced in the *Grundlagen* remained to undermine all future attempts to elucidate the manner in which the existence of the transfinite numbers is every bit as 'real' as that of the natural numbers.

The issue at stake here does not concern the psychologistic overtones of Cantor's definition of transfinite numbers in terms of powers.[15] This aspect of the problem had already been dealt with by Frege, and we might just as easily approach the matter by considering Frege's alternative explanation in terms of 'extensions of a concept'. Wittgenstein's criticisms are concentrated on Cantor's argument in §2 of *Beiträge*, where he defined the relations of 'greater than' and 'lesser than' for cardinal numbers in terms of the comparability of their corresponding powers. With this premise in place Cantor could then define the finite/infinite number system as a comprehensive and 'continuous' system that could be seen to rest on a unified ontological foundation. The definition explained how the 'actual infinite' — represented by the transfinite numbers — was constructed on the basis of the generalisation of the concept of a finite number. He employed two principal arguments to establish the demarcation between the finite and the transfinite cardinal numbers. After defining the finite numbers inductively as the successive addition of units Cantor then invoked the principle that, whereas by definition '$n + 1 \aleph_0 \, n$', '$\aleph_0 + 1 = \aleph_0$', thus indicating that $\aleph_0$ could not possibly be a finite cardinal number. (The precise account is somewhat more complicated than this, in so far as Cantor based his argument on his 'principle of abstraction'. Thus, he defined a set as finite if 'it arises from one original element by successive addition of new elements in such a way that the original element can be retrieved by successively removing in reverse order the elements of M'.[16] Wittgenstein would, of course, agree with this entirely; the proof does indeed suffice to establish that $\aleph_0$ cannot be thought of in terms of the *finite number Beweissystem*!).

The next step of the argument, however, introduced the move which transgresses this grammatical boundary. In order to establish that '$\aleph_0 > n$', Cantor argued that an infinite set can be placed in one–one correspondence with a proper subset, whereas a finite set cannot; hence the power of an infinite set is greater than (in terms of 'more units') that of a finite set. Therefore, transfinite cardinal numbers are larger than finite cardinal numbers. The argument is a simple application, therefore, of the definition of cardinal number in terms of power: 'Since a "unit" arises from every single element *m*, if one disregards its character, the cardinal number M is also a definite set, comprised of nothing but units.'[17] Wittgenstein's criticism of this argument rested firmly on the logico-syntactical distinction between *finite class/totality* and *infinite class/boundless series*. Cantor's argument proceeds on the assumption that the power/cardinal number of an 'infinite class' is categorially the same as that of a finite class. But this is the very issue which is under dispute. Moreover, there could not be a prior proof of this assumption, for it amounts to nothing less than a *Beweissysteme* confusion, and thus the attempted proof that $\aleph_0$ is larger than n is unintelligible. But if this is meaningless, then so too is Cantor's definition of an infinite class as a class that can be correlated with a proper subset (i.e. the well-known definition of 'Dedekind Infinity'). Wittgenstein's critique has thus burgeoned into a formidable assault on the fundamental ideas underlying higher number theory.

Coming to Grips with the Irrational

Wittgenstein's discussion of 'Dedekind Infinity' walks the same tightrope between clarification and reconstruction as all his other assaults on the bastions of the philosophy of mathematics; and the

language he adopted remains just as highly charged. 'In the superstition that $m = 2n$ correlates a class with its subclass', he declared,
'we merely have yet another case of ambiguous grammar' (PR
§141). 'Superstition' is a portentous term; as in the philosophy of
language, it signifies Wittgenstein's conviction that a piece of
metaphysics has resulted from conceptual confusion. In this case,
'it all hangs on the syntax of reality and possibility. $m = 2n$ contains the *possibility of correlating any number* with another, but
doesn't correlate all numbers with others' (PR §141). In other
words, Wittgenstein's invitation here is not to probe the soundness
of 'Dedekind Infinity' on quasi-epistemological grounds, but
rather, to scrutinise its logical grammatical standing on the basis of
the categorial distinction between finite totalities and infinite
series. For '$m = 2n$' must mean something entirely different in
infinite as opposed to finite contexts: 'Does the relation $m = 2n$
correlate the class of all numbers with one of its subclasses? No. It
correlates any arbitrary number with another, and in that way we
arrive at infinitely many pairs of classes, of which one is correlated
with the other, but which are *never* related as class and subclass.
Neither is this infinite process itself in some sense or other such a
pair of classes' (PR §141).

Accordingly, we arrive at the same conclusion in this investigation as was drawn in the discussion of 'infinity': '$m = 2n$ points
along the number series, and if we add "to infinity", that simply
means that it doesn't point at an object a definite distance away'
(PR §141). Thus Wittgenstein described '$m = 2n$' in the identical
terms as the symbol for the infinite series: it is an induction
'pointing' in the same manner as $(1, x, x + 1)$ along the infinite
number series. The Dedekind/Cantor definition of an 'infinite set'
violated the barrier between boundless series and totality because it
employed generality in place of induction. If we are to rectify the
confusions created by this *Beweissyteme*-transgression, therefore,
we must be careful how we interpret '$m = 2n$' when it is applied to
infinite series. In the latter context 'It is less misleading to say "m
= 2n allows the possibility of correlating every time with another"
than to say "m = 2n correlates all numbers with others". But here
too the grammar of the meaning of the expression "possibility of
correlation" has to be learnt' (PG 466). The solution, that is, must
be to cease talking in terms of magnitude, and confine ourselves
instead to expressions which pertain to limitless operations.

The implications of this argument are far-reaching: with this criticism Wittgenstein saw opening up before him a vast expanse of established philosophico-mathematical thought which rests on this venerable foundation. In number theory the idea can be traced directly back to 'Galileo's paradox': a fact which provides yet another example of the hazards inherent in the use of *reductio*.[18] In *Bridges to Infinity*, Michael Guillen describes how 'in his *Dialogues Concerning Two New Sciences*, Galileo expressed his belief that a three-inch line contains just as many points — an infinite number — as a line twice as long. He accepted the paradox as might a person for whom the universe would be no more or less accessible were it one-half or twice as large.'[19] Thus are an author's intentions lost in the mists of time. For Galileo had actually set out to show that 'the attributes "larger," "smaller," and "equal," have no place either in comparing infinite quantities with each other or in comparing infinite with finite quantities.'[20] To demonstrate this, he effected a one–one correspondence between the natural numbers and their squares in order to show that 'There are as many squares as there are numbers because they are just as numerous as their roots, and all the numbers are roots.'[21] Yet this conferred an inexplicable puzzle: the latter series certainly appears to be 'smaller' than the former — 'at the outset we said there are many more numbers than squares, since the larger portion of them are not squares'[22] — so how could the interstitial sequence of squares possibly be as 'large' as the sequence of the natural numbers? His conclusion, however — *contra* subsequent developments — was that 'the attributes "equal," "greater," and "less," are not applicable to infinite, but only to finite, quantities'.[23] The parallels between this argument and Wittgenstein's approach some 300 years later are obviously striking; all that prevented it from emerging as a perfect forerunner was Galileo's enduring commitment to the epistemological framework which had inspired so much of the confusion in the first place. For he concluded from this argument that, since the infinite cannot be viewed in terms of magnitude, it must remain ineffable: 'This is one of the difficulties which arise when we attempt, with our finite minds, to discuss the infinite, assigning to it those properties which we give to the finite and limited.'[24]

The mathematical world emerged characteristically eager to assimilate this latest paradox. A century later Leibniz extended Galileo's findings: since every number can be doubled, the number of even numbers must be the same as the number of numbers altogether: a clear example of a whole being no greater than a part of itself.[25] Perhaps the landmark in the evolution of this theory was Bolzano's posthumous *Paradoxien des Unendlichen* (1851), where both the existence of categorematic (actual) infinite collections and the theme that a part of an infinite collection is equal in number to the whole were expressly defended. Rather than scrutinising the intelligibility of applying the attributes of magnitude to the infinite, mathematicians were more than happy to embrace these paradoxes as evidence of the recondite nature of the infinite. In particular, there was virtually no deliberation over the fundamental step which occurred in Galileo's paradox: the assumption that the correspondence:

$$1,2,3, \ldots$$
$$| \quad | \quad |$$
$$1,4,9, \ldots$$

manifests that there are *just as many* squares as natural numbers. Yet what exactly licenses this inference? All that Galileo had actually demonstrated was that we can formulate a law for pairing off members of two infinite series; in Wittgenstein's words, 'a rule for generating infinitely many pairs'. To conclude that this constitutes a procedure for determining whether two infinite series contain the *same number of elements* builds into the argument from the outset the very point that should be under dispute: the question whether a concept which has a specific meaning in connection with finite totalities can carry its sense over unchanged into an infinite setting.

Proceeding from Galileo onwards, therefore, the paradoxes have multiplied on the basis of the very first move of his argument: given that correspondence establishes equinumerosity regardless of any finite/infinite distinction, how can the series of squares be as 'large' as the series of natural numbers? It is unfortunate that the paradox should have proved more beguiling than Galileo's qualms, but hardly surprising. For while Galileo may have intended to extirpate this transgression, by remaining tethered to an epistemological framework which countenances 'infinite quantities' he undermined his own insight, thereby inspiring the development of the theory which culminates in the view that 'Galileo's paradox is regularised by observing that the phenomenon it describes is a distinguishing characterisitic of an infinite set. An infinite set is, simply, a set which can be put into one-to-one correspondence with a proper subset of itself.'[26] Remove the confusion which treats infinite series as if they were finite totalities, however, and it no longer makes sense to speak of one 'infinite extension' being 'larger' than another, let alone of the 'infinite class' that is larger than all other 'infinite classes'. Dedekind's formal definition of an infinite class, however, seemed to provide mathematicians with the rationale for regarding' equi-numerous' as meaning exactly the same thing when used in either finite or infinite contexts, but yielding different results in each case, as one would intuitively expect. Two classes are equinumerous if a one–one correspondence exists between them, but for 'infinite classes' we are able to discern a one–one correspondence between the set itself and one of its proper subsets. Hence, one and the same criterion establishes what constitutes finite and infinite classes, what differentiates them, and finally, demonstrates why infinite classes are 'larger than' finite classes. A set L which can be placed in one-one correspondence with a subset of M but not with M itself is 'smaller than' M, while two infinite sets that can be placed in one–one correspondence with one another are both the same, 'infinitely large', size. They are both *countable* — an expression which explicitly betrays the *Beweissysteme*-strains which Wittgenstein detected here; they can be placed in one–one correspondence with the set of natural numbers.

Dedekind's definition of 'infinite set' was supposed to be established solely by the criterion of one–one correspondence, but it could only attain this goal on the basis of the prior assumption that it is *totalities* rather than *processes* that are being correlated. Thus Wittgenstein attacked Dedekind's conception on the grounds that his argument depends on the hidden premise that we can establish whether one–one correspondences exist between infinite series in *exactly the same way* as for finite totalities: 'The defect (circle) in Dedekind's explanation of the concept of infinity lies in its application of the concept "all" in the formal implication that holds independently — if one may put it like this — of the question whether a finite or an infinite number of objects falls under its con-cepts' (PR §130). If we are to insist that the same procedure establishes the presence or absence of equinumerosity in each case, then it can obviously only be on the understanding that we have not given the term a new meaning when speaking of infinite series. But we cannot correlate the members of two infinite series in the way in which this holds for the members of two finite classes: 'If I make the attempt with an infinite class — but already that is a piece of nonsense, for if it is infinite, I cannot make an attempt to coordinate it. — What we call "correlation of all the members of a class with others" in the case of a finite class is something quite different from what we, e.g., call a correlation of all cardinal numbers with all rational numbers' (PG 464). That is, the meaning of 'correlation' must undergo a radical shift commensurate with the move from finite to infinite contexts: 'The two correlations, or what one means by these words in the two cases, belong to different logical types. An infinite class is not a class which contains more members than a finite one, in the ordinary sense of the word "more". If we say that an infinte number if greater than a finite one, that doesn't make the two comparable, because in that statement the word "greater" *hasn't the same meaning* as it has say in the proposition $5 > 4$!' (PG 464).

The fundamental problem here is once again that, as we saw in Chapter 4, you cannot base the concept of number on that of equinumerosity. It is hardly surprising, therefore, that the notion of 'infinite sets' should have stemmed from this logico-syntactical transgression, thus demanding an operation which it is logically impossible to carry out in order to arrive at a notion which it is logically impossible to grasp. Strip the idea of magnitude from this picture, however, and what you are left with is simply a rule for mapping: full-stop. This provides no basis for the notion of magnitude to enter on its back, however; for the two concepts are not *internally* related. Thus, as Russell pointed out, to say that a mapping established that 'There are as many α's as β's' conveys no information about *how many* that is: 'It does not tell us, in the way in which counting does, *what* number of terms a collection has.'[27] But by that very token it bars us from Russell's premise that it 'tells us, to begin with, whether two collections have the same number of terms, or, if not, which is the greater'.[28] Or at least, it bars us from the implicit *mathematical* use to which Russell intended this premise; for the notions of '$=$' and '$>$' cannot be divorced from their mathematical context. Hence, while 'this method enables us to discover whether some other collection that may be mentioned has more or fewer terms',[29] it does not tell us *how many more* or *how many less*. So far all we have obtained is an empirical truth which, as such, is condemned to remain defeasible. To move from the *contingent* truth that 'There are as many α's as β's' to the *necessary* — mathematical — truth that 'the number of the set of α's = the number of the set of β's', we need an arithemtical rule which does not yet exist. Hence it is doubly misguided to conclude that 'in this way we can find any number of collections each of which has just as many terms as there are finite numbers';[30] this sins against both the correlation/calculation and the finite totality/infinite series distinctions.

The core of Wittgenstein's criticism, therefore, was a grammatical clarification of the twinned concepts *one–one correspondence* and *equinumerosity* which lie at the heart of Cantorean transfinite set theory. In terms of finite arithmetic, if we can correlate two totalities so as to achieve a one–one correspondence between the members of the two sets then we can be certain that the two sets contain the same number of elements; but only because the rules of arithmetic establish the criterion for what constitutes miscounting. That is, the rules of arithmetic provide, as it were, the missing link between one–one correspondence and equinumerosity: it is because the number of the two sets is equal that we can be *certain* that there is a one–one correspondence (cf. Chapter 7). Hence it is one thing to argue that 'If there existed some country in which, for one reason or another, it was impossible to take a census, but in which it was known that every man had a wife and every woman a husband, then (provided polygamy was not a national institution) we should know, without counting, that there were exactly as many men as there were women in that country, neither more nor less',[31] and quite another to conclude that 'If every term of a collection can be hooked on to a number, and all the finite numbers are used once, and only once, in the process, then our collection must have just as many terms as there are finite numbers.'[32] As it stands, the former example represents an empirical generalisation which, if true, is contingently so; for whatever method was used to verify that this country was free of divorce as well — short, *ex hypothesi*, of counting — it would be one which, like the Gestalt, could not exclude the possibility of doubt. Yet in the latter argument Russell has covertly introduced the illicit premises that the natural numbers can be treated as a totality and that the relation between this collection and its transfinite doppelganger is internal. For only thus could he arrive at the conclusion that 'This is the general method by which the numbers of infinite collections are defined';[33] i.e. that $m = 2n$.

Far from clearing up the muddle precipitated by Galileo's paradox, therefore, Dedekind's theory of infinity merely compounded the trouble by systematising the original source of confusion. Dedekind could hardly deny that there is something peculiar about saying that there are as many squares as there are natural numbers. Or at any rate, it certainly seems that some 'infinite sets', as they have been defined, must be 'larger' than others. The solution must thus lie in the fact that 'infinite sets' possess different properties, foreign to finite sets, which explains the divergence in their behaviour from that of finite sets.[34] We soon begin to appreciate why Wittgenstein remonstrated: 'It's almost unbelievable, the way in which a problem gets completely barricaded in by the misleading expressions which generation upon generation throw up for miles around it, so that it becomes virtually impossible to get at it' (PG 466). For Dedekind's theory was forced to adopt the following methodology: first, it assumed that, the appearance of paradox notwithstanding, the same concepts can be applied indiscriminately in finite and infinite circumstances. But then the argument was forced to clear away the air of incongruity thus engendered, so it continued: these confusions are only due to our misguided attempt to treat 'infinite sets' in the same manner as finite. Hence we need to stipulate further properties, unique to 'infinite sets', to explain what — from a finite point of view — strike us as anomalies. These properties are provided by such concepts as *density* and *continuity* (*infra*). Admittedly, these may not satisfy Galileo's apprehensions about treating the infinite series of squares and natural numbers as equal in size, but it does salvage the much more important conviction — which is integral to Cantor's vision of higher mathematics — that the set of real numbers must be *larger* than the set of rationals.

Nevertheless, it still leaves a trail of paradoxical results which strain the limits of intuition. For, given the definition of magnitude in terms of 'countability', it turns out that the 'set' of rational numbers is no 'larger' than that of the integers, since both are 'countable'. And one would expect that the cardinal number of the continuum — of the 'set of all real numbers' — would be larger than the cardinal number of a segment of the continuum. But, notoriously, the cardinal number of each turns out to be c. Furthermore, it would surely seem to be the case that a two-dimensional set of points (e.g. the number of points in a square) must have a cardinal number larger than c, but here also the two sets have the same size. It was this last 'discovery' which prompted Cantor to write to Dedekind, in tones highly reminiscent of Simplicio's perplexity in Galileo's *Two New Sciences*: 'I see it, but I don't believe it! ... What wonderful power there is in the ordinary real (rational and irrational) numbers, since one is in a position to determine uniquely, with a single coordinate, the elements of a p-dimensional continuous space.'[35] As with the initial response to Galileo's paradox, there was no thought given to the possibility that the appearance of paradox is illusory because the problem rests on the illicit use of finite-bound concepts for infinite series.

It would take us too far outside the scope of the present work — where our primary concern is to elucidate the anti-metaphysical focus of Wittgenstein's approach to the philosophy of mathematics — to digest the full implications of the various objections which he raised against this argument. For to do proper justice to the subject we would need, at the very least, to trace the history of the Continuum Hypothesis from Cantor to Cohen.[36] It does bear remarking, however, that the assaults on platonism in general and Cantorean transfinite number theory in particular which Wittgenstein had launched demanded a coordinated pincer attack on the Dedekind/Cantor theory of the continuum. For, not the least of the problems here is the manner in which the ideas infused in the latter theory can be used to bolster the former doctrines. Wittgenstein warned that 'it may sound trivial if I now say that the mistake in the set-theoretical approach consists time and again in treating laws and enumerations (lists) as essentially the same kind of thing and arranging them in parallel series so that one fills in gaps left by another' (PG 461). Since it was just this theme which inspired and in turn was consolidated by the Dedekind/Cantor theory of the continuum, Wittgenstein had no choice but to show why 'The confusion in the concept of the "actual infinite" arises from the unclear concept of irrational number, that is, from the fact that logically very different things are called "irrational numbers" without any clear limits being given to the concept' (PG 471).

Wittgenstein's discussion of irrational numbers has succeeded in antagonising platonists and intuitionists alike. For both are the targets of his attack, although why Wittgenstein should have chosen to provide the two schools with a common cause is not at all clear from the fragments gathered in *Remarks on the Foun-*

dations of Mathematics. Pasquale Frascolla has drawn attention to
the dual nature of Wittgenstein's thought in 'The Constructivist
Model in Wittgenstein's Philosophy of Mathematics', yet he by no
means finds the two sides of Wittgenstein's argument equally compelling. 'The attack on the classical theory of real numbers', he
maintains, 'can be considered fairly discounted, considering the
anti-platonistic premises of the Austrian philosopher. Much more
interesting is the fact that Wittgenstein's criticism also extends to
the typically intuitionistic procedure of generating real numbers by
means of unlimited sequences of free choices.'[37] There may be an
element of truth to this claim, given that Wittgenstein's criticism of
the Dedekind/Cantor theory of the continuum proceeds directly
from the attack on the platonist — extensional — picture of infinity
which we examined in the preceding section. But the two aspects
of Wittgenstein's approach cannot be hived off from one another
in this manner. Indeed, what is perhaps most interesting about
Wittgenstein's argument is the fact that *one and the same theme*
was ultimately meant to dispose of both the platonist and the
intuitionist conception of irrational numbers.

Dedekind and Cantor were both preoccupied — and openly
shared their results — with the problem of how to distinguish
between the real and the rational numbers. The conceptual
approach each adopted was considerably influenced by Liouville's
discovery of the 'transcendental irrationals'. The existence of
'transcendental' or 'non-algebraic' numbers can be traced at least
as far back as Euler, who described them in such terms because
they 'transcend the power of algebraic methods'. But the question
of whether there are any 'transcendental irrationals' remained
open until Liouville showed in 1844 that any number of the form:

$$a_1/10^1 + a_2/10^{2.1} + a_3/10^{3.2.1} + a_4/10^{4.3.2.1} + \ldots$$

where the numerators can be any natural number up to 9 is
transcendental. The discovery provided Dedekind and Cantor with
the rudiments that they needed to account for the 'density' of the
real number continuum. For Liouville had established that, for any
given rational number interval (a,b) we can construct 'infinitely
many' transcendental numbers between the two points. Thus, the
rationals are supposed to be 'dense' — between any two rationals
there is always a third — and like the algebraic numbers, they are
'countable'; but the rationals are not 'continuous'.

Dedekind emphasised in 'Continuity and Irrational Numbers' that his definition of irrational numbers had been guided by the picture of geometrical continuity: viz. 'If all points of the straight line fall into two classes such that every point of the first class lies to the left of every point of the second class, then there exists one and only one point which produces this division of all points into two classes, this severing of the straight line into two portions.'[38] Dedekind's method of defining the irrationals by 'cuts' on the rationals assumed *pari ratione* that, given the set of all rational numbers, it is possible to divide it into two subsets M_1 and M_2 — called the 'lower' and 'upper' sections of the cut — in such a way that every member of M_2 is larger than every member of M_1. Dedekind defined such a system as 'continuous' if, for every such cut, there is an element of the system which is either the maximum of the lower section M_1 or the minimum of the upper section M_2. There are thus just three possibilities for every cut on the set of all rational numbers: (i) there is a largest member of M_1 (e.g. if M_1 consists of all rational numbers ≤ 1 and $M_2 > 1$); (ii) there is a smallest member of M_2 (e.g. if M_1 consists of all rational numbers $<$ and M_2 of all rational numbers ≥ 1); (iii) there is neither a largest element in M_1 nor a smallest element in M_2 (e.g. if M_1 consists of all negative rational numbers, 0, and all positive rationals $< \sqrt{2}$, and M_2 of all rationals $> \sqrt{2}$; $M_1 + M_2 =$ the set of all rational numbers, therefore, since there is not rational number $= \sqrt{2}$). When this last case occurs (i.e. the cut produces two classes in which there is no largest element in M_1 or smallest element in M_2) the cut is stipulated to be an irrational number.[39] Hence the irrational number system is not continuous, since for every cut there is an element — either a rational or an irrational number — which is the largest member of M_1 or the smallest member of M_2. But the real number system — rationals and irrationals — is continuous, since for every cut there is an element — either a rational or an irrational number — which is the largest member of M_1 or the smallest member of M_2. 'Of the greatest importance' is thus 'the fact that in the straight line L there are infinitely many points which correspond to no rational number';[40] i.e. the real number continuum must be 'filled out' by the set of irrational numbers: the algebraic and non-algebraic numbers that had already been shown to exist.

Whereas Cantor criticised Dedekind for adopting a species of 'cuts' that were intrinsically alien to analysis, Wittgenstein complained on the far more general grounds that 'The Dedekind cut proceeds as if it were clear what was meant when one says: There are only three cases: either R has a last member and L a first, or, etc. In truth none of these cases can be conceived (or imagined)' (PR §173). Wittgenstein based his harsh judgement on what he identified as the theory's two interrelated infractions of the grammatical rules governing 'infinity'. The first arose from Dedekind's illicit assumption that *the set of all rational numbers* can be divided into two classes: 'if someone is dumbfounded by our talk of a class of points that lie to the right of a given point and have no beginning, and says: give us an example of such a class — we trot out the class of rational numbers; but that isn't a class of points in the original sense' (PG 461). That is, we cannot *proceed* from the assumption that the real number continuum can be defined as the collection of all real numbers: a confusion bred by considering a straight line segment as a collection of all its points: 'We don't say "among *all* its points, there is only one at which it intersects the straight line"; no, we only talk about *one* point, so to speak, about one that runs along the straight line, but not about one among all the points of the line. The straight line isn't *composed* of points' (PR §172). To compound the trouble, Dedekind's argument thence relied on an indiscriminate use of '>' and '<' which, as we can see from the above account, is similar to the misapplication which we examined in the preceding section: 'Here again, the difficulty arises from the formation of mathematical pseudo-concepts. For instance, when we say that we can arrange the cardinal numbers, but not the rational numbers, in a series according to their size, we are unconsciously presupposing that the concept of an ordering by size does have a sense *for rational numbers*, and that it turned out on investigation that the ordering was impossible (which presupposes that the *attempt* is thinkable)' (PG 461). It was solely for these reasons of logical syntax, therefore, that Wittgenstein concluded: 'The explanation of the Dedekind cut pretends to be clear when it says: there are 3 cases: either the class R has a first member and L no last member etc. In fact two of these 3 cases cannot be imagined, unless the words "class," "first member," "last member," altogether change the everyday meanings they are supposed to have retained' (PG 460). That is, (i) and (ii) from Dedekind's three possibilities are unintelligible and (iii) is admitted, but only in the sense that 'There is neither a largest element in M_1 nor a smallest element in M_2', in so far as the concepts 'large' and 'small' have no bearing in regards to the rational numbers.

The deep-rooted conceptual confusions lurking here are a direct result, Wittgenstein insisted, of the model of a 'continuous' straight line which inspired Dedekind's picture of the real number continuum: 'A misleading picture: "The rational points lie close together on the number-line"' (PG 460).[41] But why should Dedekind be denied a latitude which seems to be not only sanctioned, but indeed, demanded by Wittgenstein's account of mathematical conjectures (cf. chapter 3)? After all, Dedekind himself warned that a satisfactory foundation for the irrational numbers would have to be purely arithmetical: 'By vague remarks upon the unbroken connection in the smallest parts obviously nothing is gained; the problem is to indicate a precise characteristic of continuity that can serve as the basis for valid deductions.'[42] The geometrical origins of this concept of continuity are not the problem here, however; rather, it is that 'Originally the geometrical illustrations were *applications of Analysis*. Where they cease to be this they can be wholly misleading. ... The idea of a "cut" is one such dangerous illustration' (RFM V §29). Dangerous because 'The cut is an extensional image' (RFM V §34). That is, 'The misleading thing about Dedekind's conception is the idea that the real numbers are there spread out in the number line. They may be known or not; that does not matter. And in this way all that one needs to do is to cut or divide into classes, and one has dealt with them all' (RFM V §37).

Wittgenstein's fundamental objection, therefore, was that Dedekind's theory crossed over the boundary between heuristic and constitutive principles: 'The proof of Dedekind's theorem works with a picture which cannot justify *it*; which ought rather to be justified by the theorem' (RFM V §33). Both of the key terms, in Dedekind's theory — 'dense' and 'continuous' — reflect his desire to formalise the idea that there is a single global number system, comparable to a solid straight line, and that the absence of individual number-systems leaves 'gaps' in this comprehensive system, rendering it similar to a dotted line. It was thus the platonist foundation which sustains this picture which undermined Dedekind's theory: 'Supposing I cut at a place where there is no rational number. Then there *must* surely be approximations to this cut. But what does "closer to" mean here? *Closer* to what? For the time being I have nothing in the domain of number which I can approach' (PR §180). Despite the blatantly constructivist over-tones, however, this last point serves as an indicator that it is not just the classical definition, but the platonist picture which inspired both classical and intuitionist theories which is at issue. 'We are supposed to find that "between the everywhere dense rational points," there is still room for the irrationals (What balderdash!) What does a construction like that for $\sqrt{2}$ show? Does it show how there is yet room for this point between all the rational points? It shows that the point *yielded* by the construction, yielded by *this* construction, is *not rational*' (PG 460). The irrational number is supposed to 'fill the gap' left by the cut, but in order to generate this thesis Dedekind was forced to treat the extension created by the approximations as the definition of the number, which is the very converse of an arithmetical operation: 'Put geometrically: it's not enough that someone should — supposedly — determine a point ever more closely by narrowing down its whereabouts; we must be able to construct *it*' (PR §186). But then, this criticism can be applied to both platonist and intuitionist theories alike. Thus, even though Dedekind's cuts may have been superseded, this picture lingered on, bestowing similar confusions in its wake to those which afflicted Dedekind's abortive definition of irrational numbers.

To see this, we must examine the origins of Wittgenstein's discussion of irrational numbers in *Philosophical Remarks*. The crux — and significantly, the start — of Wittgenstein's argument is contained in §179. We are first asked to imagine that 'we are throwing a two-sided die, such as a coin. I now want to determine a point of the interval A B by continually tossing the coin, and always bisecting the side prescribed by the throw: say: heads means I bisect the right-hand interval, tails the left-hand one'. We can see what he has in mind here in the diagram printed below:

Does this method 'describe the position of a point of the interval if

I say "It is *the* point which is approached indefinitely by bisection as prescribed by the endless tossing of the coin"?' The problem is that all we have is a random procedure for bisecting the line; so *a fortiori*, if we define a real number as the single point which is contained in all of these nested intervals, we should have to say that there can be a random procedure for defining a real number. The intriguing question which this opening point raises is simply: why should Wittgenstein have chosen to approach the topic with a tacit attack on the intuitionist conception of irrational numbers?

The answer is that it was not the intuitionist position *per se* which was being assailed here, but rather, the *picture* which gave rise to both platonist and intuitionist theories. The key to Wittgenstein's ensuing argument lies in the crucial theme that this 'operation is not an arithmetical one. (And the point which I call to my aid in my endless construction can't be given arithmetically at all.)' To be sure, 'At this point many people would say: it doesn't matter that the method was geometrical, it is only the resulting *extension* itself that is our goal.' But it is this very argument which led Wittgenstein to articulate what is clearly the central motif in his discussion of the irrational numbers: 'What is the analogue in arithmetic to the geometrical process of bisection? It must be the converse process: that of determining a point by a law. (Instead of the law by a point.)' That is, if we attempt to infer the law from the point, we have merely performed an experiment. It was for this reason that he told Waismann and Schlick that 'A freely developing sequence is in the first place something empirical. It is nothing but the numbers that I write down on paper' (WWK 83). To be an arithmetical construction, the extension must be determined by the law (PR §186), for the relation between a real number and its extension is *internal* not *external*: 'there isn't a dualism: the law and the infinite series obeying it; that is to say, there isn't something in logic like description and reality' (PR §180). Hence, 'This shows clearly that an irrational number isn't the extension of an infinite decimal fraction, that it's a law' (PR §181).

It is completely misguided, therefore, to suppose that 'the law which determines the values of the digits in the sequence $[\sqrt{2}]$ is by no means obvious. In fact, no explicit formula that determines the successive digits is known, although one may calculate as many digits as desired:

$$1^2 = 1 \ < \ 2 \ < \ 2^2 = 4$$
$$(1.4)^2 = 1.96 \ < \ 2 \ < \ (1.5)^2 = 2.25$$
$$(1.41)^2 = 1.9881 \ < \ 2 \ < \ (1.42)^2 = 2.0264$$
$$(1.414)^2 = 1.999396 \ < \ 2 \ < \ (1.415)^2 = 2.002225$$
$$(1.4142)^2 = 1.99996164 \ < \ 2 \ < \ (1.4143)^2 = 2.00024449\text{'}[43]$$

For 'There must first be the rules for the digits, and then — e.g. — a root is expressed in them' (PR §182). On Courant and Robbin's account, $\sqrt{2}$ must be deemed the result of an experiment — and as such a *number* — in as much as it appears as an extension bereft of a law. The problem here does not lie in $\sqrt{2}$, however, but rather, in the perspective from which Courant and Robbins have viewed the above sequence. Admittedly, 'The idea behind $\sqrt{2}$ is this: we look for a rational number which, multiplied by itself, yields 2. There isn't one. But there are those which in this way come close to 2 and there are always some which approach 2 more closely still' (PR §183). But 'for a real number, a construction and not merely a process of approximation must be conceivable' (PR §186). And in the case of $\sqrt{2}$, 'There is a procedure permitting me to approach 2 indefinitely closely. This procedure is itself something. And I call it a real number' (PR §183). That is, it just is the rule determining the above sequence which constitutes $\sqrt{2}$. The point of the above sequence, therefore, is not that it *determines* the law, but rather, that it *manifests* it: 'I must be able to write down a part of the series, in such a way that you can *recognize* the law. ... The approximations must themselves form what is *manifestly* a series. That is, the approximations themselves must obey a law' (PR §190).

This still leaves us, however, with a serious problem: 'the way the irrationals are introduced in textbooks always makes it sound as if what is being said is: Look, that isn't a rational number, but still there is a number there. But why then do we still call what *is* there "a number"?' (PR §191) The trouble is that it only 'makes sense to call a structure a number by analogy, if it is related to the rationals in ways which are analogous to (of the same multiplicity as) greater, less and equal to' (PR §191). But the crux of the theme that 'there are no gaps in mathematics' is that you cannot compare autonomous number systems, in which case it would be as unintelligible to say that '$\sqrt{2} < 2$' as '$2 < +3$' (cf. Chapter 8). Hence we need to bring the two numbers together into the same (viz. real) number system: 'To compare rational numbers with $\sqrt{2}$,

I have to square them. — They then assume the form of $\sqrt{a}$, where $\sqrt{a}$ is now an arithmetical operation' (PR §193). The problem now, however, is that the whole point of the preceding argument is that we cannot speak of an 'infinite extension' as being 'larger than' a finite or another 'infinite extension'. To see this, we need only consider the point that, while 'we can certainly tell that π and e are different from the difference in their *first* place', we could not say of two real numbers 'that they would be equal, if all their places were equal' (PR §187); for, of course, like the wayward pupil in the rule-following argument, there is no saying what mathematical surprise the next step in the expansion might bring (RFM V §9).

The solution to the dilemma closing in here is that 'The true expansion of a number is the one which permits a direct comparison with the rationals. If we bring a rational number into the neighbourhood of the law, the law must give a definite reaction to it' (PR §191). The essence of the law for $\sqrt{2}$ is that it enables us to say, *at any specific point*, whether it is $>$ $(1.4)^2$ and $<$ $(1.5)^2$, $>$ $(1.41)^2$ and $<$ $(1.42),^2$ etc. Thus, 'decimal expansion is a method of comparison with the rationals', but only if 'it is determined in advance how many places I must expand to in order to settle the issue' (PR §195). We cannot perform an experiment to find out whether or not a decimal expansion is periodic (PR §196); 'A number as the result of an arithmetical experiment, and so the experiment as the *description* of a number, is an absurdity. The experiment would be the description, not the *representation* of a number' (PR §196). To grasp a number as rational or irrational is to see from the rule whether or not the expansion is periodic. ('0.3 simply designate[s] an induction we have seen and not — an extension' (PR §199).) We cannot *discover* whether a number is rational or irrational, therefore (e.g. by an indefinite sequence of approximations): the law — not the expansion — must show whether a number is rational or irrational (PR §196). For 'Only what can be foreseen about a sequence of digits is essential to the real number' (PR §183).

The hardest part of this argument to come to terms with is that all we are concerned with here is the logical grammar of 'real number'. A real number is quite simply 'the *general method* of comparison with the rationals'; 'squaring a and seeing whether the result is greater or less than 2', for example, 'is a method' (PR §198). To grasp an irrational number is *ipso facto* to possess a method for comparing it to a rational number in the real number system, and 'developing the extension isn't such a method, since I can never know if or when it will lead to a decision. Expanding indefinitely isn't a method, even when it leads to a result of the comparison' (PR §198). This final point is absolutely crucial: Wittgenstein's argument in no way proscribes the use of 'arithmetical experiments': it only clarifies how such a process should be described. Once again, there is nothing to prevent the heuristic use of such empirical methods in order to prepare the ground for the *subsequent* construction of the rule for an irrational number. But 'If the question how F compares with a rational number has no sense, since all expansion still hasn't given us an answer, then this question also had no sense before we tried to settle the question at random by means of an extension' (PR §198). For 'A real number *yields* extensions, it is not an extension. A real number is: an arithmetical law which endlessly yields the places of a decimal fraction' (PR §186). Thus, whether you begin with the platonist premise that the extension exists *in nubibus*, or the intuitionist premise that we construct the extension by means of unlimited sequences of free choices, both theories suffer from the same misconception: viz. that the nested point determines the law, rather than the reverse.

We shall consider in further detail in Chapter 8 the normative basis for Wittgenstein's claim that 'There isn't any gap left open by the rational numbers that is filled up by the irrationals' (PG 460), and the reason why this fundamental theme was supposed to rout platonism from the philosophy of mathematics. For the moment, however, we must be clear that it was not irrational numbers *per se* — i.e. *qua* 'rules for the formation of an infinite decimal' (RFM VII 42) — that Wittgenstein was attacking; only the confusions engendered by the misleading — extensional — picture that the relation between a rule and its expansion can be external. The parallels between this theme and the discussion of rule-following which we examined in Chapter 1 are hardly incidental; for this argument provided yet a further impetus to Wittgenstein's growing awareness of the need to clarify the nature of the *internal* relation between a rule and its applications. It was for this reason that he stressed that 'You cannot say: two real numbers are identical, if all their places coincide. You cannot say: they are different, if they disagree in one of the places of their expansion' (PR §185). For how could you be *absolutely certain* that all of their places had coincided, or would continue to do so? You can only compare *rules* — not extensions — if you are to avoid the sceptical confusions outlined in Chapter 1; and thus 'Neither may we say: Two laws are identical in the case where they yield the same result at every stage. No, they are identical if it is of their essence to yield the same result, i.e. if they are identical' (PR §179).[44] Moreover, the theme that you can only compare a rule with a rule points to a related problem of a rather different order:

> The usual conception is something like this: it is true that the real numbers have a different multiplicity from the rationals, but you can still write the two series down alongside one another to begin with, and sooner or later the series of real numbers leaves the other behind and goes infinitely further on.
>
> But my conception is: you can only put finite series alongside one another and in that way compare them; there's no point in putting dots after these finite stretches (as signs that the series goes on to infinity). Furthermore, you can compare a law with a law, but not a law with *no* law. (PR §181)

It was this point which led Wittgenstein to suggest: 'if anyone tried day-in day-out "to put all irrational numbers into a series" we could say "Leave it alone; it means nothing; don't you see, if you established a series, I should come along with the diagonal series!" This might get him to abandon his undertaking. Well, that would be useful. And it strikes me as if this were the whole and proper purpose of this method' (RFM II §13).

The celebrated 'diagonal proof', Wittgenstein indicated, grew organically out of the confusions which are rampant here. In the final stage of his argument — which has attracted the most attention — Wittgenstein traced the route leading from Cantor's initial assumption that an infinite series can be *enumerated* to the extraordinary conclusion that 'infinite classes' can be arranged in an ascending hierarchy of increasing magnitude. With all the furore that has been aroused by Wittgenstein's criticisms of the concept of *denumerability*, it is seldom noticed that the argument rests on this prior attack. In fact, the previous objections suffice to establish the point he wished to make, and one suspects that Wittgenstein only discussed the 'diagonal proof' at such length in *Remarks on the Foundations of Mathematics* because it exemplifies the type of 'charm' which an ingenious mathematical proof can exert, leading us to embrace a wholly incoherent picture. For as he told his students in 1938:

> Cantor wrote how marvellous it was that the mathematician could in his imagination transcend all limits. I would do my utmost to show it is this charm that makes one do it. ... Regarding Cantor's proofs — I would try to show that it is this charm which makes the proof attractive. ... If I describe the surroundings of the proof, then you may see that the thing could have been expressed in an entirely different way; and then you see that the similarity of $\aleph_0$ and a cardinal number is very small. The matter can be put in a way which loses the charm it has for many people. (LA 28)

The final stage of this argument thus endeavoured, on the basis of this conceptual clarification, to challenge the interpretation rather than the cogency of the 'diagonal proof'.

The diagonal proof proceeds from the very confusions that Wittgenstein hoped to extirpate from the prose of transfinitary mathematics. Given that we can speak of the 'set of all real numbers' that fills the gap between the finite interval (0,1) on the real number continuum, the proof assumes that this set is denumerable: that we could label these real numbers with the integers a_1, a_2, a_3. ... This provided Cantor with the essential grounds to establish that the set of reals is 'larger than' the set of rationals. Thus, writing each real number as a non-terminating decimal, he produced the series:

$$a_1 = 0.a_{11}a_{12}a_{13} \ldots a_{1j} \ldots$$
$$a_2 = 0.a_{21}a_{22}a_{23} \ldots a_{2j} \ldots$$
$$a_n = 0.a_{n1}a_{n2}a_{n3} \ldots a_{nj} \ldots$$

In order to show that such a list could not possibly contain all of the real numbers that exist between the interval (0,1) he simply generated another real number which is not in the list by looking at the 'diagonal' digits:

$$a_{11}a_{22}a_{33} \ldots a_{nn}.$$

He then formed the decimal fraction $d_1 d_2 d_3 \ldots$ such that d_1 differs from a_{11}, d_2 differs from a_{22}, etc (e.g. he stipulated that $d_n =$

9 if $a_{nn} \neq 9$; $d_n = 1$ if $a_{nn} = 9$). On the basis of these decimal fractions he constructed the missing real number:

$$d = 0.b_1 b_2 b_3 \ldots b_i \ldots$$

Since 'd' could only be equal to an 'a_i' in the *denumerated* list if each digit in 'b' is the same as the corresponding digit in 'a_i', and then, since $b_i \neq a_i$ (since $b_i \neq a_{11}$) and $b \neq a_2$ (since $b_2 \neq a_{22}$), and in general $b \neq a_n$ (since $b_i \neq a_i$), he had demonstrated that the list could not possibly contain all of the real numbers between the interval (0,1).

A variation on this proof then establishes the general theorem that the class of all subclasses of a given class (the 'power set') has a higher cardinal number than the class itself. The cardinal number of the set of real numbers between (0,1) is said to be 'larger than' the cardinal number of the set of natural numbers (c is 'greater than' $\aleph_0$) because by definition an infinite class M is 'smaller than' L if M can be placed in one–one correspondence with a subset of L but not with L itself. Since this proof establishes that the set of real numbers is 'larger than' the set of rationals, the reals must include the irrationals as well as the rationals. So the diagonal proof also serves as an indirect proof of the existence of the irrationals. The proof of the infinitely ascending hierarchy of increasingly 'larger' transfinite numbers begins by defining a *power set* as the set of all subsets. By a similar procedure, Cantor demonstrated that there cannot be a one–one correspondence between elements of M and the elements of its power set L. So the final result of Cantor's proof purports to be a demonstration that we have an effective means for showing how, given any set, the set of all its subsets will always be of a greater power than that of the parent set itself, and the infinite sequence of transfinite numbers is itself limitless. Here Wittgenstein would — at least partially — agree: Cantor's proof does establish that the series of transfinite numbers is infinite (to say that it is boundless is redundant); but this has nothing to do with the concept of 'larger than' as this is understood for the finite cardinals.

The fundamental problem with the diagonal proof — disregarding any misgivings about the 'non-constructivity' of 'd' — lies in the supposition that the new real number that has been constructed demonstrates that the enumerated list could not possibly contain all of the real numbers that exist between the interval

(0,1). For we cannot speak of the 'set of all reals', whether this refers to a finite interval on the continuum or to the pseudo-concept of the 'set of reals' *in toto*. Nor can we understand what it means to assume that an infinite series is *denumerable*. Once again, therefore, we see the same pattern emerge that suffuses Wittgenstein's discussion of transfinite numbers: Cantor was quite right to claim that the set of reals is non-denumerable; the trouble is that this does not at all signify what he thought. It means that the reals — *qua* infinite series — are not capable of *enumeration*: a quality which they share with all infinite series. 'When people say "The set of all transcendental numbers is greater [than] that of algebraic numbers", that's nonsense. The set is of a different kind. It isn't "no longer" denumberable, it's simply not denumberable!' (PR §174).

Given that it is unintelligible to speak of 'all the real numbers', our task is to elucidate, in a non-finitary idiom, what exactly the diagonal proof accomplishes. To do this we must overlook the 'prose' of Cantor's theory; for 'The result of a calculation expressed verbally is to be regarded with suspicion. The *calculation* illumines the meaning of the expression in words. It is the *finer* instrument for determining the meaning. If you want to know what the verbal expression means, look at the calculation; not the other way about' (RFM II §7). Thus, the purpose of Wittgenstein's discussion was not to question the cogency of the diagonal proof; rather, it was to clarify what the procedure discloses, by looking at the proof itself. The real culprit is the finite totality/infinite series categorial confusion, as embodied in 'transfinite set theory'; hence Wittgenstein suggested that 'Here it is very useful to imagine the diagonal procedure for the production of a real number as having been well-known before the invention of set theory, and familiar even to school-children, as indeed might very well have been the case. For this changes the aspect of Cantor's discovery' (RFM II §17): i.e. it frees us from the fallacy that the concept of *enumeration* can be applied *mutatis mutandis* to the infinite real number series, thereby intimating how to respond to the question 'What can the concept "non-denumerable" be used for?' (RFM II §12). The importance of the diagonal proof should lie, therefore, in its bringing us to liberate ourselves from the categorial confusion that treats an infinite series in terms of magnitude (RFM II §§10-11). Admittedly, the diagonal proof has hitherto only had a baleful influence; but this need not be the case: 'If it were said: "Consideration of the diagonal procedure shews you that the *concept* 'real number' has much less analogy with the concept 'cardinal number' than we, being misled by certain analogies, are inclined to believe", that would have a good and honest sense. But just the *opposite* happens: one pretends to compare the "set" of real numbers in magnitude with that of cardinal numbers. The difference in kind between the two conceptions is represented, by a skew form of expression, as difference of extension' (RFM App II §3).

The obvious Cantorean response to Wittgenstein's attack is that it confuses the 'potential' with the 'actual infinite'. For Cantor was careful to stress that there is a type-restriction between the two 'kinds' of infinity;[45] in a letter to Harnack he insisted: 'My conceptual grasp of the transfinite excludes properly and from the beginning "process", since this denotes a "change". According to me transfinite = definite, greater than anything finite of the same kind, but nevertheless still capable of increase.'[46] Wittgenstein's objections might be applicable to an hypostatisation of the 'potential infinite', therefore, but they are totally disarmed by the shift to the latter notion. But the starting-point for Wittgenstein's argument is that Cantor's putative type-distinction is in itself illusory: it misconstrues the hardness of the logical demarcation between finite and infinite (viz. between *totality* and *process*) and thus arrives at the fallacy that infinity, in the guise of the 'quasi-infinite' or 'transfinite', can *per impossible* be treated as a quantity, 'greater than anything finite' and 'still capable of increase'. Wittgenstein's overriding goal was to bring us to see that 'infinity' cannot be divorced from the notion of a non-ending operation, which as such erects an impassable grammatical barrier to the concepts of *limit* and *magnitude*. For these concepts are not *antithetical*; they are *incongenerous*: 'To say that a technique is unlimited does *not* mean that it goes on without ever stopping — that it increases immeasurably; but that it lacks an institution of the end, that it is not finished off' (RFM II §45).

It is not surprising, given the finitist overtones of this theme and the obvious traces of Brouwer and Weyl that can be discerned in his argument, that Wittgenstein's intentions should have been regarded as radical constructivist. The fact remains, however, that Wittgenstein's discussion was firmly based on investigating the logical syntax of 'infinity', not the 'limits of our recognitional capacities'. The question is: how else does Wittgenstein's critique differ from the intuitionist, apart from the absence of technical considerations? One noticeable feature is that, despite the harsh judgement that 'Our suspicion ought always to be aroused when a proof proves more than its means allow it. Something of this sort might be called "a puffed-up proof"' (RFM II §21), the final verdict is by no means disdainful; Cantor's proof provides an illustration of how 'A clever man got caught in this net of language. So it must be an interesting net' (RFM II §15). Herein lies the twofold key, both to the reason why Wittgenstein should have devoted so much attention to as abstruse a piece of mathematics as the diagonal proof, and the standpoint from which he approached it. Both answers lie in the metaphysical implications of Cantor's theory, and the philosophical attention which any such result commands. To be sure, an assault on an influential source of metaphysics may exhibit a pronounced streak of iconoclasm, but this does not betoken — nor can it tolerate — a lack of respect for the canons of classical mathematics. Certainly by his own lights, Wittgenstein was not in the least engaged in a *revisionist* attack on transfinite set theory; he was simply undermining a pernicious misconception by clarifying the grammatical confusions contained in Cantor and Dedekind's prose interpretations of their work. The argument none the less suffers from an obvious strain, created as much by the epistemological overtones of 'revisionism' as Wittgenstein's attempts to distance himself from the radical consequences of what certainly looks like an example of 'mathematical interference'. The questions which this in turn raises, therefore, are whether Wittgenstein was aware of this tension in his argument, and if so, why he should have countenanced it.

'Prose': The Meeting-point Between Mathematics and Philosophy

It begins to look from the foregoing considerations that, while Wittgenstein may not have been guilty of sophistry, he could be faulted for a certain measure of ingenuousness. For on the one hand Wittgenstein insisted that 'In mathematics there can only be mathematical troubles, there can't be philosophical ones' (PG 369). Yet his argument takes us *nolens volens* deep into the bowels of Cantor's proof. Just as the objection which he raised against Russell's theory of quantification was that the confusions in the prose were the direct result of the muddle produced by his symbolism (*supra*), so too Cantor was found guilty of an 'incorrect notation': the confusions suffusing Cantor's interpretation could have been avoided had Cantor employed different symbols for the various relations misleadingly grouped together under '$>$'.[47] From one point of view, however, this *prima facie* embarrassment for Wittgenstein's conception of the philosophy of mathematics is nothing of the sort, in as much as the great utility of Wittgenstein's approach lies precisely in the theme that 'The philosophy of mathematics consists in an exact scrutiny of mathematical proofs — not in surrounding mathematics with a vapour' (PG 367). But while such an argument may not be guilty of revisionism *in stricto sensu*, the emphasis on the formal demarcation between mathematics and philosophy loses much of its superficial plausibility.

The problem here is that the 'prose' of mathematics on which Wittgenstein placed so much stress pulls his argument in opposite directions: it buttresses the claim that 'The philosopher only marks what the mathematician casually throws off about his activities' (PG 369), but at the cost of initiating a process which steers us inexorably into the affairs of mathematics proper. The strain in Wittgenstein's argument is particularly manifest in his closely related discussion of Skolem's proof. Unlike his critique of Cantorean transfinite number theory, however, Wittgenstein's sustained attack in *Philosophical Remarks* and *Philosophical Grammar* on Skolem's definition of 'recursive proof' must be discomfiting for those critics who wish to portray Wittgenstein as a revisionist at heart (which no doubt explains why this topic has received so little attention from that quarter). After all, given Wittgenstein's hostility to the classical interpretation of the quantifiers, together with Skolem's declared Kroneckerian/finitist objectives,[48] one would have expected that if his interests really did lie in the direction of strict finitism Wittgenstein would have greeted Skolem's results with enthusiasm. But quite to the contrary, Wittgenstein regarded Skolem's proof as a paradigmatic example of the type of confusion which so often results when mathematicians attempt to 'translate the calculus into the signs of word-language' (PG 433). Why he should have seized on Skolem's proof to illustrate this theme, however, and what bearing this has on his remarks on the logical syntax of 'infinity', are far from immediately apparent.

It was in the context of this discussion of recursive proof that Wittgenstein maintained: 'Philosophy does not examine the calculi of mathematics, but only what mathematicians say about these calculi' (PG 396). His discussion of Skolem's proof demonstrates both the subtlety and the awkwardness of this contention. As he described it, Wittgenstein focused his criticism solely on what Skolem had said about his proof, contrasting this with the actual calculations which Skolem had performed. But in so doing Wittgenstein undertook to undermine what Skolem himself had regarded as the result of his proof. Thus, one must not mistake Wittgenstein's professed reluctance to deal with the calculi of mathematics as thereby denying himself the right to criticise the classical proofs of mathematics. To the extent that any such proofs contain or rest on *prose*, Wittgenstein forthrightly declared his intention to subject this element to philosophical scrutiny. Wittgenstein would have us distinguish, therefore, between what mathematicians prove and what they think they have proved. And provided that we see this distinction as lying between the realms of calculation and prose, we should not be confused by the air of paradoxicality engendered by this approach. The question which this raises, however, is whether there can be a hard and fast rule for where the 'prose' begins, and thence, where philosophical involvement ends.

Skolem explained in the foreword to 'Foundations of Elementary Arithmetic' that '*If we consider the general theorems of arithmetic to be functional assertions and take the recursive mode of thought as a basis, then that science can be founded in a rigorous way without use of Russell and Whitehead's notions "always" and "sometimes"*.'[49] In general terms Wittgenstein objected, of course, to the very premise underlying Skolem's argument: viz. that arithmetic needs to be 'founded in a rigorous way' (PG 420). But the brunt of his offensive was centred on Skolem's attempt to eliminate the quantifiers and express the same sort of generality that Russell and Whitehead had endeavoured to capture in quantified propositions with 'functional assertions' containing unbounded variables. Such an exercise, Wittgenstein believed, would merely replace one set of problems with another. For it proceeds on the same confusion that lies at the heart of *Principia Mathematica*: that the 'breadth' of infinity can be spanned by an appropriate proposition. What really needs to be examined, therefore, is the assumption that it makes sense to suppose that we can assert a *general (inductive) proposition* on the basis of an inductive proof. Thus, the step in Skolem's proof that Wittgenstein particularly concentrated on is the conclusion which Skolem drew in his initial proof of recursion for addition:

THEOREM 1. (The associative law.) $a + (b + c) = (a + b) + c$.
Proof. The proposition holds for $c = 1$ by virtue of Definition 1.
I assume that it holds for a certain c for arbitrary values of a and b. Necessarily, then, for arbitrary values of a and b,

(α) $a + (b + (c + 1)) = a + ((b + c) + 1)$,

since, according to Definition 1, $b + (c + 1) = (b + c) + 1$.
But according to Definition 1 necessarily also

(β) $a + ((b + c) + 1) = (a + (b + c)) + 1$.

Now, according to the assumption, $a + (b + c) = (a + b) + c$, whence,

(γ) $(a + (b + c)) + 1 = ((a + b) + c) + 1$.

According to Definition 1 we finally also have

(δ) $((a + b) + c) + 1 = (a + b) + (c + 1)$.

From (α), (β), (γ), and (δ) it follows that
$a + (b + (c + 1)) = (a + b) + (c + 1)$, which proves the proposition for $c + 1$ for unspecified a and b.

Thus the proposition holds generally. This is a typical example of a recursive proof (proof by mathematical induction).[50]

It was on the last two lines, which he identified as the 'prose' of the argument, that Wittgenstein directed his attack. (But for Wittgenstein's step-by-step analysis of the shift in the meaning — use — of the variables in the proof, cf. PR §163; PG 408 ff., 446 f.)

Wittgenstein began by reiterating a familiar theme with special relevance to Skolem's proof: 'If we want to see what has been proved, we ought to look at nothing but the proof. We ought not to confuse the infinite possibility of its application with what is actually proved. The infinite possibility of application is *not* proved!' (PR §163). To suppose otherwise is, he maintained, to violate the saying/showing distinction; for the infinite possibility of application is what is *shown*, not stated by the proof. To clarify this we are asked to consider exactly what Skolem's proof *says* versus what it *shows*:

The proof shows that the form '$a + (b + (c + 1)) = (a + b) + (c + 1)$' ... '$A(c + 1)$' follows from the form 1) '$A(c)$' in

accordance with the rule 2) $a + (b + 1) = \text{Def}$
'$A(1)$. Or, what comes to the same thing, by means of the rules
1) and 2) the form '$a + (b + (c + 1))$' can be transformed into
'$(a + b) + (c + 1)$'. This is the sum total of what is actually in
the proof. Everything else, and the whole of the usual interpretation, lies in the possibility of its application. And the usual
mistake, in confusing the extension of its application with what
it genuinely contains. (PR §163)

Wittgenstein was thus pressing us to obtain a strictly literal
reading of the proof: what Skolem *states* is that, from Theorem 1
and Def. 1, it follows that '$a + (b + (c + 1)) = (a + b) + (c + 1)$';
but the argument does not prove — in the sense that it *asserts* —
that e.g. '$a + (b + (c + 2)) = (a + b) + (c + 2)$'. The burden of
Wittgenstein's objection is thus to show that neither does it prove
— in the sense that it asserts — that '$a + (b + c) = (a + b) + c$'.[51]
To argue, *pace* Skolem, that this unbounded use of the variable
proves a 'general proposition' is to assume from the start the very
point that was supposed to have been proved (PG 412-13). Nevertheless, Skolem's proof certainly does show us how to apply this rule
to e.g. the case of '$a + (b + (c + 2)) = (a + b) + (c + 2)$ (PR
§163). The reason why Skolem's proof succeeds as a demonstration of the associative law is because it enables us to *see the rule*
governing its unbounded application: it makes the infinite possibility of applying the associative law surveyable. And it is quite
clear that such recursive techniques may play a fundamental role in
rendering mathematical rules surveyable (PG 405). The problem
with Skolem's argument, however, is that it confuses what a recursive proof *shows* with what it *says*: 'The proof shows the spiral
form of the law. But not in such a way that it comes out as the conclusion of the chain of inferences. ... What we gather from the
proof, we cannot represent in a proposition at all' (PG 405). Thus,
Wittgenstein did not deny that Skolem's proof exhibits the
infinitary scope of the associative law for addition; the challenge is
to clarify how it accomplished this, and thence, what it means to
describe Skolem's argument as a recursive *proof* of the associative
law for addition (PR §165).

The attack on Skolem's proof clearly conforms with
Wittgenstein's general intention to describe proof as a species of
grammatical construction, and to clarify that what we are concerned with are the grounds for describing an argument as a proof:

not the reliability of the judgements that the calculations are correct or that someone has grasped a proof.[52] The issue does raise, however, a special problem for us to consider: the key to understanding what constitutes a proof is that it makes the law that it is concerned with surveyable, but does it have to do this explicitly — in the sense that to be *perspicuous* is to be *asserted*; and does Skolem's proof meet this criterion? If not, does it make sense to say that what a recursive proof establishes is fully perspicuous but not assertable? Before we can answer these questions we must first recognise that the mistake which Wittgenstein attributed to Skolem is that of assuming that with his proof that from (α), (β), (γ) and (δ) [B] it follows that '$a + (b + (c + 1)) = (a + b) + (c + 1)$' he had thereby established the truth of what he described as the 'general proposition' stated as Theorem 1. Wittgenstein insisted, however, that 'The correct expression for the associative law is not a proposition, but precisely its "proof", which admittedly doesn't state the law, but shows it' (PR §165). Far from proving a 'general proposition', a recursive proof *shows* us how to use a 'basic rule of a system':"$a + (b + c) = (a + b) + c$" ... A(c) can be constructed as a basic rule of a system. As such, it can only be laid down, but not *asserted*, or denied (hence no law of the excluded middle)' (PR §163).

This return to the role of the law of excluded middle is a reminder of the point made in the discussion of the intuitionist conception of 'undecidability' (cf. Chapter 3). Only here Wittgenstein returned to his earlier theme in order to emphasise that his argument works both ways, simply because 'If the law of excluded middle doesn't hold, that can only mean that our expression isn't comparable to a proposition' (PG 400). In this case Wittgenstein showed how the criterion operates in the opposite direction: since it makes no sense to apply the law of excluded middle to A(c), it makes no sense to suppose that the recursive proof *proves a general proposition* (PR §168). 'What we gather from the proof, we cannot represent in a proposition at all and of course for the same reason we can't deny it either' (PR §164). Indeed, Wittgenstein went so far as to warn in *Philosophical Remarks* that 'If the proof that every equation has a root is a recursive proof, then that means the Fundamental Theorem of Algebra isn't a genuine mathematical *proposition*' (PR §168). It would be quite mistaken to conclude from this that Wittgenstein believed he had found some fatal flaw in Gauss's proof of the

Fundamental Theorem; his point was simply that the relation between a *recursive proof* and what it establishes is radically different from that between a standard mathematical proof and the theorem which it proves. The explanation lies in the logical syntax of the concepts of *proof* and *mathematical proposition*, not in the mathematical rigour of Gauss or Skolem's proofs.[53]

The real problem posed by Skolem's proof is thus *whether* and if so *why* it should be described as a 'proof': 'I would like to say: Do we *have* to call the recursive calculation the proof of proposition I [A(c)]? That is, won't another relationship do?' (PG 409). Wittgenstein's point was that Skolem's calculation is not so much a proof as it is an 'enumeration' or 'list' which serves as a 'signpost' for the application of the law: 'Isn't our principle: not to use a *concept-word* where one isn't necessary? — That means, in cases where the concept word really stands for an enumeration, to say so. ... What I mean is: in Skolem's calculus we don't *need* any such concept, the list *is sufficient*' (PG 417-18). We may be tempted, however, to accept Skolem's argument as a proof in so far as it satisfies the primary requirement of a grammatical construction: viz. it renders the application of the associative law for addition surveyable. It may not state the law as a general proposition, but it does manage to show us 'how to go on', and is that not all that a proof must accomplish? (PG 406). The trouble with this argument, however, is that we reserve the appellation 'proof' for constructions that stipulate the internal relations underpinning a mathematical proposition, whereas 'the recursion shows nothing but itself, just as periodicity too shows nothing but itself' (PG 406; cf. PG 450). Consonant with his overall conception of philosophy, Wittgenstein avoided the conclusion that we *cannot* employ the concept of proof in the manner which Skolem proposed; only that we should be aware of how this alters the meaning of 'proof' (PG 411,423), and in particular, the complications thus created for the internal relationship between *proof* and *entailment*: 'If you say "it follows from the complex B that $a + (b + c) = (a + b) + c$", we feel giddy. We feel that somehow or other you've said something nonsensical although outwardly it sounds correct' (PG 410; cf. PG 396-7 on the shift in the meaning of 'proved').

Wittgenstein's critique was thus concerned throughout with the conceptual complications imposed by Skolem's claim that A(c) is *proved* by mathematical induction. To illustrate this theme, Wittgenstein returned to the point which was so central to his elucidation of the concept of proof: the idea that the construction of a new *Beweissystem* provides not only a method for answering, but in so doing, a method for asking a mathematical question (cf. Chapter 3). It is precisely this process of *Beweissystem*-creation which underlines Wittgenstein's interpretation of 'proof' as a grammatical construction. But the same relation does not apply to the case of recursive calculations, and it is for that reason that 'we find it odd if we are told that the induction is a proof of the general proposition; for we feel rightly that in the language of the induction we couldn't have posed the general question at all.' That is, 'the proof by induction isn't something that settles a disputed question'; 'Prior to the proof asking about the general proposition made no sense at all, and so wasn't even a question, because the question would only have made sense if a general method of decision had been known *before* the particular proof was discovered.' As in the case of transfinite number theory, the illusion that the contrary obtains is due to the fact that 'we began with an alternative between which we had to decide. (We only seemed to, so long as we had in mind a calculus with finite classes)' (PG 402). What Skolem's argument shares with Cantor's, therefore, is the transgression of the logico-syntactical boundary between finite totalities and infinite series, from which follows such confused assumptions as that what is shown by induction can be counted, quantified over, or asserted in a 'general proposition'.

If the relation between induction and stipulation is not the same as that between proof and proposition, how then should we describe it? Not as the proof of a general law, but rather as the expression of a law, a 'signpost' indicating the 'development of the spiral': 'The construction of the induction is not *a* proof, but a certain arrangement of proofs (a pattern in the sense of an ornament)' (PG 399). Hence Wittgenstein concluded that 'A "recursive proof" is the general term of a series of proofs. So it is a law for the construction of proofs'(PG 430). That is, the recursive definition is 'a rule for constructing replacement rules, or else the general term of a series of definitions. It is a signpost that shows the *same* way to all expressions of a certain form' (PG 431). A 'recursive proof' is thus a special mathematical construction which provides 'a general guide to an arbitrary special proof. A signpost that shows every proposition of a particular form a particular way home. It says to the proposition $2 + (3 + 4) = (2 + 3) + 4$: "Go in *this* direction (run through this spiral), and you will arrive home"'

(PR §164). But while this argument may constitute a powerful attack on Skolem's interpretation of 'recursive proof' — or at least, a strong case for the clarification of the concept of a 'recursive proof' — it does so at the cost of casting considerable doubt on Wittgenstein's frequently professed claim to have scrupulously avoided meddling in mathematical affairs. Although not revisionist in the standard — 'epistemological' — sense, it would seem that Wittgenstein was far more deeply involved in the mechanics of mathematical proof than he was prepared to concede.

The moral which Wittgenstein drew from what he regarded as the prototypical failure of the Skolem proof must surely strike one as remarkably bloody-minded, even for a self-proclaimed revisionist. But in *Philosophical Remarks* and *Philosophical Grammar* Wittgenstein appears to have been somewhat divided in his own mind about the real importance of the philosophy of mathematics; or rather, the relevance of philosophy to mathematics. Of course, as long as mathematics contains prose there are likely to be conceptual confusions for the philosopher to clear up. But how important is this activity: that is, how important is the prose itself? At one point Wittgenstein seems to have been prepared to acknowledge that the prose translations of calculations may play an important role in our understanding of the significance of the calculations: provided that we do not confuse these with any so-called 'meta-mathematical' discourse *about* these calculations; rather, they are 'translations' in which proofs are presented in a different medium which might 'cast some light on' (i.e. suggest a new way of looking at) the importance or implications of a proof (PG 433). The final verdict, however, seems to come down rather more harshly against the mathematical significance of prose translations:

> An explanation in word-language of the proof (of what it proves) only translates the proof into another form of expression: because of this we can drop the explanation altogether. And if we do so, the mathematical relationships become much clearer, no longer obscured by the equivocal expressions of word-language. For example, if I put B right beside A, without interposing any expression of word-language like 'for all cardinal numbers, etc.' then the misleading appearance of a proof of A by B cannot arise. We then see quite soberly how far the relationships between B and A and $a + b = b + a$ extend

and where they stop. Only thus do we learn the real structure and important features of that relationship, and escape the confusion caused by the form of word-language, which makes everything uniform. (PG 422)

As far as the *philosophy of mathematics* is concerned this may seem to be not so much revisionism as a plea for self-immolation. But there is a subtle twist to the argument which ultimately renders Wittgenstein's conception of the affiliation between philosophy and mathematics every bit as involved and extensive as is commonly supposed in conventional attitudes to the subject.

The trouble is that the apparent inflexibility of Wittgenstein's attack on the role of 'prose' is apt to be misleading in several different respects. For one thing, it might make it look — and has done so to many — as though Wittgenstein was objecting to the 'grave imperfections of natural language'; i.e. confusions which are the direct consequence of the ambiguities inherent in 'ordinary language'. But Wittgenstein was hardly suggesting that the dangers he was trying to expose could be avoided if only we were to construct some appropriately rigorous *Begriffsschrift*. Wittgenstein's hostility to this Fregean programme was if anything even more pronounced in *Philosophical Remarks* than in the *Tractatus* (PR §3). Far from complaining about the irremediable defects of natural language for mathematical purposes, Wittgenstein adopted the — in this context, pejorative — term 'prose' to refer to *any* of the various attempts to talk about calculations: i.e. whether 'meta-mathematical' or in the vernacular. It may seem, however, that Wittgenstein's ultimate objective was to ensure that philosophy, once it is properly understood, would eventually bring about the demise of the spurious discipline presently known as the 'philosophy of mathematics'; the use of 'prose' would be banished forever, leaving mathematicians free to engage in the proper business of mathematics (WWK 149). Certainly there has been no shortage of mathematicians who shared the belief that once the authority of philosophy has withered, mathematicians will no longer be tempted to stray from their true activities. And yet it is quite obvious that the presence of 'prose' in the body of proofs is neither arbitrary nor dispensable, and hence the future of the philosophy of mathematics — on Wittgenstein's conception at any rate — is in no immediate or foreseeable danger.

The natural objection to all this criticism of the meta- (or non-)

mathematical use of 'prose' is that Wittgenstein distorted the real issue raised by Skolem's proof: viz. the use of 'prose' *within* the body of a proof. Skolem was not actually talking *about* the calculations, but was drawing a conclusion *from* those calculations, and in this context the 'prose' served as a constituent part of the proof. Granted this might have been the idea on which Wittgenstein wanted to put most pressure, the conviction will undoubtedly remain that a fundamental characteristic of mathematics is that such internal 'prose' plays an integral role in the construction of proofs, and thus, of mathematical thought, shaping as it does the development and articulation of mathematical ideas. What is potentially misleading about the manner in which Wittgenstein presented his argument is that it might seem that he was perversely denying this indispensable feature of conceptual evolution and mathematical progress. Many are thus understandably disturbed by Wittgenstein's claim that mathematics consists *solely* of calculations. But it is essential that we digest the gloss which Wittgenstein immediately placed on this radical view: 'Mathematics consists entirely of calculations. In mathematics *everything* is algorithm and *nothing* is meaning; even when it doesn't look like that because we seem to be using *words* to talk *about* mathematical things. Even these words are used to construct an algorithm' (PG 468). The final sentence in this passage is crucial to Wittgenstein's argument: such words are used in the construction of the algorithm, and hence function in precisely the same manner as the other signs which we employ. Thus, these words do not operate as *prose*, but rather are integrated symbols in the construction of the proof. Furthermore, there is no need to worry about how we are supposed to draw a formal distinction between illicit 'prose' and legitimate calculations containing words drawn from natural language. For example, it might seem that the problem suddenly arises of deciding whether the words 'the power of the natural numbers' should be disqualified from entering a mathematical proof whereas '$\aleph_0$' is all right, and if so, why this should be the case. But Wittgenstein's argument was not in the least concerned with such a spurious issue, for the simple reason that the meaning which a word/sign enjoys in some other *Satzsystem* does not determine the meaning which it acquires from the rules constructed for its use in a new proof. Whether we use 'the power of the natural numbers' or '$\aleph_0$' is completely beside the point, since the meaning of whatever signs we employ will be fixed by the specific rules of the *system*.

Thus, the distinction between *prose* and *mathematical symbols* does not concern the nature of the signs employed, nor the meaning which these might have in pre-established systems. The only issue we are genuinely involved with is the manner in which these signs relate to the proof: viz. whether they are used to say something *about* the calculations, or are actually deployed in the construction of the proof. Wittgenstein readily agreed that, in this latter sense, verbal concepts can and do play an integral role in the development of mathematical ideas. For the meanings which these concepts already possess are instrumental guides to what mathematicians think they are doing or accomplishing with their proofs.[54] But the source of the trouble which Wittgenstein was trying to pinpoint here comes back to the theme that, whatever the heuristic function of such concepts, the meaning of the symbols which occur in the construction of a proof (as e.g. with Cantor's '$>$') must be interpreted strictly according to the role which they play in the new *Beweissystem* that has been created. But now, if it should be the case that a symbol has no meaning within the proof — i.e. if no rules have been laid down for its use within that *Beweissystem*, so that its meaning derives solely from the external systems in which it operates — then it is being used as *prose* and not as an authentic element in the proof. Whatever its associations, the meaning of a concept, as has already been stressed, is *Beweissystem*-confined.

Wittgenstein certainly did not wish to deny that the whole interest and purpose of doing mathematics may lie in the mathematician's conception of the significance of his proof. And although Wittgenstein denied the intelligibility of expressing what inductive proofs *show*, he was not denying the philosophy of mathematics its central role — as he described it in the 'Bouwsma Notes' — of trying to assist mathematicians in their endeavour to interpret what their proofs establish.[55] The latter task is hardly straightforward, and it is not at all surprising that mathematicians and philosophers alike should fall victim to the confusions which arise when we try to translate the calculus into sign-language. But then, for all his talk about keeping his distance from the mechanics of mathematics, Wittgenstein was embarking on an approach to the philosophy of mathematics which would leave the philosopher even more deeply involved in the inner dynamics of mathematical interpretation than is commonly proposed by philosophers of mathematics. In a vivid metaphor he warned: 'The philosopher easily gets into the position of a ham-fisted director, who, instead of doing his own work and merely supervising his employees to see they do their work well, takes over their jobs until one day he finds himself overburdened with other people's work while his employees watch and criticize him. He is particularly inclined to saddle himself with the work of the mathematician' (PG 369). Perhaps he intended this to be reassuring, but the passage has an uncomfortably autobiographical ring to it. Wittgenstein may have wanted to leave mathematicians entirely to their own devices, but as the critiques of Cantor's and Skolem's proofs amply demonstrate, their 'charm' ineluctably lured him into their *sanctum sanctorum.*

Of course, the defence always remains open that Wittgenstein never overstepped the bounds of his philosophical task; the trouble is that, according to the logic of the argument, it is the employees who are constantly straying from their appointed duties and wandering into the realms of management, so that by merely doing his own job the even-handed director finds himself performing an ever larger amount of the labour hitherto performed by his workers. The philosopher may not have any licence to tamper with the calculations proper of mathematics, but it thus emerges that he has a fundamental role to play in the elucidation of what these calculations assert. Or rather, that when mathematicians engage in this aspect of their discipline — from which, after all, derives much of the interest of their subject — they enter a realm of conceptual discourse where they expose themselves to the cold gaze of philosophical scrutiny. And mathematicians have entered this realm so frequently that what are commonly enshrined as the most important of proofs may turn out to be nothing of the sort. The relation of philosophy to mathematics is thus anything but ornamental: 'The talk of mathematicians becomes absurd when they leave mathematics, for example, Hardy's description of mathematics as not being a creation of our minds. He conceived philosophy as a decoration, an atmosphere, around the hard realities of mathematics and science. These disciplines, on the one hand, and philosophy on the other, are thought of as being like the necessities and decoration of a room. Hardy is thinking of philosophical opinions. I conceive of philosophy as an activity of clearing up thought' (AWL 225).

Wittgenstein would no doubt seek to defend himself against the charge of remaining a ham-fisted director on the grounds that he did not actually exhibit an error in Cantor's proof; he merely showed how Cantor's interpretation was misguided. Yet Wittgenstein notoriously failed to provide us with any inkling of how a proper interpretation should proceed: a lacuna which, because of the nature of Wittgenstein's criticism, cannot — so it would follow — be fobbed back off onto the mathematician. On the other hand, if Wittgenstein had tried to reinterpret Cantor's argument, then his assurance that he would never interfere with the mathematicians would obviously become that much more suspect. Either way it is difficult to see how Wittgenstein could sustain this balancing act; for it just is the case that the mathematician's interpretation plays an integral role in the development of mathematics. The 'prose' of mathematics is hardly an incidental vehicle for the mathematician's idle whims; it provides him with the critical platform to convey what he regards as the interest or significance of his proof. It can and often will be the case that a mathematician's interpretation will be subsequently overturned, or even, that his proof will be reinterpreted along lines completely foreign to his original intentions. But far from being arbitrary or tangential, this factor provides one of the key elements in the evolution of mathematical thought. One might even argue that, in this respect, there is an inextricable synthesis of calculus and prose; after all, the use of '$\aleph_0$' is not, on Wittgenstein's own insistence, a meaningless mark; it just is the symbol for the smallest 'transfinite cardinal number', whatever that might mean, and the 'prose' which Wittgenstein seized on constitutes the *point d'appui* of Cantor's proof.

The pressures building here soon become intolerable. As is made clear in §129 of *Philosophical Remarks*, Wittgenstein felt that the proper response to the Poincaréan accusation that Cantorean set theory contains a vicious circle is that the symbol '$(1, x, x + 1)$' *shows* that the natural number series is infinite. We cannot *say* that the 'totality' of natural numbers is infinite; to do so would be to state that the 'magnitude' of the natural numbers is $\aleph_0$. But the argument does not entail — and here we look forward to the exchanges with Turing in *Lectures on the Foundations of Mathematics* — that the symbol '$\aleph_0$' is meaningless; rather, $\aleph_0$ *shows* us that the number series is infinite (viz. unbounded). 'I asked a question about a human being, namely, "How many numerals did you learn to write down?" Turing answered "$\aleph_0$" and

I agreed. In agreeing, I meant that that is the way in which the number $\aleph_0$ is used.' For that very reason 'To say that one has written down an enormous number of numerals is perfectly sensible, but to say that one has written down $\aleph_0$ is nonsense' (LFM 32). And yet, this would seem to entail that '$\aleph_0$' merely means the same thing as '$(1,x,x+1)$'! This jibs, however, with Wittgenstein's warning in *Philosophical Grammar* to avoid 'the confusion between two different meanings of the word "kind". That is, we admit that the infinite numbers are a different *kind* of number from the finite ones, but then we misunderstand what the difference between different kinds amounts to in this case' (PG 463). But '$(1, x, x + 1)$' is not a 'different *kind* of number': it is a rule for the generation of the natural numbers! Hence 'the sign "infinite" or "$\aleph_0$" does not fit into the context it was really intended for, since it would produce nonsense there' (WWK 114; AWL 117, 189).

In *Remarks on the Foundations of Mathematics* Wittgenstein struggled vainly to avoid the predicament closing in on his argument. 'We have', he suggested, 'a grammatical class "infinite sequence", and equivalent with this expression a word whose grammar has (a certain) similarity with that of a numeral: "infinity" or "$\aleph_0$".' But the only solace he could draw from this evasive compromise is that 'From the fact ... that we have an employment for a *kind* of numeral which, as it were, gives the number of the members of an infinite series, it does not follow that it also makes some kind of sense to speak of the number of the concept "infinite series"; that we have *here* some kind of employment for something like a numeral' (RFM II §38). The strain in Wittgenstein's argument which is so manifestly evident here is the direct result of his attempt to distance himself from any semblance of philosophical intrusion in mathematical affairs (PLP 398). But such neutrality is both unfeasible and undesirable. When Lewy asked 'Is "Professor Hardy believes that $\aleph_0 > \aleph$" a mathematical statement?' Wittgenstein answered: 'No. It is no more a mathematical statement than "Willie said that $7 \times 8 = 54$" is a mathematical statement' (LFM 34). But the pertinent question which this leaves us with is: how can we reconcile this conclusion with the earlier claim: 'In agreeing, I meant that that is the way in which the number $\aleph$ is used' (LFM 32). For what sort of number *could* this be? It is a question which takes us outside the domains of Cantorean transfinite number theory into the larger issue of the significance of 'prose' and *a fortiori*, the relationship between philosophy and mathematics.

Whenever Wittgenstein attacked a proof it was always on the grounds that he was not touching the calculus: only the prose. But for all intents and purposes there seems to be little genuine distinction between this subtle argument and the far simpler point that mathematicians can commit two different kinds of error: technical and conceptual. Wittgenstein's emphasis on the prose/ calculus distinction plays an important role as far as the interpretation of the calculi is concerned, but this contrast cannot be used to cover the full extent of his actual criticisms. For Wittgenstein was continually engaged in investigations of conceptual confusions which are embedded within mathematical proofs. The point is that these raise philosophical questions which vitally affect the development of mathematics, and indeed, the successful mathematician cannot afford to neglect the philosophical dimensions of his work. To be sure, the result of such a critique may not affect the cogency of a proof; but it might nevertheless have a profound effect on which areas mathematicians choose to pursue. For a misguided interpretation can all too easily stimulate activity in areas which are of little genuine mathematical importance (e.g. the construction of 'octonions'). The philosophy of mathematics — that is, the clarification of the significance of a proof — thus acts as a crucial prophylactic against this ubiquitous danger.

Hence Wittgenstein confided his hope in *Philosophical Grammar* that 'Philosophical clarity will have the same effect on the growth of mathematics as sunlight has on the growth of potato shoots. (In a dark cellar they grow yards long)' (PG 381). Hilbert had also touched on this theme when he called attention to the importance of resolving the nature of the infinite in order to complete Weierstrass's revolution in Analysis. But the solution is not, as Hilbert supposed, to eliminate all mention of the infinite; it is to understand what the term signifies. Wittgenstein's argument was not, *pace* Hilbert, that all problematic concepts must be forcibly removed from mathematics; rather, it was that the confusions generated by grammatical transgressions must be clarified in order to be rectified. Weierstrass's work in analysis did not succeed because he abolished all use of the infinite as such; rather, it was because he avoided the eighteenth-century metaphysical muddles about the infinite (viz. infinitesimals). For infinity can no more be eradicated from Analysis than from number theory. What Weierstrass really eliminated, therefore, were some of the principal misconceptions that had plagued the subject. Yet we would hardly wish to describe Weierstrass's work in the foundations of analysis as belonging to the philosophy of mathematics; any more than we would want to treat *Remarks on the Foundations of Mathematics* as an orthodox *mathematical* text! The final question which this issue leaves us with, therefore, is whether — and if so where — we can draw the line between mathematical versus philosophical conceptual clarification on Wittgenstein's approach.

It is well known that Wittgenstein criticised the influence of mathematical logic on philosophy, but the purport of this remark is often seriously misconstrued. In stark, and clearly deliberate, contrast to the kind of enthusiasm displayed by Russell at the end of 'Mathematics and Metaphysics',[56] Wittgenstein complained that '"Mathematical logic" has completely deformed the thinking of mathematicians and of philosophers, by setting up a superficial interpretation of the forms of our everyday language as an analysis of the structures of facts' (RFM V §48).[57] Wittgenstein was not implying, however, that 'philosophy and mathematics have nothing to say to one another', or that 'no mathematical discovery can have any bearing on the philosophy of mathematics'.[58] In one sense this is obviously false, if only because Wittgenstein repeatedly emphasised that it is the duty of philosophy to interpret mathematical discoveries; that is, that mathematical innovations provide *material* for philosophical reflection by throwing up new conceptual problems. If, however, the objection is that according to Wittgenstein no mathematical discovery can have any significance as far as the body of 'philosophical knowledge' is concerned, then this would simply constitute an *ignoratio elenchi*; for it would operate on the very conception of philosophy that Wittgenstein was trying to overthrow. More to the point, however, is that the upshot of Wittgenstein's argument is that there is indeed an intimate link binding mathematics and philosophy; just as there is between philosophy and psychology. But whereas the problem in psychology is that 'there are experimental methods and *conceptual confusion*' (PI p. 232), in mathematics there are normative constructions and conceptual confusion. It is because of this shared liability to conceptual confusion that 'An investigation is possible in connexion with mathematics which is entirely analogous to our investigation of psychology' (PI p. 232).

The point is that the direction of this relationship is the very
opposite from that commonly assumed by mathematical philosophers. It is not philosophy that must be governed by mathematics: it is mathematics that should be vitally influenced by
philosophy. In so far as mathematicians must continually interpret
their concepts and calculi in the course of their constructive work,
they must constantly bear in mind the results of philosophical
investigations into the logical grammar of problematic concepts.
Thus, from a position which steadfastly avoided revisionism
Wittgenstein ended up with a conclusion that has extraordinarily
far-reaching implications for our understanding and interpretation
of mathematics. The danger in all this, however, is that the frontier
between mathematics and philosophy will be not so much relaxed
as obliterated. But this worry derives from the same confusion as
that which treats Wittgenstein's approach to the philosophy of
language as a 'species of lexicography'. Just as in the latter the
philosopher's concern is not with grammatical confusions
simpliciter, but only with those transgressions of logical grammar
which result in *philosophical* questions, so too our concern in the
philosophy of mathematics is only with those violations of logical
grammar which may seem perfectly innocuous from a mathematical point of view, but which inspire metaphysical or sceptical
theses.[59] Which, of course, explains why Cantor's proof received so
much attention. For, as Cantor wrote to Father Thomas Esser: 'the
general theory of sets ... which I have begun, belongs entirely to
metaphysics. ...Nor does the fact that my work appears in mathematical journals affect its metaphysical character and content.'[60]
But if Cantor appreciated that the metaphysical character of his
theory could not be divorced from its substance, how could
Wittgenstein seriously hope to maintain the posture that only the
prose of Cantor's interpretation had been affected by his critique
while the 'calculus' had remained untouched? The quotation from
Lectures on the Foundations of Mathematics cited at the outset of
this chapter (cf. p.161 above) is thus, at best, misleading; for as the
passage from *Culture and Value* cited at the beginning of the
Preface makes clear, Wittgenstein's main intention in the philosophy of mathematics was to drive out the sources of metaphysics
from the paradise of mathematics. But not even the Archangel
Michael could accomplish a similar feat without first entering the
Garden of Eden.

Notes

1. Cf. Charles F. Kielkopf, *Strict Finitism: An Examination of Ludwig Wittgenstein's Remarks on the Foundations of Mathematics* (The Hague, Mouton, 1970).

2. Friedrich Waismann, 'The Nature of Mathematics: Wittgenstein's Standpoint', Shanker, S.G. (ed.) *Ludwig Wittgenstein: Critical Assessments*, vol. III (London, Croom Helm, 1986), p. 64.

3. Cf. Michael Dummett's explanation in *Elements of Intuitionism* of how

> The intuitionistic rejection of the completed infinite is not intended to impugn the distinction between 'limit' and '$\aleph_0$'. ... Rather, the thesis that there is no completed infinity means, simply, that to grasp an infinite structure is to grasp the process which generates it, that to refer to such a structure is to refer to that process, and that to recognise the structure as being infinite is to recognise that the process will not terminate. (Oxford, Clarendon Press, 1977), pp. 55,6.

4. Cf. Waismann, 'The Nature of Mathematics: Wittgenstein's Standpoint', op.cit., pp. 64 ff.

5. E.g. cf. A.R. Anderson, 'Mathematics and the Language Game', in *Philosophy of Mathematics*, P. Benacerraf and H. Putnam (eds) (Englewood Cliffs, Prentice-Hall, 1964); and G. Kreisel, 'Wittgenstein's Remarks', *British Journal for the Philosophy of Science*, 9, no. 34, 1958.

6. Cantor distinguished between *reelen* and *realen* numbers in *Grundlagen*.

7. Quoted in Joseph Warren Dauben, *Georg Cantor: His Mathematics and Philosophy of the Infinite* (Cambridge, Harvard University Press, 1979), p. 97.

8. Cf. Michael Hallett, *Cantorean Set Theory and Limitation of Size* (Oxford, Clarendon Press, 1984), p. 17.

9. Quoted in ibid. p. 25; cf. Frege's confidence that 'Cantor succeeds in showing that [the potential infinite] presupposes the actual infinite.' (PW 68-9).

10. Dauben, *Georg Cantor*, op.cit., p. 96.

11. Cf. ibid., p. 6.

12. Cf. ibid., p. 65.

13. Ibid., p. 98.

14. Bertrand Russell, *Introduction to Mathematical Philosophy* (London, George Allen & Unwin Ltd., 1975), pp. 89 ff.

15. Cf. Dauben, *Georg Cantor*, op.cit., p. 171.

16. Ibid., p. 224; cf. Frege's criticisms in his 'Draft towards a Review of Cantor's *Gesammelte Abhandlungen zur Lehre vom Transfiniten*', PW, pp. 68-71.

17. Ibid., p. 171.

18. Perhaps the first to emphasise this theme was Edward Kasner, in 'Galileo and the Modern Concept of Infinity', *Bulletin, American Mathematical Society*, vol. XI (1905), pp. 499-501.

19. Michael Guillen, *Bridges to Infinity: The Human Side of Mathematics* (Los Angeles, Jeremy P. Tarcher. Inc., 1983), p. 42.

20. Galileo Galilei, *Dialogues Concerning Two New Sciences*, Henry Crew and Alfonso de Salvio (trans.) (New York, Dover Publications, Inc., 1954), p. 33.

21. Ibid., p. 32

22. Ibid.

23. Ibid., pp. 32-3.

24. Ibid., p. 30.

25. Cf. Bertrand Russell, *Principles of Mathematics* (New York, W.W. Norton & Company), pp. 306 ff.

26. Philip J. Davis and Reuben Hersh, *The Mathematical Experience*

(Brighton, Sussex, The Harvester Press, 1981), p. 156.

27. Bertrand Russell, 'Mathematics and Metaphysicians', in *Mysticism and Logic and Other Essays* (London, Longmans, Green and Co., 1918), p. 87.

28. Ibid., p. 87.

29. Ibid.

30. Ibid., p. 88.

31. Ibid., pp. 87-8.

32. Ibid.

33. Ibid., p. 88.

34. Cantor sought to turn this argument to his own advantage when he wrote to Gustav Eneström:

All so-called proofs against the possibility of actually infinite numbers are faulty, as can be demonstrated in every particular case, and as can be concluded on general grounds as well. It is their *proton pseudos* that from the outset they expect or even impose all the properties of finite numbers upon the numbers in question, while on the other hand the infinite numbers, if they are to be considered in any form at all, must (in their contrast to the finite numbers) constitute an entirely new kind of number, whose nature is entirely dependent upon the nature of things and is an object of research, but not of our arbitrariness or prejudices. (Quoted in Dauben, *Georg Cantor*, op.cit., p. 125).

35. Ibid., p. 56.

36. I offer this as either an open invitation or a piece of self-exhortation: daunting as such a task might appear, an approach to Cantor's 'continuum problem' based on Wittgensteinian lines would almost certainly pay rich dividends to anyone interested in the conceptual framework of this fascinating issue.

37. Pasquale Frascolla, 'The Constructivist Model in Wittgenstein's Philosophy of Mathematics', in *Ludwig Wittgenstein: Critical Assessments*, vol. III, p. 243.

38. Richard Dedekind, 'Continuity and Irrational Numbers', in *Essays on the Theory of Numbers* (New York, Dover Publications, 1963), p. 1; cf. pp. 6 ff.

39. Or rather, Dedekind actually argued that an irrational number is then created by the mind to correspond to the cut; cf. Dedekind's letter to Weber, quoted in Ivor Grattan-Guinness (ed.), *From the Calculus to Set Theory: 1630–1910* (London, Duckworth, 1980). p. 224.

40. Ibid., p. 8.

41. Cf. Rush Rhees, 'On Continuity: Wittgenstein's Ideas, 1938', in his *Discussions of Wittgenstein* (London, Routledge & Kegan Paul, 1970), pp. 131 ff.

42. Ibid., pp. 10-11.

43. Richard Courant and Herbert Robbins, *What is Mathematics?* (Oxford, Oxford University Press, 1978), p. 62.

44. Hence,the point of Wittgenstein's vague remarks on π' was merely to draw attention to the fact that π' is — if intelligible — a *derivative rule*: 'if [the rule for π] is known, precisely *that* gives π' its sense, and if unknown, we can't speak about the law which we don't yet know, and π' is bereft of all sense' (PR §184).

45. Cf. Hallett, *Cantorian Set Theory and Limitation of Size*, op.cit., pp. 12 ff.

46. Ibid., p. 28.

47. Strictly speaking one could, of course, argue that Cantor's symbolism constituted no irrevocable obstacle to a coherent interpretation of his system, any more than the use of homonyms entails unintelligibility in natural language. Whether such a defence could carry much weight, however, the important point is that it is not a justification which Wittgenstein invoked.

48. Cf. 'The Foundations of Elementary Arithmetic Established By Means of the Recursive Mode of Thought, Without the Use of Apparent Variables Ranging Over Infinite Domains', in *From Frege to Gödel: A Source Book in Mathematical Logic, 1879–1931*, Jean van Heijenoort (ed.) (Cambridge, Mass., Harvard University Press, 1977), p. 333.

218   *The Perils of Prose*

49. Ibid., p. 304.
50. Ibid., pp. 305-6.
51. Cf. Wittgenstein's argument that tautologies show us something about the fundamental laws of logic, but they do not tell us anything about those laws. The rule of inference 'p. & p → q. → q' does not prove — in the sense that it *asserts* — that 'q' follows from 'p. & p → q'. Rather, '*That* "p. & p → q. →q"' = tautology' *shows* us that q follows from 'p. & p → q'.
52. It might be tempting to interpret this argument as leading Wittgenstein towards his putative 'scepticism' about concept-acquisition, and thus it is crucial that we see how this argument relates to the later remarks on rule-following. Wittgenstein insisted that the feature which renders Skolem's recursive proof a successful demonstration of the associative law is simply the fact that it enables us to see the 'spiral' of the law; that it renders the application of the rule surveyable:

But how can I use the sign 'f(a)' to indicate what I see in the passage from f(1) to f(2) (i.e. the possibility of repetition).
Neither can I prove that a + (b + 1) = (a + b) + 1 is a special case of a + (b + c) = (a + b) + c: I must see it. (No rule can help me here either, since I would still have to know what would be a special case of this general rule.) This is the unbridgeable gulf between rule and application, or law and special case. (PR §164)

But if the 'gulf between rule and application is unbridgeable' — if, as Wittgenstein would argue in a later context, the gulf between rule and application is 'unbridgeable by an interpretation' — how can we ever be certain that someone has grasped the direction of the spiral? Wittgenstein was already insisting in *Philosophical Remarks*, however, that you cannot hope to improve on the reliability of such an inference by extending the number of spirals in the proof: one whorl is as good as seven: if 'it really is proved, then it cannot have a still *better* proof!' The point is not, how can we be certain that someone has grasped the law, but rather, under what circumstances do we say that someone has grasped the law. The passage was not in the least concerned with entertaining or refuting the problem of scepticism about rule-following; rather, Wittgenstein was trying to show us that the reason why Skolem's argument does not constitute a proof of a 'general proposition' is because it *shows* rather than *asserts* the infinite application of the associative law.
53. It is frustrating that Wittgenstein did not explain precisely what he meant, or even whose proof he had in mind. But, assuming that it was Gauss's first proof — or some version of this — which he was thinking of, perhaps it is at least possible to reconstruct the essence of his thought. The sort of proof he would have had in mind would, of course, be one which proceeds from a particular proof to a putative general proposition. Thus, in terms of Gauss's proof, we would begin by proving that for some given integer (e.g. 3) we can construct two curves ($x^3 - 3xy^2$ and $3x^2y - y^3 - 2^2$) which must intersect each other somewhere in the angular interval $(0, \pi/3)$. The points at which these curves intersect define complex numbers which satisfy the equation:

$$(x + iy)^3 + a_1 (x + iy)^2 + a_2 (x + iy) + a_3 = 0.$$

Wittgenstein's point would then be that, if the proof that every algebraic equation has a root in the field of complex numbers appeals to this particular proof as its basis via the application of induction on *n*, then we must say that

$$(x + iy)^n + a_1 (x + iy)^{n-1} + \ldots a_{n-1} (x + iy) + a_n = 0$$

is not a *proposition*, but rather, a basic rule for deciding how many roots, in the field of complex numbers, are possessed by a general algebraic equation of degree n.

54. I discuss this issue in somewhat greater detail in 'The Foundations of the Foundations of Mathematics', in *Ludwig Wittgenstein: Critical Assessments*, vol. III .

55. Wittgenstein remarked:

> This is the age of popular science, and so this cannot be the age of philosophy. He was not objecting to this. In fact he recommended Faraday's *The Burning of the Candle* as an illustration of fine popular science. He objected to the sensationalism, and what he called the cheating. Eddington and Jeans cheat. A fine work in this order would have to be very careful, analogies would be well chosen and nicely worked out. In fact the consummation of philosophy might very well be just such fine popular science, work which does not cheat and where the confusions have been cleared up. He was especially resentful of philosophy on the radio — more sensationalism.

56. Where he concluded that if mathematical logic can be properly developed 'there is every reason to hope that the near future will be as great an epoch in pure philosophy as the immediate past has been in the principles of mathematics'. 'Mathematics and Metaphysicians', op.cit., p. 96.

57. Cf. Turing in 'The Reform of Mathematical Notation':

> mathematics has profited very little from researches in symbolic logic. The chief reason for this seems to be a lack of liaison between the logician and the mathematician-in-the-street. Symbolic logic is a very alarming mouthful for most mathematicians, and the logicians are not very much interested in making it more palatable.

(Quoted in Andrew Hodges' *Alan Turing: The Engima* (London, Burnett Books, 1983), p.215.)

58. Dummett, 'Wittgenstein's Philosophy of Mathematics' op.cit., p. 122.

59. Cf. S.G. Shanker, 'Approaching the *Investigations*', in *Ludwig Wittgenstein: Critical Assessments*, vol. II, op.cit., pp. 9 f.

60. Quoted in Herbert Meschkowski's *Ways of Thought of Great Mathematicians* (San Francisco, Holden-Day, Inc., 1964) p. 94.

6 CONSISTENCY

A foolish consistency is the hobgoblin of little minds, adored by little statesmen and philosophers and divines.

Ralph Waldo Emerson, *Self-Reliance*

Hilbert's Programme

The foregoing chapters provide us with the necessary background to approach one of the murkiest areas of Wittgenstein's remarks on the foundations of mathematics: his puzzling insistence that the consistency problem is completely vapid. Once again the cries of incompetence have been most shrill where the least effort has been made to clarify the design of Wittgenstein's attack. Perhaps the most perplexing aspect of Wittgenstein's argument is the absence of any clear statement of its purpose. Why should Wittgenstein have dwelt so heavily on a topic which was made, if not quite irrelevant, certainly of no pressing mathematical importance following the publication of Gödel's second theorem? Surely by the time he came to deliver his 1939 lectures on the foundations of mathematics, Wittgenstein had had sufficient opportunity to digest the significance of Gödel's work? Unless, of course, he was seeking in some obscure way to enhance Gödel's results: without fully realising the extent of this shared purpose! Not surprisingly, philosophers of mathematics have reacted to Wittgenstein's strictures with a mixture of bewilderment and unbridled animosity, seeing them as a crude assault on mathematical logic with little conceivable motive other than to fit in with Wittgenstein's perverse opinion that the general influence of mathematical logic on philosophy has been pernicious. Such a heresy could only be born from the seeds of technical confusion which *ergo propter hoc* is demonstrated by Wittgenstein's obtuse failure to grasp the mathematical problems involved in the discovery of a contradiction in an axiomatic system.

Once again, then, we must begin by trying to identify the focus of Wittgenstein's attention. Fortunately, two major themes in Wittgenstein's argument stand out: first, that he thought that the possibility of a hidden contradiction in a mathematical system poses no *mathematical* threat; and second, that the reason for this has something to do with the fact that mathematical propositions are rules of syntax. Curiously, despite the extensive discussions of the problem in *Wittgenstein and the Vienna Circle*, only one section deals directly with the issue in *Philosophical Remarks*: a passage which Wittgenstein apparently regarded as an adequate exposition of the fundamental confusion underlying the consistency problem: 'It seems to me that the idea of the consistency of the axioms of mathematics, by which mathematicians are so haunted these days, rests on a misunderstanding. This is tied up with the fact that the axioms of mathematics are not seen for what they are, namely, propositions of syntax. . . . A postulate is only the postulation of a form of expression. The "axioms" are postulates of the form of expression' (PR §160). Our task in this chapter is to unfold the various levels of argument contained in this brief remark. Furthermore, in so doing we must also clarify why the 'misunderstanding' which Wittgenstein referred to here, and which remained the principal theme in his later discussions of consistency, struck him as one of the foremost topics in the foundations of mathematics.

The idea that Wittgenstein failed to grasp the implications of the counter-arguments which Turing raised in *Lectures on the Foundations of Mathematics* is undoubtedly the single most dangerous source of critical prejudice in this topic. The essence of Wittgenstein's rejoinders to Turing was that his objections were beside the point, simply because he had failed to consider the logico-syntactical nature of the axioms of a system, and thence of a contradiction derived within a system. In other words, Wittgenstein never responded that Turing's arguments were themselves technically flawed; it was that they were unrelated to the *philosophical* point with which Wittgenstein was concerned. Indeed, Turing's arguments were merely a recapitulation of the standard motifs in the consistency fugue: the very themes that Wittgenstein had originally formulated his argument to expunge. Or rather, to circumvent and thence subvert. And it is this last remark which holds the key to the strategy which Wittgenstein implemented, and thus to the substance of his objections to the consistency problem and the significance which he attached to this issue as far as the philosophy of mathematics is concerned. If we are to grasp the full import of Wittgenstein's argument, therefore, we must avoid any approach which remains committed to the framework which Wittgenstein sought to undermine. In particular, we must steer clear of the two polarities which have dominated recent critical discussion: the offensives launched by Charles Chihara and the line of defence championed by Crispin Wright.

Wright strives valiantly to come to Wittgenstein's aid in *Wittgenstein on the Foundations of Mathematics*, but the premise of his apology is the very theme which Wittgenstein contested. For this reason alone, the Wright–Chihara debate proceeds on a level which sustains the fallacy that Wittgenstein was endeavouring to eradicate. Wright argues that Wittgenstein repeatedly presented 'what would amount to a kind of Cartesian doubt about mathematical certainty'.[1] He quite rightly points out that: 'Wittgenstein is not commending a scepticism about mathematical certainty, but attempting to expose what he takes to be an incoherence in the attitude of someone who thinks that a proof of consistency makes things in some way more certain; that it then becomes rational to depend upon a system in a way in which it was not before.'[2] But we must take this argument a step further: not only was Wittgenstein not commending a scepticism about mathematical certainty, he was trying to demonstrate the absurdity involved in supposing that any such possibility is feasible. It is not just that the conception of a consistency proof as a vehicle of mathematical confidence is under attack: it is the very premise that it makes sense to speak of the *reliability* of mathematical knowledge in the first place, let alone of placing it on a more rational basis. For the notion of a consistency proof rests on the sceptical thesis that Wittgenstein was struggling to overthrow. Until we grasp that according to Wittgenstein the proper response to make to the advocate of a consistency proof is that the project is otiose because the problem is unintelligible, we shall make little headway with the various arguments whereby Wittgenstein intended to prod us to see this result.

Without this vantage-point Wright is led to concede that Wittgenstein's approach 'does not seem prepossessing'.[3] In order to salvage some insight from this potential fiasco, Wright places the argument in the context of the pervasive assumption that when he talked about 'philosophical therapy' Wittgenstein was referring to emotional as much as philosophical problems. Faced with the 'neurotic who is prepared to suspect miscalculation or contradiction anywhere at all', Wright feels that Wittgenstein's 'point is a fair one'. For 'no mathematical development can refute a doubt' such as this. Hence, 'to set such a doubt at rest, it is not mathematics that is required but therapy'.[4] But this is not at all what Wittgenstein was saying. The remarks on consistency were not concerned with the Pyrrhonist who obstinately denies the certainty of mathematical truth, any more than the remarks on rule-following were concerned with the lunatic who for the sake of his argument is prepared to deny the existence of language. As the passage from *Philosophical Remarks* quoted above makes clear, it was against those who have failed to grasp the logico-grammatical status of axioms and contradictions that Wittgenstein was directing his argument. The kind of 'therapy' that Wittgenstein was talking about was strictly *philosophical*, therefore, not pseudo-Freudian: it is the therapy which enables us to stop doing philosophy because we have grasped the source of our confusion, and thus understood that we are not called upon to construct 'epistemological foundations' for our knowledge.[5] That is, it is the therapy of showing mathematicians that it makes no sense to speak of 'refuting' or 'setting such a doubt at rest': i.e. to see that such a doubt is unintelligible, and hence, that what we must recognise is the manner in which the consistency problem is logically *excluded*. Otherwise, there is a pronounced danger that we shall find ourselves landed with the conclusion that 'It is, finally, Wittgenstein's scepticism about the objectivity of sameness of use which most fundamentally underlies his attitude towards "hidden" contradictions.'[6] Rather, it was his attitude to such spurious 'sceptical' problems which most fundamentally governed Wittgenstein's attitude towards 'hidden' contradictions; the question here is not how we can be certain that an axiomatic system is consistent, but 'Is it even *possible* for mathematics to be inconsistent?' (WWK 119).

Wright is quite right, however, to draw attention to the fact that Hilbert's quest for a consistency proof is a paradigmatic example of the intrusion of sceptical worries into mathematics proper. And it is indeed this very feature which explains why Wittgenstein was so interested in the topic. Such a point may not be immediately apparent from Hilbert's presentation of 'meta-mathematics'. In 'Die Logischen Grundlagen der Mathematik' Hilbert explained that 'In this metamathematics one works with the proofs of ordinary mathematics, these latter themselves forming the object of investigation.'[7] Accordingly the predominant picture today is that the primary reason why Hilbert's Programme remains important is because Hilbert succeeded in making *proof* an object of mathematical study.[8] This makes it sound as though the issues raised by 'meta-mathematics' are purely technical: an impression which is amply corroborated by textbooks on the subject. But the whole point of 'meta-mathematics' lay in its deliberate *transgression* of the boundary between mathematics and philosophy: viz. in Hilbert's conviction that he could use this tool to resolve mathematically what were *au fond* philosophical problems. And it was for precisely this reason that Wittgenstein dismissed this approach. The method for establishing that something is a proof is always mathematical, never 'meta' or 'supra' mathematical (PR §153). To be sure, mathematical proof is a subject of *philosophical* study, but this must not be confused with 'meta-mathematics' in Hilbert's intended sense. For this activity does not constitute any sort of *mathematics*; it is solely a branch of philosophy, in which the category of concepts being examined are mathematical. Thus, we must distinguish between 'clarifying the logical syntax of proof' and Hilbert's idea that we can '*prove* that a proof is a proof', or that 'a calculus is a calculus' (WWK 175). For the logical boundary between mathematics and philosophy is inviolable, and 'What Hilbert does is mathematics and not metamathematics. It is another calculus, just like any other one' (WWK 121).

In essence Wittgenstein based this criticism on the fundamental theme that mathematical propositions are rules of syntax which fix the use of mathematical concepts rather than state mathematical facts. In which case Hilbert's conception of 'meta-mathematics' must be *au fond* misconstrued, simply because if 'meta-mathematical' propositions are to be interpreted as a species of mathematical proposition, then they cannot, *qua* norms of representation, be *about* anything, and *a fortiori*, cannot be 'supra-mathematical proofs' about mathematical proofs. To argue that 'meta-mathematics' constitutes a quasi-mathematical discipline whose 'objects of investigation' are proofs rather than numbers is thus merely to introduce a new variation on the entrenched confusion that mathematical propositions are descriptive. That certainly does not rule out the possibility that 'meta-mathematics' can be incorporated into the family of mathematics; rather, it highlights the fact that it can only do so on the same footing. It was these considerations, therefore, which led Wittgenstein to conclude that 'Hilbert's "metamathematics" must turn out to be mathematics in disguise' (WWK 136). That is, 'meta-mathematical' proofs are not a 'higher', but simply a *different* calculus: 'What Hilbert does is mathematics and not metamathematics. It's another calculus, just like any other' (PR §319).

Throughout his criticisms of Hilbert's failed attempt to develop a finitary consistency proof of arithmetic Wittgenstein embellished upon these objections; but the explicit allusions to Hilbert's thought became increasingly veiled, making it progressively difficult to identify the target of Wittgenstein's insistence that 'In mathematics, we cannot talk of systems in general, but only *within* systems' (PR §152). It is noteworthy that Wittgenstein's arguments in his conversations with Waismann and Schlick were based quite closely on Hilbert's arguments as developed in 'Neubegründung der Mathematik' and 'On the Infinite'. Moreover, the themes which Wittgenstein seized on are the very ones which relate to the general philosophical issues underlying Hilbert's Programme. By the time we reach *Remarks on the Foundations of Mathematics*, however, the attack on Hilbert's notion of 'meta-mathematics' has become a mere shadow lurking in the background of the central theme that 'mathematics is a MOTLEY of techniques of proof' (RFM III §46). In some ways this is disappointing, for apart from Wittgenstein, meta-mathematics has never received a prolonged philosophical investigation of its fundamental premises and consequences, even though it has so manifestly failed to live up to its early expectations. Unfortunately, these issues are far too complex to examine in any depth in the context of the present work.[9] There is, however, a more immediate philosophical problem underlying Hilbert's Programme which we must consider here: a fundamental difficulty about the relation of 'mathematical knowledge' to 'mathematical reality'. For it was a deep-rooted confusion on this score which gave rise to the spurious sceptical worries that Hilbert's Programme was devised to combat.

Hilbert accepted the orthodox demarcation between 'mathematical reality' and 'mathematical knowledge'; and in turn, the abiding problem whether and if so when we can be certain that the two are in harmony. To be sure, Hilbert set out to remove the seeds of scepticism which grow here; his answer to the question, 'How can we be certain that the inferences in a system are truth-preserving?' was, of course: with consistency proofs. To challenge this argument is not *ipso facto* to pursue a sceptical goal, however, if it is the framework itself — which has precipitated this dilemma — that is subjected to scrutiny. And for this reason Wittgenstein's strategy was not to try to *refute* Hilbert's version of the consistency problem: it was to *exclude* it, by showing that Hilbert's anxiety resulted from a misguided conception of mathematical truth. It is clear, therefore, that if we are to appreciate the full thrust of Wittgenstein's remarks on consistency we must first fix the manner in which we are supposed to address Hilbert's Programme. It is important that we consider, not the technical details, but rather, the *point* of his undertaking: the objectives which inspired and the philosophical assumptions which sustained his argument. There is a dangerous tendency to accept Hilbert's Programme as a purely mathematical-/meta-mathematical affair, and hence to look for the mathematical/meta-mathematical flaws and/or significance of his approach. Our first task must be to forsake this approach and identify instead the nature of the problem in strictly philosophical terms.

That is certainly not to deny that several consistency proofs may have been of great mathematical significance (such as Herbrand's investigations in proof theory, which led to the completeness theorem for quantification theory).[10] But be that as it may, it was definitely not this kind of issue that Wittgenstein was considering. Even the question of the bearing of Gödel's second theorem on Hilbert's Programme is ruled out *ab initio* on Wittgenstein's approach. Gödel's second theorem demonstrates that a consistency statement for S is unprovable in S (given that S is consistent). But what exactly does it mean to say that the consistency statement 'p' is unprovable in S? This would appear to be yet another example of the tendency to treat unprovable expressions as meaningful but unproved conjectures. Hence Wittgenstein's insistence that 'Mathematics cannot be incomplete; any more than a *sense* can be incomplete. Whatever I can understand, I must completely understand' (PR §159). Whether or not Wittgenstein's remarks on Gödel's theorem can be elucidated — much less defended — the important point here is simply that Wittgenstein did not propose a 'thesis' which (inadvertently) served as a philosophical analogue of Gödel's second theorem: the point of Wittgenstein's discussion was to stop any such argument as Gödel's before it can even begin. For Gödel accepted the intelligibility of Hilbert's Programme and attacked the cogency of Hilbert's proposed solution, thereby leaving the problem itself intact. But Wittgenstein's argument was based firmly on the premise that the issue is *conceptual*, and can only be solved by a philosophical as opposed to a mathematical approach. Gödel's second theorem can be 'bypassed', therefore, because it was a victim of the very framework which nourished it.[11] The way to resolve Hilbert's problem is rather to clarify the sources of the confusion on which it rests: that is, the solution to the problem must be one which dissolves rather than attempts to *refute* it. We must show that and why the consistency problem is at best innocuous, and at worst unintelligible.

According to Hilbert, the discovery of the paradoxes in set theory had rendered the situation in mathematics 'intolerable'. To this Wittgenstein responded that, far from this being the case, the paradoxes are harmless and the crisis is non-existent. In order to see this, we must examine the logical syntax of such concepts as *paradox, contradiction* and *hidden contradiction.* Whereas Hilbert argued that the key to a solution lies in 'completely clarifying the nature of the infinite'[12] — that the notion of consistency in elementary number theory is perspicuous and our basic problem is how to deploy this paradigm for transfinite number theory — Wittgenstein countered that infinity is irrelevant and the real problem lies in Hilbert's picture of mathematical truth. Indeed, he insisted that far from being fundamentally 'reliable' in Hilbert's terms, it makes as little sense to speak of the consistency of elementary as of higher number theory. Not, that is, because elementary arithmetical truths cannot be rendered absolutely certain, but rather, because it is unintelligible to speak of the reliability or otherwise of elementary number theory. The reason why Wittgenstein concentrated on elementary arithmetic, therefore, was simply that he intended to attack the problem at its root: the real goal of Wittgenstein's argument was to undermine the very notion of *consistency* in the mathematical or 'meta-mathematical' manner in which Hilbert — and those following him who continued to regard this as a pressing issue — employed the concept. For their understanding of 'consistency' was intrinsically committed to the possibility of 'hidden' contradictions; thus, if the latter should be unintelligible, then so too is the former. Hence Wittgenstein set out to demonstrate, not that there are no contradictions in mathematics, but rather, that their existence is both familiar and harmless, and further, that it makes no sense to speak of a *hidden* contradiction. And if there is no sceptical problem to answer, Hilbert's Programme stands exposed as the illegitimate offspring of a philosophical misadventure inspired by epistemological chimeras.

The epistemological framework of Hilbert's argument was absolutely fundamental to his Programme. He agreed with the intuitionists, he emphasised, that there is a body of mathematical truths which are grasped intuitively: 'Finitary propositions that contain only numerals are immediately intuitive and directly intelligible'.[13] For Hilbert was seeking to provide the foundations for mathematics with a species of epistemologically basic mathematical truths: mathematical truths that are intuitively self-evident.[14] An epistemologically basic set of mathematical objects exists — 'extralogical concrete objects' — and propositions about these objects are 'grasped intuitively': they are 'not subject to verification'. The trouble occurs when we shift from the level of these finitary mathematical propositions to higher mathematical truths (just as the sceptical problems so worrisome to reductionists arise when we shift from e.g. sensation to material-object language). In 'Neubegründung der Mathematik', Hilbert cautioned that 'of course, all of mathematics cannot be comprehended within this sort' of intuitively grasped finitary proposition; 'the transition to the standpoint of higher arithmetic and algebra ... already denies these intuitive procedures.'[15] As far as non-finitary mathematical propositions are concerned, we cannot know that these are true independently of having a proof for them. Furthermore, we cannot have any faith in the truth of this proof until we have constructed a 'meta-mathematical' proof which establishes that our formal proof is reliable. To be certain that a non-finitary formula is true, therefore, we must possess both the proof of the theorem and the consistency proof of the system.

The basic problem that remains, however, is to explain how we are to make sense of a consistency proof in finitary terms. It is here that Hilbert turned to the inspiration provided by Weierstrass in the foundations of Analysis: the secret is to reduce transfinite problems to finitary terms. Hilbert's solution was to argue that it is possible to do this in the construction of a consistency proof simply because the latter is a 'meta-mathematical' proof *about* the system in question, not a proof *within* the formal system. And the formal system under meta-mathematical scrutiny is itself comprised of intuitively given symbols (when 'drained of all their meaning').[16] Hence the epistemological status of a consistency proof is the same as that of the intuitively evident proofs about finitary elementary propositions (i.e. a consistency proof will not involve unbounded quantification over the symbols of a formal system). The 'final result' of all this is that: 'We gain a conviction that runs counter to the earlier endeavors of Frege and Dedekind, the conviction that, if scientific knowledge is to be possible, certain intuitive conceptions and insights are indispensable; logic alone does not suffice. The right to operate with the infinite can be secured only by means of the finite.'[17]

The most notable features of this argument are that Hilbert assumed that we are concerned with a problem of justification, and the general strategy which he consequently formulated was consciously based on classical epistemological lines. Indeed, at one point Hilbert went so far as to argue that 'Where we had propositions concerning numerals, we now have formulas which themselves are concrete objects that in their turn are considered by our perceptual intuition.'[18] The argument was phrased, therefore, in terms which deliberately mirrored the standard reductionist approach to the refutation of epistemological scepticism. Thus Hilbert explained that:

> as a condition for the use of logical inferences and the performance of logical operations, something must already be given to our faculty of representation, certain extralogical concrete objects that are intuitively present as immediate experience prior to all thought. If logical inference is to be reliable, it must be possible to survey these objects completely, in all their parts, and the fact that they occur, that they differ from one another, and that they follow each other, or are concatenated, is immediately given intuitively, together with the objects, as something that neither can be reduced to anything else nor requires reduction. This is the basic philosophical position that I consider requisite for mathematics.[19]

This, however, is the basic philosophical position that Wittgenstein wanted to demonstrate is fatally oblivious of the normative character of mathematical propositions, and thus resulted in such confusion as Hilbert's belief that mathematical truth could stand in need of a 'consistency proof'. The brunt of Wittgenstein's criticisms were therefore directed almost entirely at this level of Hilbert's argument.

The fundamental philosophical issue which Hilbert's Programme raises, therefore, is whether mathematical truth stands in need of justification. It is not just a question of whether what

Hilbert called 'ideal' propositions are reliable (e.g. whether the truths of transfinitary mathematics can be justified) for Hilbert assumed that *all* mathematical truth must be justified. In the case of elementary mathematics this is ultimately provided by intuition; and since intuition is the only means we possess for eliminating sceptical objections, we must discover some method of reducing the justification of higher mathematical truths to intuitively evident propositions. Hence Hilbert argued that the point of a consistency proof is that it 'provides us with a justification for the introduction of our ideal propositions' (i.e. non-finitary propositions about 'ideal elements' such as 'points at infinity' and 'a line at infinity'). At the beginning of 'On the Infinite' Hilbert bewailed the fact that 'in mathematics, this paragon of reliability and truth, the very notions and inferences, as everyone learns, teaches and uses them, lead to absurdities. And where else would reliability and truth be found if even mathematical thinking fails?'[20] The central premise which underlies Hilbert's Programme, therefore, and which continues to preoccupy philosophers of mathematics, is that:

> there is an obvious sceptical challenge, for which the set-theoretic paradoxes provide motivation. The sceptic should ... argue that the mathematicians who developed set theory (e.g. Cantor, Dedekind and Frege) used the same methods of justification as are used in elementary mathematics. But those methods could be used to justify claims which were later found to be false (as is shown by the derivation of the Russell and Burali-Forti paradoxes). Hence, such methods are not absolutely reliable, and our claims to mathematical knowledge can be undermined by future evidence (as Russell's famous letter undermined Frege's claims). Thus mathematical knowledge is not certain.[21]

Thus, the discovery of Gödel's second theorem may have spelled the demise of Hilbert's efforts, but it has left us with a major epistemological problem no less urgent than when Hilbert wrote. In the words of Michael Resnik: 'Given that Gödel's theorem does not rule out consistency proofs as an answer to skepticism ... how can we answer the skeptic?'[22] The theme which we must keep constantly in mind when approaching Wittgenstein's remarks on the consistency problem is that the only answer we can give to the sceptic is to reveal to him why his questions are nonsensical; to see that 'We can only ask from a standpoint from which a question is possible. From which a doubt is possible. ... We cannot ask about that which alone makes questions possible at all. Not about what first gives the system a foundation' (PR §168).

Mathematical Totems and Tabus

The exposition of the first theme in Wittgenstein's argument was formulated in response to the question: 'How can we be certain that the axioms (or theorems) of a calculus are true?' As we have just seen, Wittgenstein's main objective was to expose the epistemological confusions underlying Hilbert's Programme and those subsequent controversies which, however grudgingly, accept the presence of scepticism in the context of mathematics. Such predicaments invariably stem, Wittgenstein contended, from a persistent misconception about the logical syntax of mathematical propositions, and thence, of what it means to say that we know that a mathematical proposition is true. To bring this out, he seized on one of the more prominent themes in Hilbert's argument. Hilbert maintained in several places that to say that a mathematical proposition is intuitively grasped or self-evident entails that the truth which it expresses is 'surveyable': 'a formalised proof, like a numeral, is a concrete and surveyable object', for example, 'and this provides us with a justification for the introduction of our ideal propositions.'[23] Wittgenstein fastened on to this idea as the perfect vehicle for the point that he was trying to make: freed from any associations with some peculiar 'phenomenological feature' of the proposition concerned or some 'basic' epistemological act, what we are left with is a statement about the perspicuity of normative structures and grammatical truths (cf. Chapter 4). Thus, it might well be that Hilbert's arguments on consistency played a key role in the genesis of Wittgenstein's emphasis on the notion of the surveyability of proof.[24]

In Hilbert's hands the concept of 'surveyability' led to nothing but trouble. For Hilbert was left trying to explain how all mathematical objects (i.e. 'ideal' as well as finitary) can be surveyable in the sense in which he used this to mean 'perceptually recognisable'. But Wittgenstein rescued the notion by shifting the focus onto logical syntax. Purged of any spurious epistemological overtones, what we are left with is a criterion for what it means to say that something is true in virtue of the rules laid down by grammar: we must be able — it must be logically possible — to apply those rules. The surveyability we are concerned with is thus a direct consequence of the principle, constantly emphasised, that it only makes sense to say that we have asked a question when a method for answering it exists. And it was precisely this theme which led Wittgenstein to ask what exactly it means to speak of a 'hidden contradiction'. In his simmering argument with Waismann on this topic Wittgenstein continually insisted that it was the notion of a 'hidden' contradiction which he was attacking, not that of a contradiction *per se*. Obviously contradictions exist in mathematics, and indeed we make extensive use of their presence (e.g. in indirect proofs). But the question Wittgenstein concentrated on is 'What does it mean to speak of a "hidden" contradiction?': a contradiction which we cannot see now, but which we might encounter some time in the future? (WWK 174). The elusive point that Wittgenstein pursued was that 'all this talk about a hidden contradiction does not make sense, and the danger mathematicians talk about — as if a contradiction could be hidden in present-day mathematics like a disease — this danger is a mere figment of the imagination' (WWK 174). That is, it is *unintelligible* to ask whether a 'hidden' contradiction exists: 'this is the essential thing on which everything to do with the question of consistency depends' (WWK 127-8).

Just as many have speculated whether there is an intimate connection between consistency and completeness, so too Wittgenstein discerned a fundamental parallel between the consistency and decision problems: viz. both arise from the same illicit assimilation of 'unanswerable' with 'unanswered'. The very question whether a 'hidden' contradiction exists is similar to whether a mathematical conjecture might be true; in each case we are supposedly led to accept the possibility that the answer might transcend our recognitional abilities. But we can no more detect a 'hidden' contradiction than discover the truth of a mathematical conjecture; we can only discuss the construction of a calculus in which we can talk about *this* contradiction or proposition (WWK 174-5). The assumption that it makes sense to speak of a 'hidden' contradiction is similar, therefore, to the premises underlying the 'sceptical' rule-following argument which we examined in Chapter 2; it confuses *overlooked* with a distinctively sceptical interpretation of *hidden*. Wittgenstein acknowledged that it makes sense to say that I have overlooked a contradiction, but only in so far as I can scrutinise my rules and discover such an oversight. But I cannot then suppose that I have scrutinised my rules and yet still overlooked a contradiction: 'A contradiction is found — have I had from the very beginning a method of discovering it? If so, then only an oversight has occurred; I have forgotten to check all the possibilities. If not, then no possibility of a contradiction comes into question, for a contradiction is given only by a method of discovering it' (WWK 208). For the grammar of 'scrutinise' is such that it rules out the possibility of merely overlooking a contradiction. That is to say, we must distinguish carefully between *carelessness* and *unsurveyability*.

In order to generate the sceptical hypothesis which he then set out to refute Hilbert had to conflate these logically distinct notions. This is precisely the fallacy that he committed when he argued, for example, that 'It is necessary to make inferences everywhere as reliable as they are in ordinary elementary number theory, which no one questions and in which contradictions and paradoxes arise only through our carelessness.'[25] Wittgenstein picked up on this theme when he considered 'the case of a board-game' for which 'we already at the beginning have a method of discovering the contradiction': 'If that means " At this point, and at that point, and ...," then from the beginning there has obviously been the possibility of my discovering the contradiction, and if I did not see it, then it was my fault — perhaps I was too lazy to inspect all the cases, or I forgot about one case. ... I can always decide, however, if a contradiction is present by scrutinizing my list of rules' (WWK 195). What Wittgenstein was arguing for here is that the difference between an 'overlooked' and a 'hidden' contradiction amounts to the difference between *surveyability* and *unsurveyability*. I cannot speak of 'overlooking a contradiction' unless a method exists for definitively excluding such a possibility. And this is the crucial step which Hilbert ignored: in order to generate a sceptical problem he had to assume that it is possible to survey the rules of a system and *still* overlook a contradiction. Such a misguided assumption rests on the premise that surveyability relates to 'perceptual recognition', and hence subjects us to the same sorts of sceptical problems as those which plague classical epistemology. The answer to this argument is thus to show how 'surveyability' is a term of grammar: of the logical possibility of answering a question. To say that a problem is surveyable is to say that a method for answering it exists. Likewise, the proper answer to give to the mathematician's anxiety that a contradiction might lie hidden in an axiomatic system is that 'I am given a contradiction only by a method for discovering it!' (WWK 195).

The assumption that it makes sense to speak of a 'hidden contradiction' rests, therefore, on the spurious epistemological premise that we are compelled to answer the sceptical objection that we can never be certain, when we have surveyed our rules, whether we have not overlooked some contradiction. Just as Wittgenstein's discussion of rule-following set out, not to *refute*, but rather, to undermine the 'sceptical' argument, so too his reaction to the consistency problem was to demonstrate that the proper response to Hilbert's worry is to dissolve it: to *exclude* the possibility of such doubt. Where Wittgenstein tended to obscure and complicate the substance of this argument, however, was in his development and recapitulation of the initially discordant theme that, in those cases where I have not bothered to survey my rules, I can indeed come across an unexpected contradiction. A familiar refrain in his arguments with Waismann is that 'As long as a contradiction is not there it does not concern me. I can accordingly stay quite calm and do my calculations.' But the ensuing resolution ensured that this was not construed as a plea for philosophical quietism: 'Would the discovery of a contradiction in mathematics, then, make all the calculations cease to exist that have been established by mathematicians in the course of several hundreds of years? Should we say that they were not calculations? Absolutely not. If a contradiction is going to occur, we shall manage. *Now*, however, we need not worry about it' (WWK 195-6). It is important to see that with this argument Wittgenstein shifted his discussion to the entirely different plane of explaining what 'contradiction' means. The reason why the latter theme was so important to Wittgenstein was because he felt that in a sense it is anterior to the confusions surrounding the notion of a 'hidden' contradiction. For mathematicians are only led into their futile worry about 'hidden' contradictions because of their 'morbid fear' for contradictions *simpliciter*. Hence, the real way to stop the rot is to attack the problem at its source: the notion of a 'hidden' contradiction is unintelligible, but the real problem we want to resolve is, why were mathematicians led into this confusion in the first place?

The basic question we must answer is thus: 'Why should a

certain configuration of signs not be allowed to arise? Why this dread? Why the tabu?' (WWK 119). Once again the route to understanding lies in conceptual clarification: this time, of *contradiction*. 'The main point' in the problem of consistency, Wittgenstein told Waismann and Schlick, 'is that we should come to an understanding about the concept of contradiction. For we cannot reach agreement if you mean by it something different from me' (WWK 175). As far as Wittgenstein was concerned, 'The idea of a contradiction — and this is something I hold fast to — is that of a logical contradiction, and this can occur only in the *true-false game*, that is, only where we make statements' (WWK 124). The most important factor to bear in mind when approaching Wittgenstein's remarks on the innocuousness of contradictions, therefore, is that he adhered closely throughout his exposition to the quasi-formal definition of a contradiction presented in the *Tractatus*. A contradiction, like a tautology, does not *say* anything. So why should the former be any more worrying to mathematicians than the latter? Strictly speaking, since both types of expression function in exactly the same manner, mathematicians should be equally concerned that their axioms might one day land them with a 'hidden tautology' (WWK 131). Clearly, there is some sort of an anomaly present here which needs to be explained and if possible removed.

The essential move is to grasp that tautologies and contradictions must not be confused with *rules*. You might, of course, use a tautology or a contradiction as the basis of a rule, but the two constructions are not at all equivalent (PG 305; RPP I §44). Yet this, Wittgenstein thought, is precisely the fallacy that has nurtured the consistency problem. The example that he repeatedly gave is that the (senseless) tautology "¬(p & ¬p)' is not equivalent to the 'law of contradiction' (the prohibition of the construction of the contradiction 'p & ¬p'). Rather, the rule — in the case of the 'law of contradiction' — is 'Do not use this contradiction'. The first step is thus to clarify how rule and tautology relate to each other here: 'People always speak of "the law of contradiction." I actually think that the fear of contradictions is connected with taking a contradiction to be a *proposition*: '¬(p.¬p)".' The point is that 'I can easily take the law of contradiction to be a rule, for I prohibit the construction of the logical product "p.¬p." The tautology "¬(p.¬p)," however, in no way expresses this prohibition. How could it? It does not say anything, after all, whereas a rule does say something (WWK 131). That is, as we saw in Chapter 3 when considering the relationship between 'p v ¬p' and the Law of Excluded Middle, the conclusion here is likewise that the fundamental law of logic '¬(p.¬p)' is a tautology, and hence cannot itself function as the 'law of contradiction'. For it does not express anything: it is a 'senseless pseudo-proposition'. Rather, it is the rule '"¬(p.¬p)"' is a tautology' which formulates the fundamental feature of assertion that if we attempt to state a proposition together with its negation all information will be cancelled out.

This argument may nevertheless strike some as nothing more than an *ignoratio elenchi.* After all, why should mathematicians be restricted to Wittgenstein's formal definition of 'contradiction'? The key to Wittgenstein's response is conveyed by the above passage. The problem is that mathematicians have confused rules prohibiting certain forms of expressions, such as the 'law of contradiction', with *contradictions* as technically understood. When mathematicians speak about the damage which the discovery of a 'hidden contradiction' would inflict on a mathematical system they are thinking of the violation of a fundamental rule, such as the 'law of contradiction'. But when they come to spell out exactly what sort of thing such a 'hidden contradiction' would be they revert to a *Tractatus*-like technical definition of contradiction. Thus Wittgenstein warned Waismann that 'Hilbert calls the configuration '0 ≠ 0' a contradiction because he has a conception of contradiction in no way different from ours, i.e. "p.¬p"' [i.e. that it contradicts '0 = 0'] (WWK 176). But when Hilbert talked about the exclusion of contradictions from a system he shifted to the case of rules prohibiting certain constructions. Obviously contradictions can occur; what Hilbert was worried about, however, was a violation of the 'law of contradiction', not the construction of a contradiction *per se.* But only a contrary rule can *contradict* (as opposed to *violate*) an established rule; e.g. a rule to the effect that '"(p.¬p)"' is not a tautology'.

At this point Wittgenstein introduced an important complication into the *Tractatus* account. Wittgenstein carefully distinguished in the *Tractatus* between the technical/logical term 'contradiction' (*Kontradiktion*) and the ordinary German expression for 'contradiction', *im Widerspruch.* The former constructions are defined as *senseless* pseudo-propositions, the latter as *nonsensical* expressions;[26] the result of asserting a proposition together with its negation is *senseless*, that of breaking a rule is *nonsense.* Following the introduction of the *Satzsystem* in 1929 this division became necessarily more elaborate. It is all too easy to pass over what Wittgenstein was trying to say here, and even after he had explained the argument to Waismann and Schlick in some detail he found that he had to return to the same theme several times. The point that he was driving at is that we must distinguish between two different kinds of 'contrariety'. The idea behind this traces back directly to Wittgenstein's post-RLF distinction between 'contradiction' as technically understood in the *Tractatus* sense and 'logical exclusion' which is *Satzsystem*-defined. (It is for this reason that Wittgenstein frequently returned to the colour-exclusion problem in his attempt to elucidate his argument on consistency; cf. WWK 127, 149.) It is possible to conceive of two propositions which operate in different *Satzsysteme*, and hence are not logically exclusive of one another. The distinction we are dealing with here, therefore, is threefold: there are contradictions, which take the form '(p.¬p)'; these are well formed and senseless. Then there are 'contrary' propositions *within* a *Satzsystem*: logically exclusive statements — *Satzsystem*-confined conjunctions of the form 'p_x & q_x' — which are ill formed in a particular *Satzsystem* and hence nonsensical (e.g. 'This is red and blue all over'). Finally, there are 'contrary' propositions from two independent *Satzsysteme*, whose conjunction, 'p_x & q_y', is well formed and meaningful (e.g. we might say of a surface viewed with the naked eye that it is red, but viewed under a microscope that it is largely colourless).

Certainly, we can envisage circumstances where this last distinction will apply. 'If e.g. in geometry I conclude from one proof that the sum of the angles of a triangle is equal to 180° and from another proof that the sum of the angles is greater than 180°, then this is in no way a contradiction. Both conclusions might hold at the same time and I can even imagine a case where we would even apply such an axiom system: if the sum of angles of a triangle were by *one* method of measuring equal to one value and by a different method equal to a different value' (WWK 149). In this example we are dealing *ex hypothesi* with propositions from different *Satzsysteme*; i.e. we are confronted with a case of 'p_x & q_y' — we have two different methods of measurement — which may or may not be 'prohibited', depending on how we wish to use the system. And it is this last thought that holds the crux of Wittgenstein's argument: if, for whatever reason, we wish to prohibit 'p_x &

q_y', then we simply create a rule forbidding this product. But it is perfectly conceivable that we may wish to use 'p_x & q_y'. In any event, the crucial point is that we are dealing with a product of the form 'p_x & q_y', not an internal '*Satzsystem* contrariety' of the form 'p_x & q_x', and clearly not a contradiction of the form 'p & ¬p'. The mere fact that a proposition is *contrary* to a proposition from some other system (e.g. that we have different methods for measuring the angles of a triangle, which might yield different results) cannot *ipso facto* entail that the assertion of their product constitutes a violation of a rule; in order for this to occur there must already be a specific rule prohibiting the conjunction in question.

The reason why this argument is so important is that, because mathematicians have failed to distinguish between contradictions and contrarieties, they have misunderstood the nature of the distinction between a *senseless* and a *forbidden* expression (WWK 176). By confusing contradictions with contrarieties they have begun by arguing that it is possible to construct a contradiction in a calculus and concluded that such a result is disastrous because it is forbidden. But that in itself is a contradiction in terms; if it is forbidden to construct a given contradiction, then it is logically impossible to do so: i.e. any attempt to do so yields, not a senseless pseudo-proposition, but rather, nonsense. What has happened here is that the case of contradictions has tacitly, and unknowingly, been confused with contrarieties. The real idea underlying the consistency problem is that it is possible to construct a *contrariety*, hitherto unthought of, and *a fortiori* not prohibited in a calculus. But what should we do when such an occasion arises? When faced with an unexpected contrary conjunction, we must simply determine whether or not to prohibit such a result. We shall decide this solely according to whether or not there is any point — as considered from the purpose to which we intend to put the calculus — of permitting such a 'contrariety'. Which brings us to Wittgenstein's constantly reiterated theme that if we decide that such a 'contrariety' is undesirable, then we simply make it a rule that it is prohibited. In which case there henceforward exists a rule stating that 'p_x cannot be conjoined with q_y', and thus any violation of this rule will result in nonsense.

The distinction between 'contradictions' and 'contrarieties' leads in turn to the claim that 'if contradictions arose between the rules of the game of mathematics, it would be the easiest thing in the world to find a remedy. All we have to do is lay down a new stipulation concerning the case in which the rules conflict, and the matter is dealt with' (WWK 120). Wittgenstein approached this theme by first showing how Hilbert's argument operates at two different conceptual levels: either for a calculus of meaningless signs, or for mathematics proper. He thus began with an *argumentum ad hominem* against the formalist position: we can indeed talk of a calculus of meaningless signs, but then it obviously makes no sense to speak of contradictions. For configurations of signs cannot *contradict* one another: they are by definition meaningless marks, whereas the concept of contradiction only applies in the context of significant expressions (WWK 120, 124). Thus, just as Wittgenstein had argued *contra* Hilbert that we must distinguish between a calculus *qua* system of meaningless marks and mathematics — which consists in the rule-governed application of concepts — so too we must distinguish between the appearance of a certain configuration of signs in a formal calculus and a contradiction in a mathematical system. Hence a formalist interpretation of the 'consistency problem' is *ab initio* unintelligible. Hilbert was at least partially aware of the point operating here, but his critical mistake was that he did not appreciate its full logical implications. In 'On the Infinite' he announced: 'I, for one, have always believed that only assertions and, in so far as they lead to assertions by means of inferences, assumptions could contradict each other, and the view that facts and events themselves could come to do so seems to me the perfect example of an inanity.[27] But no less an inanity than the suggestion that configurations could contradict each other' (WWK 119, 142).

As far as the application of a mathematical system is concerned, Wittgenstein argued that the discovery of a contradiction at some later point would in no way affect the status of all the calculations that had hitherto been performed, nor need it irrevocably undermine any future use of the system in question (RFM VII §15). This is entirely a matter of the nature of the contradiction *vis-à-vis* the application of the calculus. Stated in these stark terms the argument has outraged several critics: as Wittgenstein was perfectly well aware it would (LFM 67). But the force of the argument derives from the logical syntax of 'contradiction' as it pertains to rules or propositions; not from any Bolshevist tendencies or aspirations. The first step to notice is that in mathematics a contradiction, as was emphasised above, does not itself violate a rule; rather, it marks the cancellation of two rules, leaving us with a senseless expression and thus a stalled move in an application. But that does not automatically spell the demise of a system. It might do so, as Wittgenstein suggested could be the case in noughts and crosses, but that is a matter of the bearing which the contradiction has on the nature of the application that is under consideration. But in many cases the problem can be easily circumvented, merely through the expedient of stipulating a new rule for how to deal with this case (WWK 120) (*infra*).

The standard response to this last point is that it signifies Wittgenstein's complete failure to grasp the gravity of the situation which he had so cavalierly tried to dismiss. One of the arguments most commonly cited in support of the need for a consistency proof — or at least, in defence of the thesis that Wittgenstein did not understand the technical implications of this issue — is that from a contradiction anything would follow; a calamity to which Wittgenstein naively wanted to respond: make it a rule then not to draw any inferences from a contradiction. To this argument Turing (and following him Charles Chihara) insisted that Wittgenstein had simply misunderstood the nature of the dilemma; he had merely focused his attention on one of the side-effects of the illness, when what we are really concerned with is the cancer that lies in the axioms of the system, which are capable of generating, as Chihara puts it, 'infinitely many' such contradictions. But Wittgenstein was by no means unacquainted with this objection. It is noteworthy that Waismann was already putting just this argument to Wittgenstein in 1930:

> if the formula '$0 \neq 0$' can be derived by a legitimate proof and if we, furthermore, in accordance with Hilbert, add the axiom '$0 \neq 0 \rightarrow A$', where 'A' means an arbitrary formula, then we can infer the formula 'A' from the deductive pattern.
>
> $$0 \neq 0$$
> $$0 \neq 0 \rightarrow A$$
> $$\overline{}$$
> $$A$$
>
> and write it down too. This means, however, that in this case *any* formula can be derived, and thus the game loses its character and its interest. (WWK 132)

The key point in Wittgenstein's long answer is that 'if I say, The configuration "$0 \neq 0$" is to be permitted, I once more specify a rule, I define a game, but a different one from the one where I exclude this configuration' (WWK 132). Before we consider the logico-syntactical basis for this argument, let us first examine the technical grounds for the Waismann/Turing/Chihara objection.

The problem we are meant to be dealing with is that an inconsistent system is one in which every well-formed formula is derivable; i.e. a system is consistent only if not every well-formed formula is a theorem (e.g. the negations of the theorems). To demonstrate how such a consequence would arise, we construct a system S in the propositional calculus with the following three axioms:

$$(1) \quad (p \rightarrow (q \rightarrow p))$$
$$(2) \quad ((p \rightarrow (q \rightarrow r)) \rightarrow ((p \rightarrow q) \rightarrow (p \rightarrow r)))$$
$$(3) \quad ((\neg q \rightarrow \neg p) \rightarrow ((\neg q \rightarrow p) \rightarrow q))$$

The only rule of inference in this system is Modus Ponens.

From these axioms we derive the following lemma:

$$\neg p \rightarrow (p \rightarrow q)$$

I.e. if S is inconsistent, so that we can prove both p and $\neg p$, then any wff q would be provable. The proof of the lemma proceeds as follows:

1.	$\neg p$	By Hypothesis
2.	p	By Hypothesis
3.	$p \rightarrow (\neg q \rightarrow p)$	Axiom 1
4.	$\neg p \rightarrow (\neg q \rightarrow \neg p)$	Axiom 1
5.	$\neg q \rightarrow p$	2,3 MP
6.	$\neg q \rightarrow \neg p$	1,4 MP
7.	$((\neg q \rightarrow \neg p) \rightarrow ((\neg q \rightarrow p) \rightarrow q))$	Axiom 3
8.	$(\neg q \rightarrow p) \rightarrow q$	6,7 MP
9.	q	5,8 MP

What is actually going on here? Clearly the lemma is an instantiation of axiom 3; hence, it is one of the rules of the system that from a contradiction any wff is derivable. But whereas such a rule is only contained implicitly in the axioms, the lemma is supposed to make the point explicitly. And just as axiom 3 does not mention a contradiction, neither does the lemma. How, then, does it accomplish its appointed task? We are supposed to see the lemma as running on two separate tracks — 1,4,6, and 2,3,5 — which come together in the final three steps of the proof. The lemma does not *state* that any wff is derivable from a contradiction, but rather it *shows* this. All that the lemma actually states is that, from the negation of a theorem it follows that anything can be derived from the subsequent affirmation of that theorem. The purpose of the proof of the lemma is then to show how our definition of an absolute system follows from this consequence of the axioms. It is always disquieting, however, when a non-philosophical technique — whether 'meta-mathematical or mathematico-logical — is used to create/resolve a philosophical problem. Moreover, there is a growing tendency to treat 'formal' philosophical arguments as somehow sacrosanct; which is to say that the above 'proof' is invariably trotted out in this dispute with the curt conclusion: 'therefore in an inconsistent system anything would be provable'. And it is precisely this last line that we want to scrutinise; for here is a quintessential example of the 'prose' which Wittgenstein warned against. What we want to know is, how does the proof license this conclusion: how, that is, has the proof been interpreted?

The tacit premise in this interpretation is that, in an inconsistent system we would be able to infer p on one occasion and ¬p on another, and the great danger would lie in our not being aware of these conflicting results. Passing over the substantial question of what exactly it means to say that we were not aware of these contradictory results, the fact remains that the proof itself is very much aware of this conflict. That is, the proof only begins with what in effect is the stipulation of p & ¬p. Thus Wittgenstein's — notorious — answer to this argument was, as has been stated, that we should simply make it a rule not to draw any inferences from a contradiction; or, as he put it in his discussions with Waismann and Schlick, we simply make it a rule (the law of contradiction) that '"(p & ¬p)" is prohibited'. The trouble with this answer is that 'p & ¬p' never occurs explicitly in the proof of the lemma. The key to Wittgenstein's argument, however, is that it does occur *implicitly*, and that in fact the proof of the lemma turns on this covert use. It is only the two-track nature of the proof of the lemma which obscures the fact that we have actually begun with the premise 'p & ¬p'. Thus, the strategy of Wittgenstein's objection was not to attack the *conclusion* of the lemma: it was to attack the very *premise*: to stop the proof of the lemma before it can even begin. For removed of this deceptive two-track structure what the proof of the lemma really states is:

1.	¬p & p	By Hypothesis
2.	(¬p→(¬q→¬p)) & (p→(¬q→p))	Axiom 1
3.	(¬q→¬p) & (¬q→p)	1,2, MP
4.	((¬q→¬p)→((¬q→p)→q))	Axiom 3
5.	(¬q→p) & (¬q→p)→q	3,4 MP
6.	q	3,5 MP

The objections to Wittgenstein's argument are based on the idea that Wittgenstein failed to see that it is the nature of the axiom set of the system itself, together with its rules of inference, which lead to the consequence of any formula's being derivable. Wittgenstein's *ad hoc* prohibition of a contradiction would, so the argument goes, only strike at one of the manifestations of the problem, but would leave the source of the contradiction, and hence this difficulty intact. But Wittgenstein's answer was that it is only by assuming that you can draw inferences from the contradiction that you can generate this 'proof'. And it is for this reason that we need only make it a rule that you can draw no inferences from a contradiction. In other words, the answer to Turing is that you cannot get any conclusion you like *without* going through the contradiction, and this is something we need not do: 'The only thing is to show him which way not to proceed from a contradiction' (LFM 222). The point is that if we decide in this situation that the presence of such a contradiction is intolerable then we must construct a new calculus, different from the preceding in so far as it contains this new rule. The mistake is to suppose that mathematics is composed of a single static calculus. On the contrary, mathematical systems, like language-games, are constantly fluctuating, as we add to or modify the rules (cf. Chapter 8). To be sure, the result of such an argument may seem to fly in the face of the whole thrust of axiomatics as many envisage it. For, once again, the consequence of Wittgenstein's argument is to render mathematics, in Russell's words, 'terribly complicated'; on Wittgenstein's account calculus families can indeed become heavily encumbered with subsidiary postulates. Of course, Wittgenstein's argument was not at all concerned with mathematical utility or aesthetics; his sole desire was to combat the theme that there is a *sceptical* problem which must be addressed. But apart from this point, Michael Detlefsen's enlightening instrumentalist approach to Hilbert's Programme may also suggest further grounds to clear Wittgenstein of the charge of mathematical primitivism. Most significant of all, perhaps, is Detlefsen's work on 'dynamic theory-construction', in which he shows that an instrumentalist 'may revise a theory without changing the substance of any of his axioms. Rather, he may (at least in principle) simply limit their range of application, preserving their useful applications, while discarding their problematic ones. One "bad" application of an axiom does not imply that all of its applications are to be done away with. Upon deriving a contradiction from a set of axioms, the instrumentalist need not respond by dropping any of them. He can instead simply rule out some particular uses of his axioms (i.e. some particular derivations of theorems from his axioms).'[28]

Thus we arrive from a rather different quarter at Wittgenstein's insistence that we are never compelled one way or another to permit or prohibit the presence of a contradiction. In the penultimate discussion recorded in *Wittgenstein and the Vienna Circle* he explained that 'What is misleading is the belief that everything happens through compulsion, that we are sliding into an abyss willy-nilly without any possibility of being rescued. Is it not true that we are compelled to follow the path we do? In a certain sense, it is. But by what? By an analogy — not by the calculus, but by certain implicit conditions which we want to make the calculus fit. ... It is some other characteristic that guides me here. Contradiction as such is something I can always avoid' (WWK 201). All of the controversy about 'compulsion' versus 'freedom' which has arisen in the light of this argument can be extremely misleading, however, for it can tempt one into supposing that what Wittgenstein was concerned with was the psychology of mathematical invention or with a genetic account of the development of mathematical knowledge. What Wittgenstein was really after was a technique to clarify the logical issues which are at stake: viz. the logical syntax of mathematical truths. This motive lies behind his argument on the possibility of conflicting results in geometry: 'Let us return once more to the sum of the angles of a triangle. Suppose we could at one time prove that the sum of the angles is 180° and at another time that it is 182° (and in fact from the axioms in both cases) — what then? I should say that we have simply laid down two dif-

ferent stipulations as to when to regard a measurement as correct.'
The important point is that 'I could even imagine how to apply
such rules: The one rule I use, for example, when measuring angles
by a *mechanical* method (protractor), the other one when
measuring them by an *optical* method' (WWK 198-9).

What Wittgenstein was arguing for here was the idea that if we
want to hold fast to *this* concept of geometry then we must lay
down such and such rules; we must adapt our calculus (construct a
new calculus) by stipulating a rule forbidding the 'contrariety' in
question. But there is no compulsion to hold fast to a given system:
to stipulate such a rule. There is no such thing as a 'geometrical
reality' compelling us to follow this 'uni-value' system of angular
measurement. The essence of mathematics lies in the *use* to which
we choose to apply a calculus. Given the applications that we currently demand (from Euclidean geometry!), the suggestion of two
values runs contrary to our guiding principles, and hence will be
prohibited. But that does not mean that geometry *per se* must not
yield two values; that is entirely a matter to be decided by what we
want to accomplish with our geometry (cf. Chapter 8). By the
same token, however, we could not understand someone who
spoke of geometry yielding two values unless we understood the
rules that he was employing, and hence, what he meant by
'geometry' (WWK 177). For it is one thing to imagine that someone might adopt a different system of geometry, but quite another
to imagine a different system of geometry. In the former case we
are merely supposing that someone might construct different rules
of geometry, but in the latter we are trying to imagine something
where *ex hypothesi* we have no rules to guide us. The bounds of
imagination, however, are — despite Shelley's poetic fervour —
confined by the bounds of sense.

It is only natural to ask, then, what is the point of this argument
in the first place? Simply this: not to bring out what we might do,
but rather, to clarify what we are doing: that we are dealing with
grammatical truths. Hence, we must be careful to distinguish
between saying that 'we must construct such and such rules *if* we
want these results' and 'we must construct such and such rules
because we *must* have these results'. It was the latter locution —
with its resonances of a mathematical reality — that Wittgenstein
was attacking. And it should be clear why Wittgenstein felt that
this argument was so relevant to Hilbert's Programme. The feeling
behind Hilbert's argument is that a contradiction can prevent us

from attaining the results that we want. But the logical grammar of this last expression should alert us to the fact that it is we who control the calculus, and not the reverse. Anything that threatens to undermine the results we want, whatever these might be, can be summarily dealt with whenever they arise. As, for example, we simply make it a rule that multiplication by 0 yields 0, whereas division by 0 is deemed an error. But then, one might respond that there are very good reasons why division by 0 should be construed as an error: reasons which far transcend the narrow interests of mathematical simplicity or aesthetics, and which only truly come out when we set about to apply the calculus. For it is one thing to argue that contradictions, when properly understood, will be seen to be harmless as far as the development of a theory is concerned, but quite another to conclude that the application of the theory will remain similarly unaffected. Or is it?

The Application of an 'Inconsistent System'

Chihara clearly spoke for many when he expostulated that Wittgenstein utterly failed to recognise the seriousness of the practical problems rendered by the existence of an inconsistent system, as is borne out by Wittgenstein's baffling failure to grasp the full significance of Turing's warning that 'you cannot be confident about applying your calculus until you know that there is no hidden contradiction in it'[29] (LFM 217). This took shape in the infamous 'collapsing bridge' argument. What Turing objected to 'is the bridge falling down' because we have been applying, unbeknownst to ourselves, an unsound system. Wittgenstein's insistence that this constitutes a 'question of physics' struck both Turing and Chihara as proof of a deep-seated inability to understand the damage that could be inflicted by a contradiction on an application. As Chihara sees it, Wittgenstein only distinguished between two possible causes for the collapse of a bridge: a faulty empirical theory or mistakes in calculation; whereas Turing wanted to introduce the further distinction between a faulty empirical theory based on a sound calculus and one caused by an unsound system. It was the failure to grasp this latter distinction which led to the 'strange view advanced by Wittgenstein' that 'it does not sound quite right to say that a bridge might fall down because of a contradiction'.[30] In his harsh review of *Lectures on the Foundations of*

Mathematics, Chihara then seizes on the 'collapsing bridge' problem as proof of Wittgenstein's philosophical barrenness in the foundations of mathematics *simpliciter*. One is left, however, with the uncomfortable feeling that, however well-founded Chihara's criticisms might at first appear, his attack could not but have benefited from a more sympathetic attempt at interpretation. Perhaps the most interesting way to approach this issue is to suspend judgement completely at the outset and ask: assuming that Wittgenstein *did* understand the point of Turing's objections, what could he possibly have been driving at?

The basic premise in Chihara's attack is that 'A sound system will carry one from truths to truths', whereas an inconsistent one will lead from true premises to false conclusions.[31] And yet the counter-example which Chihara provides seems *prima facie* to have little to do with the question of a 'sound' system. Indeed, his argument serves to bring into sharp focus one of the principal themes that Wittgenstein laboured to clarify in his discussion of the grammar of *proof*, for it is concerned with the case of engineers working with 'such a large number of premises and carrying out such an intricate chain of inferences that a computer is used to check their work. If we imagine that they carry out their inferences rather mechanically, following set routines in accordance with general rules of strategy (as many students in logic courses do), it is not hard to see how they could start with true premises and end with false conclusions without noticing anything wrong with their logical system.'[32] Chihara feels that this illustrates how 'the logical system they used was unsound and led them to make invalid inferences (that is, they followed the rules of derivation correctly but their calculus was wrong)'.[33] (Here at any rate is one point at which Chihara departs from Turing, who scrupulously avoided saying that it makes sense to speak of a calculus being 'wrong' (LFM 218).) Chihara thus concludes that: 'the collapse of the bridge need not be due to a faulty empirical theory or bad data. In fact, as I have described the situation, if the engineers were to recheck their data and retest their empirical theories, they would find everything in order. Hopefully, there would be some non-Wittgensteinian logicians around to discover the unsoundness of their logical system.'[34]

The key to this argument is to bear in mind that — surface appearances to the contrary — it is not supposed to be concerned with the likelihood of error in the engineer's calculations. Chihara is not interested in the case where the theory which the engineers use is so complicated that, without computers, it would be virtually impossible to avoid mistakes. Such a hazard might constitute compelling grounds for adopting a different theory for bridge-building, but it would in no way indicate any 'flaws in the calculus'. Yet neither is Chihara interested in such problems as e.g. the design of the hangers on a suspension bridge, where the engineer can either calculate the precise length each hanger should be in order to carry its proper share of the deck load or else fit the suspension rods to approximate lengths and then adjust their lengths — 'tune' the rods — in the final assembly. For we are not, *ex hypothesi*, concerned with any defects in the engineer's physical theory (e.g. about 'safe' values of design stress). In some ways the bridge example itself may be responsible for the confusions that surface here; for bridge-building seems an almost paradigmatic example of a physical theory in which the only strictly *mathematical* problems that can arise are calculating errors. To see the real force of Chihara's example, however, we need only imagine that instead of building a bridge we are dealing with an application of Hilbert's axiomatisation of kinetic gas theory which, according to Theodore von Kármán, 'is today the basis of most of our engineering calculations on the behaviour of man-made satellites'.[35]

Forgoing for the moment any consideration of where *contradictions* enter into this, the immediate problem with Chihara's opening argument is that, as it stands, it offends against the moving spirit behind Wittgenstein's remarks on the nature of proof, which in part underpinned his reaction to Turing's objections. In Chihara's words, it is because of the complexity of the theory that the engineers 'start with true premises and end with false conclusions *without noticing* anything wrong with their logical system'. This theme plays a crucial role in Chihara's polemic; for it is only this tacit emphasis on the unsurveyability of the theory which makes it seem plausible that Wittgenstein had misunderstood the gravity of the issue. But the very mention of unsurveyability should alert us to the need to scrutinise what type of *mathematical* problem has been presented. According to Wittgenstein, if it is unsurveyable it is not a proof; as in the case of the Appel–Haken solution of the four-colour problem, the engineer's faith in the theory would be purely inductive. Whereas if it is surveyable, the argument only highlights the perils of 'carelessness' (cf. Chapter 4). But this is no mere *ad hominem*: on Wittgenstein's terms, it was precisely this confusion which had led Turing to misconstrue consistency for what is either a calculation or a physical problem. Hence, whatever the merits of Wittgenstein's argument, the first point to notice is that it was expressly designed to eliminate the very objection which Chihara has only reiterated.

The brunt of Chihara's attack centres on Turing's charge that 'although you do not know that the bridge will fall if there are no contradictions, yet it is almost certain that if there are contradictions it will go wrong somewhere' (LFM 218). His main complaint was with Wittgenstein's contention that 'things can go wrong in only two ways: either the bridge breaks down or you have made a mistake in your calculation — for example, you multiplied wrongly' (LFM 218). In order to answer Chihara properly, it is crucial that we do not lose sight of the nature of Wittgenstein's response to Turing. Wittgenstein was certainly not contesting the possibility that mathematical *errors* can lead to the collapse of a bridge, and clearly a large part of his strategy was to show that and why Turing had confused contradictions with a species of mathematical error. Thus Wittgenstein's primary target was the supposition that a *contradiction* could cause such a result: and hence, that 'consistency proofs' should be a prerequisite for building bridges (or at least, that without them engineers could never afford to dispense with the use of 'open panels' to compensate for unforeseen stresses). Perhaps the most pertinent question in all this, however, is simply: 'But nothing has ever gone wrong that way yet. And why has it not?' (LFM 218). The point we must bear in mind is that, throughout his attempts to answer this last question, Wittgenstein's primary intention was to clarify the grammar of 'contradiction' *vis-à-vis* the problems that can occur in the application of a calculus.

The dominant idea behind the 'collapsing bridge' argument is that at some point in their calculations the engineers infer that e.g. $5 + 7 = 12$ while at another that $5 + 7 \neq 12$, yet because of the intricacy or length of their calculations they simply do not notice this conflict.[36] Before we can deal with this argument, however, we must be perfectly clear whether we are speaking of a contradiction, a 'contrariety', or simply a mistake: a prerequisite which is only obscured by the intrusion of the 'unsurveyability' theme. We have just seen that, if what we are concerned with is the possibility that a proof is so long or complicated that it is extremely difficult to tell when a mistake has been made, then this is *not a point* that

Wittgenstein disputed, and certainly not the claim that Turing was trying to establish. While if the point is that it is in principle *impossible* to detect such a mistake, then this can be rejected on the logical grounds that such an 'unsurveyable' construction would not be called a proof; in such a case there is simply no 'logical system' to speak of, and *a fortiori* no 'contradiction' to undermine the system. There is a deeper problem buried in this example, however, for the argument further confuses the question whether we are dealing with errors or contradictions by tacitly assuming that it is possible to prove on different occasions — via the same methods of calculation — that $5 + 7 = 12$ and $5 + 7 \neq 12$. That is, by resorting to the same notation in each case the suggestion is implicitly conveyed that we could prove contradictory results using the same mathematical rule. However, this could not constitute a *contradiction*, but must *per definiens* be a mistake. For it is a simple point of grammar that it makes no sense to speak of the same mathematical rule leading to contradictory results; this could only constitute an error, therefore: indeed, this is, so to speak, one of the defining features of mathematical errors.

If, on the other hand, what we are concerned with is a case of unnoticed *contrary* results obtained by independent *Beweissystem* methods of calculation then we can indeed say that this result might play a role in the collapse of a bridge (a possibility subsumed by engineers under the general heading of 'Murphy's Law'). Having said that, however, what we must immediately see is first, that we are not confronted with a *contradiction* in this case, and second, that this is solely an empirical problem in regard to the application of the calculus. This is precisely the point that Wittgenstein made in the following exchange with Turing:

> Wittgenstein: By 'seeing the contradiction' do you mean 'seeing that the two ways of multiplying lead to different results'?
> Turing: Yes.
> Wittgenstein: The trouble with this example is that there is no contradiction in it at all. If you have two different ways of multiplying, why call them both multiplying? Why not call one multiplying and the other dividing, or one multiplying-A and the other multiplying-B, or any damn thing? It is simply that you have two different kinds of calculations and you have not noticed that they give different results. (LFM 216)

That is, let us suppose that we are dealing with two different methods of calculation, distinguished by the symbols '+' and '⊕'. (E.g. perhaps the engineers introduced two moduli for alternative types of calculation but at some crucial stage the two methods were confused.) What we have is really a case where one method of calculation leads us to assert that '5 + 7 = 12' while the other yields '5 ⊕ 7 ≠ 12'.[37] Not, as we have seen above, a contradiction, but rather, a *contrariety*. This is the idea underlying Wittgenstein's frequent remarks that the problem lies with the application of the calculus rather than with the calculus itself; i.e. how we seek to apply these different methods, which is a problem of physics, not mathematics.

In neither of these cases, therefore, are we dealing with a contradiction *per se*; which, of course, is the point of the passage which we examined above. That still leaves us, however, with the case where we can indeed derive a contradiction from the rules of the system (e.g. Russell's paradox); that is, where different rules lead to a contradiction in some novel application. Wittgenstein offered a striking illustration of this phenomenon in his example of the statutes of a country which stipulate that on feast-days the vice-president must sit next to the president and that he must sit between two ladies (LFM 210). For whatever reason this contradiction — which in no way is 'hidden', but is simply never noticed (e.g. the vice-president has always been ill on feast-days, or the president has always been a woman) — suddenly becomes manifest. 'Then what do we do? I may say, "We must get rid of this contradiction." All right, but does that vitiate what we did before? Not at all!' (LFM 210). In order to appreciate this conclusion, we must grasp precisely what has happened in this situation. It is hardly the case that the possibility of continuing with the feast irrevocably collapses; yet it is clear that, before the banquet can proceed, some sort of decision must be made. And this is the crux of Wittgenstein's argument on the innocuousness of contradictions: the application grinds to a halt when confronted with a contradiction and cannot proceed until a decision has been made about how to deal with this blockage. The board of regents might decide to abandon the feast; equally, they might decide to construct a new rule stipulating how to deal with this situation. Inevitably they will produce reasons for whatever decision is reached; the important point is that such reasons *persuade*, they do not *compel*.

Wittgenstein's conclusion in the bridge example was thus that *it makes no sense* to speak of a contradiction's causing a bridge to collapse, for the simple reason that a contradiction cannot cause anything: it is not part of the causal chain involved in problems arising from the application of a calculus. What we choose to *do* with a contradiction may be part of such a causal chain, but not the contradiction itself; for the contradiction is a stalled move, or rather, a blocked move (WWK 120). When we are told to do two opposite things the result is that we can do nothing, we have reached the 'edge of the chess-board': 'In arithmetic, too, we reach the "edge of the chess-board", for example when we have the problem $0/0$. (If I wanted to say that $0/0 = 1$, then I could prove that $3 = 5$, and thus I would come into conflict with the other rules of the game)' (WWK 125). The argument is not concerned, therefore, with the Wright/Wrigley claim that Wittgenstein's objection turned on the theme that 'logic is antecedent to truth': that, as Wright puts it, 'our rules of inference are antecedent to truth. (That is, they are among the criteria of truth for the statements to which they are applied.)'[38] Whereas the idea behind the Turing/Chihara objection is that an 'inconsistent' system will lead us from true premises to false conclusions, the point of the Wright/Wrigley defence is that there is 'no Olympian standpoint from which it may be discerned who is giving the right account of the matter'.[39] Both of these positions rest on the very assumption that Wittgenstein wanted to rule out on strictly logical grounds: a contradiction cannot lead us from a true to a false proposition, nor from a true to a 'true-as-considered-in-this-system' proposition. For a contradiction cannot, *qua* 'stalled move in the calculus', lead anywhere.

It is for this reason that the very idea that an application could continue, unaware of the presence of a contradiction, is unintelligible. Thus the conclusion that Wittgenstein drew is that if there was a contradiction in the application of the calculus then we could never have even built the bridge: we could not *not* notice a contradiction, because in the face of a contradiction an application grinds to a halt, and cannot proceed until this blockage has been removed. This is what all of the various analogies were intended to bring out, and Wittgenstein's repeated insistence that you could not suddenly establish, on discovery of a contradiction in some new application, that all of the previous applications were really living on borrowed time. The very notion of a 'hidden' contradiction is once again demonstrated to be absurd, for it can be seen to rest on the confusion that a contradiction is a *mistake* rather than a blockage. One might, of course, argue that a bridge could collapse because of an unnoticed 'contrariety'; here it does indeed make sense to suppose that some application has gone through without our noticing the 'contrariety', in so far as the latter are not blockages. But now the force of this move in Wittgenstein's argument was to shift us from worrying about a mathematical to a physical problem. For, given that the bridge has actually been built, it must *ipso facto* be the case that the calculus was applied, and hence that there were no contradictions in the calculus. The real problem we would be left with is: what effect could an unnoticed *contrariety* have on the structure of the bridge, and this is an empirical, not a mathematical issue.

Wittgenstein was not denying, therefore, that a bridge could conceivably collapse because of an 'unnoticed contrariety'. What he was denying is that this in any way constitutes a mathematical problem — a problem *in the calculus* — and *a fortiori*, something which could be overcome by the construction of a consistency proof. For a contrariety in no way constitutes any sort of *flaw* in the calculus or our calculations: it is merely the case that, because of the different *Beweissysteme* incorporated in the theory, we have adopted different methods which can lead us to contrary results. In some cases such alternative methods — and even the contrariety which results — might indeed be a fruitful source of empirical application (as in e.g. the role of non-Euclidean alongside Euclidean geometries in astrophysics). Yet even in the case where we notice a 'contrariety' which undermines the application we have in mind, it is essential that we do not conflate such a case with the existence of an error: with the derivation, as Chihara insists, of a false proposition from true premises. What this really means is that the engineering problem should be seen to be just that: a problem in what Chihara calls the 'empirical theory'. The problem is directly one of the manner in which the engineers have applied the two different methods of calculation, which is categorially similar to the case of building a faulty bridge by misapplying a single method of calculation: 'The trouble described is something you get into if you apply the calculation in a way that leads to something breaking. This you can do with *any* calculation, contradiction or no contradiction' (LFM 219). The fact that we are dealing with a contrariety only serves to obscure this point, without affecting the general explanation that in each case we are dealing with an application problem. And this, by definition, is an empirical, not a mathematical matter.

The part of this argument which has caused perhaps the most consternation among critics, however, is Wittgenstein's consequent insistence that 'It is only when I *notice* that they contradict each other that [the rules] cease to be all right' (WWF 125). This has appeared to many as nothing more than an outrageous evasion of the problem at hand: uttering 'See no evil, hear no evil' is surely not going to make the evil disappear. But invariably such critics ignore the role of the latter part of the quotation, which contains the whole point of the argument. Wittgenstein concluded that such a contradiction 'manifests itself only in this: that I cannot apply them any more. For the logical product of the two rules is a contradiction, and a contradiction no longer tells me what to do. Thus the conflict appears only when I notice it. There was no problem as long as I was able to play the game' (WWK 125). The first point to bear in mind in order to understand what is going on here is the absurdity of suggesting that a 'hidden' contradiction could have occurred in a past application. As far as *that* application was concerned, it is obviously unintelligible to suggest that a blockage might have escaped our notice. 'If I can apply the calculus, I have applied it; there are to be no subsequent corrections. What I can do, I can do. I cannot undo the application by saying: strictly speaking that was not an application' (WWK 139; cf. WWK 129). What is feasible, however, is that the rules which were employed in that application might lead to a blockage *in an entirely different situation.* And that is the key to Wittgenstein's various arguments and analogies on this theme: the different applications on the two occasions are in no way identical, and the fact that the rules lead to a blockage in some new case in no way vitiates the fact that they led to no blockage in the previous. Or to put the matter more precisely, the distinction we have to draw here is between the first type of case where the rules permitted an application and the latter where it was impossible to apply the same rules.

The various analogies which Wittgenstein presented in *Lectures on the Foundations of Mathematics* (e.g. the prison example, the faulty seating-plan, the misguided general) were all intended to make this point. What this really means is that we need not operate with a static calculus in the course of empirical applications. Which, of course, is precisely the point that Wittgenstein stressed in his account of the dynamic and fluid structure of mathematics and language. In the course of applications we might discover that the rules lead to a blockage in some novel situation, and faced with this we might well decide to construct a new calculus by adding a rule to the pre-existing system stipulating how to deal with this complication. However, that is not to suggest that in such a case the original rules were somehow 'incomplete', for 'there are no gaps in grammar' (WWK 36, LFM 210; cf. Chapter 8). Consequently, the conclusion which Wittgenstein drew here is that, when confronted with a blockage in an application we can either ignore it and continue to operate with the calculus, aware of the fact that in these circumstances the contradiction will arise (e.g. the noughts and crosses example), or else, if we find the existence of the blockage at this point intolerable as far as the intended application is concerned, then the only remaining option is to construct a new calculus specifically designed to deal with this situation (viz. by stipulating how to proceed) (WWK 132; LFM 225). The two calculi will obviously be extremely similar to one another, but what is important is that — from a logical point of view — they are distinct, and hence autonomous. In which case the calculations of the preceding system are left undisturbed by the construction of this new calculus, and for this reason it is absurd to ask: 'Do I have to wait for the proof of consistency before I can apply the calculus? Have all previous calculations really, *sub specie aeterni,* been made on credit? And is it conceivable that one day all this will turn out to be illegitimate? Am I ignorant of what I am doing?' (WWK 140).

The tone of this passage was clearly meant to indicate that Wittgenstein's ultimate purpose was to demonstrate the unintelligibility of the sceptical thesis underlying the Hilbert Programme. For the construction of the new calculus in no way affects the calculations already performed with the superseded system. Which is why Wittgenstein insisted in *Philosophical Grammar* that what we are presented with here is a straightforward logical-syntactical problem which provides no succour for any sceptical issue:

'We may not use a system of axioms before its consistency has been proved.'
'In the rules of the game no contradictions may occur.'
Why not? 'Because then one wouldn't know how to play.'
But how does it happen that our reaction to a contradiction is a doubt?
We don't have any reaction to a contradiction. We can only

say: if it's really meant like that (if the contradiction is *supposed* to be there) I don't understand it. Or: it isn't something I've learnt. I don't understand the sign. I haven't learnt what I am to do with it, whether it is a command, etc. (PG 303)

In its simplest terms, therefore, Wittgenstein's response to the philosophical foundation of Hilbert's worry was that you cannot formulate any doubts in regards to an expression in which all information has been cancelled out. Until this anti-sceptical consequence has been grasped philosophers can be expected to pursue the question: 'What about the consistency of all mathematics or of some strong system for set theory? How do we answer the skeptic? Since here a convincing proof is not possible, we have established that the skeptic demands too much. We cannot be certain that our axioms are free from contradiction and must treat them as hypotheses which may be abandoned or modified in the face of further mathematical experience. This attitude is taken by many foundational workers who also go on to voice opinions about the *likelihood* that various systems are consistent.'[40] This conclusion must be deeply unsatisfying to the philosopher of mathematics, however. To be sure, it is very much the attitude taken up by many working mathematicians; but that is not because they have discerned some quasi-formalist truth hitherto undetected or unabsorbed by philosophers. It is because philosophical sceptical problems can make no sense in regards to mathematical truths; which is, of course, one of the points that Wittgenstein most wanted to emphasise.

The only genuine solution we can present to the above dilemma is to show, not that the sceptic has 'over-stated' his case (a claim which one also frequently encounters in the 'sceptical' discussions of rule-following) on the disturbingly *ad hoc* grounds here deployed, but rather, that the sceptic has not stated any case at all. This argument actually serves to establish, not the limitations, but rather, the incoherence of the 'sceptical' thesis. As, indeed, was Wittgenstein's chief purpose in his sustained attack on the *intelligibility* of the consistency problem. The whole force of the sceptical argument, which is becoming increasingly popular amongst philosophers of mathematics, is to push us into subverting the conceptual demarcation between mathematics and physics. It is only natural that, if you begin with a problem which by its very nature transgresses the logical demarcation between empirical and mathematical truths, you will end up with a position that deliberately enshrines the transgression of the logical demarcation between science and mathematics. What is perhaps most striking about Wittgenstein's argument is the extent to which he anticipated this trend. Indeed, the reason why Wittgenstein dwelt on the topic of consistency so extensively, and likewise, devoted so much attention to the logical distinction between hypotheses and mathematical conjectures, was to undermine this very development. Wittgenstein's strategy was thus to attack the problem at two of its most influential sources; it is to that end that Wittgenstein sought, not to refute, but rather to *exclude* the consistency and decision problems.

Notes

1. Crispin Wright, *Wittgenstein on the Foundations of Mathematics* (London, Duckworth, 1980), p. 312.
2. Ibid., pp. 312-13.
3. Ibid., p. 313.
4. Ibid.
5. Cf. PI §133, and A.J.P. Kenny, 'Wittgenstein on the Nature of Philosophy', in *Wittgenstein and his Times*, Brian McGuinness (ed.) (Oxford, Basil Blackwell, 1982), pp. 10-11.
6. Wright, *Wittgenstein on the Foundations of Mathematics*, op.cit., p. 316.
7. Quoted in Raymond Wilder's *Introduction to the Foundations of Mathematics* (New York, John Wiley & Sons, 1965), p. 265.
8. Cf. Georg Kreisel, 'Hilbert's Programme', in *Philosophy of Mathematics*, P. Benacerraf and H. Putnam (eds) (Englewood Cliffs, Prentice-Hall, 1964).
9. Indeed, they demand a book in their own right, which I am currently pursuing in a work on 'The Significance of Gödel's Theorem'.
10. Cf. Michael Resnik, 'On the Philosophical Significance of Consistency Proofs', *Journal of Philosophical Logic* (1974), p. 133.
11. Such a schematic outline of Wittgenstein's remarks on Gödel's second theorem grossly distorts both the complexity of the issues involved and the depth of Wittgenstein's argument. Mathematical philosophers will undoubtedly remain unimpressed by these glancing blows; a serious attempt to capture their attention must be forestalled, however, until my forthcoming work on 'The Significance of Gödel's Theorem'.
12. David Hilbert, 'On the Infinite', in *From Frege to Gödel: A Source Book in Mathematical Logic*, Jean van Heijenoort (ed.) (Cambridge, Mass, Harvard University Press, 1977), p. 376.
13. Ibid., p. 380.
14. Ibid., p. 377.
15. David Hilbert, 'Neubegründung der Mathematik', p. 165, in *Gesammelte Abhandlungen* (Berlin, Springer, 1935).
16. 'On the Infinite', p. 383.
17. Ibid., p. 392.
18. Ibid., p. 379.

19. Ibid., p. 376.

20. Ibid., p. 375.

21. P.S. Kitcher, 'Hilbert's Epistemology', *Philosophy of Science*, vol. 43 (1976), pp.99-100.

22. Resnik, 'On the Philosophical Significance of Consistency Proofs', op.cit., p. 133.

23. Hilbert, 'On the Infinite', op.cit., p. 383.

24. Frege had, of course, also referred to the notion in *Basic Laws*, but in *Wittgenstein and the Vienna Circle* and *Philosophical Remarks* we see Wittgenstein responding quite closely to the manner in which Hilbert had tried to employ this notion.

25. Hilbert, 'On the Infinite', op.cit., p. 376.

26. Cf. TLP 3.032, where Wittgenstein argued that it is as impossible to describe the illogical — anything that runs contrary to the laws of logic — as to construct the impossible: viz. anything that runs contrary to the laws of geometry. The subtlety of the point that Wittgenstein was making underlay his brief argument at 6.1203 on the 'law of contradiction' (significantly called the '*Gesetz des Widerspruchs*'). The 'law of contradiction' is a rule which prohibits the use of a contradiction (*Kontradiktion*); break this rule and nonsense results.

27. Hilbert, 'On the Infinite', p. 370.

28. Michael Detlefsen, 'On Dynamic Models of Theory Construction', unpublished, pp. 3-4; cf. also *Hilbert's Program: An Essay on Mathematical Instrumentalism*, forthcoming.

29. Cf. Charles S. Chihara, 'Wittgenstein's Analysis of the Paradoxes in his *Lectures on the Foundations of Mathematics*', *Philosophical Review*, vol. 86 (1977), pp.365-81, reprinted in Shanker, *Ludwig Wittgenstein: Critical Assessments*, vol.III, pp.325-37, and 'The Wright–Wing Defense of Wittgenstein's Philosophy of Logic', *Philosophical Review*, vol. 90 (1982), pp. 99-108.

30. Chihara, 'Wittgenstein's Analysis of the Paradoxes', p. 334.

31. Ibid., p. 333.

32. Ibid., pp. 333-4.

33. Ibid., p. 334.

34. Ibid.

35. cf. Constance Reid, *Hilbert* (Berlin, Springer, 1970), p. 128.

36. Lest it is felt that the argument should be presented in much more exotic terms — e.g. how can we be certain that a contradiction would not arise in the addition of 'unrealistic' numbers which are so enormous that they have never been calculated before — it is important to see that the same considerations apply to '10↑↑↑5 + 10↑↑↑↑12 = ?' as '5 + 7 = ?'. For as we saw in Chapters 4 and 5, what must be surveyable are the rules of the system: not the so-called 'size of their extensions'.

37. The point would be slightly more complicated, since we would have to distinguish between two number systems as well. e.g. $5 + 7 = 12$ and $5^* \oplus 7^* = 12^*$. For the meaning of the numerals in this alternative system would not be identical to that of the natural numbers, in so far as we are using a different addition function (cf. Chapter 8).

38. Wright, *Wittgenstein on the Foundations of Mathematics*, op.cit., p. 376.

39. Ibid., p. 311.

40. Resnik, 'On the Philosophical Significance of Consistency Proofs', op.cit., pp. 145-6.

THE RECOVERY OF CERTAINTY

> The deep of night is crept upon our talk,
> And nature must obey necessity.
>
> *Julius Caesar*, IV, iii

The Foundations of the Foundations of Mathematics

Wittgenstein did not suggest or assume that the foregoing resolution of the consistency problem would dispose of the 'foundations crisis'. On Hilbert's approach such would indeed be the
case, but Wittgenstein proceeded on the firm understanding that
the two issues are distinct albeit related areas of philosophical confusion, which thus demand independent investigation. In the
former we are concerned with the reliability of the calculi we
employ; it is not the concept of mathematical truth *per se* that is
under consideration, but rather, the problem is one of guarantee-
ing that some future mathematical discovery will not undermine
our pre-existing trust in the theorems yielded by a calculus. In
other words, the problem is one of elucidating what is meant by
regarding a calculus as sound. But the heart of the foundations
problem lies, as Frege indicated in *Foundations of Arithmetic*, at a
deeper philosophical level (FA §3). The challenge here is ultimately that of clarifying the logical status of mathematical truth in
order to establish the basis for our conviction that mathematics is,
as Hilbert described it, 'a paragon of certitude'. Thus, the 'foundations crisis' does not simply amount to the anxiety that mathematical systems might unbeknownst to us contain 'hidden' contradictions. More importantly, it derives from the fundamental
philosophical dilemma that it is not at all clear what it means to
describe a mathematical proposition as a 'necessary truth'.

It has thus been widely assumed that the origin of the foundations dispute must lie in those great nineteenth-century break-
throughs which rocked the mathematical world's faith in the
certainty of mathematical truth *simpliciter*: viz. the development
of non-Euclidean geometries and non-standard algebras. Even
before the announcement of these shattering discoveries, however,
a process had for some time been underfoot which rendered the

mathematical community anxious to obtain ever greater rigour in their theories, and for that reason, deeply susceptible to any suggestion of unwarranted confidence in their results. Hence it has generally been accepted that the impetus for the foundations of mathematics can be traced back to the revolution in Analysis; or at least, that the movements in Analysis and the birth of logicism were both part of the same search for mathematical rigour.[1] Certainly Frege saw the matter in these terms, and at the beginning of the *Foundations of Arithmetic* he carefully sought to align his efforts with the mainstream of the investigations into the foundations of Analysis (FA 1-2). There is thus abundant evidence to bear out Dummett's claim that Frege's primary motive in the construction of his *Begriffsschrift* was 'simply to attain the ideal of that rigour to which the whole of nineteenth-century mathematics had been striving'.[2] Recently, however, Philip Kitcher has questioned this interpretation, arguing that it glosses over an extremely important difference between the goals of the foundations of Analysis versus those inspiring the quest for the foundations of arithmetic upon which Frege had embarked. His arguments merit serious consideration, for they serve to highlight both the spirit and the nature of the philosophical problem underlying the foundations dispute.

Pointing to the example of Leibniz and his followers (e.g. the Bernouilli brothers) whose main concern was to *extend* the calculus rather than make it more rigorous, Kitcher argues that whereas nineteenth-century mathematicians were seeking to clarify the concepts of Analysis in order to expand their application — thereby enabling Analysis to resolve more diverse types of problem — Frege's primary purpose in his search for a 'sharp definition' of the concept of number was to place mathematical knowledge on a sure foothold of epistemological certainty. Thus, 'the foundational work of the great nineteenth-century mathematicians ... was not inspired by any exalted epistemological aims, but was, instead, an attempt to respond to the needs of mathematical research.'[3] In a detailed 'Case Study' Kitcher undertakes to substantiate this point with examples of the fundamentally *mathematical* objectives which guided the great developments in Analysis. His aim is to demonstrate that 'It is a gross caricature', for example, 'to suppose that Cauchy's work was motivated by a long-standing perception that mathematics had lapsed from high epistemological ideals and that it was accepted because it brought

relief to a troubled mathematical community.'[4] Cauchy's foundational interests were prompted 'not in response to an urgent
problem of rigorisation, but simply because his approach to *other*
analytic problems in terms of the concept of limit permitted him to
incorporate reconstructions of reasonings about infinitesimals
which had previously been offered.'[5] Similarly, Weierstrass's foundational objectives were spurred by 'his desire to extend the elliptic
function theory of Abel and Jacobi'.[6]

Kitcher is certainly quite right to draw attention to the paramount importance of the epistemological framework, not only of
Frege's logicism, but of the 'foundations crisis' in general. The only
trouble with his argument is that very much the same sentiments as
those which Frege expressed can be found in those sparse writings
which deal specifically with the foundations of Analysis. For
example, as early as 1743 d'Alembert was complaining that the
chief deficiency in mathematics was that 'Up to the present ...
more concern has been given to enlarging the building than to
illuminating the entrance, to raising it higher than to giving proper
strength to the foundations.'[7] Moreover, as Kitcher readily admits,
this was a refrain that was to become standard in introductions to
foundational writings on Analysis. Even Cauchy began the *Cours
d'Analyse*, as Kitcher acknowledges, with the declaration: 'As for
my methods, I have sought to give them all the rigour which is
demanded in geometry, in such a way as never to run back to
reasons drawn from what is usually given in algebra.'[8] There can
be no denying that Kitcher has made out a strong case for the
distinction between mathematics and philosophy, therefore, but
what are we to make of his claim that we must sharply differentiate
between two species of foundational activities in the light of such
prima facie evidence to the contrary? Significantly, Kitcher dismisses this out of hand as a matter of no importance: 'Lagrange,
like Cauchy', he protests, 'fulminates against the failure of rigour
in contemporary analysis in his preface — and quickly allows himself virtually any algebraic technique that seems useful!'[9]

The answer to this, however, is that it is precisely the preface in
which we, *qua* philosophers, are interested. For our main concern
here is precisely in the prose: the one area where mathematicians
are tempted to abandon the *terra firma* of their calculations and
venture into the unknown realms of interpreting their results. If
there is a fault to be found in Kitcher's argument, therefore, it is
not in the demarcation which he draws between the technical work

of Cauchy or Weierstrass and the philosophical thought of Frege and Russell. It is hardly surprising that professional mathematicians should be more concerned with refining and/or expanding the application of their tools whereas the philosopher of mathematics is hunting for a completely different type of quarry. The problem with Kitcher's argument is thus not that he misstates, but rather, that he is tempted to overstate his case, assuming that because someone is primarily involved in the mechanics of mathematics he is unlikely to deviate from this narrow path. Indeed, as Wittgenstein demonstrated in his discussion of Skolem's proof, it is a mistake to assume that the working mathematician is specially guarded against allowing philosophical confusions from entering his mathematical work: even within the body of a proof (cf. Chapter 5).

One manifestation of Kitcher's liability to overstatement is the extent to which he ignores the key role which Berkeley played, via his influence on the foundations of Analysis, in the genesis of the 'foundations crisis'. Kitcher contends that the influence of *The Analyst* was largely confined to British mathematicians who were eager to defend Newton from any criticism which might have been used to bolster Continental attacks on Newton's achievements in Analysis.[10] Passing over the question of whether the dispute over who should be accredited with the discovery of the calculus is quite as one-sided as Kitcher implies, what must obviously strike us here are the overtones of the debate which was later to erupt into the foundations dispute. Kitcher contends that it was because of their preoccupation with largely irrelevant philosophical issues that 'the British mathematical community fell further and further behind'.[11] On Kitcher's reading, if Berkeley's motive in his investigation into 'Whether the Object, Principles, and Inferences of the Modern Analysis Are More Distinctly Conceived, or More Evidently Deduced, than Religious Mysteries and Points of Faith' was, as Kline also suggests, to thwart 'the growing threat to religion of the mathematically inspired philosophy of mechanism and determinism',[12] then his strategy was admirably chosen; for by diverting mathematicians' attention from the concrete world of pure mathematics into the nebulous void of philosophy, Berkeley's arguments effectively retarded the British development of Analysis over the next century. But was this Berkeley's motive, or was he rather exposing a weakness in the 'Queen of the Sciences' in order to justify his demand that philosophy be accorded the same latitude that was unconsciously granted to mathematics?

It is quite true that Berkeley presented his attack as part of a general defence of religious faith, but what is perhaps most important for our purposes are the parameters which he imposed on the subsequent controversy that was immediately provoked. Berkeley asked 'Whether the mathematicians of the present age act like men of science in taking so much more pains to apply their principles than to understand them.'[13] Before Berkeley is cast in the role of religious obscurantist, it is important to notice that as far as he was concerned, there was never any question as to whether mathematics should be treated on an equal footing with science. On the contrary, the heart of his attack centred on the point that, given that mathematics quite rightly aspires to be a *bona fide* science, the truths which it yields demand precisely the same type of evidential support as applies to science. In other words, there is — or at least there ought to be — no categorial difference between mathematical and scientific truth. The importance which this assumption was to have cannot be emphasised enough. For, whatever his intentions, Berkeley introduced a disturbing sceptical element into the philosophy of mathematics, and he did so precisely because of the crucial premise which underpinned his criticism, and which has haunted the philosophy of mathematics for the past two centuries. Certainly, Wittgenstein felt that the principle confusion which he was compelled to combat time after time in the various topics which he addressed turned on the assumption that there is no categorial distinction between mathematical and scientific propositions.

The grievance that Berkeley voiced was that, as responsible scientists, it was incumbent on mathematicians to satisfy the same methodological strictures which govern science: 'in every other science men prove their conclusions by their principles, and not their principles by their conclusions. But if in yours you should allow yourselves this unnatural way of proceeding, the consequence would be that you must take up with Induction, and bid adieu to Demonstration. And if you submit to this, your authority will no longer lead the way in points of Reason and Science.' He thus concluded that he had 'no controversy about your conclusions, but only about your logic and method'.[14] Clearly no self-respecting mathematician *cum* scientist could refuse the gage thrown down here; but what exactly was the nature of this challenge? On the one hand, Berkeley conceded that Analysis had arrived at a body of truths, but then he objected: no legitimate science would be content with the lack of rigour and the metaphysical evasions whereby these results had been derived. 'That men who have been conversant only about clear points should with difficulty admit obscure ones might not seem altogether unaccountable. But he who can digest a second or third fluxion, a second or third difference, need not, methinks, be squeamish about any point in divinity.'[15] Most bitter of all, Berkeley suggested that Analysis might have advanced by a 'compensation of errors', where two mistakes had cancelled each other out, enabling mathematicians to arrive 'not at Science, yet at Truth. For Science it cannot be called, when you proceed blindfold, and arrive at the Truth not knowing how or by what means.'[16]

Berkeley's shafts found their mark. In the wave of empirical zeal sweeping Britain, few mathematicians were prepared to countenance Leibniz and Euler's bland admonition that mathematicians could happily turn a blind eye to the use of metaphysical assumptions in Analysis so long as they arrived at serviceable results.[17] But this attitude was not confined to British mathematicians. In 1784 the Berlin Academy offered a prize for 'a clear and precise theory of what is called Infinite in Mathematics'. For 'The utility derived from mathematics, the esteem it is held in, and the honorable name of "exact science" *par excellence* justly given it, are all the due of the clarity of its principles, the rigor of its proofs, and the precision of its theorems.'[18] This announcement provides what is perhaps the central theme to bear in mind in response to Kitcher's thesis. The point is that, so long as the concept of infinity had not been clarified, the foundations of Analysis had not been completed. This is precisely what Hilbert stressed at the beginning of 'On the Infinite', where he warned that discussions on the foundations of Analysis had not yet come to an end, despite Weierstrass's definitive work on the notions of minimum, function and derivative. For although Weierstrass had successfully removed infinitesimals by reducing the expressions in which they had prefigured to propositions about relations between finite magnitudes, he was nevertheless still forced to rely on the infinite in regards to number sequences.[19] Thus, the foundations of Analysis should be seen as both the source of subsequent activity in the foundations of mathematics and in its own turn dependent on these latter findings if it was to be ultimately successful in securing its own foundations.[20]

This is not the place to become embroiled in a heated controversy about Kitcher's interpretation of the development of Analysis.[21] Whatever the outcome of this debate, we can concede to Kitcher that it is crucial that we recognise the categorial difference between the mathematics of Analysis and the foundations of mathematics. But we cannot adopt this attitude to Kitcher's larger thesis that use of the same term — foundationalism — in each case does not at all signify that both are engaged in a similar type of activity. According to Kitcher, it is precisely because of the difference that is involved here — which Frege unsuccessfully tried to obfuscate — that *Foundations of Arithmetic* received so little response from the mathematical community. Hence, Frege's investigations 'failed to provoke a response because the unclarities to which Frege called attention ... did not stand in the way of mathematical research'.[22] But this is an uncharitable interpretation. One might equally well argue — as Frege himself did — that the crime, if there was one, was to bring out into the open the full implications of the foundational problems which mathematicians were struggling to contain. At any rate, Frege did provoke a sharp response, albeit not from the quarter which he had at first expected. But then, it was only a relatively short time before the ancestor to the preface to *Cours d'Analyse* found its way into the prefatory remarks in 'On the Infinite'.

The ultimate problem with Kitcher's argument is thus that it overstates the divorce between pure mathematics and the philosophy of mathematics. This is very much the point which Wittgenstein was driving at when he distinguished between mathematics and prose. One could argue that there are two strands running through the history of the foundation of Analysis: a prose and a mathematical tradition. What Kitcher has done is to focus on the latter element, ignoring — as far as the Continental mathematicians are concerned — the presence of the former. The difference between British and Continental mathematicians on this score is one of degree, however, not of kind. For it would be folly to deny the presence of both threads in the development of mathematical thought on both sides of the Channel during the nineteenth century. To some extent Kitcher weights the argument in his favour by concentrating on the century's greatest pure mathematicians, yet not even they were totally immune from the philosophical doubts sweeping the mathematical community, as is betrayed by their excursions into prose prefaces. Moreover, it is misleading to call the technical development of Analysis which Kitcher isolates the 'foundations of Analysis'; for then we should have to treat the foundations of Analysis as coterminous with the history of the calculus! Rather, the use of the term 'foundations' refers specifically to the themes that were being discussed in these important prefaces, even if the two threads were so closely intertwined that it would have been virtually impossible to try to separate this element out from the technical work which was then immediately pursued. It might well be the case that there is a sharp contrast between what nineteenth-century mathematicians *said* and what they were actually doing, therefore; but what concerns us here is that when they spoke about the urgency of providing a foundation for Analysis they were thinking of the want of evidence for the truths of Analysis. Thus, from its earliest — *epistemological* — use, the term 'foundations' has been tied to the need to secure the grounds on which a piece of knowledge is based.

Perhaps the greatest importance of Kitcher's argument lies, not in the sharp contrast which he hoped to draw, but rather, in the increasingly blurred lines between these disparate fields and the pressing need to separate out these elements at the conceptual level. It is essential that we keep these points in mind when we approach Wittgenstein's remarks on the foundations of mathematics: the nature of the categorial distinction between pure and foundational pursuits — whether in Analysis or in the use of fundamental mathematical concepts — and the extent to which this demarcation was obscured by working mathematicians and philosophers alike. Thus, it is not the calculus which concerns us, it is the prose; but in a fundamental sense, our chief interest in the calculus just does lie in the prose: in the interpretation of what has been accomplished. Of course, there is a sense in which we can use the term 'foundations' to refer to the calculus, but when we speak of the 'foundations crisis' we are referring specifically to the prose (AWL 121-2). Above all else, therefore, we must observe Wittgenstein's frequent insistence that his sole concern was with the prose: a contention based very much on the distinction which concerns Kitcher. The technical aspects which Kitcher isolates are never, Wittgenstein maintained, part of his investigation, but running beneath the surface of the advances in Analysis was an ever-present awareness of the sting contained in the tail of Berkeley's argument: how can we be certain that mathematics is 'an exact science *par excellence* — that we really are dealing with a body of truths — until we have establishd the principles whereby we have drawn our conclusions?' Indeed, Berkeley posed a problem which was soon to become an *idée fixe* of the foundations of mathematics when he asked at his twenty-third Query: 'Whether inconsistencies can be truths?'[23]

With the discovery of non-Euclidean geometries and quaternions the unreflective faith in the certainty of mathematical truth which characterises pre-Berkleian writings on the foundations of Analysis was permanently shattered: how can we be sure which — or for that matter, whether — any of these systems of geometry or algebra is true? Which brings us round to Frege's opening argument in 'Logical Defects in Mathematics': 'If you ask what constitutes the value of mathematical knowledge, the answer must be: not so much what is known as how it is known, not so much its subject-matter as the degree to which it is intellectually perspicuous and affords insight into its logical interrelations' (PW 157). Here indeed are grounds to wonder whether, at least as far as mathematics is concerned, if we can grasp the solution for one foundations problem we shall have discovered the principle for resolving them all? For in all areas of the foundational spectrum mathematicians and philosophers were responding to the same species of worry. One might thus argue that the real culprit in the surge of foundationalism was the persistent intrusion of epistemology in those areas where it has no business to meddle. Epistemology has now extended its tentacles into virtually every aspect of philosophical thought, and for two millennia philosophers have stoutly battled with the spectre of the scepticism which it invariably bestows. Despite their preoccupation with the technical problems of analysis, not even pure mathematicians were immune from the doubts being voiced by the philosophers amongst them.

There are two historical antecedents to bear in mind, therefore, when trying to fix the precise nature of the 'foundations crisis'. The more obvious is the series of what Morris Kline describes as the 'débâcles' of nineteenth-century mathematics, beginning with the construction of non-Euclidean geometries and abstract algebras and ending with the discovery of the paradoxes in set theory, which literally shook the subject down to its foundations.[24] But this in itself does not suffice to account for the dismayed reaction of philosophers and mathematicians. For why should the construction of e.g. octonions be seen as a 'débâcle'? Why should anyone be alarmed by the emergence of highly sophisticated if not always practicable methods of defining abstruse spatial structures? The answer, according to Kline, is that the creation of these recondite geometries and algebras forced mathematicians to recognise that 'mathematics was not a body of truths'. Not surprisingly, this 'discovery' 'shook their confidence in what they had created, and they undertook to re-examine their creations'. For it convinced them that they had been guilty of a false sense of security. 'The conviction that they were obtaining truths had entranced them so much that they had rushed impetuously to secure these seeming truths at the cost of sound reasoning.'[25] Ironically, in one sense Kline is absolutely right: not, that is, about the 'false sense of security' — which, as we shall see, is the major confusion which needs to be clarified in this issue — but rather, that mathematics does not contain a body of truths *in the manner which had hitherto been assumed.*

Kline's argument poses an intriguing problem: how exactly did the invention of Bolyai-Lobatchevskian geometry establish that Euclidean geometry had been based on 'unsound' reasoning? Kline, like Hilbert, would appear to have run the two separate themes — the soundness of a system and the nature of mathematical truth — together. Thus he fails to consider precisely why the construction of a new calculus should entail that the old system had not in fact yielded truths; and more to the point, would continue to do so. We would hardly say the same about e.g. Britain's recent conversion to the metric system. Those who resisted the change were not arguing that they preferred an unsound system to a sound one (nor vice versa). No one actually suggested — at least, not publicly — that for the sake of veracity Britain had no choice in how to proceed, in so far as an Imperial Standard Yard *really is* 0.9144 metres long. Here the controversy was entirely centred on the advantages as opposed to the complications of conforming to standard European usage.[26] But why should the matter be any different as far as the development of alternative geometrical or algebraic systems are concerned? As we shall see, the burden of Wittgenstein's resolution of the 'foundations crisis' revolved upon the theme that the recovery of mathematical certainty rests on the precise grammatical parallel between any such examples. But before we can approach that solution we must first try to clarify the real source of the 'foundations crisis' in the perception of mathematics which still leads some philosophers to interpret the nineteenth-century developments in geometry, algebra and set theory as resulting in the loss of mathematical certainty.

Indeed, Philip Davis and Reuben Hersh go a step further. In *The Mathematical Experience* they report that 'The loss of certainty in geometry was philosophically intolerable, because it implied the loss of all certainty in human knowledge.'[27] Both fixtures of this claim are wrong, betraying a failure to grasp the nature of empirical as much as mathematical certainty. For the purposes of the present work we shall only be concerned with the latter: the nature of the normative certainty which characterises mathematics. But it is important to note that supporters of the 'loss of mathematical certainty' thesis see the two themes as inextricably bound together. Assuming, that is, that they are even aware that we are dealing with two different species of certainty here; one approach to Wittgenstein's resolution of the foundations crisis might well be said to be the clarification of the fact that there are two grammatically distinct kinds of certainty in mathematics versus science (PI p. 224). Despite the emphasis on the fateful role which e.g. Bolyai and Lobatchevsky played in the collapse of mathematical certainty, however, this is far from being a modern dilemma. On the contrary, it was only because this confusion was so deeply entrenched in western thought that a full-blown 'foundations crisis' could emerge so swiftly. In his *Opus Majus*, Roger Bacon anticipated Davis and Hersh's alarm when he warned that 'If in other sciences we should arrive at certainty without doubt and truth without error, it behooves us to place the foundations of knowledge in mathematics.' Six hundred years later, philosophers are still haunted by the same spectre because they are still misled by the same false premise which inspires it. Paradoxical as it may sound, it is one and the same conception — the belief that 'nature is mathematical and that every natural process is subject to mathematical laws' — which accounts for both the astonishing development of mathematics over the past 600 years and the subsequent belief that the nineteenth century bore witness to, as Kline describes it, 'the withering of mathematical truth'.

Given this conceptual background, Newton's *Principia* descended on a culture which, because it believed that 'the universe is mathematical in structure and behaviour, and nature acts in accordance with inexorable and immutable laws',[28] was predisposed to accept that Newton had successfully penetrated its veil. One of the most famous expressions of this sentiment is Laplace's ringing declaration that 'There is but one universe, and Newton has discovered its laws'.[29] Clearly this conviction reflects the consequence of the assumptions built into the conception of mathematics and science which the eighteenth century had inherited. Thus, Enlightenment mathematicians and philosophers were led to exaggerate the virtues of Newton's *Principia* precisely because they had misunderstood the nature of a physical theory; and this in turn was because they transgressed the logical demarcation between mathematics and science. Of course, Einstein's 1905 papers confirmed that the Laplacean vision was distorted (or better still, Eddington's verification demonstrated this) in so far as we can employ different norms of representation to describe reality. But then, it did not require the formulation of relativity theory nor the photographs of Mercury's perihelion to show that Laplace was wrong. For his error was, not that he overestimated the accuracy of Newton's system, but rather, that he mistook the inductive certainty of a physical theory for the absolute certainty yielded by the application of a mathematical system. Equally, those who conclude on the basis of Bolyai–Lobatchevskian geometry — or Einstein's subsequent employment of it — that there is no such thing as mathematical certainty are in effect guilty of the same confusion. Had twentieth-century physicists insisted that there *must* have been some mistake in Einstein's calculations or flaws in Eddington's equipment in so far as a straight line *must* be a line which lies evenly with the points on itself, Newton's system might still reign undisturbed.

It was because of the changing demands being placed on physics that scientists were conceptually prepared to consider the merits of a rival geometrical system; or as Wittgenstein put it in 1930, of an 'alternative syntax'. In a passing reference to Einstein in the discussions with Waismann and Schlick Wittgenstein emphasised that what Einstein had effectively demonstrated is that *geometry is syntax*: a system of logical rules which lay down the grammar for describing phenomena (WWK 38, 162 f.). For example, the scientist can operate with a Euclidean or a Bolyai–Lobatchevskian definition of 'straight line', and the experiments which he subsequently performs will not establish that the Euclidean concept is in any sense incorrect; only that there may be little point in using Euclidean rather than BL geometry for the purposes of modern astrophysics, given the added complications which result from the former grammar. For there is no sense whatsoever in the assertion that 'physical straight lines are really geodesics'; such an argument merely confuses the distinction between *rule* and *application* for a distinction between *pure* and *physical* space. When a scientist chooses from amongst the alternative geometries which mathematicians have provided according to the nature of the phenomena which he is investigating, he is not ascertaining which geometry is the most 'accurate' of the various contenders for the purposes which he has in mind. What he does discover, however, is simply the advanced utility of operating with a geometry in which it is intelligible to speak e.g. of a geodesic straight line. For the behaviour of natural phenomena is not part of the geometrical concepts themselves; it is the framework against which these concepts are applied. If these framework conditions were to change, it would render these concepts not false, but most likely useless. The failure to grasp the significance of this point, and thus of the nature of the freedom which we enjoy in constructing different geometrical or arithmetical systems, lands us squarely in the 'foundations crisis' (cf. Chapter 8).

The reason why this demarcation was violated was chiefly due to the fact that mathematics had traditionally been regarded as a special — indeed, perhaps the supreme — branch of science: a confusion which quite clearly persists to this day in writings on the foundations of mathematics. Davis and Hersh suggest at the outset of *The Mathematical Experience* that 'A naive definition, adequate for the dictionary and for an initial understanding, is that *mathematics is the science of quantity and space*'.[30] But this is not so much a 'naive' as a completely misleading definition, and it is directly from this opening position that they are led into the conclusion that the discovery of non-Euclidean geometries was a 'disaster'. Likewise, Kline insists that 'The disagreements about the foundations of the "most certain" science are both surprising and, to put it mildly, disconcerting. The present state of mathematics is a mockery of the hitherto deep-rooted and widely reputed truth and logical perfection of mathematics.'[31] The essence of this approach is thus that mathematics differs from science by a matter of degree rather than of kind. Gauss's image of mathematics as the 'Queen of the Sciences' is the embodiment of this enduring misconception.[32] Even today mathematicians try to preserve some semblance of Gauss's claim; it is interesting to note that in the above quotation Kline refers to mathematics as the 'most certain' of the sciences. That is, it may not furnish us with absolutely necessary and universal truths, but at least it continues to out-perform the rest of the inductive sciences. *Primus inter pares*, then, if no longer reigning monarch.

On this reading the foundations problem reduces to the enigma of how to reconcile the demise of the Laplacean vision with the fact that, as Kline puts it, mathematics is 'effective at all'. Kline sums up the perplexity which many share when he asks whether we are 'performing miracles with imperfect tools? If man has been deceived, can nature also be deceived into yielding to man's mathematical dictates? Clearly not. Yet, do not our successful voyages to the moon and our explorations of Mars and Jupiter, made possible by technology which itself depends heavily on mathematics, confirm mathematical theories of the cosmos?'[33] It is an indication of just how wide is the gap which must be bridged when Kline offers as a clinching demonstration of the dilemma he has outlined what seems rather to be a *reductio ad absurdum* of his view. It is difficult to say whether there are two separate confusions present in Kline's picture — which are internally connected and feed off one another — or whether there is ultimately only one basic misconception operating here. To begin with this argument confuses the nature of the distinction between mathematics and science, but it does so because at a deeper level it misconstrues the nature of mathematical truth. The temptation is all too great to interpret the 'necessity and strict universality' of mathematical truth as a metaphysical thesis about the 'structure of the universe'. It is because the discovery of mathematical truths were viewed as an insight into the true essence of things — the 'laws which nature must obey' — that, when it was finally borne in that nature could be described in myriad ways, philosophers concluded, not that they had misconstrued the character of the necessity and strict uni-versality of mathematical truth, but rather, that mathematical truths must not be necessary and universal after all.

Even when the desire to avoid metaphysics is at its most pro-nounced the same fallacy is covertly present. In his 'Reflections on my Eightieth Birthday', Russell recalled his motives in turning from pure mathematics to the philosophy of mathematics: 'I wanted certainty in the kind of way in which people want religious faith. I thought that certainty is more likely to be found in mathe-matics than elsewhere. But I discovered that many mathematical demonstrations, which my teachers expected me to accept, were full of fallacies, and that, if certainty were indeed discoverable in mathematics, it would be in a new field of mathematics, with more solid foundations than those that had hitherto been thought secure.' Significantly, he was forced to report that 'after some twenty years of very arduous toil, I came to the conclusion that there was nothing more that I could do in the way of making mathematical knowledge indubitable.'[34] The fact that Russell felt that certainty was *more likely* to be found in mathematics than in any other field betrays a profound misunderstanding of the nature of the logical demarcation between mathematical and scientific truth with which we are concerned. What Russell failed to realise was that his disappointment was due, not to the enormous difficulty of the goal which he had set himself, nor to its unobtainability, but simply, to the presuppositions with which he had approached his task.

An invaluable guide to the framework of Russell's thought is provided in one of his earliest works in which he first embarked on the quest which he eventually abandoned. In 'The Study of Mathematics' Russell declared that 'Mathematics takes us still further from what is human, into the region of absolute necessity, to which not only the actual world, but every possible world, must conform'.[35] What is particularly striking in this passage is that it is explicitly concerned with a realm which transcends mortal cares; with the necessity of mathematical truth in terms of the laws to which the universe must conform regardless of human perceptions. The fact that Russell concluded in his *Portraits from Memory* that his search for the *indubitability* of mathematical knowledge was ultimately fruitless indicates his obliviousness to the possibility that there was any problem in his conception of mathematical truth, or indeed, in his conception of the indubitability of mathematical knowledge. One of the primary features of Wittgenstein's resolution of the foundations problem is his demonstration that both of these themes are mistaken, and collapse together. Once we understand the nature of the necessity which characterises mathematical truth we shall understand the nature of the 'indubitability' — the logical *exclusion* of doubt — which characterises 'mathematical knowledge'. We shall then be in a position to see how the belief in the 'withering of mathematical truth' and the resigned acceptance of the fallibility of mathematical knowledge rest firmly on a misunderstanding of the nature of this distinction, and hence of mathematical truth. Indeed, of mathematics *simpliciter*.

Equations are Rules of Syntax

One of the more subtle points of contact between the *Tractatus* reflections on mathematics and the themes developed in *Philosophical Remarks* lies in the repudiation of the thesis that mathematical propositions are tautologies. But whereas this became a central concern in the work of the 1930s, it was only indirectly expressed in the *Tractatus*. At 6.2-6.21 Wittgenstein maintained that mathematical propositions are pseudo-propositions (*Scheinsätze*) which 'do not express a thought'. Earlier (4.1272) he had explained that such pseudo-propositions are nonsensical (*unsinnig*). But at 4.461-4.4611 he explicitly stated that tautologies are *not* nonsensical, and nowhere did he suggest that they are pseudo-propositions. Rather, they are well-formed but senseless propositions (*sinnlose Sätze*). It follows, then, that mathematical propositions cannot be tautologies: something which Wittgenstein did not spell out as such for the simple reason, perhaps, that no one had ever suggested otherwise. Certainly the point is easy enough to overlook, and this indeed proved to be the case by no less a figure than Russell, who initially credited Wittgenstein with the theory that mathematical propositions are tautologies.[36] Russell's mistake might have been partly responsible for the attention which this issue received from Wittgenstein in 1930. Another likely cause is that Wittgenstein was aware that the Logical Positivists had embraced the principle as one of the central planks in their revised logicist platform, and that they regarded this as, in effect, a synthesis of the *Tractatus* and *Principia Mathematica*.[37]

On the basis of a remark in Carnap's *Autobiography* it would seem that the Logical Positivists were aware of Wittgenstein's rejection of this point at an early stage in their discussions, although it is impossible to say whether this was something they had noticed from their close reading of the *Tractatus* in 1925 or had learnt from Waismann's regular reports on Wittgenstein's progress.[38] At any rate, it seems clear that by the early 1930s both sides were conscious of their mutual divergence on the foundations of mathematics. While the Vienna Circle was preoccupied with the complications involved in treating mathematics as 'tautological' Wittgenstein embarked on a radical new conception. He remained committed to the general principle that mathematical propositions are not descriptive, but rejected the *Tractatus* argument that mathematical propositions are nonsensical (ill-formed) expressions. As opposed to this conception he introduced the bold new suggestion that mathematical propositions are 'rules of syntax' (PR §121). As we have already seen, it was a striking innovation, with profound implications for his approach to the philosophy of mathematics. To begin with, it provided the basis for his criticism of Russell's system: mathematical propositions are rules of syntax, not tautologies, for the latter are senseless, whereas mathematical propositions are norms of representation (WWK 35; PR §103). Russell, he told Waismann and Schlick, only argued that mathematical propositions are tautologies because he had a confused notion of the latter; he recognised that mathematical propositions express a sense, and hence only assumed that tautologies could perform this role because he thought that 'his logical propositions said something, that they described something' (WWK 106).

Significantly, Wittgenstein concluded that what he had said about the nature of arithmetical equations (viz. that they are rules of syntax) and about an equation's not being replaceable by a tautology, explains 'what Kant means when he insists that $7 + 5 = 12$ is not an analytic proposition, but synthetic *a priori*' (PR §108). The allusion to Kant is potentially misleading, however; for Wittgenstein certainly did not present this as a piece of literal critical exegesis (and perhaps for that reason reference to Kant was removed from the final version of the argument in *Remarks on the Foundations of Mathematics*; cf. IV §39). Yet neither did he intend this to be read as an endorsement of the intuitionist view that mathematical propositions are synthetic *a priori*. All that he was contending is that the logical behaviour which mathematical propositions *qua* rules exhibit accounts for what Kant was struggling to explain with his description of mathematical truths as synthetic *a priori* judgements. Wittgenstein was seeking to credit Kant with the recognition that mathematical propositions are not trivial nor true 'in virtue of their meanings' in order to register his shared commitment to the Kantian principle that mathematical truths must in some sense be significant. This is to be explained, however, not by postulating an arcane mental faculty, but rather, in terms of the normative grammatical character of mathematical propositions. That is, they tell us something 'which no experience will refute', and 'whenever we say that something *must* be the case we are using a norm of expression' (AWL 16).

It is nevertheless a somewhat curious argument for Wittgenstein to have introduced, let alone retained. He clearly had no interest in developing the Kantian conception of the imposition of categories of judgement on reality. Nor for that matter did he treat the concepts of *analytic* and *synthetic* as essential philosophical tools with which to elucidate the logical syntax of mathematical versus empirical propositions; if anything, his attitude tended to be the exact opposite. But then why bother to mention this Kantian theme in the first place, which is all the more striking when one considers Wittgenstein's customary reticence when it came to illustrating an argument with a reference to some notion culled from the history of philosophy? The answer to this must somehow derive from the fact that the purpose of the argument was to emphasise the rejection of the principle that mathematical propositions are analytic, but why should this have seemed so important to Wittgenstein? Presumably, because of the Vienna Circle's (and the *Tractatus*'s!) equation of 'analytic' with 'tautology'. The emphasis on the nature of mathematical propositions as rules as opposed to tautologies, and then this sudden interjection that their behaviour as rules licenses the description of them as 'synthetic *a priori*', would have immediately been seen as a direct attack on the logical positivist approach to the foundations dispute. For that reason alone, one can sense a deeper undercurrent to Hahn's curt rebuff to 'The Nature of Mathematics: Witgenstein's Standpoint' (cf. Chapter 1). But the worry posed by Hahn's reaction was that he completely misconstrued the nature of the criticisms which Wittgenstein had set Waismann to articulate at Königsberg. Hahn was obviously aware that 'Wittgenstein's Standpoint' amounted to a full-scale assault on the Russellian — and *a fortiori* the logical positivist — conception of logicism. The problem was that he did not grasp the basis for Wittgenstein's attack, with the result that he was left completely bewildered by what struck him as Wittgenstein's perverse attempt to saw off the branch on which he too was sitting.

Although the Circle were ready to register their discontent with *Principia Mathematica* they were certainly not prepared to countenance the Wittgensteinian extreme of renouncing logicism itself. In 'The Foundations of Mathematics' Hahn cautioned: 'while I do thus attack Russell's philosophical interpretation of his system, I nevertheless believe that the formal side of his system is largely in order as it is and highly suitable for the foundations of mathematics; we must only look for a different philosophical interpretation.'[39] In a series of articles various members of the Circle — in particular Carnap and Hahn — attempted to set the record straight. They subscribed to the fundamental logicist principle that all mathematical truths can be reduced to logic, and this immediately ruled out the Russell–Whitehead version, since it contained such notorious examples of synthetic propositions as the axioms of choice and infinity. The whole impetus behind logicism as far as Carnap, Neurath and Hahn were concerned was to consolidate the analytic *a priori*/synthetic *a posteriori* demarcation. It was for this reason that they had seized on logicism in their overriding zeal to eliminate any lingering vestiges of the synthetic *a priori*. But, as Hahn explained in 'Empiricism, Mathematics, and Logic', 'The place of mathematics has always presented a great difficulty for this position; for experience cannot provide us with *universal* knowledge, but mathematical knowledge seems to be universal.'[40] Needless to say, the answer to the dilemma which Hahn went on to sketch is that logical empiricism is saved by the logicist thesis that mathematical truths are tautologies, and thus, that all necessary truths are analytic *a priori* propositions. But then, wasn't this the very principle that Wittgenstein himself had established? After all, 'It was Wittgenstein who recognised the tautological character of logic and emphasized that there was nothing in the world corresponding to the so-called logical constants'.[41]

At §108 of *Philosophical Remarks* (*supra*) Wittgenstein signalled his repudiation of the Vienna Circle's logicist thesis in a manner which was intended to mark his rejection of their conception of necessary truth.[42] This has major consequences for how we approach Wittgenstein's proposed resolution of the 'foundations crisis', and hence, for the interpretation of Wittgenstein's explanation of the nature of mathematical truth and certainty. It was clearly no idle move on Wittgenstein's part that when he rejected the notion that mathematical propositions are tautologies he carefully tied this in with the assumption that they are analytic *a priori*. For the Logical Positivists the two terms were not just coextensional: in practice they became virtually synonymous.[43] This usage both accounts for and derives from the fact that the Logical Positivists placed so much emphasis on the role of a structural property in the construction of necessary truths. *Prima facie*, however, they would appear to have been guilty of running together two quite different concepts. In *Prolegomena to a Critical Grammar*, Josef Schächter chastised his colleagues for failing to see that it makes no sense to speak of mathematical propositions both as analytic and as tautologies; for the latter term applies solely to complex sentences, whereas 'analytic' is restricted to elementary propositions.[44] But the matter is rather more complicated on the logical positivist account. According to their standard definition a proposition is analytic when its truth (or falsity) depends solely on the meanings of the symbols it contains (as in e.g. the case of definitions): an explanation which deliberately leaves it open whether we are dealing with elementary or complex propositions.

As Schlick's Preface and the author's Foreword make clear, Schächter's book was written under the direct guidance of Schlick and Waismann in order to serve as a practical application of Wittgenstein's new ideas. It thus appears to have been intended as one of the counter-moves in the internecine warfare being waged within the Circle between the pro- and anti-Wittgenstein forces. But why did Wittgenstein himself not make the same point as Schächter? There are, in fact, two different problems with Schächter's argument. The first is that it oversimplified the logical positivist position. By distinguishing so carefully between *rules* and *tautologies*, Wittgenstein had certainly introduced a striking new refinement into philosophy, but although the Logical Positivists may have been oblivious of the importance of this distintion, it was for reasons which had been consciously adopted; indeed, reasons that trace back directly to the *Tractatus*. In *Language, Truth and Logic*, Ayer illustrated what a tautology is with the colour-exclusion statement.[45] It is certainly interesting that he should have seized on this, rather than the standard 'Either it is raining or not raining' type of example; perhaps this simply reflects the extent to which the distinction between *rule* and *tautology* was overlooked at the time. Notoriously, the argument has a pedigree which traces back to 6.3751 of the *Tractatus*. Even when Wittgenstein renounced the *Tractatus* argument in 'Some Remarks on Logical Form' he still insisted that the colour-exclusion statement is a tautology.[46] Moreover, when Schlick expounded Wittgenstein's RLF argument in 'An Introduction to Philosophical Thinking', he stressed throughout that the colour-exclusion statement is a tautology.[47] But in this respect Schlick had clearly failed to grasp the significance of Wittgenstein's changing position.

All of the emphasis on the distinction between tautologies and rules entailed a revised approach to the colour-exclusion statement. Thus we find Waismann explaining in 'Theses' that 'In saying, for example, that one point of my visual field cannot have two colours at the same time I am giving a rule of syntax and not an induction. For the proposition does not run, "A point never has two colours at the same time," but rather, "A point *cannot* have two colours at the same time." Here the word "can" means *logical possibility* whose expression is not a proposition but a rule of syntax. (A rule delimits the form of description)' (WWK 241). The most important question here is: what was the underlying change which accounted for this new approach to the colour-exclusion problem? As far as the Logical Positivists were concerned the fact that a proposition does not look like a tautology need not disturb us; logical analysis will establish the proposition's true tautological structure. The important point is that, by deliberately conflating the concepts of analyticity and tautology, the Logical Positivists were endeavouring to present a unified account of all 'necessary truths'. Logical analysis would reveal that all apparently synthetic *a priori* propositions reduce to complex tautological combinations. (If they tended to concentrate on the colour-exclusion problem in their writings it was largely because the phenomenologists had seized on the colour-exclusion statement as an indisputable example of a synthetic *a priori* truth.) But if we abandon the covering protection provided by the doctrine of logical analysis what we are left with is not only a fundamental distinction between rules and tautologies: we are thereby left with a crucial distinction between conventions and tautologies, and thus, between the Logical Positivists' and Wittgenstein's conceptions of mathematical truth (*infra*).

The second problem with Schächter's argument is that it ran directly contrary to Wittgenstein's purposes. Wittgenstein could certainly have argued that because of their failure to distinguish between rules and tautologies the Logical Positivists had illicitly conflated analytic propositions with tautologies (a confusion which Wittgenstein himself had propounded in the *Tractatus* at 6.11). But had Wittgenstein taken this line he would then have been committed to the position that mathematical propositions are indeed analytic albeit not tautologies: the very premise which he deliberately excluded. For it was not just the 'philosophical interpretation' of the logicist programme that Wittgenstein was attacking — whether this be the Russellian or the logical positivist version: it was the approach itself, with its basic premise that

mathematical truths are 'logical propositions', which he intended
to subvert and replace with a conventionalist emphasis on the
mathematical creation of *grammatical* propositions. To be sure,
there is a parallel between the logical positivist definition of 'analyticity' and Wittgenstein's conception of a 'rule of grammar': viz.
neither says anything about the world; but the explanation for this
lack of factual content is completely different in each case. The
'analytic' conception sees the necessary truth of a statement as
deriving from the pre-established meanings of its sub-sentential
components and the rules of syntax governing their combination.
The meaning of the words together with these syntactical rules
automatically (or mechanically) yield an expression with no factual
content. But this conception does not apply to the construction of
rules; certainly, not as Wittgenstein conceived it. There is no compositional picture of sentential meaning operating in the latter;
whether or not a sentence expresses a rule depends solely on the
manner in which it is used.

The crucial point is thus that if we are to refer to Wittgenstein's
account of mathematical truth as 'conventionalist' this must in no
way be confused with the doctrine that has devolved from the
Vienna Circle. The key to the Logical Positivist's conventionalism
is the premise that a proposition of mathematics is true in virtue of
the meaning of its constituent words together with the syntactic
rules governing their combination. But Wittgenstein was clearly not
arguing that the necessity of a mathematical proposition is a
function of the meanings of its sub-sentential terms. Such a theory
operates with a *Bedeutungskörper* conception of word-meaning
and a compositional picture of sentence-meaning, both of which
Wittgenstein now rejected. The truth of a mathematical proposition does not 'flow' from the meaning of its terms, let alone from
their unique combination. Hence Wittgenstein's account is not
subject to the problems which afflict 'modified conventionalism'.
Applying Dummett's critique (*infra*), Wright argues that the basic
problem with modified conventionalism is that it is unable to
account for all the various sorts of analytic statement which we
would intuitively want to say are true or false solely in virtue of
their meanings; i.e. that analyticity outstrips necessity on the modified account. He offers the colour-exclusion statement as a paradigmatic example of this failure; for this, he suggests, presents a
case where ostensive definition gives the meaning of 'green' and
'red' yet there is nothing in those meanings to account for the

colour-exclusion statement, which leaves us with the problem of explaining how such a truth could flow from the meaning of these unanalysable constituents.[48] But each of the premises operating in this argument violates Wittgenstein's argument.

The very concept of an 'analytic' statement is one which Wittgenstein treated at arm's length; the point he was interested in can be made without any reference to the concept of 'analytic'. In this way Wittgenstein could bypass the complications involved in dealing with a term which has received so many different explanations. Add to this the compositional theory and you have the very conception of sentence-meaning which Wittgenstein undermined. If anything, the argument reads as a *reductio* against the premise that analyticity has any bearing on conventions; or at any rate, on Wittgenstein's conception of conventionalism. There is nothing — neither metaphysical facts nor predetermined meanings — constraining us to use a *Beweissystemlos* expression as a rule. Clearly this constitutes a fundamental disparity, therefore, between the Vienna Circle and Wittgenstein's conception of mathematical truth. The Logical Positivists were *not* arguing that mathematical, and in general, necessary propositions are conventions; in *The Logical Structure of the World* Carnap explained that '*Logic (including mathematics) consists solely of conventions concerning the use of symbols, and of tautologies* on the basis of these conventions.'[49] The drift of this argument is inescapable: mathematical propositions are tautologies *because of* the syntactic and semantic conventions which have already been laid down for the use of the sub-sentential expressions. But Wittgenstein countered that the mathematical proposition itself is a convention *as opposed to* a tautology. It is all too easy to overlook the significance of this divergence in the general haste to classify both Wittgenstein's and the Logical Positivists' accounts as either species of essentially the same form of mathematical conventionalism or else as different positions within the same framework. But if Wittgenstein's argument was conventionalist, it was certainly not in the logical positivist sense.

The suggestion that Wittgenstein was a conventionalist is a highly contentious matter, but it is anything but clear how this controversy applies to what has here been claimed. Certainly this interpretation emphasises that Wittgenstein was intent on treating mathematical propositions as rules of syntax; but whether that makes him a 'conventionalist' in any of the recognised senses of the term is very much a different and far more complicated matter, hampered by the confusions which invariably surround such generic terms. The very fact that critics can be evenly divided on so fundamental a question as whether or not Wittgenstein should be described as a conventionalist should alert us to the dangers inherent in the question. It would be pointless to list all the various arguments cited on the opposing sides; rather, what we should be asking is simply: how is it possible for there to be such conflict on so basic an issue? For there can be no disputing that Wittgenstein argues that mathematical and 'grammatical' propositions are conventions — he said so repeatedly; one is thus forced to conclude that the problem must lie in our understanding of what is meant by calling Wittgenstein a 'conventionalist'. We have already seen that Wittgenstein was definitely not a conventionalist in the logical positivist sense; in the following section we shall consider the problem from Dummett's point of view. But there too the conclusion reached is that, while Wittgenstein's version of conventionalism differs radically from Dummett's framework, this need not entail that Wittgenstein was not a conventionalist: provided this is not construed as offering a '*theory of necessity*' (*infra*).

The significance of this distinction is fully borne out when we come to consider whether mathematical propositions are 'analytic' or 'synthetic'. As the parallel between his conception of mathematical propositions as rules of grammar and Kant's description of them as synthetic *a priori* judgements was meant to illustrate, this argument enabled Wittgenstein to satisfy Poincaré's objection that logicism fails to explain how mathematics can be an inventive and constantly growing discipline. If mathematics reduces in principle to an 'immense tautology', then how could we ever discover something new?[50] It was a problem which reduced the Vienna Circle to a confused psychological argument with uncharacteristically metaphysical undertones. For example, Ayer maintained in *Language, Truth and Logic* that 'The power of logic and mathematics to surprise us depends, like their usefulness, on the limitations of our reason', but that 'A being whose intellect was infinitely powerful would take no interest in logic and mathematics. For he would be able to see at a glance everything that his definitions implied, and, accordingly, could never learn anything from logical inference which he was not fully conscious of already.'[51] This was very much the standard logical positivist/logicist response to Poincaré's objection.[52] It seems likely that

Wittgenstein was led to formulate his distinction between the so-called 'synthetic' character of rules and the analyticity of tautologies with this dilemma in mind. At any rate, Wittgenstein's argument allowed him to sidestep the Logical Positivists' hopeless position while at the same time avoiding the opposite pitfall of the descriptivist conception of mathematical propositions. Mathematical propositions are autonomous rules of grammar, and this accounts for the endless growth of mathematics (cf. Chapter 8).

This left Wittgenstein with a problem of a rather different sort, however; for it now remained to reconcile the claim that mathematical propositions are rules of syntax with the time-honoured conviction that they are true and that these truths are certain (LFM 55). The difficulty here is simply that we do not ordinarily regard rules as 'true'; certainly not in the sense that they 'express a thought' or 'describe a fact'. But then, in what sense are they 'true' or 'certain'? The closest Wittgenstein came to discussing this problem was in the Ambrose Lectures, where he told his students, 'We cannot say of a grammatical rule that it conforms to or contradicts a fact. The rules of grammar are independent of the facts we describe in our language. ... The words "practical" and "impractical" characterise rules. A rule is not true or false' (AWL 65, 70). But where does that leave mathematical truth? Later in the same course of lectures we find Wittgenstein content to refer somewhat elusively to the truth of mathematical propositions as deriving from the fact that they deal with concepts as opposed to meaningless marks (AWL 146 ff.). In subsequent discussions the issue was even further downplayed; indeed, he was not prepared to say much more than to repeat the truism that a mathematical proposition is true because it has been proved, which in turn only further serves to complicate the identification of mathematical propositions with rules in as much as we hardly speak of proving a rule. But perhaps Wittgenstein only wanted to argue that mathematical propositions are *similar* to rules?

As far as the foundations problem is concerned, it is ultimately not a pressing matter to decide whether Wittgenstein wanted to establish that mathematical propositions are literally a species of rule or merely behave in the same logical syntactical fashion. Most of the evidence points to the bolder intention, but there are a few passages which could be cited in support of the alternative interpretation. In any event, the result is fundamentally the same as far as Wittgenstein's primary object was concerned: viz. to undermine the sceptical thesis lying at the heart of the 'foundations crisis'. Whether or not Wittgenstein's use of the terms 'rule' and 'equation' was unorthodox thus fades into comparative insignificance in light of the general thrust of his argument, which was to account for the certainty of mathematical truth in precisely the same terms as apply to rules in general; whatever explanation serves to elucidate the logical syntax of the latter encompasses the former as well, and it is partly for this reason that the discussion of rule-following came to play such a predominant role in the remarks on the foundations of mathematics. But there seems little more to say here, other than that there is a *categorial* difference between the *truth* of mathematical versus empirical propositions. Indeed, Waismann was perfectly happy to concede this in passing with no apprehension that anything further need be said on the subject (PLP 141, 151). The crucial point as far as he was concerned is to see that to say of a mathematical proposition that it is true has nothing whatsoever to do with correspondence to or description of a fact.

We might compare this theme to Wittgenstein's favoured example of the case of colour-grammar. If there were a rule that there are 'six' primary colours this would not be true in the way that applies to whether there are six red objects on my desk. It would be 'true' in the sense that 'The expression "primary colour number seven" has no meaning. Some people would say this means that the grammar of "colour" must conform to certain facts of nature. But there is no parallelism between "There is no seventh primary colour" and "There is no 6′2″ man who can be fitted with the six sizes of suits manufactured"' (AWL 66). In other words, unlike the case of empirical propositions, it is *unintelligible* to express a doubt about the relations fixed by an expression which I use as a mathematical proposition. Hence the certainty of mathematical truth is best elucidated by a negative explanation: it is that the possibility of uncertainty has been grammatically removed. '*What* is unshakably certain about what is proved? To accept a proposition as unshakably certain — I want to say — means to use it as a grammatical rule: this removes uncertainty from it' (RFM III §39). Strictly speaking, therefore, 'The question here is not really one of certainty but of something stipulated by us' (RFM I §122). Thus, mathematical truth is not certain in the inductive sense that we know beyond all shadow of a doubt that the proposition is true; but neither is our knowledge non-inductive. Rather, the point is that mathematical truths are 'certain' in the uniquely normative sense that all possibility of doubt has been grammatically excluded: it simply *makes no sense* to doubt the truth of mathematical propositions.

We have so far touched on the truth and certainty of mathematical propositions but neglected what many will undoubtedly see as the most important of the concepts with which we must deal: the necessity of mathematical truth. Given that it has already been argued that Wittgenstein adopted a conventionalist account of mathematical truth some might feel that — for better or for worse — this effectively disposes of the problem; but this is far from being the case. It is certainly tempting to conclude that from 1930 onwards Wittgenstein championed a conventionalist account of logical necessity and left the matter at that. The problem is that with all the attention which conventions receive in *Philosophical Remarks* logical necessity seems to get dropped by the wayside. For the term which plays such a prominent role in the *Tractatus* rarely makes an appearance in the later work. How are we to account for what *prima facie* seems such a puzzling lacuna? Perhaps the explanation can be found in a passage in *Lectures on the Foundations of Mathematics* — one of the few places where Wittgenstein dealt explicitly with the topic at any length — in which Wittgenstein returned to the themes adumbrated in the opening sections of *Philosophical Remarks*. In an exchange with von Wright he warned that we must be careful to distinguish between the 'necessity of a system' versus that of a proposition within a system (LFM 241). If we are speaking of necessity in the former sense then we have simply confused the shadows cast by grammar for metaphysical theses; grammatical systems are autonomous constructions which are not dictated by or correspond to any preexisting reality (cf. Chapter 8). If, however, what we mean is that a given proposition necessarily follows from the rules of the system, we are guilty of a solecism: 'if it means anything *at all*, [it] must be opposed to a case where there is no necessity. Or else it's a pleonasm to say you *necessarily* get this — why not simply say that you *get* it?' (LFM 242).

It would certainly seem that for the above reasons Wittgenstein was reluctant to introduce 'necessity' into the discussion, and indeed, occasionally indicated the qualms which he felt by enclosing the term in inverted commas (RFM I §5; V §41). The ultimate exegetical question here, therefore, is why did he either scrupulously avoid all mention of the term, or else allude to it in so guarded a manner that it borders on the pejorative? To understand the reasons for this attitude it is crucial to see, first, that purged of all its metaphysical overtones what we are left with is indeed a conventionalist explanation of logical necessity; but then, it is not at all clear that this can serve as a satisfactory answer to what Dummett has called 'the philosophical problem of necessity'.[53] Yet the upshot of this need not be that Wittgenstein's account of logical necessity should be found wanting; it might also be the latter which is the culprit. Dummett maintains that 'the philosophical problem of necessity is twofold': first, we must explain what the source of necessity is, and second, we must explain how we recognise it. This argument may well serve as an excellent guide to traditional attitudes to necessity, but whatever its merits as an account of the criteria which philosophers have tacitly laid down for an adequate explanation, how can we possibly apply this framework to Wittgenstein's argument? The whole thrust of this picture is in the opposite direction from Wittgenstein's approach. The very notion that there is a 'philosophical problem of necessity' which incorporates an ontological and an epistemological dimension is precisely what Wittgenstein was trying to overthrow.

By forcing us to consider the normativity of mathematics Wittgenstein was attempting to direct our attention onto logical syntax (subsequently, logical grammar) and away from such domains as possible worlds and special mathematical faculties. Hence the criteria we should be concerned with have nothing whatsoever to do with Dummett's proposed 'ontological' and 'epistemological' candidates. For what does it mean to investigate the 'source of necessity'? Wittgenstein never suggested that conventions are the source of logical necessity; this way of stating the matter would automatically leave us with the puzzle of how a convention could accomplish such a feat. The problem is that to think in terms of discovering a 'source' of necessity merely introduces confusing — metaphysical — associations and implications where the real task is one of clarifying those grammatical features which lead us to describe mathematical propositions as 'excluded from doubt'. Likewise, we are not concerned with 'how we recognise' mathematical certainty; only with what we describe as 'unshakably certain', and why this should be the case. Epistemological mandates only set us off on the doomed enterprises which we have examined throughout this work, away from our proper concern with logical syntax. The substantial issues we should be addressing are: what does it mean to describe a rule of syntax as logically necessary, how does this account for the demarcation between mathematics and science, and thence the elimination of scepticism from the philosophy of mathematics? The ultimate response to Dummett's 'twofold problem of necessity' is thus to see how both premises are undermined by the very confusions which are indicative of the pressing need to resolve the problem by dissolving it.

If the result of these criticisms was that 'logical necessity' virtually disappeared from Wittgenstein's discussion this must be construed, not as the result of a subversive attack on the concept, but rather as a consequence of the clarification of the logical syntax of mathematical propositions. Mathematicians had obviously always possessed an inchoate picture of this distinction — enough at any rate to keep the two activities operational — but by resorting to the shadowy concept of necessity in order to account for this divergence philosophers had only managed to muddy the waters by introducing metaphysical pictures as a substitute for philosophical understanding. By removing the spotlight from necessity Wittgenstein had effectively restored the focus onto normativity; to speak of the 'necessity and strict universality of mathematical truth' is to recognise that 'The mathematical Must is only another expression of the fact that mathematics forms concepts. And concepts help us to comprehend things. They correspond to a particular way of dealing with situations. Mathematics forms a network of norms' (RFM VII §67). Thus, the philosophical problem of necessity can — and perhaps must — simply drop out of our investigation, and in its place we should henceforward speak of the 'hardness of the logical must': the grammatical features which account for the logical demarcation between mathematical and scientific truth. At least, this is precisely what logical necessity does and all it could amount to; to attempt to go any further than this seriously runs the risk of proposing a 'philosophical theory of necessity'. The key to resolving the 'foundations crisis', therefore, is to grasp that the certainty which characterises mathematical truth is *categorially* as opposed to *quantitatively* different from that which applies to empirical knowledge, and mathematics is not the 'most certain' of the sciences but rather, certain in a completely different manner: one which makes it strictly unintelligible to speak, as Russell did, of rendering mathematical knowledge 'indubitable'.

The most important point to bear in mind here is that our ultimate objective is to clarify the conceptual barrier between mathematics and science in such a way as to remove rather than refute
the sceptical thesis which lies at the heart of the foundations dispute. And this task is fully accomplished by elucidating the certainty of the 'logical must': viz. of rules of syntax. The ultimate
problem with the 'philosophical problem of necessity' is that it
seeks to go beyond this need. For the essential characteristic of
necessity so perceived is that it must in principle mean more than
has thus been presented. Granted, it may be impossible to specify
what this *more* is, but that only underlines the deep metaphysical
character of the 'philosophical problem of necessity'. Even the
attempt to penetrate this mystery with possible world semantics —
which purportedly reflects the desire to remain within the boundaries of logical syntax — betrays the insuperable difficulty
involved in discussing necessity in terms which do not quickly lead
back into these metaphysical quagmires. When we prune away the
various ontological and epistemological associations and confine
ourselves solely to the area of logical grammar, what we are left
with is simply the 'logical must'. If this argument remains profoundly unsatisfactory to philosophers interested in disclosing the
hidden nature of mathematical necessity, it is precisely because to
strip necessity of its metaphysics is, as far as they are concerned,
not so much to denude as destroy it. The philosopher who resorts
to possible world semantics has not strayed unawares into some
unexpected domain; he has deliberately ventured into the void
because like Jason he thinks he can return with the golden fleece, if
only he has sufficient courage and perseverance. But at the end of
his travails he is left like Russell: a defeated Orpheus mourning
that he nearly managed to succeed, but was ultimately forced by
destiny to return empty-handed.

Unconventional Conventionalism

The greatest problem that we face in describing Wittgenstein as a
'conventionalist' is knowing precisely what we mean by the term.
There are those who resolve that, because Wittgenstein's approach
does not conform to any of the established models, the safest
course to follow is simply to desist from what they see as the futile
attempt to classify the unique.[54] But while one can sympathise with

the general spirit motivating such caution — which is merely to avert the confusions that result from trying to force Wittgenstein's thought into an inhospitable framework — it is nevertheless hardly satisfactory to leave his argument floating in a philosophical limbo. Surely it is possible to draw certain broad distinctions within the philosophy of mathematics? At the very least, it is difficult to see how we can avoid a sweeping demarcation between platonism and conventionalism in any serious inquiry into the nature of mathematical necessity. (Admittedly, this leaves out empiricism, but only because it elects to dismiss — either consciously or inadvertently — the concept of mathematical necessity *ab initio*.) Granted that Wittgenstein's remarks do not fall into any of the recognised categories of conventionalism which have proliferated in recent years, that is not so much an argument for rejecting the claim that Wittgenstein was offering a conventionalist account of mathematical truth as a case for reconsidering what is meant — or at any rate, what Wittgenstein intended — by treating mathematical propositions as rules of logical syntax.

The most commonly cited exemplar of conventionalism is the logical positivist version, whose antecedents can be traced back to the *Tractatus*.[55] As we have just seen, however, Wittgenstein's 1930 interpretation of mathematical propositions can no more be identified with the Vienna Circle than the *Tractatus* doctrine. The most serious rival to the logical positivist conception today can be found in Dummett's distinction between 'modified' and 'full-blooded' conventionalism. On the basis of this division Dummett purports to demonstrate, not just that Wittgenstein's, but indeed, that all species of conventionalism as thus defined are doomed to provide an inadequate explanation of the sources and recognition of necessity. A battle now rages, not simply over the merits of Dummett's attacks on 'full-blooded' and 'modified' conventionalism, but also whether Dummett has properly identified Wittgenstein's location in this schema. But the real question we should be addressing is, not which 'position' Wittgenstein's conception occupies, but rather, whether Dummett's framework has any genuine bearing on Wittgenstein's thought. If not, then the controversy which Dummett's argument has provoked can simply be bypassed.

According to Dummett, the 'modified' conventionalist holds that all necessary propositions can be divided into two classes: direct statements of conventions, and the subsidiary conventions which can be derived from these. 'Full-blooded' conventionalism is the thesis that there is only one class of necessary statements: those which are explicitly stipulated to be conventions. Despite this theoretical distinction, however, Dummett argues that 'modified' conventionalism — which *prima facie* strikes him as the only reasonable position to adopt if we are to provide a non-stipulative justification of mathematical truth — must either collapse into the 'full-blooded' version, or else abandon its claim that *all* necessary propositions are conventions. The problem which Dummett sees as lying at the heart of the 'modified' conventionalist's discomfiture is essentially that he is unable to identify the source of his assumption that the consequences derived from conventions are themselves conventions. If he argues that this is itself constituted by a convention, then for all intents and purposes his argument reduces to the 'full-blooded' extremity. But if he resists this move he is still left with the problem of explaining the status of the statement that one convention follows from another in anything other than metaphysical terms.

It was remarked above that Dummett's framework provides an alternative to the logical positivist species of conventionalism, and this despite the fact that Dummett cites the Vienna Circle's treatment of an axiomatic system as the *locus classicus* of 'modified' conventionalism.[56] For as it stands, this interpretation is extremely misleading given that, as we have just seen, the Logical Positivists regarded the axioms and transformation rules of a system as conventions explicitly stipulated for the use of the key mathematical concepts, but the theorems in that system as tautologies which follow from those conventions. It is thus hardly fair to say that the Logical Positivists did not have a fully worked-out position on the 'source' of the logical necessity which leads us to mathematical truths; on the contrary, the whole force of their argument just was to account for the logical necessity of mathematical propositions in these *Tractatus*-inspired terms. Most importantly, however, it is misleading to suppose that Wittgenstein's chief objection to this argument was concerned with Dummett's 'modified' versus 'full-blooded' problem; rather, Wittgenstein's criticisms were directed at the entirely different matter of defining mathematical propositions as logical truths: i.e. as senseless propositions. Wittgenstein's primary concern was to demonstrate that, far from this being the case, mathematical propositions exhibit the 'synthetic' character of rules of logical syntax. Thus, the very fact that

Wittgenstein attacked the foundation on which the Logical Positivists' argument rests was not because, as Dummett believes, he was trying to supplant their 'modified' account of conventionalism with a 'full-blooded' rendering. Rather, it was because he was trying to undermine their very way of looking at mathematical truth.

The basic problem with Dummett's interpretation of Wittgenstein's conventionalism, therefore, is that he would force Wittgenstein's argument back into the very mould which it was designed to break. Wittgenstein was not adopting the opposite or militant position within the same conventionalist framework; he was seeking to escape the confines of that framework altogether. He was not offering an account of necessary propositions which was supposed to harmonise with the compositional theory of meaning, but rather, endeavouring to undermine such a theory. The simple fact is that compositional semantics have no bearing on Wittgenstein's description of mathematical propositions, and this, far from being accidental, was a matter of deliberate design on Wittgenstein's part. The crux of the Logical Positivists' position was that a proposition is 'necessary' because of the semantic conventions determining the meanings of words and the syntactic rules that have been laid down for their combination. It simply makes no sense to try to extend this framework to cover Wittgenstein's conception of mathematical propositions as rules, and it was *precisely for that reason* that Wittgenstein had moved in this direction in the first place. By encouraging us to treat mathematical propositions as rules *rather than* tautologies, Wittgenstein was trying to bring us to see that the compositional theory of meaning has no bearing whatsoever on the question of the certainty of mathematical truth. This is entirely a matter of the normativity of mathematical propositions: of the manner in which we use mathematical propositions as standards of correct representation.

On Dummett's reading Wittgenstein subscribed to — indeed created the paradigm for — the 'full-blooded' thesis that 'the logical necessity of any statement is always the *direct* expression of a linguistic convention. That a given statement is necessary consists always in our having expressly decided to treat that very statement as unassailable'.[57] This is a distinctly odd way of stating the matter: whether a statement has been *expressly* designated or *tacitly* treated as a convention is quite irrelevant to the question of whether we should describe it as a convention on the basis of its use. Perhaps the term 'convention' itself is responsible for the pervasive assumption that Wittgenstein was actually interested in a genetic account of the evolution of mathematical knowledge: a confusion which Wittgenstein deliberately sought to remove in the Ambrose Lectures when he warned that it is 'misleading' to call '"2 + 2 = 4" the expression of a convention' because 'the situation with respect to it is comparable to the situation supposed in the Social Contract theory. We know that there was no actual contract, but it is as if such a contract had been made. Similarly for 2 + 2 = 4: it is as if a convention had been made' (AWL 156-7). The reason why Wittgenstein clarified this point was simply because so many assume that the term 'convention' implies the formal convocation and enactment of a piece of linguistic legislation. That this is unwarranted is demonstrated by e.g. our use of the term to describe manners and mores. It is frequently argued that we are only speaking metaphorically when we describe rules of grammar as 'conventions'; but the metaphor — if such, in fact, it is — works in subtle and insidious ways, and despite their awareness of this usage philosophers are nonetheless prone to treat Wittgenstein's 'conventionalism' as a covert epistemological thesis. The question of whether or not we have explicitly stipulated that a given statement is a convention is as unrelated to the problem of whether we should classify an expression as a convention on the basis of its logical syntax as would be the question whether we know that a mathematical proposition is true by acquaintance or description.

To be sure, Wittgenstein was arguing that we can only classify a mathematical expression as a theorem if it has been proved, but then, that is hardly a principle that Dummett feels he was deliberately trying to subvert. But that leaves it difficult to know what Dummett means by attributing to Wittgenstein the idea that a given statement is only necessary when we have 'explicitly stipulated' that this is to be the case. Dummett seems to worry, not just that Wittgenstein tried to reduce necessary truth to linguistic practices, but that in so doing he rendered it an entirely arbitrary matter whether on any given occasion an established convention will be adopted. Dummett's interpretation conjures up a picture — as was no doubt intended — of the individual mathematician pondering over whether to recognise a given mathematical expression as a theorem and deciding, perhaps, on the basis of his own whims or personal objectives. But such a fantasy is completely alien to Wittgenstein's purposes; and this is simply because Wittgenstein was solely concerned with the problem of what it means to describe an expression as a theorem, and not with an atomistic account of mathematical practice. Of course, the individual mathematician is free to say whatever he pleases — just as we are all free to say nonsense — but not if he wishes to engage in mathematics: what we understand and describe as mathematics. We shall consider the issue of what Wittgenstein meant when he described mathematical propositions as 'arbitrary' conventions (viz. autonomous grammatical constructions) in the following chapter; for the moment it bears remarking that the autonomy of grammar is not at all the same thing as self-autonomy.[58]

Dummett is led into his interpretation because he fails to distinguish between what Wittgenstein said about the construction of a new versus the application of an established proof-schema. The short answer to Dummett's putative dilemma is that he is quite wrong to lumber Wittgenstein with the doctrine that 'the logical necessity of any statement is always the *direct* expression of a linguistic convention'. For we must distinguish between what we have described as *Beweissysteme* and *Beweissystemlos* mathematical expressions: i.e. (meaningful) mathematical propositions which are understood against the background of a proof-schema and (nonsensical) mathematical expressions which do not operate in any proof-system. Indeed, the criterion for distinguishing between these two types of expression is that an answer to the latter can only be provided by the construction of a linguistic convention whereas answers to the former are the logical consequences of *Beweissysteme* conventions. Dummett fails to grasp the significance of this distinction largely because he misconstrues the nature of Wittgenstein's attack on the logical positivist conception of mathematical truth. The chief result of trying to read Wittgenstein's remarks in terms of the very theory which they were meant to undermine is that Dummett is predisposed to regard Wittgenstein's argument as the work of an anarchist gone out of control, leading ultimately not only to the demise of mathematical necessity, but to the very collapse of language. If Wittgenstein's 'full-blooded' account were right, Dummett objects, then 'communication would be in constant danger of simply breaking down'.[59] Against this view Dummett 'would like to say that the sense of the words in the statement may have already been fully determined, so that there is no room for any further determination';[60] i.e. the sense of the words together with the established rules of inference dictate what we can regard as a proof. As far as established proof-schemas are concerned Wittgenstein did not dispute this; but in either the case of the creation of a new or the extension of an existing proof-schema this is the very conception that Wittgenstein rejected. A new *Beweissystem* is a grammatical construction: it creates a sense for the words in that combination (cf. Chapter 3).

It is thus crucial to clarify whether we are supposed to be dealing with a proof which extends an existing or constructs an entirely new system, or with the proof of a theorem in an established proof-system. In the latter case we have no 'freedom' in our applications in so far as we can be said to understand the rules of that system, but in the former we are dealing with a novel combination of familiar words. To understand the grammatical point operating here consider once again the example, 'Do green ideas sleep furiously?' How do the meanings of these words together with the rules of syntax and inference determine whether this expression is true or false? Only a significant sentence is subject to the dictates of the Law of Excluded Middle, and this expression is strictly nonsense. A proof that this expression is true would thus have to be a grammatical construction in which rules for such a combination of concepts were laid down, thereby rendering it intelligible. That is, the proof would amount to the production of a new grammatical structure which creates the rules for the use of this expression. Dummett finds this argument 'very difficult to accept', however, and to overturn it he undertakes to demonstrate how the meaning of words together with the rules of inference compel us, if we are to remain faithful to these rules and meanings, to accept a given proof. Let us rephrase this argument in such a way that we can dispense with any allusion to the personal decisions of the individual. Dummett's essential point is that the meanings of words together with the established rules of inference pre-determine what is to count as a proof: whether in a new system or otherwise. In other words, Dummett subscribes to the *Bedeutungskörper* conception of meaning which Wittgenstein rejected (cf. Chapter 8); it is thus highly instructive to consider the example which Dummett presents in order to recognise the sorts of problem which can arise when we attempt to operate with this model.

To establish that 'face to face with a proof, we have no alternative but to accept the proof if we are to remain faithful to the understanding we already had of the expressions contained in it',

Dummett asks us to consider the case of people 'who counted as we do but did not have the concept of addition'.[61] Such a community could find out by counting that there were five boys and seven girls in a classroom, but they could only discover how many children there were by counting them all together. To this Dummett adds the complication that someone from this culture might one time be prepared to say that there were five boys, seven girls, and twelve children, and another that there were five boys, seven girls, and thirteen children. In which case it must be possible for us to prove to him that he had miscounted on the latter occasion. But in that case we would wish to say that 'even before we met this person and taught him the principles of addition, it would have been true that if he had counted five boys, seven girls, and thirteen children, he would have been wrong even according to the criteria he himself then acknowledged.' That is, 'the necessity for his having miscounted when he gets additively discordant results does not, as it were, get its whole being from his now recognising such results as a criterion for having miscounted.'[62] For it lies in the nature of numbers — in the implicit meaning of '5', '7', and '12' — that '5 + 7 = 12'. Hence someone who counts in the same way that we do, only without the concept of addition, is tacitly committed to the rule that $5 + 7 = 12$. The *Bedeutungskörper* conception of meaning which Dummett subscribes to thus maintains that the meaning of the numbers determines the rules which apply rather than vice versa, as Wittgenstein insisted. Unlike Wittgenstein's argument, however, Dummett's example does indeed seem to open up disturbing sceptical possibilities. For who is to say that the same thing might not happen to us as befell Dummett's primitive community? After all, they had no idea (*ex hypothesi*) that they might be making mistakes — according to their criteria for making a mistake — in their counting prior to their grasp of our calculating rules. Might not the same thing happen to us if someone were to discover a new criterion which revealed that we too had been mistaken in our calculations? (Once again, the argument can be read in terms of Knuth's 'unrealistic numbers' if it is felt that this would add greater verisimilitude.)

There are various ways of responding to Dummett's argument, but the basic problem with it lies in its initial assumption that we can speak straightforwardly about someone who counts the same way as we do but does not possess the concept of addition. Far

from being an innocuous premise, this contains ominous overtones. To begin with, the relation between our concepts of counting and addition is internal, not external; counting and calculating
are two different ways of reckoning a sum, but they are internally
related to one another in so far as the relations between the terms
(numbers) involved in each are identical. And this internal relation
is fundamental to the meaning of number-words as we understand
them. Furthermore, Dummett fails to mention it, but the most
pressing question we should like to pose to his example is exactly
what sort of criterion of correctness did this community possess
prior to acquiring the rules of addition? For whatever it was it
could not, according to the logic of the argument, be in the least
affected by our own criteria as set down by the rules of arithmetic.
The only relation between '5', '7' and '12' which they understand
is that '12' is more than '7' which is more than '5': but not *how
much more*. The fallacy here is to think that, if we ask them how
much larger '12' is than '7' they must answer '5'; but we have
already stipulated that they have no further knowledge — no
awareness that there is any connection between '12' and '5 + 7';
their counting would be similar to ticking off strokes or reciting the
alphabet, and thus the criteria they proceeded by would indeed
be governed by the Gestalt (cf. Chapter 4).

The temptation which Dummett succumbs to is to treat this
non-additive form of counting as an implicit arithmetical
operation. The important point to bear in mind here is that, if the
type of counting which this community performed really was conceptually divorced from the rules of calculation, then they would
be engaged in what Wittgenstein described as 'conducting an
experiment': the criteria which they employed for determining
whether they had counted correctly would be empirical (e.g.
whether a child was seen to enter or leave the room). In which
case, if it made no sense to say that a mistake had been made
according to those criteria, then no mistake had been made. To
suggest that they might none the less have committed an error
which was *indiscernible* to their techniques is merely to super-
impose our method of counting onto their activity. To be sure, if
they noticed an anomaly but could discern no error then some
explanation would be called for; but whatever form this took, it
would function as an empirical hypothesis, if not a metaphysical
thesis! Dummett remarks that 'if we came across such a person, we
should know what kind of arguments to bring to show him that in

such circumstances he must have miscounted on one occasion, and that whenever there are five boys and seven girls there are twelve children.'[63] Granted, if Dummett's native did succeed in understanding our arguments and *adopting* our criteria then it would make sense to say that we had taught him how to add; but that is a long way off from Dummett's conclusion that we would thereby have shown him 'that in such circumstances he must have miscounted on one occasion'. For this new criterion of correctness is *constitutive* of what we call adding, and thus what Dummett should have concluded was not that his agent could be shown that he had previously miscounted, but rather, that by learning how to add he had acquired the rules of calculation as his criterion of correctness. Thus, the contrast here is not between two different versions of the same operation, but rather, between two completely different types of activity: one normative and the other empirical. This is precisely the point that Wittgenstein was driving at in the Ambrose Lectures with an example which is extremely close to Dummett's. We can only be said to be adding when we use an arithmetical rule as our criterion for correctness; when this is the case we describe any discordant result as either a case of miscounting or else to be explained in terms of some (meta-)physical hypothesis. But 'When we say $2 + 3$ *must* be 5, this shows that we have determined what is to count as correct; the *must* is a sign of a calculation. The difference between a calculation and an experiment is shown by our saying that a result of counting other than 5 is incorrect' (AWL 160). But there is no such 'must' for Dummett's primitive community; there is at best an empirical probability, however high, that when they count 5 boys and 7 girls they will end up with 12 children.

There is still another way, however, in which Dummett's argument can be construed, where the contrast is not between adding versus conducting an experiment, but rather, between operating with two different types of arithmetical systems. That is, the argument can also serve to highlight the difference between two 'contrary' methods of counting, as they were conceived in the preceding chapter. Dummett assumes that the meanings of number-words are identical in the two different systems of counting: with and without the criterion of addition. But the example of the introduction of the rules of addition as the criterion of correctness provides us with an example of the very opposite: viz. of the manner in which the introduction of new rules of grammar changes

298 The Recovery of Certainty

the senses of terms. The sign '1' in the primitive series 1, 2, 3 ... —
where there is no concept of addition internally related to the concept of counting — does not at all mean the same as '1' when used
in adding. To be sure, cultures have employed different arithmetical systems of counting. But even here it would be misguided
to suppose that their terms mean the same as ours. There may be a
striking parallel, for example, between our use of '1' and the
Babylonian use of 'Υ', but the two terms are not synonymous. For
the meaning of a numeral is determined by its use in a system, and
it is only when the rules are identical (i.e. when the systems are
coextensive) that two terms are synonymous. Indeed, as we shall
see in the next chapter, Wittgenstein took great pains to explain
why '5', '5/1', and '+5' are not the same number; there may be a
considerable overlap in their logical syntactical behaviour, but the
fact remains that they belong to independent (i.e. autonomous)
systems, and in this sense are distinctive numbers.

To return to Dummett's argument, however, it is imperative to
see that this version also fails to meet Dummett's objective, for it
makes no sense to say that the construction of a new system can
reveal mistakes in the old. Certainly we can imagine someone adding according to a completely different set of arithmetical rules in
much the same way that scientists might for certain purposes
employ non-Euclidean geometries. But if we persuade someone to
adopt our arithmetical rules we have not thereby demonstrated
that he previously *miscounted*; rather, we have persuaded him to
adopt a new system of addition in order to realise alternative
results (cf. the various uses of modular arithmetics). It is solely in
the context of an existing system that the notion of 'miscounting'
has any significance; as far as the old system is concerned, there is
no mistake as long as *those* rules have been properly applied. All
that we can say is that the two systems yield different results; and,
as we saw in the chapter on consistency, it is possible to envisage
situations where either of these systems might be employed. The
scientist who switches from Euclidean to BL geometry to measure
the path of light-rays does not discover that he had made
'mistakes' in his previous employment of the Euclidean system;
rather, he decides — for pragmatic and/or aesthetic reasons — that
the new conceptual framework is preferable to the old, given the
nature of his interests. Even a primitive counting system — e.g.
Wittgenstein's '1, 2, 3, 4, 5 many' example where '3 + 4 = 4 + 5'
— is not 'wrong' compared to a sophisticated method; it is simply

designed to meet different needs: which presumably it satisfies. Thus, there is no contrast here between an 'incomplete' and an expanded system of counting; the contrast is between two autonomous conceptual frameworks. There are, as Wittgenstein insisted, no 'gaps' in mathematics. But since Dummett's argument provides a classic example of the contrary assumption, we shall not have dealt fully with his objection until we have examined Wittgenstein's reasons for insisting that 'it is impossible to move from one system to [an]other by merely extending the former' (WWK 36).

Notes

1. Cf. R. Bunn, 'Developments in the Foundations of Mathematics, 1879-1910', in *From the Calculus to Set Theory*, I. Grattan-Guinness (ed.) (London, Duckworth, 1980), p. 220.

2. Michael Dummett, *Frege: Philosophy of Language* (London, Duckworth, 1981), pp.xxxiv-v.

3. Philip Kitcher, *The Nature of Mathematical Knowledge* (New York, Oxford University Press, 1983), pp.246, 268; and 'Frege's Epistemology', *Philosophical Review*, vol. 88 (1979), pp. 238 ff.

4. Ibid., p. 248.

5. Ibid., p. 251.

6. Ibid., p. 257.

7. Quoted in Morris Kline's *Mathematics: The Loss of Certainty* (New York, Oxford University Press, 1980), p. 166.

8. Kitcher, *The Nature of Mathematical Knowledge*, op.cit., p. 247.

9. Ibid., p. 248.

10. Cf. ibid., p. 239.

11. Ibid., p. 240.

12. Kline, *Mathematics: The Loss of Certainty*, op.cit., p. 145.

13. George Berkeley, *The Analyst*, in *The Works of George Berkeley*, A.A. Luce and T.E. Jessop (eds), vol.IV (London, Thomas Nelson, 1948–57), p. 102.

14. Ibid., p.76.

15. Ibid., p. 68.

16. Ibid.

17. Cf. Kline, *Mathematics: The Loss of Certainty*, op.cit., p. 152.

18. Ibid., p. 150.

19. Cf. David Hilbert, 'On the Infinite', *From Frege to Gödel*, Jean van Heijenoort (ed.) (Cambridge, Mass., Harvard University Press, 1977). pp.763 ff.

20. Moreover, not only are the foundations of Analysis and mathematics inextricably intertwined, but it also bears noting just how important Weierstrass's work in Analysis was *vis-à-vis* the inception of Hilbert's Programme. For Hilbert explained in 'On the Infinite' that what he was trying to do in the construction of a consistency proof was emulate Weierstrass's technique in replacing mention of infinitesimals with finitary processes.

21. Cf. I. Grattan-Guinness, 'The Emergence of Mathematical Analysis and its Foundational Progress, 1780–1880', in *From the Calculus to Set Theory*, I, Grattan-Guinness (ed.), op.cit.

22. Kitcher, *The Nature of Mathematical Knowledge*, op.cit., p. 269.

23. Berkeley, *The Analyst*, op.cit., p. 95.

24. Kline, *Mathematics: The Loss of Certainty*, op.cit., *passim*.

25. Ibid., pp.4-5.

26. It is interesting to note the presence of aesthetic or cultural arguments in the debate. In 1947 Orwell was already warning against the impending switch to the metric system. In one of his 'As I Please' columns he gave the following reasons for remaining on the Imperial system:

> The names of the units in the old system are short homely words which lend themselves to vigorous speech. Putting a quart into a pint pot is a good image, which could hardly be expressed in the metric system. Also, the literature of the past deals only in the old measurements, and many passages would become an irritation if one had to do a sum in arithmetic when one read them, as one does with those tiresome versts in a Russian novel.
> > The emmet's inch and eagle's mile
> > Make lame philosophy to smile:
> fancy having to turn that into millimetres! (*The Collected Essays, Journalism and Letters of George Orwell*, Harmondsworth, Penguin Books, 1982, vol. 4 p. 352)

These, as we shall see below, are among the sorts of consideration which, as Wittgenstein emphasised, do continually enter into the decisions of which autonomous grammatical constructions to adopt.

27. Philip J. Davis and Reuben Hersh, *The Mathematical Experience* (Brighton, The Harvester Press, 1981), p. 331.

28. Morris Kline, *Mathematics in Western Culture* (Harmondsworth, Penguin Books, 1979), p. 128.

29. The same idea is echoed in the opening pages of *The Metaphysical Foundations of Natural Science*, where Kant paid tribute to Newton's genius for having achieved 'an insight into the structure of the universe that ... will remain unchanged for all time'.

30. Davis and Hersh, *The Mathematical Experience*, op.cit., p. 6.

31. Kline, *Mathematics: The Loss of Certainty*, op.cit., p. 6.

32. Cf. Schlick, 'The Future of Philosophy', in *Philosophical Papers* vol. II, op.cit.; cf. TLP 4.111, Z §455.

33. Kline, *Mathematics: The Loss of Certainty*, op. cit., p. 7.

34. Bertrand Russell, 'Reflections on my Eightieth Birthday', in *Portraits from Memory and Other Essays* (London, George Allen and Unwin, 1956), p. 53.

35. Bertrand Russell, 'The Study of Mathematics', in *Mysticism and Logic*, op.cit., p. 69.

36. Cf. Bertrand Russell, *Introduction to Mathematical Philosophy*, pp.203 ff., and the first impression of the second introduction to *Principles of Mathematics*. A subsequent correction to this introduction (in which the attribution was withdrawn) suggests that Wittgenstein must have brought this error to Russell's attention. I am indebted to Peter Hacker for drawing my own attention to this point.

37. E.g. Hans Hahn cited the *Tractatus* as the source of the tautological theory of mathematics which he presented in *Logik, Mathematik und Naturerkennen. Einheitswissenschaft*, Heft 2 (Vienna, Gerold & Co., 1933).

38. Cf. Rudolf Carnap, *Autobiography*, in *The Philosophy of Rudolf Carnap*, P.A. Schilpp ed. (La Salle, Open Court, 1963). p. 34.

39. Hans Hahn, 'Discussion about the Foundations of Mathematics', in *Empiricism, Logic, and Mathematics*, Brian McGuinness (ed.), op.cit., p. 35.

40. Hans Hahn, 'Empiricism, Mathematics, and Logic', in ibid., p. 39.

41. Hans Hahn, 'The Significance of the Scientific World View, Especially for Mathematics and Physics', in ibid., p. 24.

42. That is, the conception formally endorsed in the *Vienna Circle Manifesto*. There were, however, important divisions on this issue within the Circle; principally between Carnap, Hahn and Neurath versus Schlick, Waismann and Schächter, with Menger edging towards the latter and Kraft towards the former. In speaking of the Circle's logicist position, therefore, this is primarily based on the *Manifesto*. But it must further be borne in mind that this in itself is somewhat misleading, in so far as the *Manifesto* was written by Carnap, Neurath and Hahn during Schlick's absence in America and presented to him on his return as a *fait accompli*. I am indebted to Friedrich Stadler's papers on 'Wissenschaftsphilosophie in Österreich', which catalogue the various divisions which existed in the Circle. As far as I know, these articles are unpublished.

43. To take but one example from the countless that could be cited, Schlick explained in 'An Introduction to Philosophical Thinking' that 'Tautologies (or analytic judgements) are the only propositions *a priori*, they have absolute validity, but they owe it to their own form, not to a correspondence to facts, they tell us nothing about the world, they represent empty structures.' For the same point, cf. Rudolf Carnap, 'The Elimination of Metaphysics', p. 76 and 'The Old and New Logic', p. 143, both in *Logical Positivism*, A.J. Ayer (ed.) (New York, The Free Press, 1959); Hans Hahn, 'Logic, Mathematics and Knowledge of Nature', p. 158 in *Logical Positivism*; and A.J. Ayer, *Language, Truth and Logic* (London, Victor Gollancz, 1970), p. 84.

44. Joseph Schächter, *Prolegomena to a Critical Grammar* (Dordrecht, D. Reidel Publishing Company, 1973), pp.147 ff.

45. Ayer, *Language, Truth & Logic*, op.cit., p. 79.

46. Ludwig Wittgenstein, 'Some Remarks on Logical Form', in *Essays on Wittgenstein's Tractatus*, Irving M. Copi and Robert W. Beard (eds) (London, Routledge & Kegan Paul, 1966), p. 34.

47. Schlick, 'Introduction to Philosophical Thinking', op.cit., pp.353-4.

48. Wright, *Wittgenstein on the Foundations of Mathematics*, op.cit., pp. 345 ff.

49. Rudolf Carnap, *The Logical Structure of the World & Pseudoproblems in Philosophy*, R.A. George (trans.) (Berkeley and Los Angeles, University of California Press, 1969), p. 178.

50. Cf. Henri Poincaré, *Science and Hypothesis*, W.J. Greenstreet, (trans.) (London, 1905), Chapter 1.

51. Ayer, *Language, Truth and Logic*, op.cit., pp.85-6.

52. Virtually the identical passage appears in Hahn's 'Logic, Mathematics and Knowledge of Nature', op.cit., p. 159, and is alluded to in 'The Scienfitic World View', op.cit., p. 23.

53. Cf. Dummett, 'Wittgenstein's Philosophy of Mathematics', op.cit., pp. 123 ff.

54. Cf. Max Black, 'Verificationism and Wittgenstein's Reflections on Mathematics', where he argues: 'How misleading it is to label Wittgenstein as a finitist, conventionalist or any other kind of -ist (the lazy course followed by some mathematical reviewers of the Remarks).' in *Ludwig Wittgenstein: Critical Assessments*, vol.III, (London, Croom Helm, 1986) pp.68-9. Donald Harward reaches a similar conclusion in 'Wittgenstein and the Character of Mathematical Propositions': 'Wittgenstein was neither conventionalist nor intuitionist, formalist nor logicist, Platonist nor naturalist' in *Ludwig Wittgenstein: Critical Assessments*, vol. III, p. 259.

55. Although it is fair to say that traces can be found in Schlick's early work: e.g. cf. his 1915 paper, 'The Philosophical Significance of Relativity', pp. 169 f. in *Philosophical Papers* vol. I.

56. Dummett, 'Wittgenstein's Philosophy of Mathematics', op.cit., p. 124.

57. Ibid.

58. Dostoevsky made the converse point in *Notes from Underground*:

You will scream at me (that is, if you condescend to do so) that no one is touching my free will, that all they are concerned with is that my will should itself, of its own free will, coincide with my own normal interests, with the laws of nature and arithmetic. Good heavens, gentlemen, what sort of free will is left when we come to tabulation and arithmetic, when it will all be a case of twice two makes four. Twice two makes four without my will. As if free will meant that.

Orwell, of course, used this as one of the central leitmotifs in *1984*.

59. Dummett, 'Wittgenstein's Philosophy of Mathematics', op.cit., p. 130. It is highly significant that Dummett phrases the matter in these terms, for this is the fundamental theme of the 'sceptical' interpretation of Wittgenstein's remarks on rule-following which has proliferated in recent years. Indeed, it might very well be the case that Dummett's argument here was an influential source of that interpretation.

60. Ibid., p. 129.
61. Ibid., p. 127.
62. Ibid., p. 128.
63. Ibid., p. 127.

8 FREEDOM AND NECESSITY

I don't think necessity is the mother of invention — invention, in my opinion, arises directly from idleness, possibly also from laziness. To save oneself trouble.

Agatha Christie, *An Autobiography*

Discovering, Creating, Inventing

It is commonly argued that the real problem with a conventionalist philosophy of mathematics is that you cannot base the necessity of a mathematical truth on an arbitrary linguistic practice. The most common criticism levelled against conventionalism is that mathematical truth must be sempiternal and universal: properties that outstrip the reach of conventions, which are rooted to the decisions of a speaker or community. In a single sentence Donald Harward dismisses the entire conventionalist approach for failing to see that '"$2 + 2 = 4$" does not mean that "here and now, $2 + 2 = 4$" or "in general contexts $2 + 2 = 4$".' Hence the conventionalist simply misconstrues 'what the mathematician is most interested in: the necessity of mathematical propositions'.[1] It was stressed in Chapter 7 that it was indeed part of Wittgenstein's ultimate objective to drive out the metaphysical concept of necessity from the normative domain of mathematics, but only in order to make room for the logical certainty which characterises mathematical propositions *qua* 'rules of syntax'. But Wittgenstein certainly did not think that the rule '$2 + 2 = 4$' means 'here and now, $2 + 2 = 4$' or 'in general contexts, $2 + 2 = 4$'. The former would be like saying that the rule only applies at this instant, while the latter treats mathematical propositions as statistical generalisations. Yet neither did he hold that '$2 + 2 = 4$' means 'in all possible worlds at all possible times $2 + 2 = 4$'; both this and its denial are equally absurd. (Just as it would be to argue that 'here and now it is true that the bishop moves diagonally in chess', or to turn to possible world semantics in order to specify *when* and *where* this is true.) These misconceptions are caused by the failure to grasp that to say that $2 + 2$ *must* equal 4 is to use this rule as a standard of correct representation: i.e. that we could not *understand* anyone who denied that $2 + 2 = 4$.

The feeling behind Harward's criticism is that the conventionalist contends that a mathematical proposition only expresses either a speaker's or a community's decision to use symbols in a certain way. He fails to distinguish, however, between the argument that a convention is what Lazerowitz calls a 'verbal proposition'[2] (i.e. that a mathematical proposition *describes* the manner in which a speaker or community uses those symbols) and Wittgenstein's normative interpretation that a mathematical proposition *stipulates* the use of those concepts. Harward is led into his harsh verdict because, as the above formulations indicate, he conflates these two different conceptions. Thus he concludes that 'Where the conventionalist erred is in thinking that because the rules were applicable in different ways of life or contexts that the necessity of a mathematical proposition would be dependent on that context.'[3] Were we concerned with the 'descriptivist' version then it would indeed be the case that $2 + 2$ might not equal 4 for different communities with alternative 'verbal propositions'. The fact that this is unintelligible — since it overlooks that the meaning of these signs would thus be radically different from what we understand — illustrates the incoherence of the descriptivist interpretation. But Harward explicitly refers to the normative conception here, which renders his objection equally inexplicable; for in that case we simply could not describe anyone who denied that $2 + 2 = 4$ as operating with our arithmetical rules (WWK 177). As Gasking explains, we could only understand a Martian translation of $2 + 2 = 4$ as such if the Martians used this mathematical proposition in exactly the same manner as we do; i.e. applied the same rules of addition. [4] But then, as Gasking notes, this still leaves open the problem — which presumably is what Harward was trying to develop — of explaining how we are to reconcile the freedom which we enjoy in the construction of rules of grammar with what the platonist regards as the necessity governing the construction as well as the application of mathematical truths.

It was precisely this latter problem which Wittgenstein addressed. The point of his describing mathematical propositions as 'arbitrary rules of grammar' was to focus attention on the general theme that meaning is determined by intra-linguistic rules rather than a connection between language and reality, while at the same time retaining the basic premise underpinning the meta-physical picture of mathematical necessity that the negation of a mathematical truth yields a contradiction. But this argument has failed to soothe the anti-conventionalist's qualms, for the simple reason that what principally disturbs him is the worry that it cannot be a matter of whim that we say that $2 + 2 = 4$. He might very well appreciate that when Wittgenstein described a mathematical proposition as an 'arbitrary convention' his principal concern was to undermine the platonist assumption that a mathematical proposition is a necessary truth because it corresponds to or describes some supervenient mathematical reality, yet still feel that there must be some non-metaphysical sense in which we are *compelled* to accept that $2 + 2 = 4$. We must be careful in our response to this objection that we do not overextend Wittgenstein's argument — as e.g. does Dummett in his putative 'full-blooded convention-alist' interpretation — by overlooking the distinction between what Wittgenstein was saying about the application of an established versus the construction of a new proof-system. This contrast obviously bears strongly on how we deal with $2 + 2 = 4$. This could hardly be regarded as the *direct expression* of a linguistic convention; rather, it is a consequence of the elementary rules of arithmetic, and we would have no choice but to say of someone who insisted that $2 + 2 \neq 4$ that he did not know how to add (as we understand the term). It is thus completely misguided to fasten on to this type of example when approaching Wittgenstein's remarks on the construction of a new proof; for it totally confuses what Wittgenstein meant when he insisted that 'Arithmetical con-structions are autonomous' (PR §111), thereby undermining his intentions about what Lakatos called 'the logic of mathematical discovery': i.e. the genesis of mathematical knowledge.[5]

A widespread feeling exists — enshrined in the thesis that Wittgenstein was a 'radical' conventionalist — that he was intent on repudiating the deductivist conception of mathematics. But far from this being the case, what Wittgenstein was really subverting was the idea — common to formalists and logicists alike — that mathematics is composed of a global calculus. The crux of his new position in 1930 was that mathematics is made up of an intricate network of calculi: a suggestion, it will be recalled, which prompted Russell to remark in his letter to Moore that 'Wittgenstein's theories are certainly important and certainly very original. Whether they are true, I do not know; I devoutly hope they are not, as they make mathematics and logic almost incredibly difficult.'[6] The problem with this conception, as Russell recognised, was that the task of constructing a formal concept-script would, if Wittgenstein were right, become totally futile. But *that* problem is entirely distinct from the assumption that Wittgenstein was attacking the deductivist model of mathematics *au fond.* Waismann carefully explained this very point in *Introduction to Mathematical Thinking*; indeed, he went so far as to label Wittgenstein's new view 'axiomatic': a term which is in fact corroborated in Wittgenstein's discussions of the normative character of axioms (cf. WWK 33 f.,62,103 ff.,119; RFM IV §§1 ff.). Wittgenstein never suggested that the notion of an axiomatic system *per se* was under attack; quite the contrary, he frequently referred to it in the course of expounding his argument. What he did insist, however, was that the picture of a *single* axiomatic system encompassing the *totality* of mathematics is completely misguided. Thus Waismann explained that mathematics 'contains a series of deductive systems, which develop the inferences of arbitrarily chosen assumptions' (IMT 119). Hence, 'Mathematics is not *one* system but a multitude of systems; we must, so to speak, always begin to construct anew' (IMT 120).

To be sure, such an argument was fundamentally opposed to the views of the Vienna Circle. Not, that is, because they were committed to the idea of an amorphous calculus — there is, in fact, ample proof that they were more interested in the network model — but because it postulated an entirely different account from theirs of the genesis of mathematical truths. Waismann underscored this divergence when he argued that 'mathematics does not consist of tautologies. It is not a branch of logic, but completely autonomous and rests only on its own conventions' (IMT 118). The weakness in the Logical Positivists' argument was demonstrated, as we saw above, by their inability to deal convincingly with the discovery of mathematical truth. Lakatos seized on this flaw when he warned that you cannot account for 'the logic of mathematical discovery' in strictly deductivist terms.[7] But Lakatos's attack does not apply to Wittgenstein's conception, which threads a way between the logicist and Lakatos's own 'heuristic' theory. On Wittgenstein's approach the genesis of mathematical knowledge lies in our freedom to construct new mathematical calculi, each of which operates as an independent deductive system. The radical conventionalist interpretation thus collapses in light of Wittgenstein's account of proof; for it is this argument which accounts for his distinction between 'inferring wrongly' — i.e. making mistakes in our deductions within a system — and 'not inferring' — i.e. passing outside the rules of a system (RFM I §§8 f., VI §§48 f.). Nevertheless, the problem still remains that Wittgenstein did indeed describe the construction of a new proof-system as 'arbitrary' as well as 'autonomous'. This theme is central to his claim that 'there are no gaps in mathematics': that the construction of a calculus marks the creation of a new grammatical structure. Thus Wittgenstein emphasised in *Philosophical Remarks* that 'Where a connection is now known to exist which was previously unknown, there wasn't a gap before, something incomplete which has now been filled in! ... That is why I have said there are no gaps in mathematics' (PR §158). And this, as Wittgenstein was perfectly ready to admit, 'contradicts the usual view'.

Any anxieties that Wittgenstein had on this score were certainly well-founded, for this has become one of the chief stumbling-blocks in the interpretation of his conventionalism. To be sure, there are many who sympathise with Wittgenstein's efforts to undermine the platonist conception of mathematics; there is, however, a widely-shared feeling that the dual nature of our task — which is to account for the interdependency of mathematical truths without subsiding into platonist metaphysics — is something which escaped Wittgenstein: that in his zeal to attack the latter Wittgenstein was inclined to overlook the significance of the former problem. Wittgenstein's approach has thus been seized on as the ultimate example of the chaos and fragmentation which result when we attempt to press forward with an atomistic account of mathematical truth that strives to reduce all mathematical necessity to arbitrary conventions. Is the price that Wittgenstein paid for the elimination of the platonist scourge that he sacrificed the interrelatedness of mathematical truths? That is certainly the conclusion that Waismann drew in one of his final papers, 'Discovering, Creating, Inventing'. Waismann belaboured Wittgenstein for supposing that the law of mathematical induction is an arbitrary convention.[8] Waismann's objection was based on the idea that 'The endlessness of the number series, far from being the result of adopting an arbitrary convention, is one of the first and most significant discoveries made right at the very beginning of mathematics'. Interestingly, Waismann remarked that when a child has learned enough arithmetic to report this fact, 'What makes him say this is something more than having been habituated to follow a certain line, to follow it *blindly* — he *sees* that he can go on, he *sees* that there is an infinite possibility.'[9] As it stands this is hardly something with which Wittgenstein would have disagreed, although he might have preferred to put this point by stating that for the pupil to master the rule governing the infinite expansion of the number series just is for him to understand that the series is endless, and it is precisely when he has grasped this that we say that he is not proceeding blindly. What is particularly fascinating about this objection, however, is to encounter what is probably the first example of this theme in Wittgenstein criticism.

The real point that Waismann was concerned with here, however, was that when a mathematician constructs a new proof what he has done 'comes much nearer to a discovery than to an invention', and that it does so because his result 'is free from arbitrariness, whereas the idea of an invention always carries with it the implication that it is alterable in a good many respects.'[10] Waismann certainly did not regard himself as a platonist; indeed, it might be said that this provides — or at least, was supposed to provide — the *point d'appui* of the article. But he worried that mathematics is a 'cosmos with hidden mysterious depths' whose various branches are 'interrelated in a way which *we* seem not to have made'. The problem facing the philosopher of mathematics is thus to explain in non-Platonist terms why it appears to be the case that 'some super-human intelligence were at work in mathematics, creating a cosmos of harmonies of which now and then a good mathematician catches a single chord.' One can thus sympathise with 'those who speak of discovering a world of mathematical facts', but the problem is that they merely 'express themselves in the language of a simile'. Our task as philosophers of mathematics is to provide an explanation for this phenomenon rather than 'the giving of a label to the problem'.[11] The basic fault with Wittgenstein's explanation, therefore, is that it undermines the insight that we construct mathematics by its further assumption that we do so arbitrarily. What Wittgenstein overlooked was the fact that, although it is true that 'We *generate* the numbers, yet we have no choice to proceed otherwise. There is already something there that *guides* us. So we make, and do not make the numbers.' Waismann conceded that it is terribly disquieting for the constructivist to be confronted with this paradox, but the fact remains that 'We cannot *control* mathematics. The creation is stronger than the creator.'[12] And that is a problem which the constructivist must confront rather than seeking, as Wittgenstein attempted, simply to ignore or contravene.

The point that Waismann was driving at is that mathematics is an *interlocking* as opposed to a random network of diverse systems. It is because of this complex interdependency that 'there is no choice for us in how to build up these vast theories': 'the most disparate parts of mathematics are — without our doing anything about it, indeed without our having the least notion of it — related to each other and interwoven into one big whole.'[13] Waismann freely admitted that he found himself unable to offer any sort of explanation for this phenomenon; all that he was concerned with was to show that, although Wittgenstein rightly dismissed the platonist picture, he did so on the misguided grounds that the issue which generated that picture is itself spurious. On the contrary, there is a very real charge for the conventionalist to answer here; a problem, it should be noted, which Waismann believed it was as vain to try to answer along logicist lines as to seek to avoid altogether. For Waismann had formally rejected the Vienna Circle's logicist position in *Introduction to Mathematical Thinking*. Adhering to Wittgenstein's argument, he had explained that equations are used as rules which 'guide our behaviour (similar to a rule of chess)'. They thus contain a 'predicative' element, rendering them 'much closer to an empirical proposition than to a tautology' (IMT 119). They are 'neither true nor false, but only compatible or non-compatible with certain conventions' (IMT 120; cf. PLP 142 ff.). It is a position which he never abandoned. In *Principles of Linguistic Philosophy* and his late paper 'Equation and Tautology' he returned to this theme at some length, and in 'Discovering, Creating, Inventing' he was careful to explain, lest his attack on Wittgenstein's conventionalism give the wrong impression about his own attitude to logicism, that 'Poincaré and Brouwer were essentially right when they stressed the *non-trivial, non-analytic, non-tautologous*, character of [mathematical induction]'.[14] Yet their own explanations in terms of an '*Urintuition*' were no less opaque than the platonist picture they were meant to supplant.

Rather surprisingly, Waismann was left wondering whether perhaps there is no satisfactory answer to the mystery of how the myriad of mathematical calculi can be both constructed and interdependent, and thus that 'The existence of aesthetic values —

elegance, beauty, harmony — even if only as lodestars for the mathematician's activity, seems to point to the presence of something which, perhaps, is not entirely rational.'[15] This argument certainly marked a significant departure for Waismann from his earlier approach to the philosophy of mathematics. To begin with, he completely abandoned the — obviously Wittgensteinian — attitude to the foundations problem detailed in *Introduction to Mathematical Thinking*. At the close of 'Number' he sadly intoned that 'The attempt to give mathematics a sure foundation in logic has — in my opinion — failed', and thus 'it is time to get accustomed to the view that mathematics remains suspended in mid-air without any "foundation"'.[16] But in *Introduction to Mathematical Thinking* he had explained that the very expression '"to found arithmetic" gives us a false picture, because it gives us the idea that its structure is to be erected on certain basic truths' (IMT 121). The important point he had then believed was to see instead that 'arithmetic is a calculus which starts only from certain conventions but floats as freely as the solar system and rests on nothing'. Hence, it makes no sense to search for a foundation for mathematics, for 'Only the convention is the ultimate. Anything that looks like a foundation is, strictly speaking, already adulterated and must not satisfy us' (IMT 122).

Given his fundamental change of heart on the foundations issue it is no surprise to discover that Waismann had also completely changed his attitude to Wittgenstein's explanation of the law of mathematical induction. In *Introduction to Mathematical Thinking* Waismann had confidently explained that 'instead of being a truth [the law of mathematical induction] is merely a convention whereby, if the formula $f(x)$ is true for $x = 1$, and $f(c + 1)$ follows from $f(c)$, we say that "the formula $f(x)$ is proved for all natural numbers"' (IMT 98; cf. IMT 91-9). What could have led Waismann to renounce this view so thoroughly? *Introduction to Mathematical Thinking* was clearly written under the guiding influence of Wittgenstein's new ideas in the philosophy of mathematics, if not in fact originally intended as an exposition of those ideas.[17] Admittedly, it is puzzling that Waismann could have dealt so convincingly with Wittgenstein's arguments without understanding the full implications of the position which he so lucidly expounded. But such would appear to have been the case, for the answer to the objection which Waismann raised in 'Discovering, Creating, Inventing' is to be found in the conventionalist account presented in *Introduction to Mathematical Thinking*. With the benefit of hindsight it is, perhaps, possible to detect hints in *Introduction to Mathematical Thinking* of the confusion which was to emerge in 'Discovering, Creating, Inventing' (*infra*). One can well appreciate how, removed from Wittgenstein's commanding presence and exposed to the objections being voiced by philosophers of mathematics, any doubts which Waismann might have suppressed when writing *Introduction to Mathematical Thinking* could have blossomed into the full recantation of his conventionalism which Waismann embraced at the end of his life. Still, *Introduction to Mathematical Thinking* remains one of the most powerful expositions of conventionalism that has yet been written, so one would certainly like to know which argument in particular could have led Waismann to denounce his earlier work.

The only information we have to go on here is that provided by Waismann himself in 'Discovering, Creating, Inventing'. Waismann hoped to illustrate and substantiate his objection to conventionalism with the example of our inability to understand the behaviour of the function

$$\frac{1}{1 + x^2}$$

when the values of x are confined to the real domain. Interestingly, Waismann had touched on very much the same sort of problem in *Introduction to Mathematical Thinking* when he commented that there are 'Many phenomena [which] cannot be understood at all from the standpoint of real numbers, for example, the behaviour of the function log x' (IMT 227). It was obviously highly significant that Waismann ignored the implications of this problem at the time, pausing only to consider that 'if we restrict ourselves to the portion given by the reals' when trying to understand the behaviour of this function, 'then the vital point escapes us; we resemble the observer in the cave simile of Plato, who sees only the shadows of objects as they pass by, and to whom the actual entities remain eternally strange' (IMT 227). Twenty years later the same problem surfaced, only to lead to the opposite conclusion from that which Waismann had formulated in *Introduction to Mathematical Thinking*. Not, however, because Waismann reversed his earlier position on this issue: for the simple reason that he had not offered any argument on this problem in *Introduction to Mathe-*

matical Thinking. Rather, it would seem that the problem which led to Waismann's recantation stemmed from what he himself regarded as an oversight rather than a straightforward mistake. It is a distinction which, as we shall see, is not without some significance.

Waismann based this idea of 'explaining the behaviour' of the function

$$\frac{1}{1 + x^2}$$

which can be expanded into the series

$$\frac{1}{1 + x^2} = 1 - x^2 + x^4 - x^6 + \ldots$$

on the premise that the series converges for $|x| < 1$, but for $x = 1$ the series diverges, while for $|x| > 1$ it diverges explosively, although the function is everywhere regular. However, when we examine the function for *complex* values of x we can account for this perplexing behaviour. That is, we can see, for example, that the series must diverge when $x = i$, because the denominator of the fraction is zero (i.e. $1 + i^2 = 1 + -1$). From this it follows that the series must also diverge for all x such that $|x| > [i] = 1$, since it can be shown that its convergence for any such x would imply its convergence for $x = i$. But the philosophical problem which this raises is, how is it possible that imaginary numbers, which were originally constructed to solve recalcitrant quadratic and cubic equations by factorising polynomials, should 'suddenly intrude themselves into a department of mathematics ... where they apparently have no business?' 'What worries us', Waismann emphasised, 'is the *unrelatedness* — the *apparent* unrelatedness — between the occurrence of imaginary numbers in two quite distinct branches of mathematics'.[18]

What we are concerned with here are the philosophical dimensions of Waismann's argument: the consequences which he drew from his example, and indeed, what it means even to speak of 'explaining the behaviour of a function'. It should be noted, however, that the matter is by no means as straightforward at the technical level as Waismann implied. It would seem that, according to Waismann, the function diverges for $x = 1$ because it has a point of singularity in $x = i$.[19] All that Waismann could legitimately deduce, however, is that the series diverges if $|x| \geq 1$: the point, it will be recalled, which is known when the variables range over the real domain. The problem with his argument is that we can cite infinite series which have a singularity at $x = i$ but which none the less converge for $|x| = 1$.[20] The point is thus that what Waismann cites as the satisfactory explanation — the fact that the series has a singularity at $x = i$ — is nothing of the sort. The obvious lesson to draw from this is that what counts as a satisfactory 'explanation' may well be disputed amongst mathematicians; particularly over time. One need only read Kline's discussion of the various explanations that were given for the nature and existence of negative numbers to grasp the significance of this point. To be sure, many, if not all, of these may strike us as outrageous today; as, for example, Wallis's argument in *Arithmetica infinitorum* that since the ratio $a/0$ when a is positive is infinite, then when the denominator is changed to a negative number the ratio must be greater than $a/0$ because the denominator is smaller, in which case it follows that negative numbers are larger than infinity but less than 0.[21] The crucial point to bear in mind, however, is that these explanations may have been deemed perfectly satisfactory at the time.

What Waismann argued in 'Discovering, Creating, Inventing' is that it is not enough to respond that we have merely constructed a new rule for the use of complex numbers in function theory. For this implies that the matter was one of a free and arbitrary decision when it seems clear that the connection was there waiting for us to discover it. The tremendous temptation to resort to the platonist picture is due entirely to this underlying connection. But after we have disposed of this simile the question still remains: how else are we to account for this and the myriad such examples which characterise mathematical discovery? It is plainly no good our saying that this solution is forged by an arbitrary convention when the connection seems anything but arbitrary. Thus Waismann repudiated Wittgenstein's and his own earlier insistence that mathematical calculi are autonomous; that there are no 'gaps' in mathematical systems. 'A mathematical theory', he now concluded, 'is, in an important sense, *incomplete* — it points, as it were, beyond itself to some other part of mathematics.'[22] This is very much the opposite from what he had argued in *Introduction to Mathematical Thinking*. Indeed, one might justifiably conclude that the central theme in *Introduction to Mathematical Thinking* was that it makes no sense to speak of 'gaps' in a mathematical system. In detailed examinations of the constructions of the integers, rationals and reals, Waismann had there explained in each case why although the construction of a new number system marks an extension of the general concept of number it is misleading to speak of this new system as an expansion of an old number system.

To be sure, the motivation for the construction of a new number system is generally either to satisfy some practical need that has arisen (as in e.g. the construction of logarithms) or else to pursue some mathematical interest that has developed (e.g. the construction of imaginary numbers). The usual way of describing this is to argue that e.g. the subtraction of 7 from 5 has no solution for the natural numbers but 'this does not prove that it does not have a solution in the absolute sense, but only that the domain of natural numbers is too meagre to enable us to solve the proposition. Consequently we extend this number domain by annexing the negative numbers, and now the solution exists' (IMT 12-13). But this conception lands us, Waismann argued, with the difficulty of answering Russell's complaint that 'The method of "postulating" what we want has many advantages; they are the same as the advantages of theft over honest toil' (IMT 71). That is, if the conventionalist were operating with the naive expansion argument then he would indeed be arguing that whenever we are confronted with an 'unsolvable problem' we can escape from our dilemma simply by postulating a new kind of number to solve that particular equation. This is clearly not a practice that Waismann was prepared to condone, and thus he warned that 'We certainly should not confuse wishful thinking with wish fulfilment' (IMT 13). But how exactly did Waismann/Wittgenstein's 'conventionalist' argument differ from the postulational method?

The answer lies in the repudiation, first, of this view of the logical syntactical status of mathematical conjectures, and thence, of the naive expansion picture. Instead of postulating that e.g. subtraction can always be performed on the natural numbers, we construct 'a system of concept objects which we endow, on the authority of arbitrary conventions, with those properties which make them behave as if they were positive and negative numbers. We call these concept objects integers' (IMT 28). The wording here is not entirely perspicuous, but the idea behind it is evident; we are not simply concerned with the postulation of an arbitrary expedient: we are dealing with the construction of a new grammatical system in which our unintelligible problem finds both a meaning and a solution. We must then clarify the relation of this new number system to the old. The most important point to grasp here is that the new number system does not mark an extension of the old, but rather, of the concept *number*. For example, the integers do not provide a 'completion' of the natural numbers; the two types of number are *grammatically* distinct: '"3" and "+3" have, so to speak, a different logical grammar. ... The negative numbers are not a later complement of the natural numbers. In reality they are two entirely separate number systems ... on two different levels' (IMT 41,2). We must be extremely careful, therefore, to distinguish between the various number systems. '5', '+5', and '5/1' are by no means one and the same number: 'They only correspond to one another, which means that they play a different role in their calculi' (IMT 61). But does that mean there is no conceptual relationship whatsoever between these autonomous number-systems (apart from the bare fact that they are numbers)? Clearly not, but the problem which remains, therefore, is to elucidate the nature of these relationships and the bearing which this has on Wittgenstein's conventionalism.

Anarchy versus Autonomy

We are already in a position to see how Wittgenstein's argument avoided one major shortcoming of the postulational method. The construction of the integers does *not*, as is commonly assumed, answer an 'unsolvable' problem in the natural numbers (i.e. in an expanded cardinal number system); how could it if the two number systems operate on different conceptual levels? Rather, we must say that the original problem remains unintelligible — and hence 'unsolvable' — in the natural number system, and it is actually a correlate of the original problem which is thus answered (IMT 43-4). We shall return to this principle that each of the various kinds of number 'forms a closed system by itself, and it is quite impossible to go from one of these domains to another by adjoining new elements' (IMT 60) when we come to consider the nature of Waismann's position in 'Discovering, Creating, Inventing'. For the moment we can see how this removes the objection that the main drawback of conventionalism is that it results in an atomistic conception of mathematics. Such might indeed be the case with the 'postulational' method, but it has no force against Wittgenstein's explanation in terms of system-construction. For on the latter argument the solution of an 'unanswerable' question cannot be viewed as an isolated incident; rather, it involves the normative construction of a new system in which an analogue of the original problem can be understood and answered.

There is, however, a further complication introduced by Wittgenstein's emphasis on the principle that such a process is 'arbitrary'. After all, how could we manage to produce a 'correlate' of the original problem in our new system if we had proceeded arbitrarily in its construction? Wittgenstein's argument seems condemned to pull in opposite directions. On the one hand, we have the theme that the original problem is unintelligible in its system and that the creation of a new proof cannot affect that issue: cannot fill in any 'gaps' in the syntax of the original system. But there must be some connection between the new proof and the 'unsolvable' problem, and in order to generate the result that we have introduced a 'correlate' of the original problem the argument must accept that there are extensive parallels between the terms of the two systems. This is borne out, for example, in the case of addition, where $7 + 5 = 12$ and $+7 + +5 = +12$. Of course, the positive sign has no meaning in the natural number system, and therein lies the crux of the distinction between the two equations (i.e. it signifies that a positive integer can significantly subtract an integer larger than itself). Apart from that, however, the behaviour of the terms in the two expressions is identical for addition. But in that case, how can we say that our solution of the problem via the construction of a correlate is an *arbitrary* convention, when we could not speak of a *correlate* without this extensive overlap?

The use of the term 'arbitrary' has been the source of considerable and perhaps unnecessary dissension. There is a natural tendency to yoke the distinction between platonism and conventionalism — between the conceptions of mathematical propositions as predetermined truths or as rules of syntax — to the further properties of necessary versus arbitrary expressions. Frege clearly saw the matter in these terms, and thus he insisted that 'the rules [for the use of numbers] could not be arbitrarily established' because they must 'follow necessarily from the meaning of the signs' (BL II §158). From this point on the necessary/arbitrary dichotomy seems to have become a fixture in the platonist/ conventionalist debate, but it is not at all clear how integral it is. When Waismann maintained that a rule of grammar is 'arbitrary' (his inverted commas) in the same way that holds true for mathematical axioms — namely, that there is always the possibility of cancelling that expression and replacing it by another — one instinctively feels that this argument might serve as an important complement to the theme that mathematical propositions are autonomous conventions, but it is obscure how this contributes anything to the issue of whether such conventions are arbitrary (PLP 140). Granted, the point that Waismann was trying to make is that rules of grammar are constructed rather than discovered, and thus, that they are not answerable to any reality; hence it is always within our power to modify or abolish a rule of grammar. Still, how does this argument establish that rules of grammar are arbitrary in the sense that they are 'Derived from mere opinion or random choice' (*Concise Oxford Dictionary*). And what else does 'arbitrary' mean if not this?

The answer to Frege's platonist conception of meaning can be summed up, according to Waismann, by the principle that 'the meaning of a symbol follows from its application. The rules of application only *impart* to the symbols their meaning. Thereby, we reject the interpretation that the rules follow from the meanings of the symbols' (IMT 237-8; cf. PLP 234 ff.). This, of course, is drawn from Wittgenstein's attack on the *Bedeutungskörper* picture of meaning: the idea that every word has a 'meaning-body' underlying it, and thus that the rules for the use of words describe the combinatorial laws of these 'meaning-bodies' (PG 54; PLP 234 ff.). And Wittgenstein employed this theme in a lengthy discussion in *Philosophical Grammar* which purports to establish why rules of grammar are arbitrary (PG Chapter X). When read against the platonist *Bedeutungskörper* conception of meaning the argument presents a cogent exposition of Wittgenstein's new conception of mathematical meaning as determined by intra-linguistic rules. But whether it provides compelling grounds for the theme that these conventions are *arbitrary* is another matter. Wittgenstein himself was fully aware of the difficulties involved in describing rules of grammar as arbitrary. In one of the fragments printed in *Zettel* he asked whether the colour and number systems 'reside in *our* nature or in the nature of things'. His unequivocal answer to this was '*Not* in the nature of numbers or colours', but this still leaves us with the problem of resolving whether there is 'something arbitrary about this system?' His answer here, problematically, was 'Yes and no. It is akin both to what is arbitrary and to what is non-arbitrary' (Z §§357-8). Our problem is thus to clarify in what sense the construction of a convention is arbitrary, in what sense non-arbitrary, and finally, why Wittgenstein countenanced such complexity in his discussion and whether this was warranted.

The rules of grammar, Wittgenstein argued in *Philosophical Grammar*, can be described as arbitrary in the sense in which we apply this to 'constitutive' rules; that is, to those rules which determine the end of a rule-governed activity (e.g. chess). If you change such rules you are not then performing the same activity incorrectly: you are engaging in a different activity. (E.g. if you play a variant of chess in which the object of the game is to be mated you are not playing chess wrongly, but rather, are playing a different game from chess.) Wittgenstein then contrasted this with the case of a rule-governed activity where the rules are not constitutive of the end of the activity, as in e.g. cookery; in such a case the relation of the rules to the end result is causal, not conceptual. Thus, 'You cook badly if you are guided in your cooking by rules other than the right ones; but if you follow other rules than those of chess you are playing another game' (PG 184). The rules of grammar are akin to the constitutive rules of chess and not the regulative rules of cookery; for if you change the rules of a grammatical system you have not misused the pre-existing system: you have constructed a new grammatical system in its place. The rules of this new system determine the meaning of the terms employed; they do not follow from platonistically-conceived meanings.

Thus, the manner in which Wittgenstein thought that conventions are arbitrary can be summed up by the slogan that 'The arbitrariness of grammar is the arbitrariness of autonomy.'[23] Grammar is antecedent to truth: the rules of grammar determine what makes sense, but cannot themselves be true or false. There is no such thing as justifying grammar by reference to reality, therefore: any description of reality presupposes grammatical rules, and thus cannot be employed to justify those rules (PR §7). 'Grammar is not accountable to any reality. It is grammatical rules that determine meaning (constitute it) and so they themselves are not answerable to any meaning and to that extent are arbitrary' (PG

184). Against this argument Wittgenstein conceded that there will often be important considerations which *guide* our construction of new grammatical systems. In *Philosophical Investigations* he likened grammar to a representational style of painting, which is arbitrary in the sense that it is not dictated by external forces, but it is non-arbitrary in so far as it constitutes an established tradition which guides aesthetic judgements[24] (§§522 ff.). The external world is far from being a silent partner in these transactions, however, and it is because nature 'makes herself audible in another way' that we are constantly engaged in concept-revision: in the creation of new forms of representation which prove more useful when applied to the 'facts of nature' (Z §364). But the important point to bear in mind here is that we come up against 'facts', not 'concepts': we are free to construct grammar in any way we please, and we shall tailor our systems according to whatever we wish to accomplish. Although it is clear that certain facts might be favourable or unfavourable to the formation of certain concepts, and thus that rules of grammar may rest on certain normality conditions, it is none the less the case that these rules are not *justified* by such normality conditions[25] (PG 109-10). In the absence of such facts of nature these concepts will simply lose all their utility (e.g. consider the role of avoirdupois for chemical-refining in outer space).

The danger in the conventionalist argument, therefore, is to suppose that because we construct rules of grammar freely we must do so blindly or capriciously. Whenever Wittgenstein argued that the rules of grammar are arbitrary he was careful to exclude this impression. What he meant can thus, as Hacker pointed out, best be understood by considering the autonomy of grammar. This latter concept is completely compatible with the fact that there will generally be a host of important factors which guide us in the construction of a new grammatical structure. The crucial point to grasp is that none of these factors compels us to construct this system, but rather, that we construct whichever systems we choose because of our interest in the results which are thus obtained. This is what Wittgenstein was driving at when he argued in *Remarks on the Foundations of Mathematics* that mathematics 'is always building new roads for traffic; by extending the network of the old ones', and then immediately asked: 'But then doesn't it need a sanction for this? Can it extend the network *arbitrarily*? Well, I could say: a mathematician is always inventing new forms of description. Some, stimulated by practical needs, others, from aesthetic needs, — and yet others in a variety of ways' (RFM I §167). The problem is to distinguish between the *Bedeutungs-körper* picture, which assumes that it is invariably the meaning of mathematical concepts which compels us to construct certain rules, and Wittgenstein's 'conventionalist account' which argues that the considerations which guide our constructions for *Beweissystemlos* expressions are drawn from the uses to which we wish to put our mathematical systems or the aesthetic qualities which excite our admiration and pleasure.[26]

Where, then, does this leave the arbitrariness of conventions? We said above that the manner in which Wittgenstein thought that conventions are arbitrary can be summed up by the principle that 'The arbitrariness of grammar is the arbitrariness of autonomy'. The primary reason why Wittgenstein placed so much emphasis on the arbitrariness of conventions is that it was part of his overall strategy to dislodge the metaphysical premise underlying the platonist assumption that mathematical concepts are absolutely correct. Despite this purpose, however, we must still ask ourselves whether the conflation of the arbitrariness of conventions with the autonomy of grammar genuinely advances the argument. It is extremely illuminating when Wittgenstein compared rules of grammar with 'constitutive' rules, and yet we cannot help but feel that conventions are akin to such rules in the sense that they are autonomous rather than that they are arbitrary. Indeed, it is the divergence in respect to the latter property which largely accounts for the distinction between mathematics and games. As we saw above, Wittgenstein wanted to argue that rules of grammar are not answerable to any meaning 'and to that extent are arbitrary'; in other words, that rules of grammar are arbitrary in the sense that they are autonomous. But the two terms are by no means co-extensive. 'Arbitrary' implies the absence of any reasons in the exercise of a decision, and that is certainly not the picture which Wittgenstein wanted to present in his defence of 'conventionalism'. It is not that we lack reasons for constructing our grammatical systems, but rather, that such reasons must neither be confused with causes nor with predetermined truths: neither with com-pulsion nor necessitation (Z §352).

Our problem here is simply that, although it is always possible in principle to construct an arbitrary convention, mathematicians rarely proceed in such a fashion. Given the 'facts of nature' together with established traditions or objectives, it will generally be the case that one system has obvious advantages over another, and we shall seldom be permitted to decide such a matter arbitrarily. What really matters, however, is simply the possibility of so choosing. In other words, what concerns us here is the autonomy of grammar: the fact that the considerations which guide our concept-formations do not compel us to construct certain rules, any more than there is a reality which governs which rules it is intelligible to construct. But in that case, it is difficult to see what value remains in insisting on the arbitrariness as opposed to the autonomy of conventions, and the most prudent course would seem to be simply to redraw the division between platonism and conventionalism as lying between the doctrine that mathematical propositions are necessary descriptive truths and the (admittedly pleonastic) conception that they are autonomous conventions. It is the platonist picture which pushes us towards embracing the 'arbitrariness' of conventions, but once again we see how misleading it can be to try to respond to this picture on its own terms. In repudiating the metaphysical concept of mathematical necessity we are not forced *nolens volens* into accepting the arbitrariness of mathematical truths, but rather, we proceed in the direction of stressing the autonomy of mathematical propositions. But perhaps the real problem here lies not so much in the *autonomy* as in the *necessity* of rules of syntax? After all, it is only the latter premise which holds off the anarchy which the platonist is convinced must result from conventionalist liberties. With this in mind, the conventionalist cannot begin to rest easy at mind until he has at least seen off the rearguard action launched against him in *Naming and Necessity*.

Although the fact is not advertised as such, Kripke's *Naming and Necessity* is intended, among other things, to be read as an attack on Wittgenstein's 'conventionalism'. Both strands in Kripke's argument — the suggestion that *a priori* truths are contingent and that necessary truths can be known *a posteriori* — draw their inspiration from the theme that mathematical truths are necessary and universal. '2 + 2 = 4' must be true, Kripke tells us, not just at this particular spatio-temporal moment, but in 'every possible world'. Thus in order to undermine Wittgenstein's position, Kripke must establish that rules are contingent *a priori* truths. This theme is intended to sway the popular feeling that if the conventionalist were right then the negation of a mathematical proposition would be nothing more than a false proposition and the necessity and universality of mathematical truth would have been abandoned, since at the next moment or for a different culture a different linguistic practice might be adopted. At this stage Kripke's metaphysical conception of 'rigid designation' over possible worlds is meant to step into the breach and satisfy the basic conviction that mathematical truths are necessary and universal. That this is central to Kripke's overall strategy is made manifest when he explains that the 'peculiar character of mathematical propositions (like Goldbach's conjecture) is that one knows (*a priori*) that they cannot be contingently true; a mathematical statement, if true, is necessary.'[27] It is by tacitly relying on this assumption that Kripke hopes to deploy his putative demonstration of the contingency of *a priori* truths as the premise of an indirect proof for his bold conclusion that necessary truths can be known *a posteriori.*

The first question one wants to put to Kripke, however, is how exactly does he 'know *a priori*' that a mathematical truth cannot be contingently true? Moreover, given the preceding argument, does this mean that it is a contingent fact that mathematical propositions cannot be contingently true? Kripke vaguely remarks that 'philosophical analysis tells us that they cannot be contingently true, so any empirical knowledge of their truth is automatically empirical knowledge that they are necessary.'[28] But the closest he comes to this 'philosophical analysis' is when he argues that 'whatever truth-value [Goldbach's conjecture] has belongs to it by necessity' given that 'the results of arithmetical computations are necessary'.[29] But as it stands, the argument is either circular or else simply shifts the problem back to the necessity of arithmetical computations (not to mention the complications introduced by the issue of 'undecidable' questions; cf. Chapter 3). Nevertheless, although philosophers may generally have balked at Kripke's epistemological account of necessary truth, a surprising number have acquiesced to his conclusions, perhaps under the impression that his argument at least possesses the redeeming feature of striving to preserve mathematical necessity from what are perceived as the ravages of conventionalism. We have dealt with some of these worries above; our sole concern in what follows will be with Kripke's attempt to demonstrate the contingency of rules.

Despite his significance for the issue, Wittgenstein gets fairly short shrift in Kripke's argument. Indeed, the only reason why he is mentioned at all is because, if Wittgenstein's account of the certainty of conventions were correct it would undermine the foundation of Kripke's edifice. For Kripke's comments on the standard metre mark what is in fact a crucial step in his programme to employ his arguments on rigid designation to redraw the lines between the *a priori* and necessity, and thence, to pave the way for the conclusion that we must henceforward distinguish between contingent *a priori* and necessary *a posteriori* truths. We could, in fact, take Kripke to task on the grounds that he misrepresents Wittgenstein's remarks on the nature of the certainty of a rule of syntax as a thesis about necessary truth as metaphysically understood. But disregarding that point here, and further disregarding Kripke's comments on the existence of 'necessary *a posteriori* truths' (cf. Chapter 4), Kripke's argument on the 'contingent *a priori*' merits close attention for the deeper reason that, if he is right, the negation of a rule of syntax would indeed be a false proposition, and anarchy would be the least of our worries on this interpretation of Wittgenstein's approach to mathematical truth. Bearing in mind, then, that our intention here is in no way to defend the metaphysical interpretation of Wittgenstein's conception of mathematical necessity that is presented in *Naming and Necessity*, we must consider the reasons why Kripke's argument on the nature of the 'contingent *a priori*' breaks down.

Kripke sets out to establish that the proposition 'the standard metre is one metre long' is indeed *a priori*, but that — contrary to Wittgenstein's insistence — it is contingent. What Wittgenstein actually said is that 'There is one thing of which one can say neither that it is one metre long nor that it is not one metre long, and that is the standard metre'. The important point of this argument is that this is 'not to ascribe any extraordinary property to it, but only to mark its peculiar role in the language game of measuring with a metre rule'. That is, the point of the example is to draw attention to the fact that 'what looks as if it *had* to exist, is part of the language. It is a paradigm in our language-game; something with which comparison is made.' Hence the normative role of the standard metre is to serve 'not as something that is represented, but rather as a means of representation' (PI §50). It is in this sense that the standard metre provides us with what Wittgenstein described as the 'unshakable certainty' of a rule. To which Kripke brusquely replies that Wittgenstein 'must be wrong. If the stick is a stick, for example, 39.37 inches long (I assume we have some different standard for inches), why isn't it one metre long?'[30] Kripke wants to argue that if we can say 'the standard metre is 39.37

inches long', and 39.37 inches = one metre, then there is no reason why we cannot intelligibly state that 'the standard metre is one metre long'. But then, since the standard metre might not have been 39.37 inches long, it would follow that it is after all a contingent fact that the standard metre is one metre long.

However, Kripke's argument obviously cuts both ways. Is it a contingent fact that a yardstick measuring 39.37 inches is 39.37 inches long? Kripke's argument applies equally to the case of the 'imperial standard bar' and its role as a paradigm in the imperial system of measurement. When we say 'the standard metre is 39.37 inches long and 39.37 inches = one metre' we have implicitly shifted, via this conversion rule, from using the standard metre bar as the paradigm for the metric system to the imperial system (39.37 inches) as our criterion. But if we keep to our use of 'the standard metre bar' as the paradigm and turn Kripke's argument around on itself we must end up by saying that the imperial standard yard is 91.44 centimetres long, but it might not have been 91.44 centimetres long, and since one imperial yard = 91.44 centimetres the imperial yard might not have been one yard long. (Fortunately, we have the cubit to fall back on to end the regress which threatens here!) Kripke's argument is tacitly aided by the intrinsic conflict between a canonical sample — the standard metre — and an empirical method of calculation. Thus, we can also say, 'one metre' is one/ten-millionth of the distance along a meridian from the equator to one of the poles, and given that this is roughly 6,214 miles, a metre must be very close to 39.37 inches long. But in this case we have obviously switched from using the standard metre to the imperial standard bar as our canonical sample, and the standard metre has only a superfluous — empirical — use. It is just this sort of ambivalence which enables Kripke to distort the boundaries between logical certainty and empirical contingency.

The premise underlying Kripke's argument which leads to such a conclusion is manifest in the assumption that 'Part of the problem which is bothering Wittgenstein is, of course, that this stick serves as a standard of length and so we can't attribute length to it.' But Kripke is not at all happy with the statement that '"stick S is one metre long" [is] a necessary truth', simply because 'its length might vary in time'. 'We could', he tells us, 'make the definition more precise by stipulating that one metre is to be the length of S at a fixed time t_0'. But then, he asks, is it any more 'a necessary truth that stick S is one metre long at time t_0?' Kripke agrees that 'Someone who thinks that everything one knows *a priori* is necessary might think: "This is the definition of a metre. By definition, stick S is one metre long at t_0. That's a necessary truth."' This leads him to conclude that even on Wittgenstein's conception of the normative role of the standard metre, it is nevertheless the case that we are 'using this definition not to give the meaning of what [we] called the "metre", but to fix the reference'. Thus, even though we use this 'to fix the reference of our standard length, a metre, [we] can still say, "if heat had been applied to this stick S at t_0, then at t_0 stick S would not have been one metre long."'[31] The upshot of this argument, therefore, is that the negation of a — so it happens, true — rule is a false proposition. In showing that a rule is true in the manner which Kripke assumes, we shall likewise be demonstrating that it is as senseless to deny a rule as to suppose that a rule just happens to be true. For Kripke has run together two different themes in Wittgenstein's argument: first, that rules are autonomous, and second, that they are significant. The result is that he concludes that rules are contingent, and hence, falsifiable.

There are two interesting features which stand out in the above argument. The first is that Kripke begins by speaking of 'the stick'. Initially he accepts 'the standard metre' as meaning the metre bar, which is clearly what Wittgenstein was referring to when he said that we cannot assert or deny of it that it is one metre long. Secondly, when Kripke maintains that 'the stick serves as a standard of length and so we can't attribute length to it' he has chosen a rather roundabout way of stating that 'the stick is what measures and cannot be measured'. However, Kripke's rendering borders very closely on the formulation, 'we can't attribute *a* length to it'. Both of these features come together in Kripke's attack on Wittgenstein's argument, and Kripke shifts almost imperceptibly from talking about the metre bar to talking about the *length* of the metre bar. This may seem an innocent enough move given that we are perfectly justified in saying either that 'the standard metre' is the name of a metal bar once kept in the Louvre, or else that 'the standard metre' means that one metre is the length of that metal bar. But this is not quite the way that Kripke treats the matter. Rather, he seizes on 'the standard metre' as an ambiguous name. What he actually argues is that this name does not *mean* either the metal bar or the length of that bar; rather, it *designates* both the metre bar and the length of the metre bar. It is this prior assumption which leads him to suggest that 'There is an intuitive difference between the phrase "one metre" and the phrase "the length of S at t".' 'The first phrase is meant to designate rigidly a certain length in all possible worlds, which in the actual world happens to be the length of the stick S at t_0'. But '"the length of S at t_0" does not designate anything rigidly.'[32]

The reasoning behind Kripke's argument is that 'the standard metre' rigidly designates a metal bar and non-rigidly designates the length of that metal bar at t. This amounts to the existential quantification: 'There is a length such that the metre bar is (or is not) that length.' 'The standard metre' is the name of that length as well as of the bar, and since it is not a necessary fact that the metre bar has that length it is not a necessary fact that the metre bar is one metre long. It turns out, therefore, that *contra* Wittgenstein there is something after all with which to measure the metre bar: viz. the length which is designated by 'the standard metre'. We thus find that Kripke's argument rests on a fundamental Platonist assumption. According to Kripke 'the standard metre' is not only the name of the metre bar, it is also the name of that length. To be sure, the length of the metre bar is a property, but then, this is not some sort of mysterious entity over which we can quantify. Indeed, it is patently absurd to say of a property that it is or is not a metre long. Ultimately it is this illicit reification which misleads Kripke into thinking that the standard metre can in some sense be said to measure itself, and hence, that rules are contingent. Or rather, this illicit reification is the direct result of the formal argument which Kripke had earlier developed in his paper on the semantics of modal logic, and which he is attempting to interpret in *Naming and Necessity*. Considering the source of Kripke's argument in his work on the semantics of quantified modal logic it comes as no surprise that he should have been led into this Platonist confusion in what, following Wittgenstein, can only be described as his prose interpretation of his formal work.

Kripke's immediate purpose in *Naming and Necessity* is to overthrow Russell's argument that proper names do not exhibit the same logical behaviour as definite descriptions in modal applications. In the latter context proper names, as opposed to definite descriptions, cannot induce scope ambiguities. Russell had been led into his false account of the logical grammar of proper names because he only compared their behaviour from the viewpoint of extensional logic; but as soon as we enter the realm of modal logic we expose a radical divergence between the logical behaviour of proper names and definite descriptions. We need not delve into Kripke's formal argument in the semantics of quantified modal logic which provides the basis for this conclusion. However, it is worth noting that Kripke hopes to employ his argument as a response to Quine's attack on 'essentialism' by defining a quantificational model on a quantificational model structure in which 'necessarily $P(x)$' is true in the (actual world) G when assigned to the object a because $P(x)$ is true in both G and (the possible world) H under this assignment. Intuitively, therefore, Kripke's argument states that a falls under the extension of P in all possible worlds (i.e. G and H), and thus rests on the idea of one and the same individual existing in different possible worlds.[33] But the philosophical problem which this raises is: what does it mean to say that an object can be 'identified across all possible worlds'? Kripke's own answer is to push us into an essentialist argument: there must be some necessary property which serves to identify that object in cross-world identification (one which has to be more than simply the minimal sortal property if it is to serve as a criterion of identification for that particular object). Thus, the driving force behind Kripke's argument is to push us back into the realm of metaphysics. Kripke shares with Dummett the belief that there are two distinct problems involved in the problem of necessity, which Kripke identifies as the epistemological and the metaphysical. He contends that the Quinean critique of essentialism focuses on the epistemological aspect of the problem — viz. 'How would we identify the same individual in different possible worlds?' — whereas, on Kripke's conception, the possible world argument is only concerned with the metaphysical problem, 'What does it mean to say that an individual is the same in different possible worlds?' But the net result of his argument is that we find ourselves struggling to understand a metaphor plucked from the inner recesses of quantified modal logic.

Leonard Linsky argues in *Names and Descriptions* that 'the metaphysical question' — viz. what Kripke's metaphor really means — 'which is the only one of the two which needs answering if modal logic is to make sense, is not at all hard to answer. ... An object, in one possible world, is identical with an object in any other possible world if and only if the second object has all of the necessary properties of the first.'[34] But this is precisely the point which is totally opaque, and Linsky's argument serves, not as an elucidation, but rather a restatement of the metaphor. But then, it is not simply difficult: it is impossible to see quite what else one can say. The real solution to what Kripke's 'metaphysical metaphor' means is to see that it results in unintelligibility because it proceeds from Platonism. Both elements of Kripke's argument — the epistemological and the metaphysical — are based on a misunderstanding of the grammar of a proposition stipulating the 'essential' property of an object; the *depth* which Kripke tries to elucidate in terms of the metaphysical concept of quantification over possible worlds is simply to be accounted for in terms of the logical syntax of conventions. 'If you talk about *essence* —, you are merely noting a convention. ... To the *depth* that we see in the essence there corresponds the *deep* need for a convention' (RFM I §75).

Wittgenstein's argument thus wreaks havoc on Kripke's premise that there is a sense in which 'The standard metre might not have been one metre long' which is not to be understood in terms of scope ambiguity, but rather is to be explained in terms of the ambiguity of the modal-operator: between what Kripke calls its epistemic and metaphysical meanings. The whole force of Wittgenstein's argument that the negation of a rule yields another rule — which taken together results in a contradiction — is to prevent us from falling into just such a position as Kripke's conclusion that the sense in which the standard metre might not have been one metre long is in the 'metaphysical mode'. Wittgenstein explained that 'it is part of the grammar of the word "rule" that if "p" is a rule, "p.¬p" is not a rule': it is a contradiction (PG 304; AWL 4). Kripke thus takes a circuituous route to end up at the same destination that Wittgenstein's elucidation of the normative certainty of rules was intended to subvert. In arguing that mathematical propositions are rules of syntax Wittgenstein clarified the grammatical criterion which accounts for the reason why, as he continually stressed, it makes no sense to doubt the truth of mathematical propositions. The dissatisfaction with conventionalism which platonists feel is thus in part a consequence of the misplaced demand for preordained order that they impose on the autonomy of grammar. Still, we shall not have fully removed their fears of anarchy until we have shown how, as in the case of democracy, each of the threads in the garment of mathematics can remain autonomous, and yet still yield a seamless web.

The Interrelatedness of Mathematical Truths

Waismann may have been an enthusiastic advocate of the doctrine that mathematical propositions are arbitrary rules of syntax in *Introduction to Mathematical Thinking* and *Principles of Linguistic Philosophy*, but the various arguments which he produced to back up this position were far more concerned with the autonomy than the arbitrariness of conventions. This distinction accounts in large part for the difficulties he later found himself in when he abandoned the 'arbitrary' theme but retained his hostility to platonism. For he failed to see that the solution to his dilemma lay not in the repudiation of conventionalism, but rather, in a clearer understanding of his earlier commitment. Waismann's first mistake was to treat the autonomy of mathematical systems as a partial vindication of formalism. He argued not merely that mathematical propositions are akin to, but that in a sense they are literally constitutive game-rules for which an application has been found. In response to Frege's objection that a purely formal construction might at best be an interesting game but not a number system, Waismann explained that the imaginary numbers and quaternions were indeed constructed in the same manner as the rules of a game, but that what set them apart from the realm of games was simply that a mathematical application was subsequently discovered. 'What is more natural', Waismann asked, 'than to say: in the case of imaginary numbers, quaternions, etc. an application has been found, and for that reason are they a subject matter of science; in other cases, such an application has failed to appear, and therefore it is a game?' 'All of them', he insisted, 'were originally no more than elements of a game, until their great usefulness was uncovered' (IMT 242).

It is difficult to see how this somewhat dogmatic assertion could persuade anyone to abandon platonism, let alone embrace conventionalism. The platonist could just as easily answer that it was only when the real nature of imaginary numbers or quaternions was discovered that their great usefulness was discerned. Moreover, the platonist would certainly be justified in taking Waismann to task for his lack of concrete evidence and consequent distortion of the actual evolution of these concepts. Waismann made it sound as if e.g. quaternions were discovered long in advance of Hamilton's creation of a new species of hypercomplex numbers as ordered quadruples, and that it was only Hamilton's realisation that these constructions could be used to represent the rotations of vectors in three-dimensional space algebraically that accounted for the sudden transformation of what had previously been a mere game into a fully-fledged mathematical number system. Assuming, that is, that this is the type of application which Waismann had in mind; one of the intriguing aspects of quaternions is that Hamilton's confidence that he had discovered a mathematical instrument that would soon rival the infinitesimal calculus in importance has never been vindicated, for they have been virtually disregarded by modern physicists, and their chief interest today lies in the topological study of continuously deformed rotations. But then, perhaps that is exactly what Waismann wanted to point out; for this type of mathematical phenomenon itself provides yet more grist to the platonist mill.

Whatever Waismann's intentions his argument constituted something of an historical misrepresentation. It might be true that, as Bell reports, de Morgan offered to trace the history of quaternions for Hamilton from the Hindus to Queen Victoria;[35] but then, that would merely indicate de Morgan's own philosophical confusion on this score. Certainly we can find precursors of Hamilton's work in the writings of Gauss and Argand in so far as they were among the first to experiment with the interpretation of complex numbers as vectors, and hence with the algebraic representation of operations on vectors using complex numbers. But although Hamilton's work was an extension of the same general enterprise it marked a radical new approach to the subject. For Hamilton's initial interpretation of complex numbers as ordered pairs of real numbers signified an entirely novel definition of complex numbers. That Hamilton was constructing a completely new type of number system was borne out by his development of quaternions: an innovation which provides a classic illustration of the autonomy of mathematical systems. If this feature was not realised as such, this was primarily because Hamilton was attempting to resolve a specific problem, and since quaternions can be said to accomplish this the platonist is encouraged to see the construction of quaternions as a discovery of a new feature of mathematical reality. Gauss had already used complex numbers to represent operations performed on vectors in two-dimensional space algebraically. In particular, the multiplication of complex numbers was used to represent the rotation of a vector in two-dimensional space. Hamilton's basic problem was how to represent the rotation of a vector in three-dimensional space algebraically.

After his initial definition of complex numbers as ordered pairs of real numbers Hamilton attempted to represent the rotation of vectors in three-dimensional space with ordered triplets of real numbers.[36] But this idea proved a failure, for Hamilton found that he could not avoid contradictions in the other operations of his system when he tried to perform multiplications with these ordered triplets. After ten years of working on the problem, Hamilton hit upon his famous solution that he could represent the rotations of vectors in three-dimensional space if he used ordered quadruples instead of triplets; i.e. $a + bi + cj + dk$. These are similar to complex numbers (where $i^2 = -1$) in that $i^2 = j^2 = k^2 = -1$; but these 'quaternions' are unique in that they contain three non-real units. This was not the major innovation of Hamilton's system, however; rather it was that Hamilton could only solve his problem by abandoning the commutative law of multiplication. Thus, $jk \neq kj$. Without going into the details of his method of factorisation with quaternions, we can see that the fundamental philosophical significance of Hamilton's innovation lay in his abandonment of the 'principle of continuity': viz. that all number systems must satisfy the same fundamental laws. The new heuristic principle which guided Hamilton's work was that a mathematician must strive to preserve the basic arithmetical operations intact as far as possible in the construction of a new number system; what he had in effect resolved was that, taken as a whole, the arithmetical operations for quaternions would be least disturbed by abandoning the commutative law of multiplication. Here we have striking evidence of the autonomy of mathematical systems and the type of methodological considerations which guide mathematicians. Hamilton's decision was by no means an arbitrary postulation, but it was none the less a free act of grammatical construction which was to have a dramatic effect on the subsequent development of algebra and the creation of increasingly recherché number systems (e.g. Cayley numbers). For Hamilton had demonstrated that the mathematician can proceed as he chooses in the construction of new systems, subject only to the constraints of utility or interest. His solution was in no platonist sense the 'right' one; it was the one which best realised the goal he had set himself from the available options. But given a different approach or objective the solution arrived at will be completely different (as has, in fact, been the case).

From an historical point of view, therefore, Waismann's

account is plainly misleading; but the argument rings hollow for
other reasons as well. Not only is it difficult to see where the pre-
Hamiltonian 'games' come in, it is unclear what it even means to
suggest that this might have been the case. As far as Waismann
was concerned, 'game' denotes a calculus with no application. But
the early pioneers in the development of complex number theory
or the algebraicisation of vectors would hardly have regarded their
work as games. Waismann's argument seems to offend in both
directions: as much against the concept of game as mathematical
calculus. It is clearly not the case that the discovery of an application could turn a game into a mathematical system. The argument
here is reminiscent of Wittgenstein's early idea that chess could be
used to wage war, and that this elucidates the manner in which
mathematical systems are applied (WWK 170). However, as
Wittgenstein soon came to see, chess is logically confined to the
realm of games, and the most we could say in such a situation is
that the rules which the two nations used to wage war could be
mapped onto those of chess. The same point applies to
Waismann's argument: it is unintelligible to suppose that Hamilton
might have solved his vector problem by applying a game, or that
his system would revert to being a game if its application should
cease to operate. It is quite another matter, of course, to say that
Hamilton's solution could have been mapped onto the rules of a
game, but the important point that Waismann was struggling to
make was that the rules of a mathematical system are autonomous
in the same way as obtains for a game.

Finally, the argument did not accomplish what Waismann
demanded from it if only because the platonist could simply
respond that it was no arbitrary matter that these games proved to
be so useful; all that happened was that Hamilton discovered that
these rules describe the rotation of vectors in three-dimensional
space. The danger here is that of trying to answer Frege on his own
terms. The point is not that, *contra* Frege, mathematical systems
are indeed games (i.e. completely arbitrary systems of rules) which
we have found can be usefully applied; it is that mathematical
systems share with games the fundamental feature that their rules
are autonomous: they do not describe any reality and do not
follow from pre-established meanings. Waismann was only led into
his dilemma because of his desire to defend the argument from the
Russellian objection that conventionalism would render mathematical discovery a matter of whim. But because he had elsewhere

stoutly defended the thesis that mathematical constructions are arbitrary he was now forced to renounce this theme without conceding his intentions; that is, to argue that they may be arbitrary but they are certainly not chosen at random. But the point that he was trying to make was entirely appropriate *vis-à-vis* the autonomy of mathematical systems; viz. that the reason why conventionalism is not guilty of the same shortcoming as the postulational method is because we guide our constructions by what is considered important or aesthetically desirable. In other words, that mathematical constructions are autonomous yet far from being arbitrary.

Waismann tried to formalise this point in *Introduction to Mathematical Thinking* with his discussion of 'Hankel's principle of the permanence of the calculating rules'.[37] If we consider the significance of an expression such as a^0, we see that 'we have laid it down as an arbitrary convention that $a^0 = 1$'. By the same token, we could have stipulated that $a^0 = 5$, so how are we to defend our choice of the former over the latter convention? Here the mathematician is guided by his desire to 'form his concepts so that the rules remain valid as far as possible' (IMT 26). In which case, one convention will be preferable to another 'in as much as it leaves the calculating rules unchanged' (IMT 27). But then, what has happened to the theme that mathematical conventions are arbitrary? If anything this reads as a *reductio* on its opening premise. There are two different dangers in this argument: the first arises from the tendency to approach this topic on the postulational model, and thus, to interpret Waismann as holding that when we construct a new rule of grammar we are guided by the overriding concern to preserve the pre-existing rules intact. If, for example, we were to take Wittgenstein's case of the construction of a new rule when we discover a contradiction in chess, the temptation is to regard this as saying that we shall choose that rule which will leave the others intact. But the addition of this rule does not fill in a 'gap' in the previous rules of chess; rather it marks the construction of a new game, fundamentally similar to chess, but distinguished by the addition of this new rule. (Unless, of course, the concept of chess is viewed, historically, as a family resemblance concept.)

The second danger is to read this as a canonical rather than a methodological principle. The issue we must get clear about in Waismann's discussion is whether Hankel's principle was supposed to describe the considerations whereby mathematicians guide their constructions, or was meant to be a formal principle setting out how one must proceed. Obviously we do not call whatever we want a *number*, but is this because the concept rests on necessary properties which any construction must satisfy in terms of the basic arithmetical operations? For example, in the construction of any number system we stipulate that we must define the property of equality in that domain, but 'are we really free in the choice of a criterion?' (IMT 29). Is it not the case that since equality already possesses reflexiveness, symmetry and transitivity in the natural number domain any subsequent system must satisfy these properties? But then, as we have just seen, there are obvious counter-examples to this supposition. Hence Waismann warned that there is no 'necessary property' governing the application of the concept of equality. Rather, we must recognise that *equality* is a family resemblance concept: 'we will say that concepts can be formed which are more or less related to the concept of equality between natural numbers, and it would only be inappropriate to call concepts with entirely different properties by the same name' (IMT 63). Consequently, the arithmetical operations do not have the same meaning in each of the various number systems, and there is not e.g. 'one subtraction but as many different operations with this name as there are domains of numbers. We should not be deceived regarding this situation by the fact that we use the same signs $+$, $-$, $:$, etc. at the various levels' (IMT 61). The ultimate source of confusion in platonism lies, therefore, in the assumption that the sense of (mathematical) concepts is determinate. The theme that 'number' is a family resemblance concept provides the final step in the conventionalist argument that the solution to 'unanswerable' mathematical questions rests on the construction of new grammatical structures. It is this normative feature which accounts for the genesis of mathematical knowledge: 'The very openness, non-closure, of mathematical concepts ... gives language the freedom to comprise new discoveries in a known scheme' (IMT 237).

What could have persuaded Waismann to abandon this approach and return — in spirit, albeit not recognised as such — to the platonist fold? The most probable answer is that the objection which Waismann raised in 'Discovering, Creating, Inventing' was not strictly concerned with the above argument. In the foregoing discussion we have considered the construction of a concept in order to resolve — in a new system — a hitherto unintelligible problem. But the example which Waismann contemplated in 'Discovering, Creating, Inventing' was supposed to illustrate the case where we discover that a pre-existing concept solves an 'unsolvable problem'. In other words, Waismann was trying to draw a division between the platonist picture of the discovery of new numbers and the interdependency between mathematical truths; it is the latter and not the former problem which Waismann addressed in 'Discovering, Creating, Inventing', and which led him to abandon his conventionalism. But such a division is illusory, and the answer to the platonist conception of the interdependency of mathematical truths is *pari passu* the same as for the platonist conception of the discovery of numbers. To be sure, the explanation which Waismann cited for the behaviour of the function

$$\frac{1}{1 + x^2}$$

with x ranging over complex numbers is not arbitrary, but it is none the less an autonomous grammatical construction and not a 'discovery' of some Platonic interconnection. The key to understanding this argument is provided by Waismann's earlier explanation that the various number domains form closed systems, 'and it is quite impossible to go from one of these domains to another by adjoining new elements'.

Wittgenstein clarified that the reason why he had said that 'there are no gaps in mathematics' was that 'The discovery of the connection between two systems wasn't in the *same* space as those two systems, and if it had been in the same space, it wouldn't have been a discovery (but just a piece of homework). Where a connection is now known to exist which was previously unknown, there wasn't a gap before, something incomplete which has now been filled in! (At the time, we weren't in a position to say "I know this much about the matter, from here on it's unknown to me")' (PR §158). This is the point which Wittgenstein repeatedly made in his discussion of the significance of Sheffer's discovery of stroke-notation (WWK 122 f.; PR §§155,162). In constructing a 'super-system' which contains two previously independent systems we have laid down new grammatical tracks which render it intelligible to synthesise the elements from the two systems. But in so doing we have not *expanded* either of the two initial systems: we have created a third system which is grammatically distinct from the two sub-systems. Hence precisely the same point applies here as in Waismann's argument that the construction of the integers does not expand the natural number system. This new enlarged system 'does not contain the old one but contains a part with exactly the same structure as the old system. ... The new system is not a completion of the old one. The old system has no gaps' (WWK 35-6). Thus the 'unsolvable' question remains unintelligible in its original context, and it is precisely this point that Waismann's argument in 'Discovering, Creating, Inventing' transgressed.[38]

Waismann's error was a direct example of the confusion which Wittgenstein warned is a result of the intrusion of prose into mathematics: 'This is what creates the impression that previously there was a problem which is now solved. Verbal language seemed to permit this question both before and after, and so created the illusion that there had been a genuine problem which was succeeded by a genuine solution. ... Thus I want to say: only in our verbal language ... are there in mathematics "as yet unsolved problems"' (PR §159). If we read *Introduction to Mathematical Thinking* carefully we can detect signs of the same confusion buried within Waismann's argument. In his explanation of the considerations that guide our decisions of which calculi to construct Waismann remarked in passing that the point which the platonist must consider is: 'what if this game proves to be uncommonly fruitful for mathematics? If they enable us to solve problems which were unassailable up to then, shall we still continue to say that these numbers do not exist in actuality?' (IMT 242). The slip here — at least, as far as Wittgenstein's argument is concerned — was subtle, but extremely significant. For what Waismann should have said is that these calculi *give meaning* to problems which were *unintelligible* up to then. Indeed, this theme which as we have seen was so important to Wittgenstein is conspicuously absent from *Introduction to Mathematical Thinking*. And in this case we can see Waismann assuming quite the opposite from what Wittgenstein had argued: viz. that the problem itself is intelligible, but that we can choose to solve it in any number of ways. Phrased in these terms it is no wonder that Waismann was subsequently bewitched by the platonist conception. For nothing could be more natural than to suppose that, if the problem is meaningful, then there must be some one 'correct' answer to it.

What has gone wrong here is that this way of stating the matter violates the distinction which Wittgenstein drew between *Beweissysteme* and *Beweissystemlos* questions. In the former it certainly is the case that there is a *right* answer: an established method for answering the question such that if we do not operate with those rules we cannot be said to understand the question (to be doing our 'homework' properly). But by the same token, it thus makes no sense to speak of *constructing a calculus* in order to answer such a question. This can only make sense in the latter context, where the 'question' we are dealing with has no precise meaning since there are no rules of syntax governing the combination of words in this example. Asking how we are to explain the behaviour of the function

$$\frac{1}{1 + x^2}$$

when x is confined to the real domain is not at all the *same question* as when x ranges over complex numbers. In the former the question is simply unintelligible if it is taken to mean that there is anything *more* to be explained *beyond* the fact that the series converges for $|x| < 1$, diverges for $|x| = 1$, and diverges explosively for $|x| > 1$. These conventions form the foundations of the system, and Waismann's error was in effect a variation of the general fallacy of demanding a justification for the foundations of a language-game. Within the system of x confined to the real domain it simply makes no sense to ask why the function 'behaves' as it does — a striking example of prose — beyond recapitulating the meanings of 'converge' and 'diverge'. It is only in the extended system that the question is both intelligible and solvable; that is, it is only in this new enlarged system that it makes sense to ask why the function behaves as it does. To be sure, the rules for this new system — for our answer to the problem — are far from arbitrary, but they are not necessary. Given the demands that we place upon function theory and the type of explanation which for present purposes we deem satisfactory we place this solution 'in the archives'. The crucial point to see in all this is that we forge, we do not discover the interconnection.

Thus, to return to our starting-point in this section, Wittgenstein certainly did not wish to sacrifice the interrelatedness of mathematical truths. The fact that the calculi which we construct are autonomous — that there are no 'gaps' in mathematics — does not mean that mathematical truths, once they have been constructed, cannot be rendered interdependent. Waismann's examples illustrate such cases perfectly well. The point is that these interconnections are not somehow there, waiting for us to discover them. That, of course, is precisely the platonist picture which Waismann so resolutely wanted to overcome. What he failed to see was the very point which he explained in *Introduction to Mathematical Thinking*: that the interdependency between mathematical truths are only there once we have created them, and the considerations which guide our decisions may appertain to certain aesthetic features or to the uses to which we wish to put the new proof, but in any event, we guide ourselves by appealing to such criteria. The fact remains that mathematics is indeed a 'free-floating structure', but one which operates on certain regulative principles. With suitable qualifications, we might compare this to what Auden said about composition: 'A succession of two musical notes is an act of choice; the first causes the second, not in the scientific sense of making it occur necessarily, but in the historical sense of provoking it, of providing it with a motive for occurring. A successful melody is a self-determined history; it is freely what it intends to be, yet is a meaningful whole, not an arbitrary succession of notes.'[39] If only Auden had made some mention of the role of the composer here we would have had a very close parallel indeed to what is perhaps the central theme in Wittgenstein's remarks on the foundations of mathematics.

It would be not just unrealistic, but in some ways unwarranted to suppose that this argument could suffice to drive out metaphysics from the philosophy of mathematics. For one thing, a good many philosophers of mathematics who would be caught in the net of metaphysics as it has here been conceived would be outraged at such a gloss on their approach. But the gap between intention and outcome can be enormous; particularly where the eradication of metaphysics is concerned. Even someone as temperamentally opposed to metaphysics as Waismann could still end up with a strikingly platonist position even though — or, perhaps, especially because! — this was not at all evident to Waismann himself. For the great problem with metaphysics is simply its subtlety; the secret to its abolition lies not in the refutation or circumvention of its conclusions but in the removal of the *premises* on which it rests. But whatever the explanation, the fact remains that for all the vaunted positivism of the modern scientific spirit, atavistic metaphysical assumptions are never far beneath the surface, and we cannot rest satisfied with our efforts until we have brought these archetypal pictures to light. For that very reason it would be presumptuous to claim that this book presents an adequate account of Wittgenstein's contribution to the philosophy of mathematics. Perhaps the most glaring omission here is any serious discussion of Wittgenstein's remarks on Gödel's theorem and the metamathematical framework on which it rests. Certainly this is one of the most important lacunae, for the metaphysical repercussions of Gödel's 'intellectual symphony' continue to radiate far beyond the narrow bounds of consistency proofs. Yet the problems here are not so much a result of Gödel's theorem as the conceptual background against which this has been received; in an intellectual climate in which paradoxes begin to take on the role of an acronym, the cry of 'metaphysics' becomes a tribute to ingenuity rather than a tribulation incurred by confusion. The next task, then, is to investigate the reasons why 'the *situation*, into which [Gödel's proof] brings us, is of interest to us' (RFM VII §22). Equipped with Wittgenstein's philosophical rucksack we cán, at least, now begin to climb slowly up the mountain of metamathematics.

Notes

1. D. Harward, 'Wittgenstein and the Character of Mathematical Propositions', *International Logical Review*, vol. III (1972), reprinted in Shanker (ed.), *Ludwig Wittgenstein: Critical Assessments*, vol. III (London, Croom Helm 1986), p. 260.

2. Cf. Morris Lazerowitz, 'Necessity and Language', in Alice Ambrose and Morris Lazerowitz, *Necessity and Language* (London, Croom Helm, 1985), pp. 5 ff.

3. Harward, 'Wittgenstein and the Character of Mathematical Propositions', op.cit., p. 261.

4. D.A.T. Gasking, 'Mathematics and the World', in *Philosophy of Mathematics: Selected Readings*, Benacerraf and Putnam (eds), op.cit., pp. 394 f.

5. Cf. Imre Lakatos, 'The Deductivist versus the Heuristic Approach', in *Proofs and Refutations: The Logic of Mathematical Discovery*, op.cit.

6. Russell, *The Autobiography of Bertrand Russell*, op.cit., p. 437.

7. Lakatos, 'The Deductivist versus the Heuristic Approach', op.cit., pp. 142 ff.

8. Friedrich Waismann, 'Discovering, Creating, Inventing', in *Lectures on the Philosophy of Mathematics*, op.cit., p. 32; cf. 'Infinity and the Actual World', p. 119.

9. Ibid.

10. Ibid., p. 29.

11. Ibid., p. 33. As an attack on platonism this is reminiscent of James' precept in *What Maisie Knew* that to 'criticise is to appreciate, to appropriate, to take intellectual possession, to establish in fine a relation with the criticized thing and to make it one's own'.

12. Ibid.

13. Ibid., p. 31.

14. Idid., p. 32.

15. Ibid., p. 34.

16. Waismann, 'Number', in *Lectures on the Philosophy of Mathematics*, op.cit., p. 62.

17. Cf. The Epilogue of IMT, p. 245.

18. Waismann, 'Discovering, Creating, Inventing', p. 30.

19. Ibid.

20. E.g. the series $f(x) = x - x^3/3 + x^5/5 - x^7/7 + \ldots$. I am indebted to Peter Neumann for this example.

21. Cf. Morris Kline, *Mathematics: The Loss of Certainty* (Oxford, Oxford University Press, 1986), p. 116.

22. Waismann, 'Discovering, Creating, Inventing', op.cit., pp. 30-1.

23. Cf. P.M.S. Hacker, *Insight and Illusion* (Oxford, Oxford University Press, 1972), p. 156.

24. Cf. Plato's warning in the *Republic* that 'musical innovation is full of danger to the State, for when modes of music change, the laws of the State always change with them'.

25. Cf. G.P. Baker and P.M.S. Hacker, *Wittgenstein: Rules, Grammar and Necessity*, (Oxford, Basil Blackwell, 1985), Chapter V.

26. Cf. Rush Rhees, *Discussions of Wittgenstein*, (London, Routledge & Kegan Paul, 1970), p. 132.

27. Saul Kripke, *Naming and Necessity*, op.cit., p. 159.

28. Ibid.

29. Ibid., pp. 36-7.

30. Ibid., p. 54.

31. Ibid., pp. 54-5.

32. Ibid., p. 55.

33. Cf. Saul Kripke, 'Semantical Considerations on Modal Logic', in *Reference and Modality*, Leonard Linsky (ed.) (Oxford, Oxford University Press, 1971).

34. Leonard Linsky, *Names and Descriptions* (Chicago, The University of Chicago Press, 1977), p. 144.

35. Cf. E.T. Bell, *Men of Mathematics* (New York, Simon and Schuster, 1965), p. 354.

36. I.e. unlike complex numbers, which have a single non-real unit (i), these would contain two non-real units (i,j). Thus, where a complex number can be written as $a + bi$, these 'hypercomplex' numbers could be written as $a + bi + cj$.

37. The Kneales refer to this as Peacock's 'principle of the permanence of equivalent forms', formulated in 1833. Cf. William and Martha Kneale, *The Development of Logic* (Oxford, Clarendon Press, 1978), p. 398.

38. It almost goes without saying that Waismann's account of the manner in which the domain of infinite series was extended to range over complex numbers again amounts to a serious historical misrepresentation; this time of the evolution of complex function theory. It was not until the subject had reached an advanced state that the notion of explaining the behaviour of a function had become intelligible. In fact, probably long after the introduction of complex numbers into function theory. In this case we seem to have an example of the problem arriving long after the groundwork for its solution had been laid. Cf. Ivor Grattan-Guinness, *The*

Development of the Foundations of Mathematical Analysis from Euler to Riemann (Cambridge, 1970), particularly Chapter 2, 'The Beginnings of Nineteenth-Century Analysis'.

39. W.H. Auden, *The Dyer's Hand & Other Essays* (London, Faber and Faber, 1975), pp. 465-6. Cf. D.F. Henze, 'The Art Work as a Rule', *Ratio* vol. 11 (1969).

BIBLIOGRAPHY

Aimonetto, Italo, 'L'induzione matematica o ragionamento ricorsivo', *Filosofia*, vol. 24 (1974).

Ambrose, Alice, 'Finitism and the Limits of Empiricism', *Mind*, vol. 46 (1937).

―― 'Wittgenstein on Some Questions in Foundations of Mathematics', *Journal of Philosophy*, vol. 52 (1955), reprinted in Shanker (ed.), *Ludwig Wittgenstein: Critical Assessments*, vol.III.

―― 'Mathematical Generality', in *Ludwig Wittgenstein. Philosophy and Language*, A. Ambrose and M. Lazerowitz (eds) (London, George Allen & Unwin, 1972).

―― 'Proof and the Theorem Proved', *Journal of Philosophy*, vol. 55 (1958).

―― 'Wittgenstein on Mathematical Proof', *Mind*, vol. 91 (1982), reprinted in Shanker (ed.), *Ludwig Wittgenstein: Critical Assessments*, vol.III.

Ambrose, Alice and Lazerowitz, Morris, 'Wittgenstein: Philosophy, Experiment and Proof', in *British Philosophy in the Mid-Century*, C.A. Mace (ed.) (London, George Allen & Unwin, 1966).

―― *Necessity and Language* (London, Croom Helm, 1985).

Anderson, A.R., 'Mathematics and the Language Game', in Benacerraf and Putnam (eds), *Philosophy of Mathematics*.

Anscombe, G.E.M., *An Introduction to Wittgenstein's Tractatus* (London, Hutchinson, 1959).

Appel, K. and Haken, W., 'The Four Color Problem', in L.A. Steen (ed.), *Mathematics Today*.

Arrington, R.L., 'Wittgenstein on Contradiction', *Southern Journal of Philosophy*, vol. 7 (1969), reprinted in Shanker (ed.), *Ludwig Wittgenstein: Critical Assessments*, vol.III.

Austin, James. 'Wittgenstein's Solutions to the Color Exclusion Problem', *Philosophy and Phenomenological Research*, vol. 41 (1980), reprinted in Shanker (ed.), *Ludwig Wittgenstein: Critical Assessments*, vol. I.

Ayer, A.J. *Language Truth & Logic* (London, Victor Gollancz, 1970).

Ayer, A.J. (ed.) *Logical Positivism* (New York, The Free Press, 1959).

Baker, G.P. 'Verehrung und Verkehrung: Waismann and Wittgenstein', in C.G. Luckhardt (ed.), *Wittgenstein: Sources and Perspectives*.

Baker, G.P. and Hacker, P.M.S., 'Critical Notice: *Philosophical Grammar*', *Mind*, vol. 85 (1976), revised version reprinted in Shanker (ed.), *Ludwig Wittgenstein: Critical Assessments*, vol.I.

―― 'Wittgenstein aujourd'hui', *Critique*, vol. 399-400 (1980), translated as 'Wittgenstein Today', in S.G. Shanker (ed.), *Ludwig Wittgenstein: Critical Assessments*, vol.II, pp.24-35.

―― *Wittgenstein: Understanding and Meaning. Volume 1 of An Analytical Commentary on the Philosophical Investigations* (Oxford, Basil Blackwell, 1980).

―― *Frege: Logical Excavations* (Oxford, Basil Blackwell, 1984).

―― *Language, Sense & Nonsense* (Oxford, Basil Blackwell, 1984).

―― *Scepticism, Rules & Language* (Oxford, Basil Blackwell, 1984).

―― *Wittgenstein: Rules, Grammar and Necessity. Volume 2 of an Analytical Commentary on the Philosophical Investigations* (Oxford, Basil Blackwell, 1985).

Barker, S.F., *Philosophy of Mathematics* (Engelwood Cliffs, Prentice-Hall Inc., 1964).

Baxley, T.F., 'Wittgenstein's Theory of Quantification', *International Logic Review*, vol. 11 (1980), reprinted in Shanker (ed.), *Ludwig Wittgenstein: Critical Assessments*, vol.III.

Beckmann, Petr, *A History of π (Pi)* (New York, St Martin's Press, 1971).

Bell, E.T., *Men of Mathematics* (New York, Simon and Schuster, 1965).

Benacerraf, P., 'Mathematical Truth', *Journal of Philosophy*, vol. 70 (1973).

Benacerraf, P. and Putnam, H. (eds), *Philosophy of Mathematics: Selected Readings*, (Oxford, Basil Blackwell, 1964).

Bennett, J.F., '"On Being Forced to a Conclusion", Part 1', *Proceedings of the Aristotelian Society*, vol. 35 (1961).

Bergmann, Gustav, *The Metaphysics of Logical Positivism* (Madison, The University of Wisconsin Press, 1967).

Bernadette, Jose Amado, *Infinity: An Essay in Metaphysics* (Oxford, Clarendon Press, 1964).

Bernays, P., 'On Platonism in Mathematics', in Benacerraf and Putnam (eds), *Philosophy of Mathematics: Selected Readings*.

Black, Max, *The Nature of Mathematics* (London, Routledge & Kegan Paul, 1933).

—— 'Relation between Logical Positivism and the Cambridge School of Analysis', *Erkenntnis*, vol. 8 (1939–40).

—— *A Companion to Wittgenstein's Tractatus* (Ithaca, Cornell University Press, 1964).

—— 'Verificationism and Wittgenstein's Reflections on Mathematics', *Revue Internationale de Philosophie*, vol. 23 (1969), reprinted in Shanker (ed.), *Ludwig Wittgenstein: Critical Assessments*, vol.III.

Block, I. (ed.), *Perspectives on the Philosophy of Wittgenstein* (Cambridge, M.I.T. Press, 1981).

Bloor, David, 'Wittgenstein and Mannheim on the Sociology of Mathematics', *Studies in the History of the Philosophy of Science*, vol. 4 (1973), reprinted in Shanker (ed.), *Ludwig Wittgenstein: Critical Assessments*, vol. III.

Blumberg, A.E. and Feigl, H., 'Logical Positivism: a New Movement in European Philosphy', *Journal of Philosophy*, vol. 28 (1931).

Bogen, James, 'Wittgenstein and Skepticism', *Philosophical Review*, vol. 83 (1974), reprinted in Shanker (ed.), *Ludwig Wittgenstein: Critical Assessments*, vol.II.

Boolos, George S. and Jeffrey, R.C., *Computability and Logic* (Cambridge, Cambridge University Press, 1980).

Bourbaki, Nicholas, 'The Architecture of Mathematics', *American Mathematical Monthly*, vol. 57 (1950).

Bouvaresse, Jacques, 'Philosophie des mathématiques et thérapeutique d'une maladie philosophique: Wittgenstein et la critique de l'apparance ontologique dans les mathématiques', in *La Parole Malheureuse* (Paris, Les Editions de Minuit, 1971).

—— 'Sur le "finitisme" de Wittgenstein', in *La Parole Malheureuse*.

—— 'Le paradis de Cantor et le purgatoire de Wittgenstein', *Critique*, vol. 33 (1977).

Bouwsma, O.K., 'Conversations with Wittgenstein', unpublished notes.

Boyer, Carl B., *The History of the Calculus and its Conceptual Development* (New York, Dover Publications, 1949).

Broad, C.D., 'Wittgenstein and the Vienna Circle', *Mind*, vol. 71 (1962).

Brouwer, L.E.J., 'Mathematik, Wissenschaft und Sprache', *Monatshefte für Mathematik und Physik*, vol. 36 (1929).

—— 'Intuitionism and Formalism', in Benacerraf and Putnam (eds), *Philosophy of Mathematics: Selected Readings*.

—— 'Consciousness, Philosophy, and Mathematics', in Benacerraf and Putnam (eds), *Philosophy of Mathematics: Selected Readings.*

Calder, Allan, 'Constructive Mathematics', *Scientific American* (October 1979).

Campanale, D., 'Il problema dei fondamenti della matematica nella critica di Wittgenstein', *Rassegna di Scienze Filosofiche*, vol. 12 (1959).

Campbell, Douglas M. and Higgins, John C. (eds), *Mathematics: People Problems. Results*, 3 vols (Belmont, California, Wadsworth International, 1984).

Canfield, John, 'Critical Notice: *Lectures on the Foundations of Mathematics*', *Canadian Journal of Philosophy*, vol. 11 (1981), reprinted in Shanker (ed.), *Ludwig Wittgenstein: Critical Assessments*, vol.III.

Cantor, Georg, *Contributions to the Founding of the Theory of Transfinite Numbers* (New York, Dover Publications, Inc., 1955).

Carnap, R., 'The Logicist Foundations of Mathematics', in Benacerraf and Putnam (eds), *Philosophy of Mathematics: Selected Readings.*

—— 'Autobiography', in *The Philosophy of Rudolf Carnap*, P. Schilpp (ed.) (Illinois, Open Court, 1964).

—— *Introduction to Symbolic Logic and its Applications* (New York, Dover Publications, Inc., 1958).

—— *The Logical Structure of the World & Pseudoproblems in Philosophy*, R.A. George (trans.) (Berkeley and Los Angeles, University of California Press, 1967).

Cerutti, Elsi and Davis, P.J., 'Formac Meets Pappus', *American Mathematical Monthly*, vol. LXXVI (1969).

Chaitan, G., 'Randomness and Mathematical Proof', *Scientific American*, vol. CCXXXII (1975).

Chihara, Charles, 'Wittgenstein and Logical Compulsion', *Analysis*, vol. 21 (1961).

—— 'Mathematical Discovery and Concept Formation', *Philosophical Review*, vol. 72 (1963), reprinted in Shanker (ed.), *Ludwig Wittgenstein: Critical Assessments*, vol.III.

—— *Ontology and the Vicious-Circle Principle* (Ithaca, Cornell University Press, 1973).

—— 'Operationalism and Ordinary Language: A critique of Wittgenstein', *American Philosophical Quarterly*, vol. 24 (1973).

—— 'Wittgenstein's Analysis of the Paradoxes in his *Lectures on the Foundations of Mathematics*', *Philosophical Review*, vol. 86 (1977), reprinted in Shanker (ed.), *Ludwig Wittgenstein: Critical Assessments*, vol. III.

—— 'The Wright-wing Defense of Wittgenstein's Philosophy of Logic', *Philosophical Review*, vol. 90 (1982).

Cohen, M., 'Truth-tables and Truth', *Analysis*, vol. 35 (1974).

Cooper, Neil, 'Inconsistency', *Philosophical Quarterly*, vol. 16 (1966).

Copi, I., *The Theory of Logical Types* (London, Routledge & Kegan Paul, 1971).

—— 'Frege and Wittgenstein's *Tractatus*', *Philosophia*, vol. 6 (1971), reprinted in Shanker (ed.), *Ludwig Wittgenstein: Critical Assessments*, vol. I.

Copi, I. and Beard, R.W., *Essays on Wittgenstein's Tractatus* (London, Routledge & Kegan Paul, 1966).

Cotroneo, G., 'Un tentativo di storia di Wittgenstein sui fondamenti della matematica', *Giornale Critico della Filosofia Italiana*, vol. 44 (1965).

Courant, Richard and Robbins, Herbert, *What is Mathematics?* (Oxford, Oxford University Press, 1978).

Cowan, J.L., 'Wittgenstein's Philosophy of Logic', *Philosophical Review*, vol. 70 (1961).

Dahms, Hans-Joachim, 'Verifikationismus und Mathematik bei Wittgenstein', in Edgar Morscher und Rudolf Stranzinger (eds), *Ethik: Grundlagen, Probleme und Anwendungen* (Vienna, Hölder-Pichler-Tempsky, 1981).

Dambska, Izydora, 'Les Idées Kantiennes dans la philosophie des mathématiques

de Wittgenstein', *Organon*, vol. 12-13 (1976-77).
—— 'Les idées de Wittgenstein sur la non-contradiction et sur le caractère des propositions mathématiques', *Akten XIV International Kongress für Philosophie*, vol. 6 (1971).
Dantzig, T. *Henri Poincaré: Critic of Crises* (New York, Charles Scribner & Sons, 1954).
Dauben, J.W., *Georg Cantor: His Mathematics and Philosophy of the Infinite* (Cambridge, Harvard University Press, 1979).
Davis, Martin and Hersh, Reuben, 'Hilbert's Tenth Problem', *Scientific American* (November 1973).
Davis, Philip J., 'Fidelity in Mathematical Discourse: Is One and One Really Two?', *American Mathematical Monthly*, vol. LXXIX (1972).
Davis, Philip J. and Hersh, Reuben, *The Mathematical Experience* (Brighton, The Harvester Press, 1981).
Dedekind, Richard, *Essays on the Theory of Numbers* (New York, Dover Publications, Inc., 1963).
Desua, Frank, 'Consistency and Completeness — a Resumé', *American Mathematical Monthly*, vol. 63 (1956).
Detlefsen, M., 'On Interpreting Gödel's Second Theorem', *Journal of Philosophical Logic*, vol. 8 (1979).
—— *Hilbert's Program: An Essay on Mathematical Instrumentalism*, forthcoming.
—— 'On Dynamic Models of Theory Construction', unpublished notes.
Detlefsen, M. and Luker, Mark, 'The Four-Color Theorem and Mathematical Proof', *Journal of Philosophy*, vol. LXXVII (1980).
Dieudonné, Jean, 'The Work of Nicholas Bourbaki', *American Mathematical Monthly*, vol. 77 (1970).
Dilman, Ilham, 'Wittgenstein Philosophy and Logic', *Analysis*, vol. 31 (1970).
Dumitriu, A., 'Wittgenstein's Solution of the Paradoxes', *Journal of the History of Philosophy*, vol. 12 (1974), reprinted in Shanker (ed.), *Ludwig Wittgenstein: Critical Assessments*, vol. III.
Dummett, Michael, *Elements of Intuitionism* (Oxford, Clarendon Press, 1978).
—— 'Reckonings: Wittgenstein on Mathematics', *Encounter*, vol. L (1978), reprinted in Shanker (ed.), *Ludwig Wittgenstein: Critical Assessments*, vol. III.
—— *Truth and Other Enigmas* (London, Duckworth, 1978).
—— 'Can Analytical Philosophy be Systematic, and Ought it to be?', in *Truth and Other Enigmas*.
—— '*Constructionalism*', in *Truth and Other Enigmas*.
—— 'Is Logic Empirical', in *Truth and Other Enigmas*.
—— 'Platonism', in *Truth and Other Enigmas*.
—— 'Realism', in *Truth and Other Enigmas*.
—— 'The Justification of Deduction', in *Truth and Other Enigmas*.
—— 'The Philosophical Basis of Intuitionistic Logic', in *Truth and Other Enigmas*.
—— 'The Philosophical Significance of Gödel's Theorem', in *Truth and Other Enigmas*.
—— 'The Reality of the Past', in *Truth and Other Enigmas*.
—— 'Wittgenstein's Philosophy of Mathematics', in *Truth and Other Enigmas*, reprinted in Shanker (ed.), *Ludwig Wittgenstein: Critical Assessments*, vol. III.
—— 'Frege and Wittgenstein', in I. Block (ed.), *Perspectives on the Philosophy of Wittgenstein*.
—— *Frege: Philosophy of Language*, 2nd edn (London, Duckworth, 1981).
—— *The Interpretation of Frege's Philosophy* (London, Duckworth, 1981).
Egidi, Rosaria, 'Due tesi di Wittgenstein sui fondamenti della matematica', *Giornale Critico della Filosofia Italiana*, vol. 44 (1965).
Engel, M.S., 'Wittgenstein's Foundations and its Reception', *American Philosophical Quarterly*, vol. 4 (1967), reprinted in Shanker (ed.), *Ludwig*

Wittgenstein: Critical Assessments, vol. III.

Fann, K.T. (ed.), *Ludwig Wittgenstein: The Man and His Philosophy* (Brighton, Harvester Press, 1967).

Feigl, Herbert, 'Moritz Schlick, A Memoir', in Schlick, *Philosohical Papers. Volume I*

—— 'No Pot of Message', in *Inquiries and Provocations: Selected Writings. 1929–1974*, R.S. Cohen (ed.) (Dordrecht, D. Reidel Publishing Company, 1981).

Ferguson, T.A., 'Quine, Carnap, and Wittgenstein: Analyticity and Logical Compulsion', *Dialogue*, vol. 12 (1970).

Field, Hartry, *Science Without Numbers* (Oxford, Basil Blackwell, 1980).

Fiorentini, M., 'Oggetto e fondamenti della matematica', *Scientia*, vol. 106 (1971).

Fogelin, R., 'Wittgenstein and Intuitionism', *American Philosophical Quarterly*, vol. 5 (1968), reprinted in Shanker (ed.), *Ludwig Wittgenstein: Critical Assessments*, vol. III.

—— *Wittgenstein* (London, Routledge & Kegan Paul, 1976).

—— 'Wittgenstein and Classical Scepticism', *International Philosophical Quarterly*, vol. 21 (1981), reprinted in Shanker (ed.), *Ludwig Wittgenstein: Critical Assessments*, vol. II.

Fraenkel, A., 'On the Crisis of the Principle of the Excluded Middle', *Scripta Mathematica*, vol. 17 (1951).

—— 'The Recent Controversies About the Foundations of Mathematics', *Scripta Mathematica*, vol. 13 (1947).

Frascolla, Pasquale, 'Il modello construttivistico nella filosofia della matematica di Wittgenstein', *Revista Filosofia*, vol. 71 (1980), translated as 'The Constructivist Model in Wittgenstein's Philosophy of Mathematics', in Shanker (ed.), *Ludwig Wittgenstein: Critical Assessments*, vol. III.

Frege, G. *The Foundations of Arithmetic*, J.L. Austin (trans.) (Oxford, Basil Blackwell, 1950).

—— *Translations from the Philosophical Writings of Gottlob Frege*, P. Geach and M. Black (trans.) (Oxford, Basil Blackwell, 1977).

—— *Posthumous Writings*, H. Hermes, F. Kambartel and F. Kaulbach (eds), P. Long and R. White (trans.) (Oxford, Basil Blackwell, 1979).

—— *Philosophical and Mathematical Correspondence*, G. Gabriel, H. Hermes, F. Kambartel, C. Thiel, and A. Veraart (eds), H. Kaal (trans.) (Oxford, Basil Blackwell, 1980).

Gasking, D., 'Mathematics and the World', in Benacerraf and Putnam, *Philosophy of Mathematics: Selected Readings*.

Gödel, K., 'Russell's Mathematical Logic', in Benacerraf and Putnam, *Philosophy of Mathematics: Selected Readings*.

Goodstein, R.L., *Essays in the Philosophy of Mathematics* (Leicester, Leicester University Press, 1965).

—— 'Wittgenstein's Philosophy of Mathematics', in *Ludwig Wittgenstein: Philosophy and Language*, A. Ambrose and M. Lazerowitz (eds) (London, George Allen & Unwin, 1973).

Granger, G., 'Wittgenstein et la metalangue', *Revue Internationale de Philosophie*, vol. 23 (1969).

Grattan-Guinness, I., *The Development of the Foundations of Mathematical Analysis from Euler to Riemann* (Cambridge, Cambridge Univeristy Press, 1970).

—— *From the Calculus to Set Theory: 1630-1910* (London, Duckworth, 1980).

Griffin, James, *Wittgenstein's Logical Atomism* (Oxford, Clarendon Press, 1964).

Grosholz, Emily, 'Wittgenstein and the Correlation of Logic and Arithmetic', *Ratio*, vol. 23 (1982), reprinted in Shanker (ed.), *Ludwig Wittgenstein: Critical Assessments*, vol. III.

Hacker, P.M.S., *Insight and Illusion: Wittgenstein on Philosophy and the Metaphysics of Experience* (Oxford, Clarendon Press, 1972).

—— 'Laying the Ghost of the *Tractatus*', *Review of Metaphysics*, vol. 29 (1975), reprinted in Shanker (ed.), *Ludwig Wittgenstein: Critical Assessments*, vol. I.

—— 'The Rise and Fall of the Picture Theory', in Block (ed.), *Perspectives on the Philosophy of Wittgenstein*, revised version in Shanker (ed.), *Ludwig Wittgenstein: Critical Assessments*, vol. I.

—— 'Semantic Holism: Frege and Wittgenstein', in C.G. Luckhardt (ed.), *Wittgenstein: Sources and Perspectives.*

Hahn, Hans, 'Logic, Mathematics, and Knowledge of Nature', in Ayer (ed.), *Logical Positivism.*

—— *Empiricism. Logic and Mathematics: Philosophical Papers*, Brian McGuinness (ed.) (Dordrecht, D. Reidel Publishing Company, 1980).

Haller, Rudolf, 'Österreichische Philosophie', *Conceptus* vol. II (1977).

Hallett, Garth, *A Companion to Wittgenstein's 'Philosophical Investigations'* (Ithaca, Cornell University Press, 1977).

Hallett, Michael, *Cantorean Set Theory and Limitation of Size* (Oxford, Clarendon Press, 1984).

Hanfling, Oswald, *Logical Positivism* (New York, Columbia University Press, 1981).

Hardy, G.H., 'Mathematical Proof', *Mind*, vol. 38 (1929).

—— *A Mathematician's Apology* (Cambridge, Cambridge University Press, 1941).

Harrison, Bernard, *An Introduction to the Philosophy of Language* (London, The Macmillan Press, 1979).

Harward, D., 'Wittgenstein and the Character of Mathematical Propositions', *International Logic Review*, vol. 3 (1972), reprinted in Shanker (ed.), *Ludwig Wittgenstein: Critical Assessments*, vol. III.

—— *Wittgenstein's Saying and Showing Themes* (Bonn, Bouvier Verlag, 1976).

Hempel, C., 'On the Nature of Mathematical Truth', in Benacerraf and Putnam (eds) *Philosophy of Mathematics: Selected Readings.*

Heyting, A., 'The Intuitionist Foundations of Mathematics', in Benacerraf and Putnam (eds), *Philosophy of Mathematics: Selected Readings.*

Heyting, A., *Intuitionism* (Amsterdam, North-Holland, 1956).

Hilbert, David, 'Mathematical Problems', *Proceedings of Symposia in Pure Mathematics*, vol. 28 (1976).

—— 'On the Foundations of Logic and Arithmetic' (1904), in J. van Heijenoort (ed.), *From Frege to Gödel: A Source Book in Mathematical Logic.*

—— 'Neubegründung der Mathematik' (1922), in *Gesammelte Abhandlungen* (Berlin, Springer, 1935).

—— 'On the Infinite' (1925), in J. van Heijenoort (ed.), *From Frege to Gödel: A Source Book in Mathematical Logic.*

—— 'The Foundations of Mathematics' (1927), in J. van Heijenoort (ed.), *From Frege to Gödel: A Source Book in Mathematical Logic.*

Hintikka, J., 'Are Logical Truths Analytic?', *Philosophical Review*, vol. 74 (1965).

—— 'Quantification and the Picture Theory of Language', *Monist*, vol. 53 (1969).

—— 'Partially Ordered Quantifiers versus Partially Ordered Ideas', *Dialectica*, vol. 30 (1976).

Hodges, Andrew, *Alan Turing: The Enigma* (London, Burnett Books, 1983).

Hofstadter, Douglas R., *Gödel, Escher, Bach: An Eternal Golden Braid* (Harmondsworth, Penguin Books, 1979).

Holtzmann, S. and Leich, C. (eds), *Wittgenstein: To Follow a Rule* (London, Routledge & Kegan Paul, 1981).

Huff, Douglas, 'Wittgenstein and Mathematical Foundations', *Dianoia*, vol, 10 (1974).

Ishiguro, Hidé, 'Wittgenstein and the Theory of Types', in I. Block (ed.),

Perspectives on the Philosophy of Wittgenstein.

Joergensen, Joergen, *The Development of Logical Empiricism* (Chicago, University of Chicago Press, 1951).

Jourdain, Philip, *The Nature of Mathematics*, in Newman (ed.), *The World of Mathematics.*

Juhos, Béla, *Selected Papers on Epistemology and Physics*, G. Frey (ed.) (Dordrecht, D. Reidel Publishing Company, 1976).

Kaufmann, Felix, *The Infinite in Mathematics*, B. McGuinness (ed.) (Dordrecht, D. Reidel Publishing Company, 1978).

Kenny, A.J.P., *Wittgenstein* (London, Allen Lane, 1973).

—— 'Wittgenstein on the Nature of Philosophy', in B. McGuinness (ed.), *Wittgenstein and His Times* (Oxford, Basil Blackwell, 1982).

Kielkopf, C., *Strict Finitism: An Examination of Ludwig Wittgenstein's Remarks on the Foundations of Mathematics* (The Hague, Mouton, 1970).

—— 'Wittgenstein, "*A posteriori*" Necessity and Logic for Entailment', *Philosophica*, vol. 9 (1979), reprinted in Shanker (ed.), *Ludwig Wittgenstein: Critical Assessments*, vol. III.

Kitcher, P., 'Hilbert's Epistemology', *Philosophy of Science*, vol. 43 (1976).

—— 'Frege's Epistemology', *Philosophical Review*, vol. 88 (1980).

—— *The Nature of Mathematical Knowledge* (Oxford, Oxford University Press, 1983).

Klenk, V., *Wittgenstein's Philosophy of Mathematics* (The Hague, Nijhoff, 1976).

Kline, Morris, *Mathematics in Western Culture* (Harmondsworth, Penguin Books, 1979).

—— *Mathematics: The Loss of Certainty* (Oxford, Oxford University Press, 1980).

Kneale, W. and Kneale, M., *The Development of Logic* (Oxford, Clarendon Press, 1978).

Knuth, D.E., 'Mathematics and Computer Science: Coping with Finiteness', *Science*, vol. 194 (1976).

Koestler, Arthur, *The Act of Creation* (London, Picador, 1969).

Kolata, G.B., 'Mathematical Proofs: The Genesis of Reasonable Doubt', *Science*, vol. 192 (1976).

Kraft, Victor, *The Vienna Circle: The Origin of Neo-Positivism* (New York, Greenwood Press, 1953).

Kreisel, G., 'Hilbert's Programme', in Benacarraf and Putnam (eds), *Philosophy of Mathematics: Selected Readings.*

—— 'Wittgenstein's Remarks', *British Journal for the Philosophy of Science*, vol. 9 (1958).

—— 'Wittgenstein's *Lectures on the Foundations of Mathematics*', *Bulletin of the American Mathematical Society*, vol. 84 (1978), reprinted in Shanker (ed.), *Ludwig Wittgenstein: Critical Assessments*, vol. III.

—— 'Zu Wittgensteins Gesprächen und Vorlesungen über die Grundlagen der Mathematik', in *Wittgenstein and his Impact on Contemporary Thought* (Vienna, Hölder-Pichler-Tempsky, 1978).

Kripke, Saul, *Naming and Necessity* (Oxford, Basil Blackwell, 1980).

—— *Wittgenstein: On Rules and Private Language* (Oxford, Basil Blackwell, 1982).

Lakatos, Imre, *Mathematics, Science and Epistemology*, J. Worrall and G. Currie (eds) (Cambridge, Cambridge University Press, 1980).

—— *Proofs and Refutations: The Logic of Mathematical Discovery*, J. Worrall and Elie Zahar (eds) (Cambridge, Cambridge University Press, 1981).

Lazerowitz, M., 'Necessity and Language', Ambrose and Lazerowitz, *Necessity and Language.*

Levison, A.B., 'Frege on Proof', *Philosophy and Phenomenological Research*, vol. 22 (1961).

—— 'Wittgenstein and Logical Laws', *Philosophical Quarterly*, vol. 14 (1964).

—— 'Wittgenstein and Logical Necessity', *Inquiry*, vol. 6 (1964).

C.G. Luckhardt (ed.), *Wittgenstein: Sources and Perspectives*, (New York, Cornell University Press, 1979).

Malcolm, N., 'Wittgenstein's *Philosophische Bemerkungen*', *Philosophical Review*, vol. 76 (1967), reprinted in Shanker (ed.), *Ludwig Wittgenstein: Critical Assessments*, vol. I.

McGuinness, Brian (ed.), *Wittgenstein and His Times* (Oxford, Basil Blackwell, 1982).

Mendelson, E., *Introduction to Mathematical Logic* (New York, D. Van Nostrand Company, 1979).

Menger, Karl, *Selected Papers in Logic and Foundations, Didactics, Economics* (Dordrecht, D. Reidel Publishing Company, 1979).

Molitur, Arnulf, 'Bemerkungen zu Ludwig Wittgensteins posthumer philosophie der Mathematik', *Salzburger Jahrbuch Philosophie*, vols. 10-11 (1966-7).

Moore, G.E., 'Wittgenstein's Lectures in 1930-33', *Mind*, vol. 63 (1954).

Morawetz, T.H., 'Wittgenstein and Synthetic *a priori* Judgements', *Philosophy*, vol. 49 (1974).

Nagel, E. and Newman, J.R., *Gödel's Proof* (New York, New York University Press, 1958).

Neurath, O., *Empiricism and Sociology*, Marie Neurath and R.S. Cohen (eds) (Dordrecht, D. Reidel Publishing Company, 1973).

Newman, James R. (ed.), *The World of Mathematics*, 4 vols (New York, Simon and Schuster, 1956).

Nyiri, J.C., 'Ludwig Wittgenstein as a Conservative Philosopher', *Continuity* no. 8 (1984), reprinted as 'Wittgenstein 1929-31: the Return', in Shanker (ed.), *Ludwig Wittgenstein: Critical Assessments*, vol. IV.

Odegard, Douglas, 'Two Types of Scepticism', *Philosophy*, vol. 54 (1979).

Olscamp, P.J., 'Wittgenstein's Refutation of Skepticism', *Philosophy and Phenomenological Research*, vol. 26 (1965).

Pears, D.F., *Bertrand Russell and the British Tradition in Philosophy* (London, Collins/Fontana, 1967).

—— *Wittgenstein* (London, Fontana, 1971).

—— 'The Relation between Wittgenstein's Picture Theory of Propositions and Russell's Theories of Judgement', *Philosophical Review*, vol. 86 (1977), reprinted in Shanker (ed.), *Ludwig Wittgenstein: Critical Assessments*, vol. I.

—— 'The Logical Independence of Elementary Propositions', in I. Block (ed.), *Perspectives on the Philosophy of Wittgenstein*.

Peppinghaus, Benedikt, 'Some Aspects of Wittgenstein's Philosophy of Mathematics', in *Proceedings of the Bertrand Russell Memorial Logic Conference* (Leeds, University of Leeds, 1973).

Phillips, D., *Wittgenstein and Scientific Knowledge* (New York, Macmillan, 1977).

Pitcher, G., (ed.) *Wittgenstein* (London, Macmillan, 1968).

Plantinga, A., *The Nature of Necessity* (Oxford, Clarendon Press, 1978).

Plochmann, G.K., 'Mathematics in Wittgenstein's *Tractatus*', *Philosophica Mathematica*, vol. 2 (1965).

Poincaré, H., *Science and Hypothesis*, W.J. Greenstreet (trans.) (London, 1905).

—— 'On the Nature of Mathematical Reasoning', in Benacerraf and Putnam (eds), *Philosophy of Mathematics: Selected Readings*.

Popper, Karl, *Conjectures and Refutations: The Growth of Scientific Knowledge* (New York, Harper Torchbooks, 1965).

Priest, G., 'A Bedside Reader's Guide to the Conventionalist Philosophy of Mathematics', in *The Proceedings of the Bertrand Russell Memorial Logic Conference* (Leeds, University of Leeds, 1973).

Prior, A.N., *Objects of Thought*, P.T. Geach and A.J.P. Kenny (eds) (Oxford, Oxford University Press, 1971).

Putnam, H., *Mathematics, Matter and Method* (Cambridge, Cambridge University Press, 1979).
—— 'Analyticity and Apriority: Beyond Wittgenstein and Quine', *Midwest Studies in Philosophy*, vol. 4 (1979).
Quine, W.V.O., *From a Logical Point of View* (New York, Harper Torchbooks, 1961).
Rabin, M.O., 'Probabilistic Algorithms', in *Algorithms and Complexity: New Directions and Recent Results*, J.F. Traub (ed.) (New York, Academic Press, 1976).
Ramsey, Frank, 'Critical Notice of the *Tractatus*', *Mind*, vol. 32 (1923), reprinted in Shanker (ed.), *Ludwig Wittgenstein: Critical Assessments*, vol. I.
—— *Foundations of Mathematics and other Logical Essays*, R.B. Braithwaite (ed.) (London, Paul, Trench, Trubner, 1931).
Reid, C., *Hilbert* (Berlin, Springer, 1970).
Resnik, M.D., 'On the Philosophical Significance of Consistency Proofs', *Journal of Philosophical Logic*, vol. III (1974).
Rhees, Rush, *Discussions of Wittgenstein* (London, Routledge & Kegan Paul, 1970).
Rorty, Richard, *Philosophy and the Mirror of Nature* (Oxford, Basil Blackwell, 1980).
Rundle, Bede, *Grammar in Philosophy* (Oxford, Clarendon Press, 1979).
Russell, Bertrand, *Principles of Mathematics* (New York, W.W. Norton & Company, n.d.).
—— *Mysticism and Logic and Other Essays* (London, Longmans, Green and Co., 1918).
—— *My Philosophical Development* (London, George Allen & Unwin, 1959).
—— *Introduction to Mathematical Philosophy* (London, George Allen & Unwin, 1975).
—— *The Autobiography of Bertrand Russell* (London, Unwin Books, 1975).
—— *Logic and Knowledge: Essays 1901–1950*, R.C. Marsh (ed.) (London, George Allen & Unwin, 1977).
—— *Theory of Knowledge: The 1913 Manuscript*, E.R. Eames (ed.) (London, George Allen & Unwin, 1984).
Saaty, T.L. and Kainen, P., *The Four Colour Problem: Assaults and Conquest* (New York, McGraw-Hill, 1977).
Savitt, S.F., 'Wittgenstein's Early Philosophy of Mathematics', *Philosophy Research Archives*, vol. 5 (1979), reprinted in Shanker (ed.), *Ludwig Wittgenstein: Critical Assessments*, vol. III.
Schächter, Josef, *Prolegomena to a Critical Grammar* (Dordrecht, D. Reidel Publishing Company, 1973).
Schlick, Moritz, 'The Future of Philosophy' (1930), in *Philosophical Papers* vol. II.
—— 'The Turning-Point in Philosophy' (1930), in *Philosophical Papers*, vol. II.
—— *Philosophical Papers Vol. I (1909–22)*, J.L. Mulder and B. van de Velde-Schlick (eds) (Dordrecht, D. Reidel Publishing Company, 1979).
—— *Philosophical Papers Vol. II (1925–36)*, H. Mulder and B. van de Velde-Schlick (eds) (Dordrecht, D. Reidel Publishing Company, 1979).
Shanker, S.G., 'Sceptical Confusions about Rule-Following', *Mind*, vol. XCIII (1984), reprinted in Shanker (ed.) *Ludwig Wittgenstein: Critical Assessments*, vol. II.
—— 'Wittgenstein's Solution of the "Hermeneutic Problem"', *Conceptus*, vol.XVIII, no.44 (1984), reprinted in Shanker (ed.), *Ludwig Wittgenstein: Critical Assessments*, vol. IV.
—— (ed.), *Ludwig Wittgenstein: Critical Assessments. Vol. I. From the* Notebooks *to* Philosophical Grammar: *The Construction and Dismantling of the* Tractatus (London, Croom Helm Publishers, 1986).

—— (ed.), *Ludwig Wittgenstein: Critical Assessments. Vol. II. From* Philosophical Investigations *to* On Certainty: *Wittgenstein's Later Philosophy* (London, Croom Helm Publishers, 1986).

—— (ed.), *Ludwig Wittgenstein: Critical Assessments. Vol. III. From the* Tractatus *to* Remarks on the Foundations of Mathematics: *Wittgenstein on the Philosophy of Mathematics* (London, Croom Helm Publishers, Ltd., 1986).

—— (ed.), *Ludwig Wittgenstein: Critical Assessments. Vol. IV From Theology to Sociology: Wittgenstein's Impact on Contemporary Thought* (London, Croom Helm Publishers, 1986).

—— 'The Philosophical Significance of the *Tractatus*', in *Ludwig Wittgenstein: Critical Assessments*, vol. I.

—— 'Approaching the *Investigations*', in *Ludwig Wittgenstein: Critical Assessments*, vol. II.

—— 'The Portals of Discovery', in *Ludwig Wittgenstein: Critical Assessments*, vol. III.

—— 'The Foundations of the Foundations of Mathematics', in *Ludwig Wittgenstein: Critical Assessments*, vol. III.

—— 'The Appel-Haken Solution of the Four-Colour Problem', in *Ludwig Wittgenstein: Critical Assessments*, vol. III.

—— 'The Nature of Philosophy', in *Ludwig Wittgenstein: Critical Assessments*, vol. IV.

Shanker, V.A. and S.G., *Ludwig Wittgenstein: Critical Assessments. Vol. V.A. Wittgenstein Bibliography* (London, Croom Helm Publishers, 1986).

Shwayder, D., 'Wittgenstein on Mathematics', in P. Winch (ed.) *Studies in the Philosophy of Wittgenstein.*

Skolem, T., 'The Foundations of Elementary Arithmetic', in J. van Heijenoort (ed.), *From Frege to Gödel: A Source Book in Mathematical Logic.*

Sluga, Hans, *Gottlob Frege* (London, Routledge & Kegan Paul, 1980).

Sondheimer, E. and Rogerson, A., *Numbers and Infinity* (Cambridge, Cambridge University Press, 1981).

Spiegelberg, H., 'The Puzzle of Wittgenstein's "Phänomenologie"', *American Philosophical Quarterly*, vol. 5 (1968), reprinted in Shanker (ed.), *Ludwig Wittgenstein: Critical Assessments*, vol. IV.

Steen, L.A. (ed.), *Mathematics Today: Twelve Informal Essays* (New York, Springer-Verlag, 1978).

Steiner, Mark, *Mathematical Knowledge* (New York, Cornell University Press, 1975).

Stewart, Ian, *Concepts of Modern Mathematics* (Harmondsworth, Penguin Books, 1981).

Stewart, I. and Tall, D., *The Foundations of Mathematics* (Oxford, Oxford University Press, 1977).

Stolzenberg, G., 'Can an Inquiry into the Foundations of Mathematics Tell Us Anything Interesting about Mind?', in George Miller (ed.), *Psychology and Biology of Language and Thought* (New York, Academic Press, n.d.).

Stroud, B., 'Wittgenstein and Logical Necessity', *Philosophical Review*, vol. 74 (1965), reprinted in Shanker (ed.), *Ludwig Wittgenstein: Critical Assessments*, vol. III.

Teller, Paul, 'Computer Proof', *Journal of Philosophy*, vol. LXXVII (1980).

Torretti, Roberto, *Philosophy of Geometry from Riemann to Poincaré* (Dordrecht, D. Reidel Publishing Company, 1984).

Troelstra, A.S., *Principles of Intuitionism* (Heidelberg, Springer-Verlag, 1969).

Tymoczko, Thomas, 'The Four-Colour Problem and its Philosophical Significance', *Journal of Philosophy*, vol. 76 (1979).

ul-Haque, Intisar, 'Wittgenstein on Numbers', *International Philosophical Quarterly*, vol. 18 (1978), reprinted in Shanker (ed.), *Ludwig Wittgenstein: Critical Assessments*, vol. III.

van Heijenoort, Jean (ed.), *From Frege to Gödel: A Source Book in Mathematical Logic, 1879–1931* (Cambridge, Harvard University Press, 1977).

Vesey, G. (ed.), *Understanding Wittgenstein* (London, Macmillan, 1974).

von Neumann, J., 'The Formalist Foundations of Mathematics', in Benacerraf and Putnam (eds), *Philosophy of Mathematics: Selected Readings*.

von Wright, G.H., *Wittgenstein* (Oxford, Basil Blackwell, 1982).

Wang, Hao, *From Mathematics to Philosophy* (London, Routledge & Kegan Paul, 1974).

Waismann, F. *Introduction to Mathematical Thinking* (New York, Harper & Row, 1959).

—— *How I see Philosophy*, R. Harré (ed.) (London, Macmillan, 1968).

—— *The Principles of Linguistic Philosophy*, R. Harré (ed.) (London, Macmillan, 1968).

—— *Philosophical Papers*, B. McGuinness (ed.) (Dordrecht, D. Reidel Publishing Company, 1977).

—— *Lectures on the Philosophy of Mathematics*, Wolfgang Grassl (ed.) (Amsterdam, Rodopi, 1982).

—— 'The Nature of Mathematics: Wittgenstein's Standpoint', S.G. Shanker (trans.), in Shanker (ed.), *Ludwig Wittgenstein: Critical Assessments*, vol. III.

Webb, J.C., *Mechanism, Mentalism, and Metamathematics*, (Dordrecht, D. Reidel Publishing Company, 1980).

Weyl, H., 'Über die neue Grundlagenkrise der Mathematik', *Mathematische Zeitschrift*, vol. 10 (1921).

—— 'Die heutige Erkenntnislage in der Mathematik', *Symposion* 1 (1927).

—— 'Consistency in Mathematics', *The Rice Institute Pamphlet* 16 (1929).

—— *Philosophy of Mathematics and Natural Science* (Princeton, Princeton University Press, 1949).

Whitehead, A. and Russell, B., *Principia Mathematica to *56* (Cambridge, Cambridge University Press, 1973).

Wilder, R.L., 'The Nature of Mathematical Proof', *American Mathematical Monthly*, vol. 51 (1944).

—— *Introduction to the Foundations of Mathematics* (New York, John Wiley and Sons, 1965).

—— *Evolution of Mathematical Concepts* (Milton Keynes, The Open University Press, 1973).

Winch, P. (ed.), *Studies in the Philosophy of Wittgenstein* (London, Routledge & Kegan Paul, 1969).

Wittgenstein, L. *Remarks on Colour*, G.E.M. Anscombe (ed.), L. McAlister and M. Schüttle (trans.) (Oxford, Basil Blackwell, n.d.).

—— *Philosophical Remarks*, Rush Rhees (ed.), R. Hargreaves and R. White (trans.) (Oxford, Basil Blackwell, 1964).

—— *Lectures and Conversations on Aesthetics, Psychology & Religious Belief*, C. Barrett (ed.), (Oxford, Basil Blackwell, 1966).

—— *Zettel*, G.E.M. Anscombe and G.H. von Wright (eds), G.E.M. Anscombe (trans.) (Oxford, Basil Blackwell, 1967).

—— *Tractatus Logico-Philosophicus*, D.F. Pears & B.F. McGuinness (trans.) (London, Routledge & Kegan Paul, 1972).

—— *Philosophical Grammar*, Rush Rhees (ed.), Anthony Kenny (trans.) (Oxford, Basil Blackwell, 1974).

—— *Philosophical Investigations*, G.E.M. Anscombe (trans.) (Oxford, Basil Blackwell, 1976).

—— *Wittgenstein's Lectures on the Foundations of Mathematics*, Cora Diamond (ed.) (Hassocks, The Harvester Press, 1976).

—— *On Certainty*, G.E.M. Anscombe and G.H. von Wright (eds), D. Paul and G.E.M. Anscombe (trans.) (Oxford, Basil Blackwell, 1977).

—— *The Blue and Brown Books* (Oxford, Basil Blackwell, 1978).

—— *Remarks on the Foundations of Mathematics*, G.H. von Wright, R. Rhees, and G.E.M. Anscombe (eds), G.E.M. Anscombe (trans.), 2nd edn (Oxford, Basil Blackwell, 1978).

—— *Notebooks 1914–1916*, G.H. von Wright and G.E.M. Anscombe (eds), G.E.M. Anscombe (trans.) (Oxford, Basil Blackwell, 1979).

—— *Wittgenstein's Lectures: Cambridge 1932–1935*, Alice Ambrose (ed.) (Oxford, Basil Blackwell, 1979).

—— *Culture and Value*, G.H. von Wright (ed.), Peter Winch (trans.) (Oxford, Basil Blackwell,1980).

—— *Wittgenstein's Lectures: Cambridge 1930–1932*, D. Lee (ed.) (Oxford, Basil Blackwell, 1980).

Weinberg, J., *An Examination of Logical Positivism* (London, Routledge & Kegan Paul, 1936).

White, Alan, 'Logical Atomism: Russell and Wittgenstein', in *G.E. Moore: a Critical Exposition* (Oxford, Basil Blackwell, 1958).

Williams, Michael, *Groundless Belief* (Oxford, Basil Blackwell, 1977).

Wright, Crispin, 'Rule-following, Objectivity and the Theory of Meaning', in Holtzmann and Leich (eds), *Wittgenstein: To Follow A Rule*.

—— *Wittgenstein on the Foundations of Mathematics* (London, Duckworth, 1980).

—— 'Strict Finitism', *Synthese*, vol. 51 (1982).

—— *Frege's Conception of Numbers as Objects* (Aberdeen, Aberdeen University Press, 1983).

Wrigley, Michael, 'Wittgenstein on Inconsistency', *Philosophy*, vol. 55 (1980), reprinted in Shanker (ed.), *Ludwig Wittgenstein: Critical Assessments*, vol. III.

—— 'Wittgenstein's Philosophy of Mathematics', *Philosophical Quarterly*, vol. 27 (1977), reprinted in Shanker (ed.), *Ludwig Wittgenstein: Critical Assessments*, vol. III.

INDEX